AFTER the Lemons

The Glory Years of Bath rugby

This book is dedicated to the memory of Mollie Hall. As a daughter, wife and mother of Bath players, her unstinting support for the club spanned eight decades.

AFTER the Lemons

The Glory Years of Bath rugby

A history of Bath Football Club (RFU) 1965-1996

By Kevin Coughlan, Peter Hall and Colin Gale

Published by Montroy Media Ltd
The Loft Room
6 Montroy Close
Henleaze, Bristol BS9 4RS

A CIP catalogue record for this book is available from the British Library

ISBN 978-0-9567541-0-3

Cover design by sweetdesign (uk) ltd
Typeset in Sabon and Frutiger by sweetdesign (uk) ltd
Printed in Great Britain by Midway Colour Print

www.montroymedia.com

www.sweetdesignuk.com

CONTENTS

Contents

ACKNOWLEDGEMENTS

The originators of this work wish especially to thank The Bath Chronicle and its library staff for their help in allowing access to the newspaper's archives over a period of years. Without their assistance it would not have been possible to provide such a detailed account of the club's fortunes, particularly in the 1960s and 70s.

Historical assistance

Since it is so difficult to identify separately those individuals who have helped us to create this two-part history of the club, the following list includes those who made valuable contributions to the whole story: Lyn Alvis, Ted Arnold, George Atchison, Mrs Phil Arnold, Bath Rugby plc, Stuart Barnes, The Bath Library, Dorrien Belson, John Brennan, Steven and Louis Bush, Gareth Chilcott, 'Patchy' Davies, Philip de Glanville, John Dolman, Bill Donnelly, John Downey, Chris Ducker, Mrs Lorna Ebdon, John Edwards, David Egerton, Roger Elliott, Mike Etheridge, Morton Evans, Roy Farnham, Nevil Field, Jacqui Fisher (NZ), Kevin Ford, Peter Frankcom, Nigel Gaymond, Russell Gibbs, Tony Guest, Geoff Hancock, Andrew Hall, Gordon Hall, John Hall, Phil Hall, N Halse, Mick Hanna, Richard Harding, Phil Hardy, Tim Harris, Ben Hartley (Oldfield Old Boys RFC), Freddie Hayman, Peter Heindorff (dec'd), Brian Henson, Malcolm Henson, Tommy Hicks, Richard Hill, Eric Hopton, Brian Jenkins, Simon Jones, Len Hughes, Mrs Elizabeth Higgins, M Hoskins (Bristol), Ken Johnstone, Jerry Keeling, Glen Leat, Tom Martland, Les Matthews, Richard Mawditt, J M 'Bertie' Meddick, Angus Meek, John Monahan, Reg Monk, Gerry Moore, Bob Orledge, John Palmer, Brendan Perry, Chris Perry, David Peters, Geoff Pillinger, Major John Quin, Nigel Redman, H D Rees, John Roberts, Andy Robinson, David Robson (dec'd), Jack Rowell, The Royal Engineers Museum of Military Engineering, Peter Sibley, The Royal Navy, Danny Sacco, Mrs Florence Simpkins, Jed Smith (Curator, RFU Museum), Malcolm Spark, Roger Spurrell, Mrs Rosemary St John-Davies, Michel van der Loos, Ken Watts, Mrs Joyce Weiss, Gerry Wheeler and Dr John Wroughton. To anyone we have inadvertently omitted, please accept our apologies. Sadly, some of the people mentioned are now deceased.

Photographic, technical and other assistance

Thanks to the generosity of The Bath Chronicle, the Bristol Evening Post, Getty Images, Val Cooper and Chas Williamson, of CW Sports, we have been able to illustrate this book with contemporary images. We owe our thanks too to John Taylor, of Montroy Media, for his expertise and enthusiasm in steering the book through the design, typesetting and print process and to Maria Sweet, of Sweet Design, for the jacket cover design, also to Timothy Coughlan for his efforts in sorting and archiving 25 years of match programmes and other research material.

Last but not least, the authors are immensely grateful to Bath Football Club Trustees Ltd and, in particular to Jack Rowell, Nick Maslen and Richard Seaman, for their encouragement and vital support.

Return of the lemons ... on being introduced to the Bath team before the 1994 Pilkington Cup final against Leicester, His Royal Highness Prince Edward is surprised to be offered a lemon drop by Audley Lumsden, much to the amusement of captain John Hall (left) and Ed Rayner.

Cover pictures

FRONT: Richard Lee, Graham Dawe and Gareth Chilcott ready for the fray against Leicester in the 1989 Pilkington Cup final.

BACK: Brothers in arms ... Roger Spurrell and John Hall celebrate victory at Gloucester in the 1985 semi-final of the John Player Cup.

INTRODUCTION

We owe readers an explanation regarding the esoteric title. Why *After The Lemons*? But what else could we call it after choosing *Before The Lemons* for its precursor?

It's not so long ago that players sucked slices of orange at half-time but the times when lemons provided a 'sharpener' at the interval belong in those dear dead days beyond recall when correspondents would refer to the two halves of a game as 'before – and after – the lemons'.

So for the first volume, covering the first 100 years, the reference was entirely appropriate, perhaps less so for this book. But at least it removed the temptation to adopt something more clichéd.

If there is an apology due, it is because our 'lemons interval' between the two volumes has been rather longer than any of us anticipated – seven years. Yet it has allowed us to look back on events with a greater sense of detachment, particularly the advent of the professional game.

For those who lived through the 'glory days' at the Rec, we hope this book brings back happy memories. For those who didn't (but wished they had), perhaps it will explain why their companion on the clubhouse terrace keeps talking about Jim Waterman's runs from full-back, 'that Cardiff match in 1985', Barnesy's drop goal against Quins or 'that pub we always stopped at on the way home from Twickenham'.

It may also settle some arguments about exactly what happened when, particularly as we are incorporating fixtures and results from each season. Happy reading!

Kevin Coughlan, Peter Hall, Colin Gale

ABOUT THE AUTHORS

Kevin Coughlan

Kevin has reported on rugby on the Rec for 25 years. He was educated at
Prior Park College in Bath and trained as a journalist in South Devon before
moving in 1979 to the sports desk of the Bristol Evening Post; assignments
there included the 1984 Olympic Games in Los Angeles and the 1991 World Cup.
After a spell as Business Editor of the Evening Post, he moved into public relations
and now runs his own business as a media and communications consultant.
Kevin has continued his association with Bath rugby as a freelance journalist.

Peter Hall

Peter is a Past President of the Bath Football Club and a former player, having
first played for the club in the 1950s. Family associations with the club extend
over half a century – married to Mollie, his father-in-law was Harry Vowles, a
brilliant half-back immediately after the Great War, while their son, John, was
at one time Bath's most capped international. Now retired, Peter's background
in banking prepared him for the many months of meticulous research which
prepared the ground for this definitive record.

Colin Gale

Colin is a former Local Director of NatWest Bank and was the club's Honorary
Treasurer until the end of the amateur days. Educated at Bristol Grammar School,
he has enjoyed a life-long interest in rugby and diligently researched this work
together with Peter Hall over a period of more than five years.

Chapter 1

THE MYOPIC VISIONARY

As the Bath Football Club prepared to celebrate its centenary in September 1965 there was precious little to suggest that the club and rugby union football itself were ripe for revolution.

The Recreation Ground fixture list for the coming season even persisted with the antiquated, anglicised spelling of Llanelli - with a 'y'.

At a wider level, patience had been strained two years earlier with the most tedious of matches between Scotland and Wales at Murrayfield. Distinguished, if that is the word, by a record 111 line-outs, it forced the International Board to give serious consideration to a radical law change preventing kicks direct to touch from outside the 25-yard line, as it then was.

Meanwhile, the equally effective law of serendipity intervened at Bath when former Oxford University student Peter Sibley accepted a teaching post at Monkton Combe School. Having been a regular at Blackheath, he was duly invited to join the Recreation Ground squad by the team secretary, Roger Berry.

Sibley, who had intended to keep quiet the fact that he was already 30 and rather short-sighted, recalls: "I was made most welcome – although in a 'West Country' sort of way, as Roy Farnham informed me that he knew just how old I really was." After a run-out for the United against Cinderford, he made his first team debut at Leicester on 11 September, a game Bath lost 9-3.

Peter Sibley in full flight.

"A try beckoned early on, as I ran across from the right wing to over-lap on the left, only for the left wing, Graham Hand, to be tackled in possession with me screaming for the scoring pass. And then I was told that he was the left wing in this club and that I should 'bugger off' to my proper position!"

Centenary or not, it was hardly the most successful of campaigns, disrupted by mid-winter flooding and featuring too many narrow defeats. But the newcomer enjoyed the camaraderie, not to mention playing for a city club with a passionate following, the support of a dedicated committee and good local press coverage. He quickly built up a good rapport with John Stevens, rugby correspondent of The Bath Chronicle.

Nine tries came Sibley's way from 27 appearances and he pays tribute to "that powerful pack, a mixture of the old brigade – Phil Hall, Peter Heindorff, Peter Parfitt and Tom Martland – and some exciting youngsters, David Gay and Bob Orledge."

Gordon Margretts, who had the honour of leading the club in its centenary season, was an astute captain but was part of a back line perceived as lacking pace and thrust to match the forward effort inspired by veteran pack leader Parfitt. There were some victories in the first half of the season but only against medical students, servicemen and West Country opposition of the calibre of Penzance, Bridgwater and Clifton.

After a 6-3 defeat at Bridgend on 30 October a few of the committee trooped into the dressing room to congratulate the team on a good performance. Sibley did not appreciate the condescension, however well intentioned.

"I muttered to Phil Hall, unlacing his boots next to me, that if we had run the ball more, we could have won. 'Right', he said, 'you skipper us next year and we'll back you'. I was duly elected and asked the doughty Phil to be my vice-captain. Although I had enjoyed my rugby immensely in Oxford with both 'town' and 'gown' and my time at Blackheath, I now embarked on a few years that far exceeded my expectations both on and off the field. And it all began in the year that England won the World Cup with the round ball – 1966."

Meanwhile Bath's centenary fortunes improved after the New Year, primarily with a 6-nil win in a downpour at Wasps, but also with a 19-13 home victory over Gloucester in which Vaughan Williams, half-back partner of a certain Gareth Edwards at Millfield School, made his debut. Even better was a first success over Harlequins in a decade, Bath holding on to win 8-5 on the Rec as Bob Hiller missed a last-minute penalty amid a cacophony of boos.

Wing John Cousins finished top scorer with 15 of the 107 tries as Margretts' side finished their programme of 48 fixtures with 19 victories, 28 defeats and a draw. Having made 43 appearances, more than any other player, Margretts handed the captaincy over to Sibley.

University rugby had taught Sibley a great deal about possession and effective use of the ball. It was only his poor eyesight that had deprived him of a Blue.

*On tour in France: Clive Buckle, Bob Orledge and Tom Martland (left) take a breather
against Nice as the referee is carried off with cramp.*

He continues: "I had always been a keen advocate of the nearest person to the breakdown, be he back or forward, going in to retrieve the ball, thus releasing forwards to take the ensuing ball at speed close to the maul or ruck. Bath had the ideal players for this as Orledge, Gay, Martland and even Heindorff came into their own. Some of us still remember backs turning round and scuttling back to their position in the line rather than going in to get the ball! The new RFU coaching manual also appeared that year, advocating the same – long overdue in my opinion.

"I will always remember the powerful John Donovan turning round to me during one of the early games and shouting: 'It's really working, skipper!' "

Work it did. After losing 14-nil at Llanelli (sic) and 6-3 at home to Broughton Park in September 1966, the forwards suddenly found inspiration at home to Leicester, Sibley running in two tries. Centre Bryn Jenkins crossed for the other with Vaughan Williams adding the conversion to an earlier penalty as Bath scored all their points in the first half and relied on simple teamwork to secure a 14-8 victory.

"Williams was outstanding," recalls Sibley, "and an American torpedo-style throw across half the pitch from John Cousins to put me in at the corner, stands in the memory."

With hooker Brian Collins winning plenty of possession and the ball being moved wide at every opportunity, success followed success. Notably, Hall poached a try at Pontypool to give Bath their first win in Wales since 1959 and there were also victories over Saracens and London Irish before Sibley led his side with some panache to a 19-14 victory at Gloucester on 11 February 1967 – their first at Kingsholm since 1948. Centre Paddy Hillyard scored a try and there were two more for the enigmatic

Bath team 1967-68 – back row (from left): Jim Messer (Baggageman), Allen Gay,
John Monahan, Peter Parfitt, Bob Orledge, John Parsons, David Gay, Jack Thomas,
Jim Galley, Ron Ludlow (masseur). Front row: Bill Lye, Geoff Frankcom, Phil Hall,
Peter Sibley (Captain), Peter Heindorff, John Donovan, Ben Hartley.

ex-Royal Marine officer Ian Duckworth, both converted by Gordon Mobley, who added two penalties.

After a run of five defeats against Wasps, Leicester Bristol, Moseley and Harlequins, Bath strung together nine victories, including an 11-3 win over Llanelli. Sibley was missing through injury for the Rag Doll contest but his stand-in, schoolboy international Michael Bull, celebrated his debut with a try. Barry John was well shackled and the home pack eventually took control with Collins claiming several strikes against the head.

Sibley's first season as captain had yielded 29 wins, 20 defeats and a draw, including an end-of-season tour victory over Combined Services at Guttersloh in West Germany in which all 11 tries were scored by the wings – eight to John Monahan and five to Sibley, who finished leading try scorer with 21.

"That equalled the record number of wins in a season, and led to my re-election for another year," says Sibley. "It had been great fun. Handling skills and mobility were improving fast, and I reckoned the best was yet to come."

Rugby in the 1960s was not always such a playful romp. A trip to the Gnoll the following November produced one of Sibley's favourite rugby stories:

"Neath always played combative football – even Gloucester had dropped them that year for rough play – so we knew we were in for a tough encounter. And it was raining, as usual.

"Malcolm Lloyd suffered a badly cut head; Tom Martland was late tackled into the stand; and punches began to fly. As the referee called the two captains together with tempers running high, I showed him the bite marks on my rib cage sustained in the previous maul.

"To his eternal credit, Neath's gnarled, grey-haired old hooker – Morlais Williams, I think – defused the situation by giving me a tooth-less grin, and saying: 'It can't be me, Pete, my teeth are in the ref's pocket'! In my chat with my opposite number, Brian Thomas I had also said that if there was any more rough play I would take Bath off the field and Neath would lose another fixture against an English club. At the selection meeting the following Monday, John Roberts took me to task for attempting to change the club's fixtures!"

Sibley admits he was not above pulling rank when the occasion demanded: "Jim Galley, incumbent scrum-half during the 1966-67 season, was the new PE teacher at Monkton Combe School and I was temporarily running the hockey there. On the same Saturday as the Bristol game, the member of staff taking the 1st XI hockey team away fell ill. Jim and I were the only possible replacements but I was the senior colleague and also captain of the club. Poor Jim, he took ages to forgive me. He was later to travel home in the boot of the coach from Ebbw Vale, but that is another story!"

Bath lost that derby match 24-6 but the expansive style continued to develop, with Jack Thomas, Hillyard, Monahan and Donovan making important contributions. Irish wing forward-turned-prop Niall Carter bolstered the pack too but the biggest asset had been the arrival of the maverick Duckworth, a fast, powerful runner on the wing and a destructive tackler too. "He was a law unto himself, spending the night with his motor bike in the changing room before some games, but what a player!" says Sibley.

Ian Duckworth: missed out on an England call–up.

It was on the eve of the England Wales game at Twickenham in January 1968 – Bath were playing at Met Police next morning – that club secretary Jack Simpkins famously received a call at Bath's London hotel from Dickie Jeeps, chairman of the England selectors. He asked if Duckworth could report to Twickenham because of an injury to David Duckham. Sibley recalls: "Jack replied that Ian was in bed with 'flu back in Bath and was therefore not available but that Peter Sibley was. Jeeps' reply was unprintable as he put the phone down!"

Bath No 8 David Gay, son of Bill, who had been elected Bath captain for the abortive 1939-40 season, did take his place against Wales, however. The 19-year-old had made eight of his 52 first team appearances for the club while still at Bath Technical School. He was to play in all four of England's matches, packing down with fellow schoolboy international Bryan West, of Northampton. England drew the first two matches, then lost in Paris but salvaged some respect by beating the Scots at Murrayfield. Gay moved to Harlequins the following season in order to pursue law qualifications in the capital but was denied further international honours, despite a strongly worded letter to the England selectors by Sibley.

New faces had begun to appear as Bath's reputation flourished under Sibley's leadership. Pilot Officer Geoff Frankcom, educated at King Edward's School and groomed by Bath but capped in 1965 while at Bedford, returned to his home club after being posted to RAF South Cerney for flying training. His subtle skills were ideally suited to the Sibley regime but early in 1968 he was transferred again to Yorkshire. He turned out for Headingley for two seasons, eventually captaining the RAF side in 1972; his recollections show that his military career was as distinguished as that of any Bath player in the previous century.

Brothers Alan, Peter and Robert Parfitt in Oldfield Old Boys kit.

"From 1970 I flew Phantom F4s, including a tour in Germany. My last first-class game was in 1972 for the South West of England against the Rest of the World team at Bristol; not a bad way to finish! In 1976 I went to France for three years as an instructor of French Air Force students on their final stage before becoming fighter pilots. This was near Bordeaux; I played in the Second Division for La Teste, which was great fun – a wonderful experience, as much gastronomic as sporting. I left the RAF in 1983 as a Squadron Leader having flown for 16 years."

Some rugby histories list another RAF serviceman, Peter Glover, as a Bath player when he was capped against Australia in January 1967 but he was not to make his debut at the Recreation Ground until April 1969.

These had not been the only recruits with international experience, however. There was also former England scrum-half Simon Clarke, an old friend of Sibley's from Blackheath days, and he was joined by Gloucester stalwart Terry Hopson, a mobile prop in Mike Hannell and a promising product of Oldfield Old Boys, Roger Elliott.

Bath had begun that 1967-68 season well, with wins on a Northern tour and eventually the double over Bristol, the first for 17 years and one that Sibley remembers with particular satisfaction.

"In the home match on the Rec, my old Oxford pal Jim Glover, playing in the centre for Bristol, delivered a relieving kick in my direction, fully expecting me to drop the ball in the gloomy conditions because of my well known short-sightedness. But, unbeknown to Jim, the club had bought me contact lenses (subsequently repaid on a monthly basis) and I caught the ball cleanly and ran in from half way for the winning try. It was a closely fought game, with the injured Allen Gay returning in heroic fashion to help us withstand the final Bristol onslaught.

"There was another win at Gloucester; Richmond, Rosslyn Park and Moseley succumbed, as did Llanelli in the 'rag doll' match, Peter Parfitt's record breaking 365th appearance for Bath. Annoyingly, by careless play we still lost matches that we should have won comfortably. But our running style was catching on."

John Roberts, who had set the old appearances record, presented prop Parfitt with an engraved tankard and supply of drinks to mark the occasion on 16 April 1968. It had been a magnificent team performance, particularly in the forwards; Alan Parfitt won several heels against the head and Orledge reigned supreme in the line-out. Barry Fry was a last minute addition to a scratch back division – and he had only turned up to watch! Sibley and Martland scored the Bath tries.

Martland, troubled by a persistent knee injury, had performed as remarkably as any other player in the resurgence of the Bath club under Sibley. Early in 1968, playing on the wing, he scored a drop goal, try and conversion to force an 11-11 draw at home to Leicester, earning the description "that versatile master of the unexpected" from John Stevens, of The Chronicle. A month later, at the request of the Somerset

Scrum-half Malcolm Lloyd fields an awkward tap from Bob Orledge
against Leicester on 14 September 1968.

selectors, Martland appeared at full-back against Gloucester, drawing the following observation from a correspondent of The Daily Telegraph:

> **"His last appearance in the championship – when Somerset lost 14-18 to Gloucestershire in October 1965 – was at wing forward. This season, he has played openside, blindside, wing, centre and emergency full back for Bath, helping himself to six tries and 54 points in the process."**

By the end of the 1967-68 campaign, 27-year-old Martland had made 164 first team appearances, helping Sibley achieve a playing record of 24 victories, 14 defeats and five draws from his second season in charge. For 1968-69, Bath handed Sibley the reins for the third successive season, with Martland his vice-captain.

Among the newcomers was a Bristol University student by the name of Jim Waterman and he scored a try on his debut at full-back against Ebbw Vale on 21 September. A week later, there was also a scoring debut for 19-year-old Mike Beese, selected at fly-half against Clifton after promising performances for Keynsham Colts. He had only recently opted for rugby over soccer and had represented Somerset Schools at cricket and in the triple jump. Studies at Liverpool Polytechnic were to deprive Bath of his services for much of the next six years.

Sibley continues: "The change in the laws suited the 'new' Bath down to the ground, but meant that loyal servants at full-back such as the strong-tackling Allen Gay, the stylish David Dolman and John Hiles and such a good kicker as Gordon Mobley had to give way to the darting Waterman, with his incursions from the back and wriggling runs out of defence. There have been few players since to match Jim's lines of running, in my opinion. And what a loyal servant to the club he was to become."

Gates were increasing, heavy grounds were no longer welcome and Bath were unbeaten in 11 games between the end of September and mid-November 1969. The sequence included another win at Bristol with Sibley crossing twice. It took an outrageous individual score from the great Phil Bennett, breaking from his own 25, for Llanelli to sneak a 10-8 victory at Stradey Park on 21 December but Sibley remembers the visit for other reasons:

"That day we were just tucking into George Brown's sandwiches in the team bus when the pipe of committee man Dennis Curran disappeared through the front door, courtesy of Ian Duckworth, who objected to the smoke. Dennis stopped the coach, stated that he would not continue the journey and made his way back to Bath, having searched unsuccessfully for the ill fated pipe; we continued down to Stradey minus one of our selectors.

Peter Glover: debut against Llanelli.

"My team talk was short and to the point: 'Lads, this could well be Ian's last game for the club. Make it a good one!' They certainly did, making light of an early injury to young Alan Parfitt, and harassing Bennett and Co all afternoon, with Duckworth appearing here, there and everywhere. We received a standing ovation as we left the pitch and Dennis Curran did not press charges!

"Mike Beese was already making his presence felt in the centre as we lost at Leicester by only a point – and then at home to London Welsh, complete with six British Lions, in one of the most thrilling games that I had played in for Bath and surely that many spectators had seen." The Bath Chronicle was in total agreement:

> **Bath and London Welsh fought out a magnificent match under difficult conditions on the Recreation Ground on Saturday which fully justified all the superlatives heaped upon it by friend and foe alike. It simply bubbled with vintage, sophisticated football and with the result in doubt almost to the final whistle, lived up to the classic hopes everyone had beforeit started**
>
> **In the end the Welsh triumphed – and who can deny that they deserved to on the strength of their superb team-work and touches of individual genius – but what inspired opposition this up-and-coming young Bath side provided.**

John Mason of The Daily Telegraph concurred:

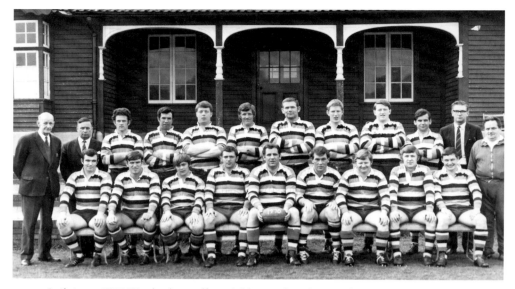

Bath team 1970-71 – back row (from left): R Ludlow (masseur), D Curran (committee), I Duckworth, I Holmes, Hannell, R Lye, K Plummer, R Walkey, N Carter, J Thomas, J Vassiere (Committee), P Pothecary (sponge man). Seated: John Donovan, Peter Glover, Alan Parfitt, Tom Martland, Peter Heindorff, Phil Hall, Malcolm Lloyd, Roger Elliott, Brendan Perry.

Here was a contest, an entertainment, an exercise of ability in which London Welsh's eager willingness to turn a defensive situation into an attacking one finally meant defeat for Bath. But they did not fall easily."

Harlequins were run off their feet at the start of their Easter tour, with Brian Collins taking seven against the head and Hall swallowing Nigel Starmer-Smith's attempted breaks. And as Sibley ran round the newly capped wing, John Novak, England full-back Bob Hiller's voice was heard to boom across the Rec: 'For God's sake, Novak, do something in this game, even if it is scratching your own f***ing arse!'

Bath were no means unbeatable, however. England wing Peter Glover made his debut against Llanelli at the Rec but the Scarlets won 11-nil and Orledge was afterwards dropped for disciplinary reasons after speaking out of turn to the referee. Newbridge, Gloucester and Bedford also proved too strong but Sibley's third season in charge yielded 24 wins from 44 games, with 17 defeats and three draws. The points total of 645 was the highest in the club's history, yet even that record was short-lived.

With house master duties calling at Monkton Combe, Sibley stood down and Martland was elected captain for 1969-70. The outgoing skipper was looking forward to turning out for another year at least but dislocated a knee against Pontypool in one of the first matches and did not play seriously again. In February he conceded defeat, offering his services as club coach for the remainder of the season.

"But," says Sibley, "there were wonderful memories and some great fun over the four years since Roger Berry's invitation to join the club. How glad I am that I accepted. It is nice to think that perhaps we did pave the way for those exciting, successful years to come."

Martland's plans were first disrupted by David Gay's departure to Harlequins and later by the loss of Glover who broke his leg just above the ankle against Bridgwater in early October. The following week at Aberavon, winger Barstow suffered an identical injury and as if things could not get any worse, the captain then suffered torn knee ligaments and was forced to hand over the reins to Peter Heindorff.

Under Heindorff's forthright leadership, Bath had hit a purple patch during the autumn of 1969, following up the 17-10 win at Aberavon with an 11-9 victory at London Irish. The match featured the comeback of 'glamour boy' Tony O'Reilly at 33, who actually carried the ball over the line at one point but was denied a try when Elliott's tackle forced the ex-Lions star's foot into touch. O'Reilly's resurrection was to culminate in an improbable – and largely ineffectual – recall to the Irish team against England.

It was honours even with Bristol a week later – 11-11 at the Rec – and then Welsh-born Roger Walkey reinforced his status as 'find of the season' by scoring a hat-trick in a 35-14 victory at Pontypool, adding four conversions and a penalty for good measure. Frankcom, who had masterminded much of the attacking play, crossed for the final try. The other four tries had been shared by Casey and Perry.

There was sadness in December at the sudden death at 21 of former lock Jamie Monahan, 21-year-old brother of John. The Sporting Chronicle recorded:

> **He had been a London Irish player for the past two seasons, but the strongest of connections remained through his Bath family, his Kingswood School connection, and his brother, John. At Cambridge he had achieved an Honours degree and a Rugby Blue, and had opted for London Irish in furtherance of International aspirations. He had appeared in two Irish trials. A gentle giant off the field, this popular young man was sadly missed.**

Despite a sequence of six defeats in the New Year, Bath were quickly into their stride again with a rare victory at Swansea. Martland marked his comeback in a 14-4 win over Sale with an assured display at full-back and a 35-yard dropped goal into the bargain. The only black mark was incurred by touch judge Jim Vaissiere, sent from the field by international referee Mike Titcomb for shouting at the players

Only one of the last 12 games was lost and Bath hit top form to beat Llanelli 16-8 on the Rec on 11 April 1970. Although Phil Bennett threatened to tear the home side apart with his runs from full-back, he was finally stifled and the home back row of Hall, Lye and Walkey set the stage for Perry to turn in an immaculate performance at fly-half, as The Chronicle noted:

Combining more determination with his usual brilliant acceleration, he knifed through the Welsh defence several times and once decisively, Heindorff backing him up to provide the scoring pass for Walkey to touch down and convert... There were Bath jerseys everywhere, cutting down one movement after another in a game so admirably controlled by Mike Titcomb.

The club record of 27 wins in a season, established by Alec Lewis's team of 1950-51, was eclipsed against Bedford, England's unofficial club champions. A new mark of 29 was eventually set, from 43 matches, with 13 defeats and a draw. Points for were also the highest ever at 730 with 480 against Entertaining stuff!

Heindorff became captain in his own right for 1970-71, a season which marked the long-awaited introduction of the new law penalising direct kicks to touch from outside the 25. In Waterman, Bath had a player with a range of skills perfectly suited to the new tactical environment. Joy at the return of David Gay from Harlequins turned to exasperation when the international No 8 cracked a bone in his leg during an early England trial; Walkey was also injured in the same match, although not so seriously

A measure of the club's progress was the sense of dissatisfaction with the quality of performance at Pontypool where Waterman converted his own try and also kicked three penalties in a 17-9 victory. Glover scored the other try.

For the visit of Leicester on 12 September 1970 – Heindorff's 300th game – a fit-again Martland appeared in the back row with Hall and Lye. Heindorff packed down with Orledge and the front row comprised Hannell, Alan Parfitt and Carter. Half-backs were Lloyd and Perry with Waterman at full-back, while the threequarter line-up featured Mario Polledri, Donovan, Elliott and Duckworth, making his 100th appearance.

After Perry had a pass intercepted for an opening try by Leicester, Bath responded in extravagant style with a break from his own half by Orledge, carried on by Duckworth, Elliott, Donovan and Polledri, before scrum-half Lloyd cut through to lay on the try for Duckworth. Another fumble let the Tigers in for a second try to lead 6-3 at the break but the second half was all Bath as Lye dummied his way through to provide a try for Hannell, converted by Waterman, and Lloyd slipped over for the third to secure an 11-9 victory.

No sooner had Glover been restored to the side than he obliged with two tries in a 17-13 win over Moseley and Bath continued on a run of nine successive victories until London Irish nicked an 18-17 win at the Rec on 10 October. Waterman was absent, appearing against the Fijian tourists, with Lloyd on the bench.

Next up, though, was a visit to Bristol – a typically tense, rugged and occasionally bad-tempered West Country derby. Early on Lloyd wriggled through for a try, converted by Waterman, but home scrum-half Alan Pearn landed two penalties before Waterman replied to give Bath an 8-6 lead at the interval. Then Alan Morley broke from defence and his kick ahead provided a try for Dave Tyler. Pearn kicked another penalty and it was nip and tuck throughout the second half as Hannell plunged over for Bath, Waterman converting, only for Pearn to snatch the lead with his third penalty.

Almost immediately, however, Duckworth sped away for Bath's third try and victory was theirs by 16-15. In the clubhouse afterwards, there were dark mutterings from Bristol that Duckworth had put a foot in touch but the man with the flag, Bath's long-serving secretary Jack Simpkins, was adamant. Ah, the days of 'impartial' touch judges ...

> **A glorious finish to a fine game at Bristol last Saturday, and those of us who have been privileged to watch many Bath and Bristol games will probably agree that this was one of the best ever.**
> *(Programme notes 24 October 1970)*

That initiated another winning sequence of five games, including a 9-3 victory at Bridgend which kept Bath at the top of the Anglo-Welsh Merit Table. Nevertheless, the club's only representative in the final England trial at Wilmslow on 19 December was Glover.

After an 11-3 defeat at Bridgwater, Bath's fortunes began to turn sour as the winter weather closed in. With Martland still suffering knee ligament problems, they also lost the services of scrum-half Lloyd with a torn Achilles tendon, suffered 30 minutes into a nil-nil draw with Gloucester. His place was taken by John Deverell, later to become Major General Sir John Deverell OBE.

Reverses against Llanelli and Cardiff were followed by the visit to the Rec on 9 January 1971 by London Welsh, arguably the best club side in the world at the time. J P R Williams, Gerald Davies, John Dawes, Mervyn Davies, John Taylor and Trevor Evans – all destined to play significant roles in the British Isles' historic series win in New Zealand that summer – strutted their stuff as the Exiles saw off a spirited Bath challenge to win 14-6. Despite winning at Rugby and Rosslyn Park and then earning a 9-9 draw against Gloucester under the Kingsholm floodlights, Bath lost their unbeaten record against English opposition by tripping up at Cheltenham on 22 February.

A week later, after a four-year exile from international rugby, Glover won his second cap in a 14-14 draw against France but was then dropped, only to reappear in an England shirt in the RFU centenary match against a President's XV on 17 April. He was also selected for their summer tour to the Far East.

Meanwhile Bath continued their Anglo-Welsh rivalry, losing 14-13 at home to Swansea when referee Titcomb awarded a late penalty try, then restoring links with Newport for the first time since 1952 and beating the Black and Ambers 12-8 on the Rec. Hopes of achieving a 'double' over Bristol quickly evaporated in the first half, however, as The Chronicle reported:

In the end all Bath's woeful limitations in tackling and covering and their lack of experience in key positions were exposed for all to see. But undoubtedly the most lasting damage was done in the first 25 minutes during which Bath, with one schoolboy error after another, allowed Bristol to build up a 4-6 lead. They were body blows from which Bath never recovered. If the crowd was stunned into silence, one could imagine the demoralising effect on the Bath players, who groped their way through the rest of the game without ever finding their true touch... To say the crowd were disappointed was an understatement, and Bath's lack of real fighting spirit must have been doubly hard to bear.

With Somerset Cup and tour fixtures excluded from first team records, Bath's 26th and last victory of a 41-match season was against Old Merchant Taylors on Easter Monday. The visit of Llanelli a week later again became a 'master class' from Bennett who scored all but six of their points in a 28-19 win for the Scarlets. A run of defeats to the end of April was not the best preparation for the Somerset Cup final against Somerset Police on 8 May but tries by David Gay and Perry, both converted by Elliott who also kicked a penalty, secured a 13-8 win. Yet the champions looked jaded.

Meanwhile the Management Committee were in negotiations on an extended lease on the Rec, prompting the chairman, Cyril Beazer, to draw up plans for improvements to the North Stand and dressing rooms at a cost of £10,000.

Bath was setting its sights on becoming a thoroughly modern rugby union club. There was though no tokenism, as we might say these days, in the election of Mrs Mollie Gerrard to the club presidency on 26 June 1971. She was not only the widow of the club's most-capped England player, R A Gerrard (1932-36), but also an accomplished architect in her own right and a former member of the Management Committee valued for her business expertise; it was however a sign of the times.

It was not long before difficulties arose. When asked to send representatives to the Somerset RFU dinner, Bath's Honorary Secretary, Jack Simpkins, did not think to demand an invitation for his President, having ascertained with his counterpart at the county body that it was a men-only function. Mrs Gerrard, taking 'executive action', turned up at Fortt's Restaurant without a ticket and eventually sat down to dinner as the guest of the Somerset committee. Inevitably, the matter was raised at a Management Committee meeting on 25 October 1971.

From the Chair, Mr Cyril Beazer ruled that in future Mrs Gerrard, as Club President, should always be invited to official functions and she should be allowed to decide if she wanted to attend. The Secretary said he thought this might embarrass some Clubs. No one disagreed with the Chairman's ruling.

Chapter 2

THE LIONS INSPIRE A NINE-YEAR-OLD

It would not happen these days, certainly not on a school pitch casually roped off for the occasion. But back in 1971, the best players in the world could be persuaded to turn out on a Sunday afternoon to play for scratch sides.

So it was that Gareth Edwards, Barry John, Mike Gibson, John Bevan and John Pullin – heroes of the Lions tour to New Zealand barely two months before – appeared for an International XV raised by referee Mike Titcomb to celebrate 50 years of rugby at St Brendan's College, Bristol.

Among the 2,000 or so spectators straining at the touchline ropes was a nine-year-old boy from Bath. The young John Hall's enthusiasm for rugby was fired from that moment, to such a degree in fact, that he was to forge a reputation as arguably the finest forward that Bath has ever produced.

"I do recall going over and watching it," he says now. "I remember thinking how fantastic these players were. It would have been just after the '71 Lions tour. The memory is of all these amazing players – seeing Barry John and John Bevan.

"I wasn't playing rugby at that age. I didn't start until I was 11 but there was a rugby tradition within my family so I knew a lot about the game. A lot of my childhood was spent in Cardiff and I was a Welsh supporter during the great days of the 1970s, those halcyon days in Wales."

No-one really cared about the final scoreline at St Brendan's that day but it ended up 77-44, enhanced by the new law elevating the try to four points. They just feasted on a banquet of rugby skills ... Edwards' delivering the most extravagant reverse passes, 'The King' John a sublime mix of guile and perfect balance, Gibson immaculate in everything he did and Bevan all pace and power on the left wing. Pullin was rightly feted as the local hero while Bath interest was sustained by Peter Glover's presence on the right wing for the International XV and by Brendan Perry, also in the No 14 shirt, for the Old Boys.

There was not a lot to celebrate back at the Recreation Ground at that time, Bath being in the middle of a nine-match losing run. They were already out of the new RFU Knock-out Cup, defeated 12-3 at home in the first round by eventual champions Gloucester, while Bristol spoiled veteran wing forward Phil Hall's

400th appearance by winning 12-3 at the Rec. On one county championship Saturday, Bath, suffering from a lack of pace in the backs and a dearth of experience overall, even lost to St Mary's Hospital.

Problems had been apparent even before the season began as the Management Committee forced through the appointment of Roger Walkey as captain against the wishes of the majority of players, who had been rooting for Hall. It split the club and the depth of feeling was evidenced by Orledge's departure for Bristol and Waterman opting to join Clifton, although he returned to the fold before the end of the year.

Bath marked New Year's Day 1972 – and agreement on a new 75-year lease on the Rec – with a 17-15 victory over Leicester but the wheels came off again a week later when they had the temerity to to travel to London Welsh without seven players required for county duty. In contrast, the Exiles were welcoming back their seven British Lions and fielded 11 internationals in all. They ran in 10 tries, converting seven, to win 54-nil.

Another sequence of six successive defeats sapped morale even further. Heindorff was sent off for a short-arm tackle in a 16-3 defeat at Cheltenham, although his punishment was confined to a mere reprimand from the disciplinary committee, confirming most observers' view – and The Bath Chronicle's – that he was not the main instigator of the violence.

> "From a bright start, both sides suddenly deteriorated into niggling brawls with fists flying openly, and after one set scrum, while Norris was speeding down one wing, Parfitt was prone on the other side of the field and had to be carried off... More penalties did not stop the fighting and just before half-time, after Walkey had been fouled, Heindorff was sent off for an alleged short-arm tackle."

Hall, no shrinking violet himself and chuckling at the memory, recalls that Heindorff finally reacted to being called "a fat German bastard."

It was a rough and tough introduction to first-class rugby for 18-year-old scrum-half Richard Harding, persuaded to play by his Millfield schoolmaster, Geoff Phillips. Although blooded on that day by Bath, it was with his home town club, Bristol, that Harding went on to establish his reputation as an astute and stylish performer, winning 12 caps for England (1985-88) and also captaining his country.

Meanwhile Walkey's powers of leadership were being tested by the worst spell of form for some years. The commitment of the ex-Welsh Secondary Schools captain was not in doubt – he would turn out in the back line when required, kicked some fine goals and made 43 appearances, more than any other. On and off the field, a gregarious Roger Elliott fulfilled a vital supporting role as vice-captain.

Wistful Bath eyes must have been cast to the north, though, when one of their own, Keynsham-born Mike Beese, was selected from the Liverpool club to make his England debut against Wales on 15 January 1972. The centre also appeared against Ireland and France but did not survive a record 37-12 defeat in Paris. Beese's career as a town planner took him back to Bath in the summer but he never again wore an England shirt.

Although Waterman had returned from Clifton before Christmas, differences with the hierarchy were not immediately patched up. His comeback game on 18 December as a somewhat reluctant right wing had coincided with a superlative Llanelli display at the Rec, the 34-nil scoreline leaving Bath "lifeless and bitterly disappointed." Waterman then opted to play for the United XV at full-back rather than continue on the wing and was soon restored to his preferred position in the first team.

The punch-up with Cheltenham, continuing an unfortunate tradition of bad feeling which stretched back to the previous century, was followed by a 12-9 win at Wasps and a 20-27 defeat at Swansea, a match Bath let slip from their grasp.

Roger Elliott: a vital supporting role.

Having been advised at the start of the season that a proposed rebuilding of the North Stand and dressing rooms would cost £8,000-9,000 and that the maximum loan available from the RFU would be £1,184, the club set about making up the difference. On 3 March 1972, a sub-committee was given a fund-raising target of £6,000 with the following individuals handed responsibility for specific events:

Sponsored Walk	*R A Berry*
Indoor Race Night	*C H Beazer*
Firework Display	*R A Berry*
Derby Draw	*A Meek and L Newton*
Dance and Tombola	*G S Brown*
Combined event with Somerset County Cricket	*L Hughes.*
There would be a Ladies Coffee evening.	

The sponsored walk raised £680, a remarkable sum at a time when entry to the ground cost just 20p and gate takings from the home game with Cardiff on 23 March amounted to a mere £120. Hearty congratulations were accorded to Roger Berry and

Len Hughes but the Management Committee also received the unwelcome news that the RFU's loan scheme to clubs had been temporarily suspended.

Nevertheless, the sense of collective effort seemed to be felt throughout the club. On the field, after losses to Cardiff and Richmond, Bath began to turn the corner, stringing together six wins against the likes of Harlequins and other Easter tourists before going down 15-33 at Llanelli.

They then made hard work of beating Somerset & Bath Police 13-8 in the final of the Somerset Knock-Out Cup, a competition which had engendered mixed feelings at the Rec ever since its inception in 1906-7. This time there was wrangling over a venue for the final and it was no great shock when the winners announced they would no longer be entering the competition, despite the fact it guaranteed them entry to the National Knock-out Cup the following season. Bath would take their chances with the seedings from first-class fixtures in 1972-73 – but only for one year, as it turned out.

Throughout an undistinguished season, the forwards had carried the fight to the opposition – literally, on occasions – and were strong enough to subdue Northampton 15-6 but Bristol came from behind at the interval to win 24-12 at the Memorial Ground.

The 50th and final match of 1971-72 was at home to Bedford on a rain-drenched Rec. It marked the retirement after 358 games of the supreme clubman, Heindorff, but the team, lacked inspiration and lost 7-10 – their 27th defeat. He was not the only influential figure within the club to hang up his boots. A recurrence of a knee problem finally forced Martland to call time on his Bath career, which had begun in 1963 and covered more than 220 games for the first XV, although his recent involvement had been restricted to captaincy of the United. The second string had benefited hugely from his leadership, winning 22 of their 34 games, and it was hoped, nay expected, that the Culverhay schoolmaster, still only 30, would develop his obvious talents for coaching alongside David Dolman, who had been appointed first team coach in February.

Needless to say, given Bath's recent record, there were no players among the England party to tour South Africa that summer. But the manager was the affable Alec Lewis, back row forward for Bath and England in the early 1950s, so there was great satisfaction at the Rec when they returned unbeaten, including a wholly unexpected 18-9 victory over the Springboks at Ellis Park. And this was a team that had been 'whitewashed' in the Five Nations.

Back at Bath, after the breakdown in relations between players and committee over Walkey's appointment, Hall had been the obvious choice for the 1972-73 captaincy, the wing forward approaching pre-season training with his peculiarly gritty style of 'follow me' leadership. A hectic September programme was to include a Scottish tour, each player having to contribute a minimum £5 towards the cost (at Hall's suggestion) and all the squad being collectively responsible for raising the balance. The Management Committee agreed that team captains be provided with cash to buy beer for visiting teams – £3 per match for first XV and United and £1.50 for Spartans and Youth XVs – and players Allen Gay and Chris Perry were authorised to organise discotheques in the clubhouse.

Within a month, however, day-to-day finances became a cause for concern. The Finance Sub Committee suggested cancellation of coaches for all but the first team, free beer only to be supplied to first XV visitors and a review of playing kit expense. Players were also to pay their subs by 31 October. A fruit machine had been installed in the clubhouse, yielding £2 profit in the first week and it was agreed to charge 10p for parking for the President's XV match on 28 September.

The Scottish tour had been costly in another sense, skipper Hall suffering a knee injury that would rule him out of action until the end of October.

Much of the obligatory pre-season optimism had been dissipated over the first month by displays of "fumbling ineptitude", in the words of The Chronicle's seasoned rugby reporter, John Stevens. They included 30-point defeats at Leicester and Hawick and, most disturbingly, a 59-4 hammering at Moseley. David Gay galloped down the touchline for an unconverted try but the rest of the afternoon was dominated by Moseley's internationals, full-back Sam Doble and fly-half John Finlan. The previous season Doble had set a world club record of 450 points and on England's triumphant tour of South Africa, he scored 47 points in five appearances, including four penalties and a conversion of Alan Morley's try in the Test. There was a universal sense of loss at his death from cancer in 1977 at the age of 33.

Doble was absent from the star-studded line-up of 13 England internationals that Alec Lewis brought to the Rec for the President's XV fixture, a crowd of 4,000 seeing the select team win 30-15 as the visitors paraded their full portfolio of skills.

Having negotiated a potentially tricky qualifying round tie at Matson in the RFU Knock-out Cup, the heavier Bath pack eventually subduing their spirited opponents to secure an 18-6 victory, they found themselves drawn away to Gloucester in the first round proper. The tie was set for Monday evening, 30 October, but first there was the little matter of a 'derby' at Bristol.

Under the Memorial Ground floodlights, Bath rose to the challenge magnificently, running themselves to a standstill in support of each other and never letting Bristol slip into the devastating attacking rhythm for which they were renowned. With Holley and Hughes scoring tries, both converted by Thompson, Bath won 12-7.

With a tremendous team performance belying their indifferent record this season, they knocked Bristol right out of their stride, and by the end were audaciously dictating terms against a side previously beaten only at Cardiff.

Bath completed their cup preparations with a nine-try rout of St Mary's Hospital. On the same afternoon, Ian Kirkpatrick's Seventh All Blacks announced their arrival in the British Isles by thrashing the Western Counties 39-12 at Kingsholm. Bath's Robbie Lye watched from the Reserves' bench as the New Zealanders ran in seven tries, including a hat-trick by right wing Bryan Williams.

Gloucester had supplied seven players – five of them forwards – to that chastened Western Counties XV and they took it out on Bath barely 48 hours later under the Kingsholm floodlights. Bath, steamrollered by the Cherry & Whites' pack, occupied the home 25 just twice in a one-sided match and even with Hall back to lead the side were lucky to lose only 16-nil.

Wins were very much at a premium during the winter of 1972-73 – just three in 15 matches, against St Luke's College, US Portsmouth and, bizarrely, a 42-nil rout of Leicester at The Rec on 6 January as England were losing 9-nil to New Zealand.

The victory was notable for the selection of David, Peter and Brian Jenkins; the last time that three brothers had appeared in the Bath team had been on 30 December 1893 when B H, G G and H T Vincent turned out against Wellington.

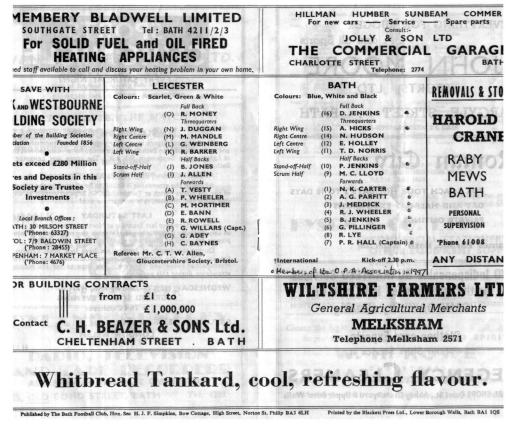

Brothers David, Peter and Brian Jenkins line up against Leicester on 6 January 1973.

Bath won 42-nil.

Among the defeats were a 41-10 trouncing at Llanelli – no surprise there, against the team that beat the All Blacks – but also against Clifton who secured a rare 22-18 victory at the Rec in the traditional Boxing Day fixture.

After the romp against Leicester, cold reality returned in the shape of London Welsh who inflicted a 30-10 defeat at Bath with the help of a superb Gerald Davies try. This was the first of four successive home losses, watched by ever-diminishing crowds as televised internationals provided irresistible counter-attractions, but there were distinct signs of improvement in the second visit to Kingsholm on the evening of Friday, 10 February. After outplaying the home side for much of the game, it was only Bath's indiscipline that allowed Peter Butler to kick his side to an 18-16 victory. The full-back's final penalty was only within range because Bath failed to retreat 10 yards.

Nevertheless with spirits and confidence restored, there followed a run of 10 games unbeaten, starting with a 24-7 victory at Cheltenham and then a 25-3 win at home to Wasps. Next up was the home derby with Bristol who fielded seven internationals but found Bath in unyielding mood, taking a 9-nil lead with a David Gay try, converted by Thompson, who also kicked a penalty. Bristol scrum-half Alan Pearn, who was to amass 557 points during the season, was in uncharacteristically poor form with the boot, missing seven goal attempts. Bristol eventually drew level with penalty and a converted try by Peter Knight but Gay dribbled through for his second try to take Bath 13-9 ahead. Tremendous Bristol pressure led to a late equalising try in the corner for Pearn but he could not kick the conversion to earn victory.

A 15-9 home win over Swansea maintained the momentum and the side achieved their only success in Wales that season by winning 22-21 at Ebbw Vale. They also beat Richmond (31-12) and Bridgend (21-nil) before setting off for Sale early on the morning of 7 April; the committee had rejected on grounds of cost Dolman's request that they travel by coach on the Friday evening.

The reason for the parsimony was that at a time of rampant inflation, accompanied by statutory wage and price controls, projected costs for clubhouse improvements had risen to £12,000, prompting the Management Committee to apply again to the RFU for an £8,000 loan. Admission charges were also raised to 25p from 1 April, with transfer to the West Stand an extra 15p; OAPs and juveniles to pay 10p. The average wage was barely £40 a week.

Starting hesitantly after the long trip to Cheshire, Bath conceded a try in the third minute but eventually earned a 16-16 draw with two tries from centre Chris Perry, both converted by Thompson, plus another touchdown by wing Tony Hicks. Perry was lectured by the referee for a late tackle on the Sale fly-half, John Horton. Notwithstanding that rude introduction, Bath soon received word that Horton might be taking up a teaching post in the Roman City.

Few would have guessed how big an influence he was to become as a creative force, ushering in an era of unparalleled success.

Martin "Nellie" Gould fires out a pass in Bath's 16-7 win over Gloucester on 25 April 1973.
Bath players (from left): Frank Carter, Radley Wheeler, Malcolm Lloyd (background),
Brian Jenkins, Gould, Robbie Lye.

Back in April 1973, the unbeaten run was ended by Newport, winning 12-11 at the Rec after Thompson missed a last-minute touchline conversion, and the full-back kicked Bath's only points four days later as a formidable Llanelli line-up repeated the dose 17-3. Three 30-pointers over Easter against Harlequins, Otley and Old Merchant Taylors restored confidence nicely for the visit of Gloucester and Bath found their form to win 16-8. The back row of Hall, Lye and Gay dominated the loose, affording critical time and space to fly-half Phillips who gave a fine exhibition of tactical kicking and also dropped a goal. Thompson kicked three penalties while left wing Peter Burrowes powered through two tackles for the Bath try.

The season was brought to an end by a 4-nil defeat at Bedford which saw Bath represented by no fewer than nine players originating from local clubs – David Gay (Walcot Old Boys and Oldfield Old Boys), Martyn Gould (Oldfield OB), Brian and David Jenkins (Combe Down), Tony Hicks (Walcot OB), Robbie Lye (Walcot OB), John 'Bert' Meddick (Stothert & Pitt), Chris Perry (Oldfield OB), Radley Wheeler (Frome) – plus Malcolm Lloyd and Phil Hall who had played for Bath since leaving school at 15. They bade farewell to Geoff Phillips who was leaving for an overseas teaching appointment and had made 102 first team appearances since joining from Rosslyn Park in 1970.

On 5 May 1973 the Management Committee, accepting a builder's estimate of £11,000, voted to begin work on the North Stand. It was by no means a unanimous decision, with three votes against from those who, given the uncertain economic conditions, were wary about work starting before any RFU loan had been sanctioned.

Roger Berry, demonstrating a far-sighted approach to the commercial possibilities of the sport, asked if it might be possible to raise funds by selling advertising space around the ground.

Despite mixed results over previous seasons, the progressive elements in the committee held sway and by the time they next met, on 4 June, estimates had been received for the installation of floodlighting. At that time, however, the club was very much dependent on individuals giving freely of their spare time and it was reported that the 'lady helpers' had been entertained to dinner by the committee in appreciation of their work throughout the season.

However, real progress was judged solely by results on the field and the same meeting heard with obvious delight that Mike Beese, capped three times during his exile in Liverpool, was returning to his home club for the 1973-74 season. Soon afterwards it was learned that Sale fly-half Horton, who had played for North West Counties against the Fijians in 1970 at the age of 19, had indeed been successful in applying for a teaching post in the PE department at Bath Technical College.

The return of Beese and Horton's subsequent arrival were not entirely coincidental, as Horton conceded later in conversation with Brian Jones, author of *Bath Ace of Clubs*: "Knowing Mike from his time at Liverpool when I was also in Lancashire persuaded me to play at Bath. It seemed the obvious thing to do." It appeared to come as something of a surprise to Beese though. Visiting his wife, Christine, who worked in the same PE department, he only vaguely recognised the curly-headed youngster standing in the corridor. "Don't I know you?" he ventured.

Already the England Under-23 fly-half, Horton came as a gift from the gods to Bath where there was increasing concern about the fitness of 29-year-old solicitor Brendan Perry, who had managed only one first XV appearance the previous season owing to leg muscle problems. Perry did line up at fly-half in the opening match of the 1973-74 season at home to Pontypool but they were beaten 7-nil; flanker Terry

Bath pair first on the scene of air tragedy

Among the absentees on the opening day of the 1973-74 season were Brian Jenkins and Roger Wilcox, on holiday together in South Devon. On Monday, 3 September, they were walking near Brixham Rugby Club when they noticed a light aircraft in difficulties. The pilot, apparently looking to make a forced landing on the club's Astley Park ground, lost control when the engine failed and crashed into the roof of a nearby bungalow. Among the first on the scene, the Bath pair found the pilot's wife badly injured in the wreckage but could do nothing to save her husband or their two young children.

Bath v Pontypool (1 September 1973) – back row: B Thompson, P Burrowes, R Lye, R J Wheeler, K M Plummer, P R Hall, D J Gay, J M Meddick, P Pothecary (sponge man) Front: A Hicks, M C Lloyd, A Sparkes, M Gould, R Elliott, C Perry, B Perry.

Cobner, who was to be capped by Wales later in the season, sent Waters in for the only try.

The defeat by Pontypool highlighted a number of selection problems following the departure of key players and long-term injuries to others, such as Irish-born prop Niall Carter, whose weight and power had been missed since seriously injuring his knee the previous February.

That did however leave the door open for Bert Meddick to make the loosehead position his own. After an ill-tempered 16-3 defeat in sweltering temperatures at Leicester – Meddick was at one point left prone by a punch – there was a 34-8 win at home to Taunton and an even more impressive 43-7 rout of Moseley, sweet revenge for the previous season's annihilation. Meddick, who crossed for the first of six tries, eventually made 43 appearances in a punishing programme of 55 matches but was missing for the trip to Newport on 19 September. Bath's front row was propelled skywards at the first scrum and it was only the Black and Ambers' inability to make good use of ample possession that restricted their winning margin to 10-4.

One positive was the performance of 34-year-old scrum-half Malcolm Lloyd, courageous behind a beaten pack on his 200th appearance for the first XV. Lloyd had arrived at the club as a Colt, already the proud bearer of an England Schools Under 15 cap while a pupil at Wellsway, Keynsham. It had been a long hard road, first understudying a string of other scrum-halves and when finally established, then severing an Achilles tendon. It was an injury which would have finished many a lesser character so it was greatly to the stocky Lloyd's credit that he had come bouncing back after 12 months absence.

Those who played rugby in the 1960s and 70s must shake their heads in wry amusement at the way the professional game and its all-seeing TV coverage exposes almost every incidence of foul play, even to the mildest bout of 'handbags'. Make no mistake, the game in those days could be brutal and the RFU had already issued an instruction that clubs should take a hand in eradicating ungentlemanly conduct.

There is no evidence that Bath were more culpable than other teams but having already voiced concern about standards of discipline, the committee were left in an awkward position when skipper Hall was sent off during a 22-4 defeat at Exeter, Bath's fourth defeat in six matches. They suspended the Tormarton farmer for two matches although on this occasion it was felt that he had been more sinned against than sinning. If there was a mitigating factor, it was his tendency to absorb more punishment than he dished out! Off the field, he was a gentle man.

The former Wales centre, Bleddyn Williams, wrote in his Sunday People column on 30 September 1973:

> **"I did not see the game in which Hall was sent off, but I'm delighted that Bath are not prepared to accept anything other than a high standard of conduct from their players."**

Hall remembers a slightly unreal atmosphere surrounding his appearance before the club disciplinary committee of former players John Roberts, George Brown and Tom Smith. "In front of me were the three filthiest players ever to turn out for Bath – and as John Roberts delivered their verdict, I could see Tom was grinning at me!"

With Lye leading the side in Hall's absence, Bristol won 18-9 at The Rec and the skipper was still missing when Horton finally made his debut on 29 September 1973 against the Irish tourists, Terenure. Aside from the wins against Taunton and Moseley, it was a wretched September for Bath and the 12-9 defeat at the hands of the Irish club was the sixth loss. Horton must have wondered what he had let himself in for.

A midweek visit to Clifton four days later provided an early glimpse of Horton's skills as he retrieved his own short kick-ahead and fed Nick Hudson for a try under the posts; two drop goals in a 15-6 victory provided further confirmation of his talent. Ironically, on his return from suspension Hall found himself at the centre of another sending-off. This time he was the target – collecting eight stitches in his ear – and Clifton back row Ian Elvin was dismissed for illegal use of the boot.

It was four matches before Bath won again, a scrambled 4-3 victory at Cheltenham, and it was no great surprise that no-one from the club merited selection in the South Western Counties XV to face the touring Wallabies on 27 October – not even on

Robbie Lye: 457 first XV appearances 1970-86.

the bench. It was doubly embarrassing because the match was played on the Rec. Instead the Bath players turned out against Midsomer Norton the following day in the first round of the Somerset Cup, winning 33-nil.

With only five wins to mid-November 1973, discussion behind the scenes focused on the need to attract more talent, so a scouting sub-committee was set up under the chairmanship of John Cousins. It was not long before junior clubs Old Redcliffians and Old Sulians voiced their displeasure about attempts to poach players.

The immediate concern, however, was the poor form displayed to date. Morale was lifted temporarily with a 20-3 win over Newbridge, Horton scoring an early try, and they progressed to the third round of the county cup the next day, beating Stothert & Pitt 23-3. But it was achieved at a cost, Hall being sent off for the second time in two months in a contest of simmering aggression. The captain eventually received a second two-week suspension but not before Bath had negotiated the first round of the RFU Knock-out competition by defeating Royal Military College of Science Shrivenham 27-6. David Gay then took over as skipper for two of the toughest matches on the fixture list.

At Kingsholm, Bath had to borrow a British Police forward, Jerry Herniman, after turning up minus Brian Jenkins but they actually led 8-7 before Gloucester took control to win 18-8. And although a Horton drop goal gave his side an early lead at home to Llanelli, the visitors eased to a 12-3 win.

The year ended on an unfortunate note with Lloyd breaking his leg during a 10-3 defeat at home to Northampton, the second serious injury of his career. He was to be badly missed, not only as an experienced and resourceful scrum-half but also as a 'fourth back row forward'. The incident persuaded the Management Committee to urge all players to take out personal accident insurance.

1974 was ushered in with a 53-6 New Year's Day rout against Cheddar Valley as Bath continued their progress through the Somerset Cup. They were also to beat St Brendan's Old Boys, Bridgwater and Weston-super-Mare on their way to winning the competition, scoring 180 points in the six rounds without conceding a try.

Progress in the RFU Knock-out Cup was halted on 9 February by Wilmslow, semi-finalists two years earlier. With the Recreation Ground unfit, the tie was moved to the exposed Kingswood School pitch on Lansdown where the gusting wind made handling movements near impossible. Bath led 6-nil at half-time with two wind-assisted penalties but the Cheshire club's forwards took control after the break and were by no means flattered by the 19-6 scoreline.

A presentation by club president George Brown to Phil Hall on his 500th appearance.

Faced with the counter-attraction of England's home match with Ireland the following weekend, Bath experimented with a Sunday fixture at home to Cheltenham. Although a financial success and a 6-4 win for the home team, as a spectacle it was best forgotten.

Phil Hall must have spilt more blood in the Bath cause than any other player in the club's 139-year history. Against Wasps at Sudbury, he had only just returned to the action with stitches in a badly gashed head when he scored a try from a tapped penalty to force a 16-15 win. The following weekend he marked his 500th appearance in characteristic fashion by crashing through two defenders to score in the derby match against Bristol at the Memorial Ground. His fellow players presented him that afternoon with a pewter tankard inscribed prosaically but with feeling:

To Phil – a great player's player
The Players

By this time, this most durable of back row forwards was a folk hero at the Rec. Regarded with awe, even fear, by opposing fly-halves, he was a player who typified the earthy nature of West Country rugby. Uncompromising, uncomplaining, intensely competitive, Hall would stand toe-to-toe with the most intimidating opponents. As such he was a worthy successor to hard-bitten characters such as Frank 'Buster' Soane and Fred 'Chumpy' Russell from the early years of the club's existence; Roger Spurrell, Gareth Chilcott and Graham Dawe would carry on that tradition

As Hall received the plaudits with characteristic modesty, there was sad news regarding a former team mate, Mike Hannell, who had joined Bristol. The Newport-

Mike Hannell: a sad loss.

born prop, who had captained Dorset & Wilts and also won representative honours with the South of England against the Springboks and Fiji before being asked to tour Japan with England in 1971, was terminally ill. He had made 141 first XV appearances for Bath, his last being against Exeter on 23 September 1972.

Chris Ducker remembers Hannell as "a lovely bloke". In those days newspaper reporters often used to give players a lift home from away matches. Ducker continues: "Driving him home from a Bristol game at Sale one Saturday evening, he showed me a lump on his hand which needed 'minor surgery'. He was putting it off for fear of losing his hard-earned first team place at Bristol. Sadly, the lump was cancerous and he was dead within a few weeks. All very sad."

Undoubtedly there had been happier times at the Rec. The only significant victory from late February to mid-April 1974 was at home to an understrength Neath when Tony Hicks showed a welcome return to form to cross twice, also chasing his own kick-ahead to send in Beese for a try in a 21-18 win. David Gay, Robbie Lye and scrum-half Gary Pudney played major roles in a second-half comeback and Bath were also well served in the line-out by Clive Harry and Brian Jenkins. Spirits were lifted by a courageous performance at home to Gloucester on 2 April when Bath moved the ball at every opportunity only to be undone by handling errors and missed penalty chances. Their rivals won 19-15 but the match was memorable for a remarkable solo try by Horton, as The Bath Chronicle recorded:

> **Receiving the ball almost alone on the blind-side, he wrong-footed the cover defence with a magnificent sidestep and his acceleration took him clean through to the posts from where he also converted... Lye, Gay and Hall gave the Gloucester halves some of their own medicine and determined running and handling, involving Beese, Hicks and Waterman in particular, had the visiting defence gasping.**

Horton found himself up against his old team-mates in the next game as Sale lost 26-6 at the Rec. It was the start of a run of five victories over the Easter break but the sequence ended abruptly at Stradey Park on 20 April with a 43-19 defeat by Llanelli. Prolific Scarlets wing Andy Hill kicked a penalty to open the scoring, bagged two tries and kicked five penalties to top 300 individual points for the season.

After overcoming Weston-super-Mare 22-3 in a scrappy Somerset Cup final, Bath failed to win either of their concluding matches – at home to Bedford (32-19)

*Bristol's Mike Fry outnumbered by Radley Wheeler (left), Geoff Pudney,
Steve Horton, Robbie Lye and David Gay as Chris Perry gets the ball away at the
Memorial Ground on 3 March 1974.*

and away to Stroud, a 15-11 defeat which rounded off the Gloucestershire club's centenary season.

David Dolman, who had worked with tremendous enthusiasm during his two years as Club Coach and had introduced Mini Rugby to the club during the previous Christmas holiday, confirmed his resignation at the 6 June meeting of the management committee, citing business pressures. It was unanimously agreed that the club should write to Tom Hudson at the University of Bath, inviting him to meet the committee to discuss coaching issues.

It was also decided that work should proceed on ground improvements and the installation of floodlighting at an estimated cost of £18,000, prompting a reminder from treasurer Tom Smith of the financial liability which would be incurred. In view of the results from a season in which the first XV won just 26 of their 55 fixtures and the United suffered their worst season on record, with only seven wins, some trepidation was understandable.

If Bath could have picked a less auspicious time to embark on wholesale ground improvements and an ambitious floodlighting scheme, it would have been early 1974. Ted Heath's outgoing Conservative Government, crippled by the oil crisis induced by OPEC following the Yom Kippur war and a miners' overtime ban, imposed a three-day working week and even printed petrol coupons ready for rationing. Inflation soared to 26 per cent in little over a year and by October 1975 there was concern that the projected cost of extending the clubhouse had doubled in 18 months to £24,000. Some 30 years later that figure would represent less than one per cent of the annual salary bill for players!

Bath were grateful for the fundraising efforts of individuals such as Mrs Doris Churchouse, who had paid £11.75 into Club Funds, proceeds of the Christmas Raffle. She was ever-present at home games, enlivening proceedings with her heartfelt cry of "Come on, my Luvvers." It echoed around the West Stand for many years to come.

Even Doris might have been drowned out by The Bay City Rollers and The Troggs, who performed on The Rec in June 1974 to raise funds for the club's German tour. The 'promoter' was Joint Treasurer Les Newton who received a letter of complaint from the council about "excessive noise" but cheerfully banked £175 on the club's behalf.

The captaincy passed to Chris Perry for 1974-75. A wing forward-turned-scrum-half-turned-centre-turned-scrum-half again, Perry had been at the club for five years and was a popular choice. A true all-rounder, he was also a cricketer for Lansdown and Somerset Second XI and had played football for Somerset Schools as well as earning a trial with Swindon Town.

Harvesting duties on his Tormarton farm were to prevent Hall from adding to his tally of 523 first XV appearances until late October and he let it be known that Perry should have time and space to organise affairs in his own way. In any case, Geoff Pillinger stepped up into the openside flanker slot with aplomb, scoring a try in a 15-9 win over Leicester and earning county recognition.

Off the field, the committee had been supervising the major upgrade of facilities at the Rec. The club was still paying off the residue of a £11,000 bill for modernisation of the changing rooms and it was estimated that around £30,000 would be needed to clear all projects. With the President, George Brown, a real driving force, pledges of donations and interest free loans were received from committeemen and members and by the next Management Committee meeting, £3,944 was in hand and £3,000 more promised.

By the end of that 1974-75 season, the club had completed work on the changing rooms, installed floodlights and begun an elaborate renovation of the clubhouse. There had been an exceedingly good response to the appeal from the President but not least among his achievements was his success in healing breaches between players and management.

Commercially, rugby was still in nappies and there was still no sponsor for the 'National Club Knock-Out Competition' when Bath found themselves involved in one of the more bizarre episodes in its history. They had been forced to play off with Falmouth for a place in the competition proper because of their indifferent showing in the South West Merit Table the previous season. They won 13-11 thanks to a brilliant try created and finished off by John Horton, only to find they had been drawn against themselves in the first round!

> **"But Bath's opponents as a result of Saturday's victory are none other than Bath themselves – for at the annual meeting of the RFU in July, they were included in the draw as a nominated club, which presumably means that Bath earn themselves a bye into the second round."**
> **(The Guardian, 1 October 1974)**

That would have been too easy for the RFU! Instead they reinstated Falmouth for the first round tie and somehow contrived to award the Cornishmen home advantage, much to the irritation of Bath Secretary Jack Simpkins who snapped: "It's absolutely ridiculous. Is this a knock-out cup or isn't it?"

The 'second leg' on 16 November 1974 produced further drama as Bath progressed only by virtue of being the away side following a 9-9 draw. Unsurprisingly, it was an emotionally charged occasion and the closing stages became particularly heated, as John Stevens of The Bath Chronicle reported:

> **"One particularly nasty incident in front of the stands saw fists thrown freely and Bath touch judge John Cousins went on to the field to pull a Falmouth player away. Several other spectators were dragged away by officials."**

The Recreation Ground's first floodlit match on 15 January 1975,
with the Royal Navy providing the opposition.

Bath would have won the tie outright but for a try-saving tackle on Hicks by the Falmouth wing, Barry Trevaskis, who was soon to enjoy rather more cup success in Bath colours. In the meantime, however, Bath found themselves drawn away again in the second round, at Liverpool. By the time the teams met on 8 February, Liverpool had gone 16 games unbeaten but four penalties by left wing Richardson earned 12-6 win for Bath and a place in the quarter-finals for the first time. Horton, playing behind a dominant pack, kicked astutely and showed some deft touches in attack.

The quarter-final at home to unfancied Morpeth could not have been more of an anti-climax. Again, the match had to be switched to the Kingswood School pitch on Lansdown because the Rec was flooded and the Yorkshire team settled more quickly into their stride, relying on a rock-hard defence to protect their lead and running out 13-9 winners. Bar takings exceeded £1,000 for the first time as home players, officials and supporters returned to the Rec to drown their sorrows.

The highs and lows of the 1974-75 season were typified by Malcolm Lloyd, who turned in a number of virtuoso performances at scrum-half, notably in scoring the only try in the 10-9 win at Bristol on 19 October and, again at his destructive best, in the 13-4 victory at home on 28 February. It was the first time since 1967-68 that they had achieved the double over their neighbours. Lloyd had also set up the winning try against Newport on 11 February, inflicting on the Black and Ambers their first defeat in 21 games.

Yet Lloyd had been sent off for the first time in his 11-year career during a 49-4 hammering at London Scottish on 7 December, apparently for dissent,

John Palmer: schoolboy prodigy.

and his season ended prematurely on 9 April when he broke his leg against Northampton. It was a repeat of the injury he had suffered 15 months earlier – against the same opponents. The 15-3 defeat at Franklins Gardens also marked the debut of a Prior Park College sixth-former, John Palmer, partnering the unfortunate Lloyd at half-back.

Palmer made an immediate impact, as teammate Bert Meddick remembers. "The team coach had to pick this boy up from the school. There wasn't much of him, to be honest, but on the field he'd take a pass, there'd be a gap and he'd be through it in a flash. Who is this boy, we asked ourselves?"

Bath v Pontypool (6 September 1975) – back row (from left): Bob Campbell, Mike Beese, Lindsay Pritchard, Geoff Pudney, Radley Wheeler, Brian Jenkins, Robbie Lye, Ian Dunbar, Tom Martland (coach). Front: Chris Perry, Alan Parfitt, John Davies, John Horton, Jim Waterman (captain), Terry Norris, Geoff Pillinger. Bath beat the Welsh champions 30-15.

But it was after matches that Palmer made his biggest impression on the experienced Meddick, who prided himself on always being first to the bar. "Every match, I'd be showered and changed before everybody else. But this time, when I got to the bar, this schoolboy was there first – fag in hand and on his second pint!"

Palmer himself, without wishing to diminish Meddick's reputation as a storyteller, insists that his housemaster at Prior Park had warned that if he broke the 10pm curfew he would not be allowed to play for Bath again. And that was the reason for his rapid departure!

The regular fixture list was rounded off in style with a 16-9 victory over Llanelli before Bath trounced Old Redcliffians 41-3 in the Somerset Cup final, finishing with 28 wins and one draw from 46 matches.

John Stevens summed it all up in The Bath Chronicle: "A season of considerable achievement with a notable double over Bristol and victories over Gloucester, Leicester, Saracens, Wasps, Harlequins and Llanelli. However, the two of the most memorable games were the marvellous encounters with London Welsh and the equally pulsating match with Newport both of which Bath won. Newport will not want to recall how their much vaunted pack was systematically torn apart by the Bath forwards and their defence torn apart by John Horton. Horton's inability to impress English selectors reminded one of the mysteries of the season. Bath's away win over Liverpool in John Player Cup was a great tactical success, but was overshadowed by the shock defeat by Morpeth in the Quarter Finals."

The one worry had been the lack of tries – just 75 – and this was something that the new captain, Jim Waterman, was determined to remedy; he was in a perfect position to do so as a free-running full-back blessed with a near mystical sense of timing when it came to entering the line. After a 30-point run-out against Taunton, Bath repeated the dose against the reigning Welsh champions Pontypool, winning 30-15 and scoring five tries with newcomer Ian Dunbar, an Oxford Blue, crossing twice. John Stevens was impressed:

> **"New skipper Jim Waterman is to be congratulated not only on the positively adventurous approach he has instilled into his side but for generating a general air of bubbling enthusiasm throughout the club."**

Trouble was, Horton and his speedy three-quarters were relying for possession on the lightest pack that Bath had fielded in several seasons.

A tobacco manufacturer had come forward to sponsor the national cup competition for 1975-76. The newly-christened John Player Cup was to become synonymous with Bath but their first experience left a rather nasty after-taste as Bristol won 24-15 at the Rec on 18 October 1975 in an ill-tempered tie. There was an ugly brawl after just ten minutes, with fists flying in all directions, and Waterman was laid out in another unsavoury incident.

After a one-point victory over Bridgend, revenge was gained over Bristol when Horton dropped three goals and Perry another in a 12-6 victory. It ended a run of 11 successive wins by Bristol for whom Dave Alred, now better known as England's kicking guru during the triumphant World Cup campaign in 2003, had an uncomfortable time at full-back.

In contrast, Horton, profiting from the dominance of the loose play by Hall, Harry and Pillinger, dominated all aspects of play from fly-half with his immaculate tactical kicking. Later in November came news that he had been selected by the Western Counties to face the Wallabies at Bristol.

Chapter 3

THE HUNTER HUNTED

John Horton's dancing feet were guaranteed to brighten many a dull afternoon at the Rec yet the form fly-half in the country was still Llanelli's Phil Bennett and he proved it by masterminding a 36-4 victory over Bath on 22 December 1976.

It was Phil Hall's last tussle with Bennett and his respect for the dazzling Welshman endures to this day:

"In one match I took him late and he said: 'You're dead, Hally!' Obviously, he wasn't going to do anything about it himself – he had his 'protectors' – but he was the best fly-half I ever played against, better than Barry John."

At a Bath dinner in more recent times, when Bennett was guest speaker he made special mention of his adversary from three decades before in a reference to "that bloody madman!"

While goal-kicking right wing John Davies became the first Bath player to top 400 points in a season and weaker teams such as Clifton and the Royal Navy could be run off their feet by Horton, Beese, Waterman and Co, heavyweight opposition found it much easier to curb Bath's attacking game. Gloucester proved a predictable stumbling block, winning 18-15 at Bath and completing the double 12-13 at Kingsholm in February 1976. There were also defeats at the hands of Leicester, Northampton, London Welsh and Swansea while Bristol won a featureless game 12-10 at the Memorial Ground in March.

There were 32 victories from a programme of 50 matches though and occasionally Waterman's team could hack it with the best. Such a match was the home game with Cardiff on St Valentine's

A fresh-faced Phil Hall at the start of a career totalling 580 games and 78 tries.

Day when John Horton displayed his full range of skills and no little courage in a 9-4 victory, as John Stevens, of The Bath Chronicle reported:

"He first toyed with Cardiff, then destroyed them with his superb kicking and running and finally thwarted them with at least three superb cover tackles which definitely nailed the lie that he is weak in defence."

Hall took it upon himself to quell the threat posed by the great Gareth Edwards: "He came blind and I left an arm out. The ref said: "Hally! Behave yourself." Half an hour later I was running full-tilt, covering across and defending like hell, when I suddenly felt a set of studs gouging down my calf. It was Edwards – we were quits."

That encounter had a dark and malevolent sequel, played out in the home game with Newport in early April. Again Bath won 9-4 but for Hall, who had already announced that he would be retiring at the end of the season, the match ended in the most gruesome fashion.

He recalls the events quite matter-of-factly: "Apparently, there was huge feeling among the players in Wales – because of the Cardiff game when I'd laid out Edwards. The word was that someone would 'get' me. Anyway, I was on the floor and I felt fingers pulling at each side of my mouth; I managed to bite one of them but the other just tore through my cheek.

"I remember Dave Protheroe, our doctor, immediately putting a syringe in my leg … but not much else. Apparently the ref made sure we won the game. At the hospital, they put 60 stitches in me – 30 outside and 30 inside my mouth and I also had some plastic surgery. First though, I had to get someone to ring my wife to say I wouldn't be able to milk the cows that night!"

Hall had only just returned to the field after having six stitches inserted behind his ear. It was one of several instances of foul play which enraged Protheroe and he took the unusual step for an Honorary Team Doctor of issuing a statement to the Bristol Evening Post: "There are certain injuries which in my opinion have been deliberately caused with malice aforethought. You get stud-marks with a full rotation, which means someone has put the boot on and twisted it. This is usually found on the back or buttocks area."

Hall was urged to take further action regarding his dreadful injury but, as invariably happened in those days, it was all smoothed over. "I was asked if I wanted to do anything about it and a few people wanted to make a fuss. But I had a meeting with the Club Secretary, Jack Simpkins, and we agreed to let it lie." One can only imagine the furore that would have ensued today.

An interview with Chris Ducker, of the Bristol Evening Post, a few weeks later provided an insight into Hall's approach to the game:

"I know there are plenty of players who hate my guts. But while I have given some stick at times, I have always been prepared to take it."

These days he can laugh about it. "I remember once looking at our prop, John Parsons, as we came off the pitch at the end of a match. He had two black eyes, gouges and blood on his face. And do you know what he said? 'What a great game that was, Hally!'

"Over in Wales though, if you didn't stand up for yourself, you got stamped on, literally. Every Welsh side was hard in those days but we had a few hard men too

Clive Harry: accidentally broke John Taylor's jaw.

– Niall Carter, Bob Orledge and Clive Harry, who once broke John Taylor's jaw in six place with a perfectly legal tackle. On the other side, there were people like Neath's Brian Thomas – you wouldn't have guessed he was a Cambridge Blue – and from Gloucester, Mike Nicholls and Robin Cowling."

Hall's 580th and final game was a 10-6 win over Nottingham at the Rec on May Day 1976, ending a first team career that had begun at Torquay on Christmas Eve 1960.

"I had actually never seen a rugby ball till I went to school but I knew straight away it was my kind of game. I just enjoyed rugby, enjoyed the camaraderie. There are lots of memories ... of battles in Wales, long hours on the coach to Sale, tours to France ...of the time when Fred Hicks, our No 8, threw his passport into the sea at Nice insisting he didn't want to go home.

"But at the end my pace had gone – even at the best of times I had to run flat-out to keep up."

Hall continued to turn out for the United, casting an expert eye over the promising youngsters and reviving the Youth XV, but the times they were a-changing at the Rec.

In the very week of Hall's retirement, the Management Committee considered a letter from former prop Dave Robson, by then part of the coaching set-up under Tom Martland, suggesting certain improvements in the way players should prepare for the season ahead. It was agreed that players should attend the Sports Centre in the close season for weight and fitness training.

Before Robson's untimely death he recalled for this history: "I finished playing for the United – my Achilles was playing up too much – and initially went down to Charmouth and played soccer for half a season. Then I got a call from Tom Martland asking me to help out with some coaching."

Tom Hudson, Director of Sport at the University of Bath, was another early influence on playing aims and strategies, having first been approached by the Management Committee in late 1973 to provide expertise in the area of preparation and fitness, nowadays called 'conditioning'. A former Olympic athlete and an imposing personality, he had helped Carwyn James prepare the Llanelli side that had famously defeated the All Blacks in October 1972.

His opinions were forthright and farsighted. He maintained that a team could not realistically expect to win every game, but should plan ahead, targeting certain games. To this end, a squad system should be introduced and his view, as expressed to The Bath Chronicle on 7 July 1976 was: "What you really have to do is to win the games that really matter and win something big." The Merit Table games and the John Player Cup, were therefore to be their prime targets.

John Horton: 125 drop goals for Bath in 15 years.

In September 1976, under John Horton's captaincy, some of the pieces were beginning to come together but no-one was talking of cup triumphs or league titles after Ray Prosser's intimidating Pontypool side demolished Bath 46-6 on the first weekend of the new season. It was Alan Parfitt's 300th game and all the more distressing given the hard work the players had put in during the summer but John Stevens of The Bath Chronicle told it as it was:

"Bath's utter failure to combat them in any shape or form came as a big blow to local pride. The answer was simple enough – a complete lack of aggression in the front five from whom Pontypool took the ball as easily as snatching candy from a baby."

Right wing Richardson kicked two penalties but John Palmer, the Prior Park College prodigy of the previous season, assumed kicking duties for the following game, a midweek defeat at Newport. The only reward for a hard afternoon's work was a Palmer penalty but the match did mark the return at scrum-half of Malcolm Lloyd after a succession of serious injuries.

Three days later Leicester arrived at the Rec for the opening fixture in the new Anglo-Welsh Merit Table. Although their 18-year-old centre, Paul Dodge, was already looking an England prospect the dominant figure was Horton who scored a try and a drop goal in addition to a try from Wyatt and two penalties from Richardson. However, Bath lost 14-3 the following weekend at Moseley for whom the other Horton – England lock Nigel – dominated the line-out

As Merit Tables met the desire for more competition in rugby – without ever fully satisfying it – traditional fixtures increasingly became mis-matches. Clifton were hammered 44-7 on their new purpose-built ground at Cribbs Causeway while Bath won 32-nil at Weston-super-Mare. Wins over South West Merit Table opponents Exeter and Plymouth Albion completed a busy September.

The promise of Palmer was evident when Bath became the first side to beat Aberavon, winning 12-9 through three John Davies penalties and a Horton drop goal.

> **Last season's Prior Park College captain came in as a last minute full back replacement and turned on a second half performance which was reminiscent of J P R Williams himself. His sudden change of pace and power in the thighs bemused the Welshmen at times and with only a shade more luck he could have created at least two tries. Three superb runs out of defence, however, will remain vividly in the memory for a long time to come, as for that matter will a rip-roaring game which developed from very tentative beginnings. (The Bath Chronicle 3 October 1976)**

Palmer kept his place for the trip to Bristol two weeks later but Bath were annihilated 35-10, with only Horton's kicking saving his side from a heavier defeat. There was also a 35-19 lesson at Neath before Bath registered their first victory in Wales since 1973, winning 9-7 at Bridgend thanks to Brian Jenkins' late try converted by Davies, who had earlier landed a 40-yard penalty.

Bath lost only three of their next 13 games but the sequence included a visit to Stradey Park where they had not won for 17 years. With Bennett again in top form, the Scarlets ran in seven tries to win 36-nil.

The John Player Cup campaign saw Bath drawn away to London Welsh and 200 supporters travelled to Richmond on a distinctly chilly 4 December 1976. The Bath team were ready to play but Exiles' skipper Jim Shanklin refused to take the

Bath v Bedford (30 April 1977 – back row: R Lye, R Holman, B Jenkins, R Wheeler, R Hill, M Beese, R Miller, D Barry, J M 'Bert' Meddick, D Spavan. Front row: Trainer, A Mason, C Perry, G Townsend, J Horton, J Palmer, J Waterman.

field, saying the ground was dangerously hard. Bath made their point by playing an impromptu game of touch rugby on the adjoining second team pitch. Frost caused the tie to be postponed again the following weekend and it was 8 January before the teams eventually met. Bath played poorly, losing 18-3 as London Welsh's England fly-half, Neil Bennett, kicked five long-range penalties and a drop goal in reply to Palmer's early penalty.

It was the third week of February before Bath lost again, going down 4-nil at Coventry in a game they should have won, and the return with Bristol was drawn 3-3. A week later, on 12 March, they surrendered their unbeaten home record in losing 12-6 to Swansea.

After an heroic performance in defeat at Ebbw Vale – Bath played most of the game with 13 players, occasionally 12, and won a scrum against the head with just a front row – they capitulated completely the following week at Gloucester. The 51-7 scoreline reflected a display "utterly lacking in any sort of fighting spirit" in the words of John Stevens.

Newport, whose second team inflicted a devastating double over the United by scores of 91-6 and 58-12 during the season, became the second team to triumph at the Rec, their heavyweight pack laying the foundations for a 32-7 success. Llanelli repeated the dose 21-3 on a bone-hard pitch devoid of grass on 16 April and Bath were deprived of their first win at Northampton in 45 years by a last-minute penalty (14-12). The 1976-77 domestic season ended with a whimper in a 44-15 rout at Bedford and then, touring in the Bordeaux region with a depleted squad, Bath went down 52-6 to Begles.

Excluding the French tour, Bath had used 43 players, of whom 18 had made first XV debuts. Of 45 matches played, there had been 26 victories and 17 defeats, with two draws. A former Bath player, David Burcher, was selected for that summer's Lions tour of New Zealand, one of three players from Newport in a Wales-dominated squad captained by Bennett.

Back at Bath, Robson, appointed Club Coach for the 1977-78 season, was thanked by the committee for his efforts in obtaining match sponsors. The 4 March fixture with Bristol had been the first to be fully supported by a local business, a local firm of stockbrokers who provided a full set of shirts as well as bearing the costs of staging the match. Similar arrangements had been agreed for the home matches with Newport and Llanelli; the match ball was regularly sponsored and another local business had provided a set of tracksuits. The value to club finances was some £1,000 over the season. Negotiations were soon under way for a kit sponsorship deal and before the start of the season, the club signed a three-year, £3,000 agreement with Adidas

Crowds at a number of first team matches had been treated to curtain-raisers involving youngsters from the club's Mini Rugby section and the committee report of 1977 noted with some satisfaction the continuing development of this "new innovation":

This has proved beneficial to the youngsters and given joy and satisfaction to the proud watching parents. We hope the organisers will continue the good work but we must beware in case the game of Mini Rugby becomes over-competitive for our young enthusiasts."

Gareth Chilcott: made his first team debut on 28 September 1977 against Leonard Cheshire's International XV.

Among their number was one Jeremy Clayton Guscott, then only 11 years old but destined to play a starring role for Bath, England and the Lions.

The Youth section continued to rely on stalwart figures such as Harry Fiddes, who had given 30 years of his life to the club in various capacities. The 20 June 1977 meeting of Management Committee resolved to reward his loyalty with a Life Membership but within a couple of months found themselves mourning his death.

As characters faded from the scene, others arrived to establish their own place in the annals of the club. So it was that Bath's increasingly vigorous scouting policy directed by Robson attracted a young prop from Old Redcliffians. Twenty-year-old Gareth James Chilcott had been educated at Ashton Park School where first indulged his passion for sport as a goalkeeper; he remains an enthusiastic supporter of Bristol City.

After several run-outs for the United and a place on the bench at Clifton, it was 28 September 1977 before he made his first XV debut against Leonard Cheshire's International XV on the Rec, packing down at tight head alongside Bert Meddick and hooker Tony Mason. Waterman, Horton and Beese had their moments but Bath lost 24-18 in front of a crowd of 4,000.

"Bath had a nice fluent side with people like Horton and Beese," recalls Chilcott. "But then Dave Robson did a trawl of local clubs, looking for some hairy-arsed forwards. I was playing for Old Reds first team and so was Derrick Barry. He wasn't a typical second row forward, being not much more than 13 stones dripping wet, but he had incredible spring in his jump and that was what we needed in the line-out. There was no lifting in those days, of course.

"Dave recruited me as a prop. I was lacking in technique in those early days but I had plenty of aggression – possibly too much! The reason I was playing rugby was that I had got into a bit of trouble at the City ground and 'the authorities' suggested I take up the game to work off that aggression. I found that first season at Bath so daunting though. I was so much out of my normal environment. Rough and ready … a bit of a handful, I suppose.

"The first player to come up and introduce himself was one of the other props, Chris Lilley. The following week though I was in Bristol city centre when there was a bit of a ruckus with some Welsh lads. Sadly, I was involved – and as I looked around, who did I see standing in a taxi queue? Chris Lilley. "It was all round the club in no time, of course. They must have been thinking: 'God, what have we got here.' But having that reputation gave me time to learn the trade of propping. With my lack of technique, I had to make up for that by being just, I don't know … 'orrible!"

After his full debut against the Leonard Cheshire XV, a gentlemanly affair refereed by Air Vice Marshal G C 'Larry' Lamb, with Air Marshal Sir Augustus Walker as one of the touch judges, Chilcott was quickly introduced to a different kind of kind of rugby altogether – and it involved a trip across the Severn Bridge.

Aberavon were then one of the best teams in the principality and had three of the 1977 Lions in fly-half John Bevan, prop Clive Williams and that peerless line-out technician, Allan Martin, paired in the second row with formidable Billy Mainwaring, so it was no surprise that Bath lost 29-12.

Chilcott recalls such experiences all too vividly: "You'd go down to Aberavon or Neath and you weren't bothered with the ball. It wasn't in anyone's game plan because in those days it was a fight for survival. There were no citing officers or cameras and the crowd expected people to be 'sorted out'. I suppose it was the ultimate 'spectator sport' – a bit like a battle. The injuries you got would be scratches, cuts, gouges, head wounds. You don't get that these days … the kicking, the biting or the off-the-ball cheap shots. You had to have eyes in the back of your head.

"You knew who would be putting it about, of course. There was a hard man, an enforcer, in every club – people like Billy Mainwaring or Brian Thomas at Neath or John Perkins at Pontypool. You had to be a bit of a streetfighter. That's what I was and it was why Jack Rowell picked me for so many years. Bath got respect because we fought fire with fire. Yes, there were times when I got sent off for things I didn't do but there were other times I should have been sent off and wasn't."

Trips into Wales on a Wednesday night to play Pontypridd, Swansea or Newport are just as firmly fixed in the memory of John Hall, of later vintage. "They were really, really tough games" he says. "While now if you go into a changing room in the modern era, you see lots of bruises and injuries through hard contact, in our day you'd come off the pitch and your back would be in absolute tatters. You'd have scars all over your body, scrapes and wounds needing stitches. And that was because there were a lot of studs flying around, much more than there is now, although the actual physical contact is so much greater these days.

"It was scary ... it was very, very scary. At the time I didn't think about it but you would go down to Wales and you knew you would get kicked in the head. And I would come home from lots of games with 10-15 stitches in my scalp.

"We would dish it out, too. We were tough enough to do that, when you had characters around like Chilcott and Spurrell, Richard Lee and Nigel Redman – I wasn't frightened to mix it, either. We'd stand up to anybody and give it back a bit as well.

"Traditionally, Phil Hall would have been the man who stood up to people in the 1970s. In the 1980s and onwards it was about having a group of people. The foundation for that was Chilcott, as the man who would stand up to people. The reason why we beat those sides was that we could match them physically, if not beat them physically, and also have the more skilful side as well, the best players."

Chilcott remembers "a great buzz about the club" in his early days at the Rec.

"It was a great time. I learned about the 'facts of life' from people like Bertie Meddick and there were other characters such as Brian Jenkins. It was a family club where the first XV, the United and the Spartans were all one group. Some of my long-time friends never played anything other than Spartans rugby. But that contributed to that 'rugby club feel' and was where we eventually had the advantage over Bristol and Gloucester, in my view. When Jack Rowell arrived, he fostered that and took it on to another dimension with a unique blend of players.

Peter Polledri, of Bristol, under pressure from Bath wing forward Geoff Pillinger at the Rec on 15 October 1997. Bristol won 16-10.

The Hunter Hunted

"And we became more pro-active in supporting each other. The players started up the 'Blue, Black and White Fund' which was money raised for teammates who had fallen on hard times."

Although now a successful entrepreneur, in the tough economic times of the late 70s-early 80s the young Chilcott had to take work where he could find it in – as a club doorman, a tree feller, a French polisher. "We didn't get paid for playing rugby but we had good times," he says.

The young Chilcott was selected against his 'home town club' on 15 October 1977, a date that clashed with an England XV's non-cap international against the USA. It meant that Bath were missing Horton and Palmer, named as reserve after his selection for the England Under 23 side earlier in the year. Bristol won the first derby of the season 12-10 but coach Robson was encouraged by the performance of the pack, particularly Chilcott and Barry.

One of Bath's most impressive displays of the 1977-78 campaign was a 25-9 victory over Neath at the Rec. – Then it was off to the cavernous confines of Twickenham where Palmer kicked two penalties in a lacklustre performance against Harlequins, winners by 14-6. One of Quins' fixtures still played at 'HQ', it was watched in eerie silence by some 200 spectators.

Coventry were then one of the elite sides in Britain and a trip to Coundon Road was not for the faint-hearted. Bath were given a 42-4 hiding on 19 November 1977 as former England full-back Peter Rossborough scored the last of his team's five tries, converted the lot and added two penalties and a dropped goal for good measure.

As Bath's injury list lengthened – Chilcott was among the casualties from the Coventry debacle – they succumbed in December to London Scottish, Gloucester and Harlequins. It was the first home defeat by Quins in a decade and Brian Jenkins was sent off along with opponent Stefan Purdy, the Bath man incurring a four week suspension.

At least the Christmas fixtures provided some cause for celebration as Rugby were hammered 57-3, the highest total in the club's history. Horton and Waterman

John Davies: 1,000 points in three and a half seasons.

made light of the heavy pitch and Somerset policeman Gerry Parsons enjoyed an impressive debut on the flank. Just 24 hours after dismissing Clifton with similar ease on Boxing Day, Bath restricted Llanelli to a 10-7 winning margin at Stradey Park.

The main talking point was John Davies's record-breaking feats, not only in setting an individual points total of 26 against Rugby, but also in becoming the first Bath player in the club's history to amass 1,000 points. This was all achieved in just three and a half seasons. After a short time with Bristol without ever playing first team rugby, the dark-haired Welshman was recruited as fly-half cover for John Horton. Davies had only taken over the goal-kicking mid-season because other players were injured and finished with a modest 118 points at the end of 1974-75. The following season he almost trebled the previous best with 425 and in 1976-77, despite injury problems, broke the club try scoring record by touching down 25 times and totalled 297 points.

That most durable of back row forwards, the late Robbie Lye, reached another significant landmark in the 28-16 win over Leicester on 7 January 1978, making his 300th appearance on an afternoon when John Palmer scored an interception try, three conversions and a drop goal.

Bath-born Simon Jones joined the Bath squad late in 1977 after being spotted scoring two tries for Dorset , where he had secured his first teaching post. Jones had also played for Plymouth Albion while studying at the College of St Mark and St John. A knee injury restricted his involvement in his first season at Bath to a few United games but Lye made a strong impression.

"The thing about Robbie was his generosity of spirit," says Jones. "He was always laughing, always friendly, never had a bad word to say about anybody. And he was always keeping an eye out for the the younger players. When I eventually made my home debut, he knew I was a bit nervous so he made a point of meeting me two or three hours before kick-off and we went up and had a coffee in town and then strolled down Milsom Street chatting and looking at the shops. It became a bit of a routine during my early games. I was always very grateful to him for sparing the time."

On the field, Lye was just as reassuring a presence for his back row partner. "He was a stonemason by trade and had such big hands," recalls Jones. "He was able to just pick and go from the back of the scrum, bumping people off with his huge chest and amazing upper body strength."

Lye's death in April 2008 at the tragically early age of 62 shocked the rugby community across Bath, but particularly at Walcot Old Boys where he began his career. After calling time on his first team career at the Rec he had continued to play for the United and Spartans, taking his tally for Bath to 450 appearances over 16 years.

Back in January 1977 Palmer was the only player to emerge with credit from a feeble 46-nil defeat at London Welsh. But with a John Player Cup first round tie at Exeter in their sights, Bath returned to winning ways against the RAF when the match programme had the same player, John Hickey, on both sides! Back row Hickey eventually opted to turn out in Bath colours and played his part in a 17-12 home victory. Met Police provided stiffer resistance, going down 11-10, but the Exeter pack proved too strong in the cup-tie on 28 January and Bath caved in miserably, managing only two penalties from Davies in a 20-6 defeat.

Derek Wyatt: England wing.

A week later Horton became the first Bath player to be capped by England for seven years but his old adversary, Phil Bennett, spoiled the occasion by landing three penalties to two from Bristol full-back Alastair Hignell as the eventual Grand Slam winners won 9-6 at Twickenham. Horton and England had to be content with wins over Scotland (15-nil) and Ireland (15-9) to round off their campaign.

Returning to the Rec and many plaudits, the little fly-half helped Bath win 10 or their last 13 games, defeated only by Llanelli, Newbridge and Gloucester without ever being overrun. Highlight of the closing fixtures was a 15-9 victory over Newport and Bath completed the campaign with an entertaining 45-28 romp against Bedford to finish with 28 wins from 49 matches under Waterman's captaincy.

Bedford's fightback was led by England wing Derek Wyatt, destined to join Bath a few months later, but another summer arrival was to make an even bigger impact.

Chapter 4

'DEAR MR ROWELL, THANK YOU FOR YOUR LETTER, BUT ...'

Jack Rowell's name will forever be associated with rugby at Bath – a union that has produced a veritable dynasty of playing and coaching talent – so it is all the more surprising to learn that the club initially rebuffed his advances.

A newly arrived Jack Rowell casts a critical eye over pre-season training.

Back in 1977 he was certainly not a household name, not even in rugby circles. However, those with their fingers on the pulse were very much aware that he had coached the Gosforth club to win the National Knock-out Cup in 1976, a feat they repeated the following season when Rowell's business career had already brought him to the South West.

Jack and Sue Rowell had decided that they wanted live in Bath, rather than in Bristol where he worked. So he wrote to the Bath club's Honorary Secretary, Jack Simpkins, offering his services. Rowell takes up the story: "I had been approached by a number of people – first, the England coach Peter Colston asking if I would be interested in coming to Bristol and then Dickie Rossiter who said 'how about coaching at Clifton?'

"I didn't go to Bristol but I did write a letter to Jack Simpkins, saying I had just come down to take a job in Bristol, that I was coming to live in Bath, that I had been captain and coach of Gosforth and that I'd be keen to join the club if there was an opportunity.

"I received a letter back saying: 'Dear Mr Rowell. Thank you for your letter ... but we have enough coaches at Bath at the moment.'

"Fair enough, I thought. But Dickie Rossiter had been persistent so I turned up at Clifton to have a chat with him only to discover that he'd already announced to the players that I was going to coach them. And when he did appear, he drove straight across the training pitch in his Rolls-Royce to meet me!" Rowell recalls with fondness the 1977-78 campaign at Clifton: "It was a lot of fun. There was a great buzz about the place and some good players. I think we had a record-equalling season."

Eventually, however, Sue Rowell took a call at home from a slightly chastened Jack Simpkins who said: "I think I may have made a mistake. I hadn't realised who Jack Rowell was. Actually we would like him to be our coach." It turned out that England centre Mike Beese, elected captain for the 1978-79 season, had been a prime mover in restoring contact.

So began a 30-year association with the Rec, one that brought unparalleled success for the venerable old club and eclipsed anything previously achieved in the English amateur game. Forwards Brian Jenkins and Bert Meddick were the first players to meet Rowell. "This very tall bloke appeared on the touchline one Tuesday night and we went over to speak to him," recalls Jenkins. "There had been rumours that the ex-Gosforth coach, Jack Rowell, had moved down South and that he was interested in getting involved with Bath so we guessed who it was.

"Other than he had coached Gosforth to win the cup final we didn't know a lot about him. I said to him: 'Why don't you come and coach us, Jack?' But that was obviously why he was there." When asked if he could put a date on that first encounter, Meddick says helpfully: "Yes, 'twere a Tuesday."

Meeting Rowell in the flesh – all 6ft 6in of him – the Bath contingent would have guessed quite rightly that he had been a second row. The idiosyncratic, sometimes abrasive manner could be attributed to (or excused by) his North Eastern roots – not a Geordie, mind you, but a native of Hartlepool.

A little more digging would have revealed that Rowell was an Oxford graduate – but not a Blue because his rugby career had been ended by badly torn back and neck muscles in a Freshers' trial. Employed by Lucas Food Ingredients in Bristol, he was building a reputation as a capable and ambitious manager in the industry.

Rowell had timed his arrival perfectly because Bath were ready for change and the incumbent coaches, Robson and Hudson, already had a few ideas of their own. The late Dave Robson certainly had no hesitation in welcoming the newcomer, recalling: "At first it was me, Tom and Brendan Perry but then I coached for one season on my own. When Jack arrived, I said: 'You run it, I'll help you.'

So what did Rowell find when he arrived at the Rec? The set-up was none too promising – a very conservative club, accustomed to playing second fiddle to Bristol and with gates often measured in the hundreds rather than thousands. Tradition had left the club with a formidable fixture list, featuring virtually all the top Welsh clubs, but without the depth of personnel to deliver anything other than the occasional bloody nose.

The triumvirate: Dave Robson, Tom Hudson and Jack Rowell.

"The team used to travel over the Bridge and get 'Welsh flu'," observed Rowell. "To change all that, we needed to train properly and systematically. Some people thought it was too tough and in the early days some of the players melted away.

"So we started training properly; there were talented individuals, especially in the backs … people like Beese, John Horton, John Palmer and Jim Waterman. They had been used to living on scraps because the forwards couldn't deliver. My job was to put a decent pack together – it wasn't long before we were winning."

Horton relates in Brian Jones's excellent book *Bath, Ace of Clubs* how training was transformed under Rowell, particularly for the forwards: "He would spend hours with them on details of technique. He had great technical knowledge of the game." Beese was just as taken with the new regime: "There was a new confidence born out of Jack's being over us. We took on an extra dimension as a team. He was someone we respected and he respected us and we were confident playing under his guidance."

In fact the impact had been more or less immediate. Bath won their very first game under Rowell. It was no gentle introduction either, a trip to Pontypool on 2 September 1978, but Bath never looked back after taking the lead with a first minute dropped goal from Horton and triumphed 26-10 with tries by John Davies, Waterman, Beese and Horton. The Ponty pack, led by Lions prop Graham Price, dominated possession but the Bath back division was at its inventive best and Waterman was heroic in defence. Jack Arnold, former player, team secretary and club president and latterly appointed press officer, penned a series of pen portrait for the match programme, including this summary on Waterman:

JIM WATERMAN

Position: Full-back.

Honours: Somerset, Oxford University and Western Counties.

Height: 5ft 8ins.

Weight: 12 stone 8lbs.

Jim Waterman was born in Middlesex on 21st January 1945. He learned his rugby at Isleworth Grammar School. He then studied at Bristol University whose rugby team he captained after playing briefly in the West Wales League, joined Bath in 1968-69 season where his exciting full-back style earned him a first team place. He made his debut at Ebbw Vale in September 1968, had played over 300 first team games, mainly at full-back, but also occasionally at centre, on the wing, or at fly-half. He has scored more than 600 points including 43 tries. He has played on numerous occasions for Somerset whom he has captained, and for Western Counties against the Fijians the Springboks. He went to Oxford University in 1974 to further his teaching career and won a Blue there. Since, he has captained Bath twice, in 1975-76 and again last season.

The match marked debuts for Dauntsey's schoolmaster Derek Wyatt on the left wing and for another teacher, Simon Jones, teaming up in the back row with Parsons and Lye in a Bath side as follows: J S Waterman; J Davies, M C Beese, J Palmer, D Wyatt; J Horton, D Murphy; R R Speed, A Mason, J M Meddick, B J Jenkins, C Chappell, G Parsons, S Jones, R Lye.

Four days later, the same Bath XV faced just as tough a test against Newport at Rodney Parade, where they had never won. A 4-4 draw was therefore more than satisfying as Bath produced, according to The Chronicle, "some thrilling running, followed by spirited, tenacious defence." Characteristically, their 31st minute try was started in their own 22 by Murphy and Davies and carried on by Colin Chappell on the right touchline before Horton took the lock's inside pass to score in the corner.

Not for the first time – and not for the last – Welford Road then provided a reality check as Leicester won 25-6 to put a dampener on Beese's 200th appearance for Bath. Taking the field just three days after their efforts at Rodney Parade, the Bath forwards were overpowered and the backs given little chance to shine. There was something of a hangover the following Wednesday evening as Bath struggled to subdue a spirited Clifton side, keen to make a point against their erstwhile coach. Beese scored his 81st try for the club in an 18-3 victory but there was no escaping the fact that the pack had again been outplayed by a home eight in which Somerset forwards Simon Luxmoore and Nick Williams were outstanding.

This was a time when clubs made the most of the early autumn evenings to stage a succession of midweek matches. Bath had played 12 games by the second week of October but Rowell's influence was already being felt. The win at Clifton initiated a run of eight victories, the highlight being a first-ever success at Neath on 30 September 1978. This was a bruising affair and the referee offered little protection to players being trampled, flanker Jones being particularly roughly treated, but the 12-8 scoreline was remarkably effective in easing the pain.

Leicester's Dusty Hare on collision course with John Davies as flanker Simon Jones moves in (9 September 1978).

Jones did catch the referee's attention a couple of weeks later when Bath travelled to his former club, Plymouth, for a South West Merit Table fixture. He was sent off, along with his opposite number, in a game notable only for late tackles, flailing boots, fistfights and stampings. The other miscreant? A blond-haired ex-Para called Roger Spurrell. The match ended 13-12 to Bath who edged ahead with a try and penalty from John Davies before hostilities broke out.

Jones recalls: "Albion had been talking up how they were going to get me because I had left them for the job in Hampshire. And the press had built up the fact that Roger and I were best pals and this was the first game we had played against each other.

> **"The referee was a guy called Terry Friend, a no-nonsense type. There was a scrum and I remember the prop just whacked me one so I started punching him and Roger came in from the other side. He had his arms around me – we didn't even hit each other – while the fighting was going on around us. The referee just looked at us and said: 'Right, you two, off!' The only time I ever got sent off in my career was with Roger and we never laid a punch on each other."**

The winning run came to an end four days later at London Irish whose pack laid the foundations for a 15-9 win at the Rec, three tries to nil telling the story. There was a week to recover before the local derby with Bristol where Bath matched the home side's four tries with a hat-trick from Wyatt who also laid on another for Beese.

Gerry Parsons moves in on Bristol scrum-half Richard Harding as home players Kevin Bogira, Malcolm Baker, Nigel Pomphrey, Mike Rafter and Mike Fry provide protection from Robbie Lye, Steve Lewis and Geoff Pillinger (21 October 1978).

The skipper's verdict was "We only got good possession six times, scored four tries and nearly scored from the others as well." Unfortunately, Bath's problems up front were ruthlessly exploited by their neighbours who ran in three tries in six minutes and held out to win 24-16.

Not before time, Chilcott made his first appearance of the season in a County Championship day fixture against St Mary's Hospital and, having proved his fitness, was a late addition to the team travelling to Harlequins. With second row Barry also prominent, the 22-year-old prop provided much-needed solidity to the scrum and, helped lay the foundations for a 15-4 win. Scrum-half Steve Lewis scored an early touchdown and added a dropped goal while further tries were added by centre Paul Simmons and Palmer, playing at fly-half. Yet another member of the Bath contingent fell foul of the referee, however, as touch judge David Jenkins was relieved off his flag five minutes from time after an audible aside.

While Jones earned a two-week ban from the Somerset RFU disciplinary committee for his dismissal at Plymouth, Jenkins escaped further censure from his own Management Committee. There was considerable satisfaction though in the news that Beese and Palmer had been selected in the South West squad to face the All Blacks at Bristol, Palmer being in the starting line-up at fly-half. A crowd of 15,000 at the Memorial Ground saw the New Zealanders win 20-nil on a wet and windy Wednesday afternoon.

After a hiccup at home to Newbridge, losing 6-3, Bath recovered their form against Coventry (23-3) and United Services Portsmouth (25-10) before making the trip to Stradey Park for a midweek match on 29 November. Neither side was at full-strength but blindside flanker Gerry Parsons was outstanding; the big postman, with his distinctive 'mutton chop' sideburns, engineered a last-quarter try with a diagonal kick for Derek Wyatt to earn a 7-7 draw.

A poor start left Bath far too much to do against London Scottish and they lost 18-12 but they rose to the challenge against Gloucester, winning 20-10 at the Rec with tries by Meddick, Jones and Wyatt, running in from 60 yards. Horton dropped a goal and Palmer added a penalty and conversion. The double was achieved over Harlequins but Horton, although recently capped for the fourth time against New Zealand, looked strangely hesitant and the whole side misfired before winning 21-10.

The year ended positively with wins at Rugby and at home to Clifton (although postal workers Parsons and Jenkins were absent, dealing with the Christmas mail), and on the last weekend of 1978, a 10-10 draw at Northampton. The New Year brought an announcement from the Management Committee that work was to begin on an extension to the rear of the North Stand in May. Meanwhile, it was 2 February before Rowell's team lost again, falling foul of referee Roger Quittenton and Rosslyn Park's international forwards Neil Mantell and the late Andy Ripley who scored three tries between them in the last quarter to win 25-14. Charlie Ralston, later to join Bath, converted two and dropped a goal after Wyatt, Harry and Simmons had touched down for the visitors.

The first round draw for the John Player Cup handed Bath a trip to London Welsh on 10 February, pitting Horton against Neil Bennett, the man who had taken his England No 10 shirt for the opening Five Nations Championship fixture against Scotland a week previously. Although Bath led 11-10 at the break, Bennett kicked 16 points in a 28-18 victory to underline his pre-eminence. Horton, after missing a straightforward dropped goal attempt early in the second half, received poor service from a pack lacking Parsons, Jenkins and Meddick. Simmons (2) and Lewis scored tries with Lewis adding two penalties.

After initially blowing this out of their system with a record 68-4 romp against Exeter University, Bath lost 23-7 at home to Bristol whose back row of Mike Rafter, Malcolm Baker and new No 8 Bob Hesford were outstanding as a 'hunting' combination. An early Wyatt touchdown, from an inch-perfect chip by Horton, and a Palmer penalty kept the home side in contention but Bristol confirmed their superiority with four tries. Just three days later it was back over the Severn Bridge for a rain-drenched night at Bridgend, the Brewery Field far too boggy for Bath's running game, not that they managed to gain much possession in losing 15-6. Nevertheless, it was their first defeat in five visits to Wales in Rowell's first season as coach.

In the absence of neutral touch judges, let alone citing commissioners, and with referees often unsighted – or turning a blind eye to all but the worst excesses – English clubs travelled to Wales with justifiable trepidation. At Cross Keys on Friday, 2 March, Bath eventually prevailed by 22-nil but it was a sub-standard, thoroughly unpleasant affair which erupted before the interval into a full-scale fight between the forwards. As the referee lectured the packs, a wag shouted from the crowd: "Don't spoil it ref. It's the best we've seen so far!" but the violence continued until centre Lyn Jones (punching) and flanker Peter Sparkes (use of the boot) were sent off in separate incidents, reducing Bridgend to 13 men. Palmer completed the hat-trick with a try, two conversions, a dropped goal and a penalty to add to tries by Jones and Wyatt.

There was far more rugby played at home to Swansea the following weekend and Bath continued to build their reputation with an 18-6 victory, notable for a busy display by Murphy at scrum-half. He scored the first try and there were others from Simmons and Wyatt, plus two penalties from Mark Sutton. Again, Waterman was the master of the timely intervention from full-back and Beese was fulsome in his praise for the forwards: "It was one of their best performances for a long time. They really stuck at it, controlled the ball they got and came round to spoil Swansea's as well." With an outstanding performance from the back row of Jones, Parsons and Lye and important defensive kicking from Murphy and Horton, the rest of the team took their cue in putting in some fine tackles.

That weekend it emerged that the Plymouth Albion flanker, Roger Spurrell, was to join Bath. His imminent arrival was viewed with disquiet in some quarters because since his dismissal against Bath in October he had since served a second ban for being sent off against Exeter. He had also been ruled 'persona non grata' by the Cornish selectors after an alleged incident at a Bristol hotel in November. One person who had no doubts about his suitability for Bath, however, was his ex-Plymouth teammate and sparring partner from the October clash, Simon Jones, who had rung him up, saying: "Come up to Bath. It's real rugby up here." Jones told The Bath Chronicle at the time:

> **"I think things have just all piled up together on Roger who is basically a very nice guy. He's also a very good rugby player, very much in the Mike Rafter digging mould, who could go a long way. I'm not saying he isn't a very hard player but he's not dirty and I have every confidence in saying he would be an asset rather than a liability to Bath considering he could so easily keep me out of the team."**

Spurrell, aged 23, had begun his career with Launceston and then served as a paratrooper, playing for Combined Services. On returning to Cornwall to take over his father's farm, he became a regular member of the Cornwall side. He had since sold the farm and was looking for a job in the Bath area.

Apart from a lacklustre 11-6 defeat at Gloucester, Kingsholm never having been a happy hunting ground for Bath, they romped through the rest of the 1978-79 campaign, registering home wins over Newport (15-6), Pontypridd (20-18), South Wales Police (36-16) and Llanelli (22-6) to bring the Rag Doll back to the Rec for the first time in four years. This display on the 24 April ranked as one of the best ever seen, with Wyatt claiming a hat-trick to equal George Haydon's 48-year-old record of 29 tries. With Beese and Palmer superb in midfield and Waterman, playing his 350th game, making timely incursions from fullback, the rest of the points came from two conversions and a penalty by John Davies and a Horton dropped goal.

It was a notable triumph against a superb Llanelli side and Bath's ninth win against Welsh opposition, confirming them as runners-up to Bridgend in the Daily Mail Anglo-Welsh Pennant merit table. Although Spurrell's arrival was to add an even steelier edge to the forward effort, the idea that Bath were a 'soft touch' was already being revised in Rowell's first season as coach.

That was the breakthrough, as Rowell himself recalls: "From the time I joined, there was no 'Welsh flu'. I said to them, that as soon as we could win in Wales systematically – and the refs were never giving us any freebies – we would dominate English rugby. That's what happened."

As Margaret Thatcher moved into Downing Street to initiate a political revolution founded on market economics, Rowell was formulating his own radical plans to transform the fortunes and reputation of one of the oldest rugby clubs in the country. As one of the true pioneers, founded in 1865 even before the RFU itself, the club still rejoiced in the name 'Bath Football Club (RFU)', a title whose continuing relevance was questioned at a Special General Meeting:

> **Major Chiverell asked if the club could be called the Bath Rugby Football Club instead of Bath Football Club. In reply, Mr. H J Simpkins, Secretary, said that the Club was privileged, as were some eight or nine other rugby football clubs in the country, to call themselves 'Football Clubs' and it was an old tradition of the Club. Rugby football was started before the game which is now called soccer and the Club were privileged that they were still allowed to use their original name of Bath Football Club and put the letters (R.F.U.) after it.**

However, a fundamental change of culture was obvious for all to see. To Rowell, it was just "management and leadership", applying business principles to the game he loved.

Although still vulnerable against the top sides such as Bristol or Gloucester, the potent mix of exciting back play and a more effective ball-winning pack began to have an impact on recruitment. Towards the end of the season Bath had handed a debut to an 18-year-old Bryanston schoolboy, David Trick. Playing on the right wing against South Wales Police, he scored three tries, rounding things off with an 80-yard dash past three hapless defenders. It was to become his party piece.

Horton took over as captain from Beese for the 1979-80 season, one of his first duties being to endorse the acceptance of Spurrell as a playing member of the club at the July meeting of the Management Committee, although it was midway through the season before the Cornish flanker fully established himself in the first XV.

At the next meeting on 29 August, Horton and Rowell were "pleased to announce that the club now had strength in depth and that the players were looking forward to a successful season." However, before the campaign began flanker Geoff Pillinger announced his imminent retirement at the age of 30 owing to a recurring back problem.

Spirits were high, though, especially after a pre-season tour to California which included five matches and a successful foray at the San Jose Sevens tournament. Thanks were extended to former skipper John Roberts as organiser and manager before business moved on to other matters such as a donation of tables and chairs for the clubhouse from the Old Players Association and whether to charge Bath Croquet Club £3 for hire of a clubhouse room for their regular bridge sessions.

With greater interest in rugby on the Rec, efforts were being made to drum up commercial support for home games. A sponsor had been found for the Neath fixture at the end of September and local business people were being invited to the pre-match luncheon with a view to sparking their interest.

The early season results did nothing to dampen the pre-season optimism. Visitors on the opening day were a formidable Pontypool side who, with Geoff Squire, Bobby Windsor and Eddie Butler prominent, led 9-nil at the break. But Bath eventually won 16-9 with a remarkable second-half comeback spearheaded by scrum-half Murphy, who crossed twice. Palmer converted both tries and also laid on a try for Simmons. Horton's verdict: "It was a very satisfying match to win considering the mess we had got ourselves into. It showed our strength of character."

History was made the following Wednesday evening when Bath recorded their first success at Rodney Parade, beating Newport 6-3 with a Wyatt dropped goal and a Palmer penalty. The Black and Ambers' Leighton Davies had a nightmare with the boot, eventually missing a kick in front of the posts in the last minute but Bath deserved the win, if only for their tenacity. The watching Lions selectors learned very little.

Now on something of a roll, Bath patched themselves up for the trip to Leicester just three days later and again came away with the spoils for only their second win at Welford Road since the war. The 10-9 scoreline was testament to a fine forward effort, with Parsons, Jones and Lye impressive as both creators and destroyers while the front row of Meddick, Tony Mason and Chilcott gave Peter Wheeler's stand-in, Ian Bridgwood, a torrid time in the scrums.

With Bath in this sort of form, it was no surprise to see England's Chairman of Selectors, Budge Rogers, in the West Stand for the home game against Moseley. With 15 minutes to go, Bath had managed only a touchdown by Murphy and trailed 11-4 but the forwards roused themselves to provide the scrum-half with his second try before Waterman twice attacked out of defence to set up tries for Wyatt and Beese, Palmer converting all three. An admiring Rogers commented afterwards: "They just

Roger Spurrell on his debut against San Jose Seahawks (18 September 1979).

don't know when to stop attacking – even when things aren't going right for them – and they're a very exciting side to watch."

Spurrell had to wait until the visit of Californian tourists San Jose Seahawks to make his debut, as did another Cornishman destined to give outstanding service to the Bath club, wing Barry Trevaskis. Of the 11 tries scored in a 58-nil win, one went to Chilcott, his first in senior rugby.

Bath's winning run was halted at Stradey Park where they were leading 6-4 with five minutes left on the clock. The dam broke when Murphy had a kick charged down for a score by Ray Gravell who then broke a tackle to set up a try for right wing Lyndon Jones and Llanelli squeezed home 14-6. It was Lye's 350th game for Bath but there was little to celebrate, particularly as Chilcott suffered a dislocated kneecap, an injury which was to rule him out for the rest of the season.

Fortunately, front row resources had been bolstered by the arrival of an affable tighthead prop from Somerset who made his debut in a 33-13 win at Clifton the following Wednesday night. Richard Lee, a foursquare character in every sense of the word, was to be the unsung hero of the Bath pack for the next decade, underrated by all except his teammates and opposing front rows. A farmer from Wellington, he was as strong as an ox and the only possible flaw in his game was a propensity to cause as much damage to fellow players as to the opposition. Hence the affectionate nickname 'Oafie'.

It took an injury-time penalty by John Davies to force a 22-22 draw at home to Neath, although Bath scored three tries to none, and they managed a scrappy 13-4 win away to South Wales Police as the injury list began to lengthen. Barry then lasted only 12 minutes at Aberavon on 5 October before taking a punch in the eye which ruled him out for five weeks but it was only in the closing minutes that the Wizards snatched a 17-15 victory thanks to an interception of Lye's pass at the base of a scrum.

With the advantage of a couple of weeks' break before the eagerly awaited derby against Bristol at the Rec, Rowell considered his options and selected 18-year-old

Trick on the right wing for only his third senior game. If it was a gamble, it paid off handsomely as the Bryanston schoolboy scorched past bewildered opponents for a hat-trick of tries in a stunning 38-17 win. Bristol were handicapped by the dismissal of hooker Kevin Bogira after 30 minutes but there was no holding the home side as they rattled up 23 points in one 14-minute spell. Wyatt crossed twice while Palmer converted four and added two penalties. Bristol were to turn the tables later in the season but never again under Rowell's tutelage could Bath be accused of labouring under an inferiority complex against their nearest rivals.

Barry Trevaskis: another Cornishman joins the Rec ranks.

As if to reiterate the 'new order' of things, Bath then fulfilled for the last time a fixture against St Mary's College, winning 28-6. It was a poignant parting for older members, particularly for 84-year-old Arnold Ridley, established as one of the nation's best loved TV characters in his role as Private Godfrey of 'Dad's Army'. The ex-Club President had originated the association with the medical students while Bath's fixtures secretary between the wars. Matches between the clubs had featured England 'greats' such as Norman 'Nim' Hall, Lewis Cannell and Trevor Wintle but there was no room for such rheumy-eyed sentiment in Rowell's grand strategy.

Given these traditions it was no surprise that in the early days of Rowell's tenure as coach, there was a degree of uneasiness in some quarters at the scale of his ambitions and the commitment he demanded from players. That disquiet was voiced by an unidentified club official who told him: 'Your problem, Jack, is that you want to win all the time...' But others in the club with impeccable rugby pedigrees had already been won over. Rowell recalls how Alec Lewis, the illustrious former international and recent chairman of England selectors, took him aside and said: "Jack, there's a bit of tension around the place about what's going on. But let me assure you that Bath have never played as well as this."

That was acknowledged also by the selection of five players in the South & South West Counties XV to face the All Blacks at Exeter on 20 November – more than any other club. Jones, Murphy, Horton and John Palmer were joined by Mike Beese as captain.

To Jones, Beese was "a very serious, rather elegant figure, quite a contrast to the rougher lads like Bertie but a quiet, strong character." Unfortunately Beese was laid out and taken off in the first half, to be replaced by Bristol's Alan Morley. For Jones, eventually to be ousted from the Bath side by his mate, Spurrell, the clash with the New Zealanders represented the pinnacle of his career: "It had been raining quite a lot and the surface was heavy, although it was a nice day. I remember arriving at a line-out, chest heaving, gasping for breath, and Graham Mourie was already there, hardly breathing. It was just a different level of fitness.

"I really enjoyed the game though. At one point Paul Ackford was driving for the line and all he had to do was flick the ball up and I was over. He got held and didn't pass. Then Eddie Dunn, their fly-half, booted the ball downfield, our full-back knocked on and they scored."

So Mourie's team eased to a 16-nil victory on the same County Ground where Dave Gallaher's pioneering 1905 'Originals' had made their first appearance in the British Isles. On that occasion, so disbelieving had English rugby types been at the 55-4 scoreline against a highly-regarded Devon side that the scoreline was reversed in the newspapers!

As Bath cut a swathe through the remainder of 1979, they accounted for other time-honoured opponents who would in time fade from the fixture list – Cheltenham, Newbridge, Coventry, United Services Portsmouth, London Scottish, Plymouth Albion and Clifton. Predictably, only Gloucester lowered Bath's colours, winning 10-3 on a filthy Monday night at Kingsholm thanks to the iron grip exerted by the home pack.

Cardiff were in no more generous a mood on New Year's Day at the Arms Park where, despite good work from the back row of Spurrell, Parsons and Jones and apart from a smart try by Waterman, Bath failed to take their chances and lost 14-6 in front of a 10,000 crowd. Parsons, Jones and Horton were summoned to the final England trial four days later and were therefore absent when Bath surrendered their home record to Leicester, who possessed more strength in depth and won 22-12.

After a midweek 'sinking' of the Royal Navy, as the newspaper headlines would always have it, rather than watching his side at London Welsh, Rowell took the afternoon off to check on John Player Cup opponents Marlow. With Horton restored to the England team and the opening Five Nations game just a week away, the skipper was also absent as Bath turned in by far their worst display of the season, losing 37-7 to London Welsh – a performance that had to be seen to be believed according to John Stephens, of The Bath Chronicle:

> **"It was not so much that Bath lost. It was the way they lost. Hardly a gesture of defiance was shown to a Welsh side made to look like world beaters by Bath's non-tackling, dispirited rabble who were unrecognisable as the side that has swept virtually all before them this season. The crowd shrugged with disbelief as Bath missed tackle after tackle, were eclipsed up front and compounded it all with woeful errors in their own handling which at times almost completely disintegrated."**

There was no doubt that confidence had been dented and although Met Police and then Marlow were dispatched without too much difficulty, Lee scoring two tries in the cup-tie, Rosslyn Park earned a 10-9 win at the Rec. That was on the eve of England's 17-13 victory over France at the Parc des Princes where Horton dropped two goals. He did not return until the second round John Player Cup match at Liverpool where he dropped another goal in a 19-12 victory. Tries were scored by Wyatt and Trick with Palmer contributing two penalties and a conversion.

Bath's cup ambitions ended on the Rec on 8 March when, for the first time in 35 matches, they failed to score a try and lost 6-3 to London Irish in the quarter-final. While Horton sat out the game ahead of England's historic Grand Slam decider against Scotland, Ireland's John O'Driscoll was outstanding at the head of a rampaging Exiles back row and it was no surprise that they reached the final or that O'Driscoll figured prominently in the Lions Test team in South Africa that summer.

Michel van der Loos: line-out expertise.

Horton's return to action after the Grand Slam celebrations – Palmer had also been involved as a replacement without ever taking the field – saw Bath back into their stride, winning 11 out of 13 matches to the end of the season. At the Rec on 26 March Gloucester lost flanker Mike Teague, sent off for use of the boot six minutes into the second half, and the home side made light of the poor conditions to win 24-9 with tries by Trick, Beese and Jones. The impeccable Horton dropped two goals and three days later put on a masterclass of fly-half play at Exeter, steering his side to a 19-4 victory and scoring a fine solo try into the bargain.

The pack was being led at this time by a Dutchman from Ebbw Vale, line-out expert Michel van der Loos, who had scored a try on his debut against London Scottish in December. A colourful character who was one of seven rugby-playing brothers, the lock had been working as a chef in Cardiff and then turned to labouring in Bath before the effects of the recession led him for a brief period to seek his fortune in Australia in 1981. Capped by the Netherlands at 18 he amassed 94 caps before retiring and when last in contact with the club in 2002 was running a bar in Ibiza.

Van der Loos also scored a try against Bristol in the return match on 5 April 1980 but Bath were overwhelmed by a home side in unstoppable form. The 44-6 scoreline represented the heaviest defeat to date although Bath were handicapped by the absence of Horton and the loss through injury during the match of Murphy, replaced by a prop, Chris Lilley, and Wyatt.

The double was achieved over Newport for the first time although the Welsh side were enduring the worst season in their history. This was their 32nd defeat and Bath did not even need to put out a full-strength line-up to win 17-7. An unbeaten home record against Welsh opposition was completed with a 13-6 victory against Llanelli three days later, David Trick scoring his 22nd and arguably best try to date. It was an 80-metre effort and not a finger was laid on him as he evaded a clutch of defenders.

An outstanding season ended with a strange whimper as Bath surrendered 49-3 at Pontypridd on 30 April but the statistics showed 37 wins from 48 matches – a club record. In accepting the Clubman of the Year award, Rowell told the Management Committee that they must now look forward and plan for the RFU leagues "which will be with us in a few years." The Young Player award went to prop Richard Lee.

For newcomer Spurrell, it was the sort of rugby he had been looking for: "There was a lot of good rugby being played when I got there and it was down to a lot of people," he recalls. "There was Jim Waterman, who was quite influential in that period, also John Horton and John Palmer. It was those backs and the way they played rugby, exciting rugby. You did come up against hard, forward-dominated sides and quite often we got stuffed but there was a gradual evolving of the side."

Summer 1980 was a busy time for recruitment with Simon Luxmoore and Nick Williams joining from Clifton and the Richmond fullback Charlie Ralston and Swansea forward Andy Marriott also arriving at the Rec. Robbie Lye, veteran of 375 appearances, was handed the captaincy with John Palmer as vice-captain.

While Rowell planned the next steps in the playing side's development, the Management Committee had to write a letter to Walcot Old Boys apologising for damage to the Lambridge pitches caused by the exploits of motorcycle stunt rider Eddie Kidd; Mr Les Pring was concerned that players were deserting the club bar early in the evening to drink at the nearby Boater; and it was unanimously agreed that a portrait of Her Majesty be hung in the clubhouse.

From the very first match of the 1980-81 season, a 39-nil run-out against Bridgwater, there arose problems in the place-kicking department, with Palmer giving way to Ralston who enjoyed no greater success. It was the same story at Pontypool who ran out 23-13 winners and at Newport (7-13) but the blame could not be laid entirely at Palmer's feet because this was generally a poor team performance. The ever-dependable Davies was then recalled to the left wing to land two crucial kicks in a confidence-boosting 13-4 home win over Leicester who included Dusty Hare, Clive Woodward, Paul Dodge and Les Cusworth behind the scrum; and the tireless Spurrell and his pack laid the foundations for a 7-3 success at Moseley.

In restoring Davies to the team as goalkicker however, Bath lost pace on the wing and this was identified as a factor in losing 17-4 at Llanelli when they might

Bath v Bridgwater (3 September 1980) - back row (from left): Simon Luxmoore-Ball, Andy Marriott, Simon Jefferies, Mike Beese, Gerry Parsons, Simon Jones, Derek Wyatt, Charlie Ralston, Michel van der Loos. Front: Jim Waterman, Paul Simmons, John Horton, Damian Murphy, Robbie Lye (captain), John Palmer, Bert Meddick, Gareth Chilcott. Bath won 39-nil.

have snatched their first win in two decades. The short trip over to Clifton's Cribbs Causeway ground in Bristol the following Wednesday evening, 1 October, was an opportunity to get things back on track – but it all went horribly wrong. Never mind that Bath won 22-3; Horton caught an accidental knee in the face from Clifton flanker Neil Morgan and was ruled out for more than two months with a fractured cheekbone.

Without their playmaker, Bath relied on tenacity and will-to-win rather than fluency and free running to subdue Aberavon (19-13) and Maesteg (25-22), a match which marked Waterman's 400th appearance and where the result was in doubt until Sutton's penalty five minutes from time. Ralston took over at fly-half for the visit to Bristol but the home pack and David Sorrell's accurate boot engineered a comfortable 16-3 scoreline. Plymouth snatched a 9-9 all draw with a late penalty at Beacon Park a few days later, although Ralston had an even later penalty chance to take the Merit Table points. One encouraging aspect was the debut performance at full-back of Cornishman Chris Martin.

Successive defeats at Harlequins and Newbridge in early November exposed shortcomings behind the scrum where Bath had been so devastating and although 19-year-old Martin was impressive in a 19-14 win over Coventry, running in a spectacular try, kicking goals and making massive touch kicks, a 3-3 draw at Exeter set alarm bells ringing. Qualification for the later rounds of the John Player Cup in the following season depended on a respectable showing in the South West Merit Table and this was by no means a certainty. Bath had opted for an all-or-nothing strategy by declining to enter the Somerset Cup, which offered entry to the first round of the national competition.

Spurrell roused his teammates with a man-of-the-match display at Neath where Bath won 13-6, their first success in five visits to Wales. Ralston was equally impressive, kicking two penalties and making the break which set up a try for Simmons, but in a brutally hard match Lye needed stitches after being punched in the eye and Jones fractured his right hand, an injury which kept him out of the side for two months. Skipper Horton, Beese and Palmer were also absent for the visit of a well-organised Gloucester team a week later and the unbeaten home record was lost 19-nil but Horton, heavily strapped to protect a dodgy hamstring, then rallied to the cause just before Christmas to inspire a 16-nil victory over Harlequins.

The second half of the 1980-81 season was a similarly stuttering affair, featuring a third round John Player Cup win at Richmond (12-6) before Bath exited the competition at Nottingham (3-4) on 28 February when the tie turned on a mix-up between Ralston and Parsons, allowing winger Clive Pitts to hack on through the Beeston mud for the winning try.

That was followed by a 12-3 defeat at the Rec by Pontypridd and there were further home defeats against Wasps (12-27) and, more humiliatingly by Richmond (13-25), the poorest performance for some years in some people's eyes. Coming on top of Simon Jones's departure with van der Loos to play rugby in Australia, it also brought a new crop of injuries to wing Simmons (knee) and props Lee (neck) and Kelvin Neale (knee).

Time to stop the rot then. Back into the pack for the home game with Newport came experienced campaigners Meddick, Mason and Barry while Murphy returned from injury to partner Horton and inspire a confidence-boosting 9-3 victory. Horton initiated the try from his own 22, combining with Ralston who sent Trick away before taking the return from the right wing and handing on for skipper Lye to score. The Murphy-Horton partnership again paid dividends in a 16-3 win over Llanelli, in which Spurrell got the best out of his forwards and Martin and Murphy crossed the line. Horton dropped two goals.

After maintaining the winning sequence against South Wales Police (21-3) and with Chilcott back after injury, Bath prepared to entertain Bristol on Easter Saturday, very much aware that defeat would rule them out of the following season's John Player Cup. Bristol opened up a six-point lead but a superb second-half display by Horton, calmly dropping a 40-metre goal and then fielding his own chip ahead to touch down, turned the tide. Martin's conversion made it 9—6 and it was left to Horton to deliver the killer blow, another dropped goal from an even more difficult angle.

With the weight of John Player Cup qualification off their minds, Bath walloped New Brighton 44-13 on Easter Monday and recorded a memorable 18-11 victory over a strong Cardiff XV three days later. Trick's 23rd try of the season 10 minutes from time was a spectacular effort launched from the 22 by Horton who had earlier collected one of his trademark chips to score himself; Martin converted both and added two penalties.

Apart from an ill-tempered 6-3 win at Bedford in which flanker Phil Turner and the home team's Nick Youngs were sent off, there was then only a finale against an RFU President's XV at the Rec, arranged to raise funds for a club tour to Miami in August. The RFU president was John Kendall-Carpenter, capped with Alec Lewis as a Bath back row pairing in the early 1950s, and the invitation side included Irish international lock Ronnie Hakin, who was to join the club the following season.

The match marked farewells by Mike Beese (316 appearances) and Bert Meddick (334), one an elegant centre of international pedigree, the other a 'salt of the earth' prop from the Stothert & Pitt club, who had been bending his back in the Bath cause since January 1971. As a kid he occasionally jumped into the River Avon to retrieve balls kicked over the West Stand – and received a half-crown from Jack Simpkins. Meddick had had first hand experience of Rowell's demanding new training regime and refusal to accept excuses for anything less than total commitment.

> "We had a match at Harlequins once and I cried off because I had to look after our young 'un," recalls Meddick. "Jack couldn't see a problem – 'You've got to play; just bring the boy with you,' he said. You had to do things Jack's way. There wasn't room in the squad for anyone who didn't. So I ended up on the team coach with the baby, giving him his feed and changing his nappy. And when we got to the Stoop I had to give him to this woman in the crowd to look after – but I was bit upset when the Harlequins committee wouldn't et me take him into the changing room afterwards. How old was my boy? Five months."

Both Meddick and Beese had given sterling service to the Bath club yet had caught a glimpse of Rowell's "promised land." Totally unexpected, however, was the revelation in The Sun newspaper on 9 July 1981 that David Trick had signed a £25,000 contract to sell sportswear in the United States, South America and South Africa and was flying out to New York the following Monday. He told the paper:

> "I have always hated training. But that did not stop one Rugby League scout waylaying me in a car park when I was a 17-year-old sixth-former and offering me £6,000. He had it all there in a briefcase – no questions asked."

Reputed to be the fastest winger in the rugby union game, he had since been pestered by other Rugby League clubs, receiving one bid of £21,000 from Oldham. He added: "I would love to have won a cap- but there's more to life than playing rugby." 'Tricky' was to return to Bath but remained an enigma, exciting and exasperating in equal measure.

In September 1981, the Bath club was very much at a crossroads, struggling to cope with a string of casualties from the Florida tour and with some of their most experienced players either already in retirement or in the case of 36-year-old Jim Waterman in contemplation of it. There were talented youngsters but doubts persisted about their readiness for the fray. It would only take a few more injuries to key personnel to tip the delicate balance – and that is what happened in the early part of the season.

Nine of the first 14 fixtures were lost, including at home to Pontypool (19-22) and away to Newport (10-24), where a Welsh Schools cap called Stuart Barnes looked a good prospect at fullback, before Leicester handed out a 44-6 thrashing at Welford Road. New skipper Murphy did not figure at all after the Pontypool defeat and resources began to look even more threadbare when the midfield playmaker, Palmer, announced in mid-October that a pre-season shoulder injury would rule him out until April 1982.

Even the youngsters were not immune. Nineteen-year-old John Hall, a product of Beechen Cliff school, had made such an impression on his first XV debut as a replacement against Pontypool that once recalled to the side at Leicester, he kept his place against Plymouth (20-nil) and Moseley (27-16). Selected for Somerset against Middlesex on 26 September, he was stretchered off at Roehampton with damaged knee ligaments after colliding with teammate Spurrell.

"I had started to make a name for myself. It was the first time I had been watched by the England selectors but Somerset were getting beaten quite badly," recalls Hall. "I collided with Roger, my studs got caught in his shirt and I tore the ligaments in my knee. That was the first of my bad injuries."

It was no great surprise that a typically lively Llanelli team won 17-9 at the Rec but a 46-9 hammering at Aberavon was a humbling experience, even for a depleted Bath side. The Welsh onslaught continued when Gareth Davies inspired Cardiff to a seven-try rout as Bath tried yet another fresh face at hooker, Paul Knight, and the back row of Spurrell, Parsons and No 8 Mitch Patching worked vainly to hold the score to 32-3 at the Arms Park.

What more could possibly go wrong? They found out after losing 19-6 at home to Bristol on 19 October, when Chilcott was dismissed by Welsh international referee Clive Norling for kicking No 8 Bob Hesford with 15 minutes left on the clock. Somerset RFU's disciplinary committee handed out an unprecedented suspension of ONE YEAR, a sentence whose severity left the 25-year-old prop "absolutely shattered". Fortunately for Chilcott – Cooch, as he was popularly known – the penalty was reduced on appeal and he was able to resume at the start of the following season.

Gerry Parsons announced he was leaving to join London Welsh and turned in another commanding performance in his farewell game at Harlequins, although his loss was tempered by the emergence of Hall in the blindside role and the return of Simon Jones from Australia. Less easy to take was a third round exit from the John Player Cup on 23 January 1982, Rosslyn Park dominating the line-out from start to finish through Paul Ackford and squeezing through 11-9.

The announcement of Murphy's retirement – not entirely unexpected – followed soon after but perhaps the most significant result was a second defeat by Gloucester on 21 April, not so much for the 33-15 scoreline but because it meant that Bath could not now qualify for the John Player Cup the following year. Before the end of the campaign Jack Simpkins announced that Bath would re-enter the Somerset RFU Knock-out Cup in the 1982-83 season in order to ensure John Player Cup qualification the following year.

'Doubles' inflicted by both Gloucester and Bristol were among the 19 defeats suffered by Bath during an immensely frustrating season. The end-of-term report revealed that 69 players had taken the field. What was not realised at the time, however, was that some of the newcomers were to establish themselves as key individuals in a golden era for the Bath club. Among those

John Hall arrives on the scene as a replacement in the 19-22 home defeat by Pontypool (5 September 1981).

who made debuts, apart from Hall, were Oxford University centre Simon Halliday and a fresh-faced lock, Nigel Gaymond, who appeared together in the Christmas game against Clifton. Scottish prospect Rob Cunningham made the hooking position his own and another centre, Alun Rees, followed Gaymond from Bristol. It was Halliday who made the greatest impression, however, and by the end of the season he was a worthy successor to Beese.

Sometimes it was worth casting a closer eye over the opposition. Swansea right wing Tony Swift, later to become a Rec favourite, scored two tries in the 41-nil humiliation at St Helen's on 13 March; and the visit of Exeter University 12 days later saw the first appearance on the Rec of Richard Hill and David Sole, two players destined to forge illustrious international careers through the Bath club.

So extraordinary would be the transformation wrought by players of this calibre that Bath would not lose another cup match for nearly six years.

Chapter 5

'THIS CLUB USED TO BE CAPTAINED BY GENTLEMEN!'

The captaincy may have come to Roger Spurrell by accident, or at least prematurely, but no-one was better fitted than the former paratrooper to drive the team forward. Actually, he led from the front, invariably placing his own body in the firing line – and there was a sense that teammates found him more intimidating than any opponent.

He fulfilled exactly Rowell's requirement for an uncompromising individual who would motivate the people around him, generating a collective desire to overcome even the toughest opposition, home or away.

Whether it was derived from his military training as a Physical Training Instructor or some inner force of nature, probably both, Spurrell would not back away from confrontation. Like Phil Hall, of the previous generation, it was not in his character to be intimidated.

It certainly came as a shock to some Welsh sides to witness their backs being terrorised and their loose ball being pilfered by this fearless, aggressive open side, with his shock of curly blond hair. He just didn't seem to feel pain – and he certainly didn't show it. Blood and bruises were his stock in trade. "He had to be hard to take the kicks," says Rowell, "and there were a lot of them. He was physically and mentally strong, a real motivator."

And Spurrell himself. Why does he think he was so successful? "In hindsight I played for fun," he says. "But there's never any fun in losing. And I was in a very lucky position because we were winning so much."

Spurrell's motivational skills were far more sophisticated than people gave him credit for, according to Richard Hill, one of a string of Bath captains who were to carry the Cornishman's mantle with distinction. "People tend to forget that Roger was far more than a scrapper and tub-thumper," says Hill. "First of all, he was a highly-skilled openside who was well worth an England cap, but he was also a supreme motivator.

"Like a good Company Sergeant-Major, he had the knack of summing up a person within five minutes of meeting him, so that he instantly knew how to get under their skin. He tapped in to their psyche, knew what everyone's Achilles heel was and, whether it was a sharp word or a quiet one, it was designed to get the very best out of them."

Gareth Chilcott concurs: "Roger was the best captain I played under. He knew exactly what it took to motivate people. He understood my fear of losing – it was what made me perform. He also had that 'Martin Johnson factor' in that if we won by 40 points you never saw him, but if it was 6-6 in Cardiff in the rain Roger would come to the fore. He was abrasive, loyal and, of course, he had that strange insight into people."

So what was Spurrell's secret, if there was one? "I'm very lucky," he says. "I obviously had natural leadership qualities. But to develop and evolve them you've got to think about them, haven't you. And so you think about people and, at that time, how you could get the best out of them.

"Simon Halliday, who if he hadn't broken his ankle would have been one of the best centres in the world ... ever, was a perfect example. He was always the quiet one. I couldn't shout and scream at him. But there were ways to motivate him."

Nigel Gaymond remembers sitting in the changing room before a game, waiting with some trepidation for his turn to get the Spurrell treatment, short but hardly sweet and delivered with a scornful snarl: "And you, are you going to play today ... you tart?" "Er, yes Roger."

But these days Spurrell insists that his was a more balanced approach than legend would sometimes have it: "You can't shout at everybody – and if you do, you've got to have a quiet word with them afterwards. It's why it's such a lovely game – you have so many different characters. We had doctors and lawyers, whereas the professional game now hasn't got so many highly intelligent people. I had Charlie Ralston living with me for a few months – he's now a hospital consultant in the Midlands – and the two who always sat together and bunked together were Charlie and Coochie. It was the classic pairing that you used to see in rugby."

John Hall remembers Spurrell's the 1981-82 period as "a time of change, old hands going out and new people coming in. "I was one of the new people. Spurrell was established – but not initially as a captain. Yes, he could lead from the front but like all the successful Bath captains he was someone who could stand up to Jack Rowell, although not in a confrontational way, and have their say, not be walked over by Jack. So Spurrell had his own thoughts on things. He was and is an intelligent person and didn't really get the recognition that was due to him as a player and as a captain."

Of course, Spurrell was destined never to win an England cap (an ill-advised exchange with RFU luminary Bob Weighill at Twickenham in his second full season as captain did not help) but Hill believes it was the nation's loss.

Roger Spurrell outside his club, known to all as 'Bog Island.'

"Roger should have gone to New Zealand in the summer of 1985 – as should Gareth Chilcott – but their disciplinary record told against them. Instead they picked David Cooke, of Harlequins, and Paul Huntsman, from Headingley," says Hill. "The All Blacks beat them up and we lost both Tests." Neither Cooke, nor Huntsman played again for England.

"Paul Huntsman was a nice man," says Chilcott, "but the All Blacks of that era used the rolling maul very effectively and you had to have people to pull it down. Me and Spurrell might have got the crap kicked out of us – but we would have kept doing it, if that's what it took to stop them. I had actually been told I was in the tour party but I got into trouble with the RFU after being sent off and was told to ignore the first letter." Fortunately, Chilcott was to get a second, even a third chance.

Spurrell's view now is that he "didn't fit the mould." Sitting at home – a converted boat house beside his restaurant overlooking the harbour at Newquay – he continues: "I live in a hut on the beach now, which about sums me up, really. I've always been pretty alternative. And some people didn't see through the facade which I sometimes put on. Some of that came from my upbringing, some of it from the Forces."

He was never one to walk away from a challenge though and while Damian Murphy, sidelined by a persistent back problem, pondered his own playing future throughout the winter of 1981-82 his vice-captain struggled manfully to lead an injury-ravaged team. Results were mixed, if not downright discouraging, but Spurrell was Murphy's firm recommendation to the Management Committee on 3 March 1982 when faced with the painful, if inevitable, decision to retire.

There were those on the management committee who thought that the abrasive Cornishman was definitely not the man to lead the club into 1982-83, as Spurrell recalls: " When I first became captain, they did everything they could to stop me. One of my proposers was John Palmer and they conveniently 'discovered' that he hadn't paid his subs. Jack Simpkins, the club secretary, came out with the line: 'This club used to be captained by gentlemen!' But that was typical Jack. I ended up best friends with him and used to spend all my time in Tucker's Grave (Simpkins' local in the village of Faulkland)."

In the early days Spurrell spent his time between matches and training sessions

Jack Simkins: later became firm friends with Roger Spurrell.

tending sheep on the Mendips although he eventually acquired derelict public conveniences on the Grand Parade and turned them into a nightspot called 'The Island Club' but known to all, naturally enough, as 'Bog Island'.

The passage of time tends to blur precise recollection of those exciting early years under Rowell and it has to be said that Spurrell's first full season as captain began none too auspiciously. Despite the arrival of a formidable back row presence in Paul Simpson from Gosforth and the emergence of the promising young Jon Morrison, soon paired with Gaymond at lock, the frantic fixture list of September-October yielded fewer wins than losses. A closer look would reveal however that only four of the 14 matches were at home and that Bath players were much in demand among county selectors.

The burly Simpson had been introduced to the club by Simon Jones after the pair had met on the Barbarians' Easter Tour of South Wales. "The Bath boys always take the mickey out of me," says Jones. "I got two of the best back rows the club ever had – Roger Spurrell and Paul Simpson – at the cost of my own place in the side. But I've got no regrets about that at all. If you're not good enough, you're not good enough."

Pontypool, led by Eddie Butler, provided a lesson in power play to win 37-16 on the opening weekend but the prodigal David Trick had returned in time to take his place on the right wing against Leicester at the Rec, adding to earlier tries by Barry Trevaskis and Chris Stanley to clinch a 24-15 victory. Despite further wins over Newport and Aberavon, Spurrell's men suffered four successive defeats on the road against Liverpool (4-12), Bristol (4-6), United Services Portsmouth (16-18 on a county day) and Neath (21-22). The derby match at the Memorial Ground was a close-fought affair, literally, as Bristol survived the loss of John Doubleday, sent off for kicking Gaymond.

Once the seasonal round of County Championship matches had been completed, Bath were able to field a settled side, although they could not resist hosting Newbridge on Monday 15 November, barely 48 hours after many players had been involved in the county programme. Paul Turner, just one of a clutch of magical young Welsh playmakers at that time, masterminded a 12-3 victory for the Gwent team, their 15th in 18 games – but that was to be the last home defeat for Spurrell's men that season.

The momentum was hardly checked by a 21-9 reverse at Leicester on New Year's Day or a 7-7 draw at Gloucester in the second week of February or even a 6-6 draw against Exeter University. The records show that, following the defeat at Welford Road, Bath went 26 games unbeaten to finish their 50-match programme with 38 wins, nine defeats and three draws. It was breathtaking stuff, and the points total was a staggering 1,278, with just 555 conceded.

Admittedly, the tally was bolstered by a successful Somerset Cup campaign – Old Redcliffians were beaten in the final at Weston-super-mare on 28 April – but John Player Cup qualification had already been secured when Bristol were beaten 21-16 at the Rec earlier that month. The derby victory, in which Spurrell was a makeshift but highly combative scrum-half, also brought up 1,000 points for the season.

After two years absence from the England team, Horton was recalled to face Scotland and then Ireland, a game which also marked the international debut of Trick, inexplicably selected on the left wing rather than the right. England finished bottom of the Five Nations Championship having added three defeats to a draw in Cardiff. On the way home from Dublin a gaggle of England supporters formed the Wooden Spoon Society, which continues to do so much good work for needy children – so it was not altogether a wasted effort!

Back at Bath, as a memorable season drew to a close, the performances just got better and better with seasoned commentators queuing up to offer their tributes. As always, the benchmarks were set by matches against Welsh opposition and Newport's 10-match winning run was ended 13-7 at the Rec before Halliday's searing pace laid on tries for Trick (2) and Trevaskis in a 31-28 home victory over Llanelli the following weekend. The stage was set for a memorable contest a week later when Cardiff were visitors to a sunny Recreation Ground.

With Spurrell urging on his pack until they gained mastery, Horton was able to conduct affairs with his customary precision. Trick glided in after a Palmer break and Trevaskis chalked up a club record 32 tries for the season before the capacity crowd savoured a characteristic Horton chip ahead which he re-gathered to send in Halliday. The best was saved to last as full-back Martin, impressive all afternoon, ran 70 yards to score. Palmer converted three and added two penalties.

Spurrell believes that Bath's remarkable form in the spring of '83 represented a watershed in the development of the team: "We just took everybody apart. I think that was the turning point. Once you start getting to that standard and above, the physical abilities go up too but really it's all to do with mental ability. All the little bits that come into people's heads that help them improve, a lot came from the last month of that season. It was a phenomenal run.

> **"You went on the field, all fifteen of you, believing there was no way you were going to lose. Once you build that mental strength, that incredible self-belief, it's a hugely imposing position to be in.'"**

Bath's scrum-half position was by this time occupied by Richard Hill, the Exeter University student who had so impressed in the 6-6 draw before Easter. Approached after that game, he had no hesitation in agreeing to join the club he had supported since at school although he was only midway through his degree course. "When I was at Bishop Wordsworth School in Salisbury where we lived, my father used to take me to Bath to watch the rugby," he recalls. "So when Roger Spurrell spoke to me it wasn't a difficult decision." He was to be unchallenged as the wearer of the Bath No 9 jersey until his retirement in 1994.

Back in April 1983, many of the building blocks for enduring success were already in place – a battle-hardened, ball-winning pack, a potent three-quarter line and now a fresh-faced but intensely ambitious scrum-half to ensure a ready supply of ammunition. There might be changes in personnel but the formula was to be astonishingly effective when fuelled by an insatiable desire for excellence and success.

But Spurrell believes a lot of it all started with a huge dose of good fortune. "Jack turning up, for instance," he says. "It was a huge amount of luck that a group of people were in the same place at the same time. People came for very different reasons, sometimes not for the rugby but because it was good craic. It was incredible. That year we weren't in the cup and had a brilliant run from January was a major, major part of what happened.

"We used to go out on the piss on a Friday night. And then it got to the point where we wouldn't go out on the Friday, just on the Thursday night after training. By the time I had finished, if someone had been seen out on a Wednesday night, it was: 'What were you doing out?' It was peer group pressure right through."

As head coach, Rowell determined tactics, assisted by Dave Robson overseeing the scrummaging and Hudson on the fitness and conditioning side. "Each of us was a forceful and dynamic individual," recalls Rowell. "The head coach's job is a lot about management so it was a matter of establishing the goals and how we were going to get there. Dave was very good on the recruitment side too. It wasn't until we started winning that people wanted to come to Bath but he did a great deal helping people find jobs."

"Bath wasn't really big enough as a pool of talent so we had this clear focus – that we were a South West club. We needed to get quality players to play it properly and to have the proper tactical and mental approach. And while at the beginning other clubs might have had better squads than us, we were winning. We evolved in terms of the quality of people and the way they played the game.

"Guys got caught up in it. It wasn't top-down management. It was the sheer collectivity of it. If you wanted to play for Bath, training was challenging and high-intensity. That was the preparation for the way you needed to play on the Saturday."

The commitment was undeniably top-to-bottom though, as Robson remembered shortly before his untimely death: "Jack was marvellous. In later years, he was working much of the time at Golden Wonder up in Market Harborough, yet he would invariably be there at training – sometimes taking a session in his suit!"

The man himself characteristically defers to Mrs Rowell for a perspective on his own approach: "As my wife points out, you get committed – you don't back off. On a training night, it was just expected that you were there. I coached Bath for 17 years and I would miss literally less than a handful of games. And Mrs Rowell will tell you that even if I was abroad on business I would always try to be back for training nights, certainly for games. And you expected players to buy into it.

"To start with, as with running a business, you get a grip, get everyone involved doing their bit. And they would do extra training of their own volition … people like Richard Hill, who would spend their lunch break on the training field, people like Nigel Gaymond and Richard Lee, who were outstanding too … unsung heroes.

"Guys like this became part of the success. They were big people," adds Rowell. "Then you get an environment that aims high all the time – that challenges everyone to the point where they want to be involved. That's basically what we started off with.

"The word on the street soon became 'Join Bath and become a better player'. It is a team game but individuals can make a great contribution. I ran it – but it was all about us as a group, not whoever the coach might be."

Behind the scenes, the machinery of the club began to pick up the pace too. Jack Simpkins, already installed as club president, handed over the responsibilities of Honorary Secretary to Clive Howard, a local building society manager. This brought to a close the remarkable Simpkins 'dynasty' which had held sway in this post since 1911 when his father, Eddie, had been appointed Joint Honorary Secretary alongside one J T Piper, whose own tenure extended from 1890 to 1940. The Simpkins family were a living link to the very early years of the club.

Jack, who succeeded Eddie as Honorary Secretary from 1957, worked for Burningham & Brown Solicitors, their offices at 20 Queen Square being the de facto administrative hub of Bath Football Club (RFU) since they accommodated such luminaries as Brendan Perry (fly-half and later Club President), David Gay (England and Bath), Mike Curling (Referees Assessor), Mick Watts (Old Sulians), Duncan McDaniel (Old Edwardians and Referees' Society), and stalwart Peter Brown. The firm also acted for the Club.

Peter Hall has vivid memories of Jack as the "quintessence of conviviality." He recalls: "On Saturdays during the season Jack would be at the Rec or travelling to a match; on Sundays, after a 'cheerio' to his dear wife, Florence, it was but a short walk from Bow Cottage to the George Inn at Norton St Philip. Otherwise, he could be found at the 'time warp' that was the Tucker's Grave Inn, Faulkland, where pipe-smoking Jack and his farmer mates would sit around in a smoky huddle. With broad Somerset accents, they all seemed to talk at once, with Butcombe, Bass and scrumpy cider quaffed in goodly measure.

"Jack often extolled the virtues of gardening and loved his cricket too, but his forte was anything related to rugby. Anybody stumped for an answer, would simply say: 'Ask Jack.' If one could attempt to sum him up – he was a man with his feet on the ground, authoritative, always ready to dispense common sense, totally dedicated to the Bath Club."

In the summer of '83 there were two Jacks, the traditionalist as custodian of the history and lore of the club, the other a modernist ushering in the future, creating the stuff of legend, 'professional' before the concept could ever be contemplated. Naturally, that was anathema to Jack Simpkins but he enjoyed the success as much as anyone.

Ambition came at a price so for the 1983-84 season entry to the ground was raised to £1.20 for adults with concessions for Senior Citizens and Students set at 60p. Transfer to the stand was raised from 30p to 50p. To accommodate the burgeoning interest, half a dozen six-tier stands were purchased for the 'Flower Pots' terrace at a cost of £6,916. At a Management Committee meeting on 6 September 1983, Jack Simpkins reported that he and Duncan McDaniel, of Burningham and Brown, had met with the Council, as the Club's landlords, to discuss a new lease.

A problem had arisen in that the North Stand belonged to the City Council, the Club owned the clubhouse, and as a result of the extension work, the two buildings were now communicating. It had been suggested that the North Stand be conveyed to the Club. It was resolved that the Club seek to purchase the North Stand, subject to the price being acceptable. The Secretary advised that the Council wished to maintain sole responsibility for the pitch and that a new draft lease was awaited.

On the field, after opening with a 41-3 win over Plymouth Albion, Bath's winning run of 24 matches was ended by Leicester at Welford Road. Although leading 15-3 at half-time with three Palmer penalties and two Horton drop goals, they conceded too many penalties to Les Cusworth and lost 18-15.

Welsh fly-half Gary Pearce was just as unforgiving as Llanelli withstood a second-half comeback at Stradey Park to win 19-13 and Bath also lost 25-16 at Aberavon the following weekend, 1 October. More significant perhaps was the debut of England Colts second row Nigel Redman just six weeks after his 19th birthday; but the youngster from Weston-super-Mare and his fellow forwards were treated to a masterclass in line-out play from Allan Martin, veteran of 34 internationals from 1973-81.

Honours were now coming Bath's way though. Halliday was called up for an England XV fixture against Canada, with Hall on the bench. Unfortunately, the Twickenham fixture clashed with the local derby against John Player Cup holders Bristol at the Rec on 15 October so the club asked for the match not to count towards the South West Merit Table. Perversely they won, Ralston kicking three penalties and Horton dropping a goal in a 12-10 victory in muddy conditions.

When the full side did come together – against Welsh Merit Table leaders Neath at the Rec on 29 October 1983 – it provided an unforgettable spectacle. Horton orchestrated affairs as Bath racked up 67 points without reply, the backs profiting from excellent work by the forwards to carve their opponents into tiny little pieces. John Palmer converted ten of the 11 tries and Spurrell marked the occasion by paying for drinks all round.

A first win at Newbridge in 30 years (22-12) featured an outstanding line-out display by Ronnie Hakin but a week later Bath lost their unbeaten record against English clubs stretching back to February 1982. The honour fell to Wakefield who won 19-16 at the Rec on a day when both sides were ravaged by county calls. Coventry repeated the dose of humble pie at Coundon Road six days later on the eve of England's clash with New Zealand.

Halliday should have won his first England cap in that game but had suffered a badly broken ankle playing for Somerset against Middlesex at Bridgwater while his clubmates were losing to Wakefield. The author was in the press box that day and can testify that it was the kind of injury – a dislocation and compound fracture - that rips the competitive guts out of a game. To a man, the players looked as if they wanted to be somewhere else and the match drifted to some sort of conclusion.

In the dressing room at Bridgwater & Albion's old Broadway ground, facilities were inadequate to provide the stricken Halliday with the immediate care he needed before transfer by ambulance to hospital. For several days afterwards, there were doubts whether he would play again – even whether his leg might be saved.

At Twickenham, however, England found a new hero in Halliday's teammate, Simpson, who rampaged through the All Black ranks, taking the game to the tourists with a perpetual and vaguely menacing grin on his face. England won 15-6 with a try by Maurice Colclough, converted by Dusty Hare, who added three penalties.

Four days earlier, the South & South West had taken on the All Blacks at Bristol, losing 18-6 in front of a crowd estimated at 17,000. With Simpson kept back for Twickenham, the South West selectors picked seven Gloucester forwards, adding Bath's Hall as the sole 'outsider'. Behind the scrum, the only Bristol representative was Stuart Barnes, included at centre rather than fly-half. Bath supplied Horton, Palmer, Trick and Martin. It was 21-year-old Hall who caught the eye, however, clearly relishing the physical and mental challenge posed by Murray Mexted and Co.

Halliday's pace at outside centre and his ability to off-load in the tackle had provided so much of the attacking thrust that it seemed to take some time for Bath to refocus, both tactically and mentally. Following wins over Camborne and London Scottish, December 1983 brought defeat at Gloucester and at home to both Harlequins and Pontypool.

The tide turned with wins over Clifton and Northampton over the holiday before Leicester were beaten 14-nil at the Rec on 7 January 1984, although 18 players on both sides were absent on international trial duty. A first win at London Welsh in 24 years (40-9) and a further 40-pointer at home to the Royal Navy built momentum nicely for the opening round of the John Player Cup against Headingley at the Rec.

England and Lions flanker Peter Winterbottom was at the height of his powers in the Yorkshire club's pack and such was the intensity of the contest that there was no score until after half-time. With England chairman of selectors Derek Morgan watching approvingly, Hill combined with Hakin and centre Rees to set up a try for Trevaskis. Martin added another from full-back and then Hill broke clear again to feed Horton who dummied, shimmied and sidestepped three defenders to score.

Rowell declared himself satisfied with the club's "best-ever cup performance" and waited for Monday's draw for the fourth round, which handed Bath a trip to Blackheath. There was further reward for Simpson who kept his place in the England team to play Scotland at Murrayfield a week later while the form of Hill and Hall earned them places on the replacements' bench. An injury to Winterbottom then allowed Hall to join Simpson for his first cap, to the delight of his parents, Peter and Mollie, in the stands but the elation was tempered by the Scots' 18-6 victory.

The Simpson-Hall combination was short-lived, England's selectors deciding that only one of them could wear the No 6 shirt. While Hall kept his place for the visit of Ireland to Twickenham, his clubmate was discarded and had to wait another three years for his third and final cap.

With John Scott a fixture at No 8, the man chosen to replace Winterbottom on the open side was Harlequins' Cooke although Spurrell continued to impress. Just a week after the Calcutta Cup match Bath hosted Gloucester in a South West Merit Table match which gave Mike Teague and John Gadd the opportunity to prove a

Spurrell ticked off as Bath beat Headingley 17-nil in the John Player Cup (28 January 1984).

point against Simpson and Hall. But it was Spurrell who emerged as the elemental force, both ball-winner and destroyer in Bath's 13-6 victory.

The following week Hall made his first start for England and was able to celebrate a 12-9 win over the Irish. On the eve of the international, Bath recorded their tenth straight win, overcoming a lively Bridgend side 25-19 in a second half fightback which featured tries by Martin and Trick. Palmer's goalkicking – four penalties and a conversion – was decisive.

It was an effective dress rehearsal for the cup date with Blackheath who were swept aside 41-12 in a relentless display of forward power coupled with speed of thought and execution behind the scrum. A young Mickey Skinner was in the home pack but there was no way past the Bath back row "of whom Hall, in particular, could deter most men with a sideways glance." The tries went to Trick (2), Hill, Cunningham, Gaymond and Simpson, with Palmer converting four and adding three penalties.

No sooner had Bath learned that their prize was a home quarter-final against Wasps than Chilcott was sent off again in a Tuesday night game at Exeter. Bath won 27-3 but there was an anxious wait to discover the length of the prop's inevitable ban for butting an opponent. At the very least he was going to miss the quarter-final and any semi-final date.

His absence did provide opportunities for others, however. Exeter University student David Sole, who had made his debut against the Royal Navy in January, packed down again with hooker Greg Bess and Richard Lee in a 50-24 home win over Launceston, a result which consolidated Bath's leadership of the South West Merit Table.

For the visit of cup opponents Wasps a week later, Bath selected Chris Lilley at loosehead, partnering Cunningham and Lee, with Gaymond packing down alongside Hakin and a back row of Spurrell, Simpson and Hall, who had won his third cap in Paris seven days earlier. Despite having to replace Hill with Chris Stanley at scrum-half and Cunningham with Bess, Bath maintained their poise to win 26-12. Although the Londoners dominated the set piece, the home back row took control of the loose, allowing Horton to dictate the tempo. Trick crossed twice and Gaymond scored the third try, with Palmer adding a conversion and four penalties.

> **"Bath's defence was equal to any challenge and for all the tidying up and covering of Dun on behalf of Wasps later on, the Bath back row was never far from the ball in one capacity or another – and the ruck, not the maul, was king." (John Mason – The Daily Telegraph)**

Having so often fallen short in the national cup competition, Bath appeared at last to be getting the hang of it. The semi-final draw was a tough one, Nottingham away, but at least they had avoided the holders, Bristol. While Bristol confirmed their place at Twickenham with an 18-15 home defeat of Harlequins, relying heavily on the goal-kicking of fly-half Barnes, there was a sense of anti-climax when Bath's tie was postponed, owing to the state of the Beeston pitch.

But Bath's powerful squad had also lifted Somerset's fortunes and on 31 March 1984 they filled all but one position – Bristol lock Peter Stiff being the odd man out – when they confronted Gloucestershire at Twickenham in the County Championship final. Yet it was a chastening experience as Gloucestershire, inspired by Barnes, won 36-18 although a third of the Bath cup team was not available to Somerset, either because they were injured (Hill, Cunningham), suspended (Chilcott) or were qualified for other counties (Trevaskis, Martin).

Trick and Spurrell did not finish the game but were fit to make the trip to Nottingham a week later when the John Player Cup semi-final eventually took place. Not so Hill, Cunningham or Hakin whose positions were filled by Stanley, Bess and Redman, but it was another stand-in who proved the un-likely hero.

With Bath leading 6-3 in injury time but the tie still very much in the balance, Chris Lilley, captain of the United, found himself in possession in the Nottingham half, confronted by three opponents. Showing commendable nerve and no little skill for a loosehead prop, he steered a delicate chip into the right hand corner and Trick swooped on the bouncing ball to score the game's only try. Ralston, who had kicked two penalties after replacing the injured Palmer, converted the try to complete a 12-3 victory that exacted a degree of retribution for the fourth round exit three years earlier.

'This Club Used To Be Captained By Gentlemen!'

The build-up was going to be unlike any previous Twickenham final, although there was an assumption in some quarters that the cup-holders would dispatch the challengers in much the same way that Gloucestershire had dealt with Somerset.

> When Bath's management committee met on the Monday night to plan for the club's first visit to Twickenham, they voted to hire a train, at £6 per head. They also learned that there was to be no post-match dinner. Instead, they accepted an offer from The Bath Chronicle to sponsor a buffet and drinks for squad players, wives and committee back at the Rec, with a disco to follow from 10.30pm. Bizarrely, the committee's agenda also asked them to consider the grazing of sheep on the Lambridge training ground – and that was also nodded through in the general air of bonhomie.

With the John Player Cup final still nearly three weeks away, attention then turned to the home game with Llanelli on 14 April – the last run-out for the majority of the first team. Palmer, Hill, Cunningham and Lee were absentees but the winning run extended to a 17th game as Spurrell focused his teammates' minds on the task in hand rather than a cup final two weeks away

Five days before the final, an evening match at home to Glamorgan Wanderers provided a final opportunity to give game time to Hill and Cunningham, returning from injury, plus Chilcott who had now completed his suspension. Hill laid on the only try for wing Peter Drewett but a team composed largely of second and third string players lost 6-9.

The inclusion of Redman at lock for this inconsequential fixture had suggested that he was merely keeping the No 5 shirt warm for the popular Irish international, Hakin, who had originally been selected to face Nottingham but was unfit for the rearranged tie. So when the team was announced for the final, there was a good deal of sympathy for Hakin and a degree of surprise when the 19-year-old was preferred. "An awful decision to have to leave him out," said Rowell later.

> Spurrell also has sympathy for Hakin – but no regrets: "Ronnie was a lovely, lovely footballer. We had been the greatest of friends before I dropped him for the Twickenham final, which was the greatest shame, and he wouldn't talk to us after. I had no regrets because I picked the right man in Nigel Redman, a stunning young player who might have lacked a bit of height but made up for it with everything else."

On the big day, 28 April 1984, they travelled in their thousands from the West Country, although the recorded attendance of 21,000 fell a long way short of the record 34,000 achieved when Bristol beat Leicester the previous year. Bristol's preparations were disrupted by the late withdrawal of England No 8 Hesford, who was replaced by the little known Dave Chidgey, and concerns over the match fitness of other players.

BATH: *C Martin; D Trick, J Palmer, A Rees, B Trevaskis; J Horton, R Hill; G Chilcott, R Cunningham, R Lee, N Gaymond, N Redman, R Spurrell, J Hall, P Simpson.*

BRISTOL: *P Cue; A Morley, R Knibbs, S Hogg, J Carr; S Barnes, R Harding; J Doubleday, D Palmer, A Sheppard, N Pomphrey, P Stiff, P Polledri, M Rafter, D Chidgey.*

REFEREE: *R C Quittenton* (London).

Bath were quickest out of the blocks, the back row of Spurrell, Hall and Simpson wasting no time in imposing themselves on the opposition and Horton opening the scoring with a dropped goal after five minutes. Simpson drove off the back of a scrum to touch down in the 18th minute but Palmer missed the conversion – and four first-half penalty chances.

Barnes put Bristol on the scoreboard with a penalty but Palmer found the target to give Bath a 10-3 interval lead. After Harding nipped over from a tapped penalty, with Barnes converting to bring the holders within one point, it could not have been more tense. Horton was narrowly off-target with another dropped goal attempt and a double tackle by Barnes and Polledri prevented Simpson scoring a second try.

Then in the third minute of injury time came the moment that decided the 1984 John Player Cup final. As right wing and world record try scorer Alan Morley

Nigel Gaymond ties in a Bristol forward as John Hall, Roger Spurrell and Paul Simpson ensure that Richard Hill gets tidy ball.

prepared to take a pass in space – and Bristol supporters held their breaths for the trademark sidestep and inevitable burst to the line – Trevaskis made the tackle a fraction early, taking man without the ball. Roger Quittenton considered awarding a penalty try ("five metres closer and I would have done," he said afterwards) but Barnes was left with a 30-metre kick that seemed straightforward enough except for the stiffening breeze and the nerve-shredding circumstances. As Spurrell turned his back, the ball drifted wide, Quittenton blew for no-side and the celebrations began – among one set of supporters at least.

Famously, Rowell was absent for the denouement. The tension of the closing minutes had proved too much for him and he was pacing the West Car Park as Barnes missed the kick. Who should Rowell bump into? Only his Bristol counterpart, the late David Tyler, who could not bear the tension either.

It couldn't have been closer. Had Bristol been caught on an off-day? Or was there a peculiar hunger and ambition in this Bath side?

The squad came home the toast of the city. After a memorable night at the club the players were guests of honour on the Sunday at a civic reception hosted by the Mayor of Bath, Elgar Jenkins, who declared: "Saturday's match was the greatest moment in our sporting history." He also admitted to winning a £5 bet with the Lord Mayor of Bristol and another side bet with the wife of an Avon county councillor for a pound of cheese. Meanwhile Spurrell sat himself down opposite the Cup – and stared at it for hours!

Not surprisingly, none of the cup squad was available for the trip to Newport on the Monday night and the season ended with a 52-7 defeat, one Jon Callard landing three conversions for the Black and Ambers.

> **Bath were still voted Victoria Wine Rugby Team of the Season, earning ten cases of Moet & Chandon champagne and a trophy. The club finished second to Wasps in the English clubs table and fifth in the English-Welsh Sunday Telegraph table, whose readers named them 'Team of the Season'. "As I understand it that's 120 bottles, which must be an excuse for a party," said the club's Honorary Secretary, Clive Howard, with masterful understatement.**

Meanwhile England's selectors were mulling over contenders for the summer tour to South Africa, their first to the Southern Hemisphere for nine years and one that flouted the anti-apartheid sporting boycott adhered to by the majority of nations. When announced, the squad included Trick, the club's top try scorer with 19, along with Palmer, Horton, Hill and Hall. A measure of Bath's sudden emergence as a rugby force was that the club had had no representative on England's previous tours to the Southern Hemisphere.

All five appeared in the first Test in Port Elizabeth on 2 June, Palmer and Hill making their international debuts, but this was a particularly powerful South African side. With Errol Tobias, the first black player to wear the Springbok shirt, pulling the strings at fly-half and Danie Gerber in imperious form in the centre, the home team won 33-15. Horton dropped a goal and Dusty Hare kicked four penalties. For the second Test a week later at Ellis Park, Johannesburg, Trick lost his place to Swansea's Tony Swift and the Gloucester front row of Phil Blakeway, Steve Mills and Malcolm Preedy were demoted en bloc. It made no difference as Gerber ran in a hat-trick of tries in a 35-9 victory, which remained their biggest winning margin over England until the World Cup pool match of 2007.

> Asked if there was any aspect of England's performance that might be regarded as noteworthy, skipper John Scott replied deadpan: "I thought that we ran out on to the field rather well ..." This was South Africa's last international against a recognised Test nation until normal relations were restored, post-apartheid, in 1992.

All five Bath players – plus Redman who had been with England Under-23 in Spain – were on tour again within a couple of months, later albeit on a much less demanding pre-season jaunt to Canada, starting in Calgary and finishing in Vancouver. Having won four and lost one, with hooker Kevin Adams suffering a dislocated shoulder, they arrived back just two days before the 1984-85 season's opener at Plymouth Albion. There were some signs of jet-lag but, with seven internationals in the ranks, Bath eventually found some rhythm to win 26-10.

The cup holders' first appearance at the Rec since their Twickenham triumph was something of an anti-climax as they scraped a 10-10 draw against South Wales Police. But that was followed by wins against Leicester, Moseley and Llanelli. That 27-9 victory, their biggest at Stradey, also brought Bath their first success there since 1959 but a return to West Wales the following weekend saw them beaten 28-13 at Neath, the home side exacting revenge for the 67-nil thrashing at the Rec 11 months earlier.

Meanwhile Halliday was close to match fitness after a remarkable recovery from the dreadful ankle injury suffered in the previous season's County Championship. But blocking his path to the first team was the flame-haired Rees, whose rugged defence and ability to stay on his feet in the tackle earned him selection for the South & South West Division against the touring Australians at Exeter on Saturday, 20 October. More than half the side was drawn from the Bath club – Martin, Trick, Palmer, Chilcott, Redman, Hall and Spurrell being the others – and the line-up also included Barnes and Swift, both destined to join the club at the end of the season. Barnes matched the 19-year-old Michael Lynagh's tally of four penalty goals to earn a 12-12 draw.

Attention quickly turned to the cup final re-run at the Memorial Ground three days later – and no-one was looking forward to it more eagerly than former Bristol man Rees. But the team included only two others from the tour match, Hall and Spurrell, and Bath found themselves 6-16 down going into the final quarter. Horton then delivered a perfect kick to the corner for Trevaskis to score, with Irish B international Roy Palmer adding the conversion. Palmer followed up with a penalty and the forwards then set Horton up for a drop goal to steal a two point lead. When Barnes was given an opportunity to win the match with a penalty, Bristol supporters prayed that history would not repeat itself. It did though, and Bath embarked on an astonishing winning sequence against their neighbours that would last nearly two decades.

Meanwhile Halliday had marked his return to first team action at Liverpool on 13 October in a largely reserve selection which lost 22-16. The England selectors made no secret of their desire to see him back at a higher level. For the time being however, they had to pick a side to face Andrew Slack's Wallabies at Twickenham. Hall was again in the starting line-up and among the new caps were Redman, just 20, and Chilcott, whose occupation was revealed in the match programme as 'tree feller', plus Barnes of Bristol. Hill and Simpson were on the bench.

England never really posed much of a challenge to the tourists who scored three tries to win 19-3, with Lynagh contributing 11 points on his debut, the first leg of an historic Grand Slam. The main talking point was Chilcott's flooring of Wallabies scrum-half Nick Farr-Jones, the punch a sign of his frustration at his own team's lack of guts. The fall-out came immediately, but from an unexpected quarter, as Chilcott recalls: "Mickey Steele-Bodger, of the Barbarian club, came up to me at the Hilton Hotel and said: 'Chilcott, I have to tell you that you're not the sort of player we could ever consider playing for the Barbarians.' Of course, virtually all the lads at Bath became Barbarians and sometimes they'd all turn up at the club wearing their ties, just to wind me up.

> **"Quite a few years later, I got a phone call from Steele-Bodger asking if I was available to tour Russia with them. I told him I'd have to check on my other commitments and would ring him back. I left him stewing for an hour or two and then called to say: 'Sorry Mickey, I'm afraid your tour clashes with a skittles match down the Bristol Dockers Club'!"**

After tripping up at Maesteg, Bath recovered their poise with Merit Table wins over Exeter (64-3) and Gloucester (19-9) before defeating Harlequins 21-12 at Twickenham, where they experimented with John Palmer at fly-half to accommodate a centre pairing of both Rees and Halliday. Horton, who had announced his decision to retire at the end of the season, was not at all amused, as Brian Jones related in his book, *Bath, Ace of Clubs*:

> **"If I had been playing badly, I would expect to be dropped. At present, Bath are saying I am rested and will be back in the side next week. But that only means that one of the other players will be left out. That's no way to establish team spirit. I believe the club have to make a firm decision and pick what**

is considered the best side. If the team tomorrow is considered the best, I would rather the selectors say that. In discussion at training last night, the club seemed to think I wouldn't mind standing down for a week, but they were wrong."

A rota system was nevertheless introduced and Horton was recalled at Rees's expense for the trip to Pontypool on 22 December, a day when Bath fulfilled two first team fixtures, losing both. The other match, at home to Sale, featured a debut at centre for a 19-year-old product of Bath's mini-rugby section, Jeremy Guscott. An injury to Rees gave Guscott a chance to partner Halliday at Waterloo on 5 January 1985 and the youngster showed obvious promise. He should have scored a try but dropped the ball over the line and had to be content with four penalties in a 23-13 win.

Suddenly, Bath were into their defence of the John Player Cup, first clearing a potentially tricky hurdle by beating Berry Hill 24-3 to earn a fourth round tie at Blackheath although hooker Rob Cunningham broke his arm. Then, after defeating Rosslyn Park on 1 February, a prolonged freeze threatened to leave the defending champions without any meaningful preparation until the cup-tie on 23 February.

In stepped Brixham with an offer of a fixture at their Astley Park ground, which was one of the very few playable pitches in the country. Although the visitors fielded a Bath XV it was virtually full strength, lacking only Cunningham, Simpson and Hall. The result was surely a foregone conclusion ... except that no-one told the home team, who got stuck in from the first whistle and won 9-6 to end Bath's unbeaten record against English opposition. Even Palmer's try and conversion came too late to influence matters against the raw-boned 'Fishermen' from the South West Leagues.

David Green, of The Daily Telegraph, described it thus: "One of the most extraordinary results of this or any other season occurred at Brixham yesterday where Bath, arguably the best team in England, lost by a dropped goal and two penalty goals to a goal."

The visitors' dressing room door was kept firmly shut for the best part of 45 minutes afterwards as a few home truths were shared. Typically, first out was Chilcott to buy drinks for the home side. For some years afterwards, he was accustomed to growl, "Just remember Brixham," if he thought anyone was not taking the opposition seriously enough.

Blackheath did not stand a chance the following week as Trevaskis ran in a hat-trick of tries in a 37-3 win. Perhaps the lesson was applied rather too ruthlessly though. Hooker Bobby Howe, who needed four stitches in his head, was found to be suffering from delayed concussion and Blackheath's captain, Rick Bodenham, did not mince his words: "Someone tried to rip my lip off while I was lying at the bottom of a ruck. It was probably the worst game I've ever played in for the frequency of violence. The violence went on through 80 minutes. Some of our players had their eyes gouged, and others were stamped on. I'm annoyed my players were hurt like this. It makes me wonder whether it is worth playing the game if we have to go home looking like we've been in a war."

Whether justified or not, comments like these began to create an image of Bath that gained currency ... of an uncompromising, unsmiling team intent on forward domination and prepared to take few prisoners in their quest for success, particularly in the John Player Cup. It was five years or so before they really cut loose.

Meanwhile, the South West Merit Table was no longer a challenge – Redruth were thrashed 67-nil on their own ground – and in any case the new National Merit Table was under way. At the same time, Horton announced that he was "not altogether ruling out the possibility of carrying on" instead of retiring at the end of the season.

The following Saturday, 9 March 1985, Horton returned to his former club, Sale, for the quarter-finals of the John Player Cup. With the back row of Spurrell, Hall and Simpson controlling possession and the Hill-Horton axis directing operations, Simpson battered his way over for the opening try on 26 minutes before Hill ran wide to lay on a try for Trick, cutting back through the spreadeagled defence. After Palmer landed a conversion and penalty, Trick took over the kicking, succeeding with three penalties before Horton landed a drop goal.

Guscott gave further signs of his raw talent at Ebbw Vale the following midweek, carving through for a spectacular try in a 15-10 win. That completed a sequence of 11 straight wins leading up to a semi-final at Kingsholm and while most opponents might be intimidated by Bath's forward power, Gloucester certainly did not fall into that category.

Chris Martin, who had won his first cap in the 9-9 draw against France on 2 February – memorable for Richard Harding's in-goal try-saving tackle against Patrick Esteve – was retained along with flanker Hall for the Calcutta Cup match on 16 March, Scotland being beaten 10-7.

Martin, an immensely powerful figure at full-back for Bath, played a full championship season for England but it was memorable for the wrong reasons. Ireland celebrated the Triple Crown after Martin's charged down clearance kick presented Brendan Mullin with a try and an uncharacteristic fumble under the high ball gifted Jonathan Davies a try in Cardiff. The only other Bath player to feature in the Five Nations was Hill, replacement for Nigel Melville after 20 minutes in Dublin.

Club rugby in England was now reaching an intensity not far removed from internationals and the semi-final at Gloucester the following weekend was no less gripping. Bath had not won there for 17 years and their preparation was far from ideal, Halliday being ruled out by injury and 34-year-old second row Hakin refusing to be content with a place on the bench. Even with a strapped up thumb, the younger and more athletic Redman was regarded by Rowell and the selectors as the indispensable partner for Gaymond.

Give us a hug! Roger Spurrell and John Hall celebrate the 12-11 John Player Cup semi-final victory over Gloucester at Kingsholm (23 March 1985), flanked by hooker Greg Bess (left).

It was the wettest of West Country afternoons and Bath took their chances to lead 9-nil after half an hour, Horton dropping a goal and Palmer converting a Hill try. Gloucester edged back into the game but Palmer added another penalty to make it 12-11 and it was then left to unyielding defence and the odd slice of luck.

'Match-winner' was not normally a description applied to Richard Lee, Bath's utterly dependable tighthead prop, but his tackle on John Gadd late in the game as the Gloucester flanker plunged for the line exemplified the total commitment.

Moments later Lee looked disbelievingly as referee Laurie Prideaux penalised him for going over the top at a ruck, presenting full-back Tim Smith with a very kickable penalty. He failed – and Bath were looking forward to another trip to Twickenham five weeks hence, pitted against London Welsh.

With their sights fixed firmly on that final, Bath did not lose too much sleep when an under-strength side lost at Cheltenham and, after winning 35-3 at London Irish, they accounted for Bristol in a conclusive 25-3 victory at the Memorial Ground.

Although Trick scored 17 points, the outstanding figure was Hill who scored the first try and laid on others for Gaymond and Trick.

An 11-nil defeat at Newport eradicated any complacency before a cup final dress rehearsal against Llanelli which Bath won 21-10 to complete their first 'double' over the Scarlets.

BATH: *C Martin; D Trick, J Palmer, S Halliday, B Trevaskis; J Horton, R Hill; G Chilcott, G Bess, R Lee, N Redman, N Gaymond, R Spurrell* (capt), *J Hall, P Simpson.*

LONDON WELSH: *M Ebsworth; J Hughes, R Ackerman, D Fouhy, C Rees; C Price, M Douglas; T Jones, B Light, B Bradley, E Lewis, J Collins, S Russell, K Bowring, M Watkins.*

REFEREE: *R C Quittenton* (London).

From breakfast time on Saturday, 27 April, there was an exodus by car, coach and train from Bath of expectant supporters in blue, white and black. This time, Bath were overwhelming favourites against a famous club already struggling in the new competitive club environment and conscious that this might be their last hurrah. Skipper Clive Rees, a speedy and resourceful wing, had support from fellow internationals Mark Douglas at scrum-half and Rob Ackerman in the centre but opted to play against the wind, hoping that his forwards would remain in the game long enough for the backs to take advantage in the second half.

Express delivery ... Richard Hill receives quality ball from Paul Simpson, Nigel Redman, Roger Spurrell and Gareth Chilcott.

*John Hall, John Palmer, Nigel Redman, Richard Hill, Roger Spurrell and Chris Martin
with 'the family silver'.*

It made no difference. Bath's back row simply snuffed out Douglas and once Halliday's trademark 'round the corner pass' had allowed Trick to outpace the remaining defender with ridiculous ease for the first try, there was little doubt over the outcome. Chilcott then added a try to enhance his growing folk hero status among the 34,000 spectators and Palmer converted both tries as well as kicking two penalties. After leading 18-nil at the break there was even a sense of anti-climax as Bath contented themselves with two more penalties from Palmer against five successful kicks from Exiles fly-half Colin Price. Hall, who had been ever-present in the England side all season, summed it up at the time:

> **"Whatever the Welsh tried, we knocked them back. It was all down to careful preparation and the build-up from Friday night. Coach Jack Rowell stressed that we were like one big family who could pull together when it really mattered – and that's what happened."**

Hall was a shoo-in for England's squad to tour New Zealand a month later and he was to be joined by Martin and Hill. But it was another member of that tour party who really stirred things up, not for the first time – and not for the last.

Chapter 6

IN AND OUT, A TALE OF TWO TENS

At 22 years of age, Stuart Barnes did not lack confidence in his ability, nor was he slow to air his opinions on rugby … or anything else for that matter.

But as the 1984-85 season drifted to a close at Bristol even he did not know quite how to tell his club captain, flanker Peter Polledri, that he was quitting to join Bath. There was plenty of opportunity – they shared a house after all. And if he really wanted to drop this bombshell on Bristol's chairman of selectors, Alan Ramsey, they worked in the same site office at housebuilder Wimpey, where Bristol had found the newly-graduated Barnes a job.

Eventually, it was Polledri who broached the subject, asking the clearly unsettled Barnes what his intentions were. The fly-half had wanted to keep his move under wraps until the summer but if the rumours had started, it was only a matter of time before everyone else knew.

On the Monday after Bath's cup final victory over London Welsh and almost before the hangovers had subsided, the story of Barnes's defection was broken on the back page of the Bristol Evening Post. He told its rugby correspondent, Chris Ducker.

> **"I didn't want this to come out now. I wanted the rugby season to be well and truly over. But rumours were flying around and so I told Peter Polledri of my decision today. The time comes when you have to think about your future. In the end rugby is an amateur game which you play for enjoyment. I am ambitious and I believe that to achieve my goals the only answer is to join the best club in the land."**

He also rated Jack Rowell "the best coach in England." The 25-3 defeat by Bath less than a month earlier had confirmed his view that they represented all that was innovative and progressive in club rugby and he added: "Their speed in producing ruck ball will be vital to me."

And in his autobiography, Smelling of Roses, Barnes pinpointed the essential difference between the clubs at that time:

"Bath was more cosmopolitan, more ambitious... In Bath I believed I would recapture my form and still have my fun. I left Bristol, a club proud of its traditions, for Bath, a club proud of its performance."

The feelings of disappointment, hurt and even betrayal at Bristol were understandable. They still considered themselves the senior club, yet here was their chief playmaker and points scorer rejecting them for the blandishments of the team down the road.

John Hall had initiated contact in 1983 when he and Barnes found themselves on a tour to Kenya with the Penguins. "I said to him: 'You've got to come to Bath. We're building a side and we've got some great players. John Horton's not going to go on forever and you've got to join us.' It was really on that trip that it was settled that he would join at some stage over the next couple of years – largely down to our friendship. Of course, he played against us in the 1984 final and missed the kick – I always tease him, saying he missed it on purpose!"

It has to be said that the reaction of people at Bath was mixed, particularly all those supporters who treasured John Horton's contribution over 12 seasons as a loyal club man and an inspirational No 10. Horton himself learned of Barnes's arrival from the press and, not unnaturally, he was not best pleased. Since his debut against Terenure on 29 September 1973, he had made 380 appearances, scoring 90 tries, 12 conversions, 125 drop goals and eight penalties, with a total points tally of 908. He partnered 15 scrum halves in an illustrious career which brought him 13 England caps, including a Grand Slam in 1980.

Rather than retire, however, the 34-year-old Horton decided he had one last season in him – and joined Bristol. Club captain John Palmer tried to persuade him to stay but Horton's mind was made up as he told John Stevens, of The Bath Chronicle:

"It's going to be a terrible wrench but perhaps it's for the best. I think it would have been impossible having us both vying for the same position on the Rec and could have led to unpleasantness, which I want to avoid. So I feel it would be better to make a clean break ..."

Sadly, a succession of injuries meant that he was never seen at his best in Bristol colours before finally taking up a teaching appointment in Oxfordshire. Despite their distinctly unsentimental approach to recruitment, Bath's playing hierarchy did feel lingering disquiet at the manner of Horton's departure and, happily, he returned to Bath colours for a couple of hugely popular guest appearances in 1988.

In the days after the announcement of Barnes's recruitment, however, emotions were running high – and not just in the vicinity of the Memorial Ground. Tensions within the Bath Football Club surfaced as early as the annual dinner on the following Wednesday evening, 1 May, unfortunately under the noses of Albert Agar and Bob Weighill, respectively president and honorary secretary of the Rugby Football Union.

In And Out, A Tale Of Two Tens

As chronicled by the now retired Derek Wyatt in his column in The Observer (5 May, 1985): "It all went horribly wrong." It kicked off, as they say these days, with some pointed remarks by outgoing club captain Roger Spurrell, directed at the committee. The riposte came from the club's elder statesman, retiring president Jack Simpkins, who questioned the game's state of health when a player could move clubs just to further his career. He did not mention the name Stuart Barnes but the reference was obvious to Wyatt, who continued:

> "This was too much for Jack Rowell, the club coach, who along with Dave Robson and recently Tom Hudson, has been responsible for the upturn in the club's fortunes. Rowell asked permission to respond to Simpkins. Simpkins, rightly, would not give way at the microphone. A brouhaha resulted and when Rowell finally started to speak members of the committee walked out.
>
> "A private argument has now become public. It's an argument about the search for excellence in the amateur game. In Bath's case, the players feel they have attained it but the committee haven't. The players believe they know more about the game and they know the potential that exists for them. England could feel this strain in New Zealand and in the World Cup in 1987. If the differences are recognised, the events in Bath on Wednesday evening might yet be a cause for celebration."

Hall remembers the occasion all too vividly: "It made me cringe because it was supposed to be a celebration. But Jack was right – he wanted something that was much more professional and in the end he had his way. But, being Jack, he would always want to make his point, even in the most inappropriate of circumstances. I think a lot of the committee stuff was exaggerated. We were largely allowed to get on with what we wanted to do."

It was as if the pace of change was too rapid for some. But change was everywhere in 1985: Margaret Thatcher was in her pomp, ripping up age-old conventions; Mikhail Gorbachev had taken over in March as General Secretary of the Soviet Communist Party; and South Africa had ended its ban on inter-racial marriage. Even the red telephone box was being phased out as successful tests were carried out on something called 'cell phone technology'. Why should rugby union remain untouched?

The summer of 1985 also saw the departure from the Rec of two other key players – Nigel Gaymond and Alun Rees. Gaymond, an engaging and extraordinarily hard working second row, opted to start a new life across the Atlantic while Rees, not content to play second fiddle to Halliday, joined Gloucester where he had taken up work. There was no ill feeling over his move: "The club have been very good to me. But once you have tasted first team rugby it's hard to accept anything else for too long."

Meanwhile, after coming off the bench against Romania in January and then being overlooked for the 1985 Five Nations Championship, Barnes won his third and fourth caps against New Zealand on the summer tour, finally getting to partner Richard Hill when the scrum-half came on as replacement during the second Test in Wellington. England had gone close in the first Test in Christchurch (18-13) before being overrun in Wellington (42-15). John Hall, who scored from a line-out in the second Test before the All Blacks took control, was one of the few players to enhance his reputation.

Amid all the comings and goings, Bath were confident that some of the younger players were coming through nicely for the 1985-86 season. Jon Morrison, lately of Bristol, was ready to partner Redman in the second row and Scotland B prop David Sole added mobility and footballing ability to the front row resources while the rangy David Egerton promised to provide an extra dimension at No 8. Prolific Swansea wing Tony Swift had also taken up an accountancy position with the firm of Robson Taylor (senior partner, David Robson, chairman of Bath selectors) but, as the season began, all eyes were on Barnes.

Bath had first encountered Barnes as a young Newport full-back. Born in Essex, he had been educated at Bassaleg School, captaining Welsh Schools at both 15 and 19 Group. He also represented Gwent Schools at cricket and athletics. Such was his precocious talent that as an 18-year-old he was chosen for the Welsh national squad for its centenary against a WRU President's XV in 1981 but he opted instead to join an England Under-23 tour to Italy.

Winning Blues with Oxford in 1981 and 1982, he joined Bristol in his third year at St Edmund Hall and after appearing in a third Varsity match – he was on the losing side on each occasion – he helped his club win the John Player Cup against Leicester in a thrilling final. He provided many of the important points in Bristol's surge to the final in 1984 – and the missed kick in the dramatic finale – but the 1984-85 season had been a disappointment, punctuated by injury and loss of form.

His debut for Bath, against Plymouth Albion at the Recreation Ground on 7 September, was a fairly gentle introduction to the 1985-86 season, yielding a try and six conversions in a 40-nil victory. Apart from scoring two of the seven tries, new skipper Palmer was in inspirational form at centre. The warm-up continued with a midweek match against Canadian tourists Alberta Province who provided rather stiffer opposition than expected, although Swift celebrated his first appearance – and the birth of a son earlier in the day – with a brace of tries.

That slightly distracted display left nobody prepared for the five-star performance which followed at Welford Road three days later. Leicester were determined to give a certain Clive Woodward the appropriate send-off before leaving to join the Manly club in Australia.

But to borrow my own words, writing for the Bristol Evening Post: "ruthless Bath wrecked the party and left Woodward's team-mates wishing they could join him on the plane." The scoreline, 40-15, was due to an immense performance by the pack who ensured that Bath turned round at 9-9 after facing a stiff wind, Redman scoring the only try. The second half was a humbling experience for the Tigers as further

Jon Morrison prepares to contest a line-out throw in the season's opener, a 40-nil win against Plymouth Albion (7 September 1985). Bath players pictured (from left) are: John Hall, Richard Hill, David Egerton, Paul Simpson, Nigel Redman, Gareth Chilcott (rear view!), Morrison, David Sole and Greg Bess.

tries went to Hill, Trevaskis (2), Trick and Martin, who had stood firm in the face of a barrage of high balls early in the game from Les Cusworth and Dusty Hare. Barnes converted five and kicked two penalties.

Noting that Bath's previous best at Leicester had been a 16-3 win back in 1919, fellow journalist John Stevens put the result into perspective when he wrote in The Bath Chronicle:

> **"It was one of the most devastating performances I have ever seen Bath give on a major opponent's ground in 30 years of rugby reporting, even allowing for some of last season's efforts, including the win at Llanelli."**

Leicester captain Les Cusworth described Bath's display as "phenomenal", adding: "It's a very long time since I've seen any senior club performance like that."

The result would have been the story of the day on most weekends but all the headlines were made at the Memorial Ground where referee George Crawford walked off the field in protest at the constant brawling between Bristol and Newport. Virtually unnoticed was the debut at full-back of a 22-year-old medical student – Jonathan Webb.

Bath attracted their own unwelcome publicity when the club had to apologise to the RFU for incidents on the club's North American tour. Club secretary Clive Howard revealed that one or two players had been spoken to and a general tightening up of discipline had been ordered throughout the club.

With Egerton again providing a new dimension to the forward play and Chilcott coming on as reserve hooker – throwing in accurately and even claiming a strike against the head – Bath beat Pontypridd 45-19. But the occasion was marred by a serious head wound to hooker Mark Roberts against his former club. Bath clearly believed that the injury was the result of foul play.

Despite then being without the injured Palmer and Hall for the visit of Moseley, Bath ran in 50 points in front of England's new chairman of selectors Mike Weston. "Our attitude is one of absolute greed," said Halliday afterwards. "We're not satisfied to win by 20 points – we want to win by as many as possible." And Barnes delivered a cautionary note to their rivals by declaring:

> **"We are nowhere near perfection. We don't want to congratulate ourselves for winning, we concentrate on putting right the wrongs. With that kind of professional attitude at the club the sky's the limit... I've never played with or against a better organised club than Bath. That is not being disparaging to Bristol or anybody else, it's simply a fact."**

Barnes returned to his first club, Newport, the following Wednesday evening when Bath were relieved to come away with a 16-16 draw. Halliday was the pick of the backs, scoring the first try and setting up the equalising score for Morrison. Newport could still have snatched victory but full-back Jon Callard missed two angled penalties from the 22. Next up were Llanelli, just three days later, and Halliday was again outstanding in an 18-15 win at Stradey Park, providing the cutting edge for tries by Kevin Withey and Trick.

Eight games in 25 days left the players unbeaten – but physically and mentally drained. With Cardiff and Bristol lying in wait amid the assault course of October fixtures and an England squad session squeezed in for good measure, Rowell was concerned about his squad's ability to last the season and at the time confided to your author: "I honestly don't know how we are going to cope. You can't really do much to alleviate the pressure on players the way rugby is organised at the moment."

One suggestion being floated within the playing hierarchy and "half seriously put forward by chairman of selectors Brian Jenkins" was to send the players abroad for a week in the sun around Christmas. Jenkins explained: "That's what they need at that stage of the season. But I don't know what the treasurer would say about it." It was typical of the forward-thinking, innovative player management that characterised Bath's approach at that time. Ideas that seemed quite 'off the wall' were initially viewed with some scepticism, even distaste, but were eventually seen to be highly effective and adopted by everybody else.

It was too much for some, however, especially when Messrs Rowell, Hudson and Robson announced they were to spend three days in November with Rugby League's leading lights, Hull Kingston Rovers and their coach, Roger Millward, to study training methods, coaching and the build-up to a big game. Hudson, also Bath University's director of physical education, told the Bristol Evening Post he couldn't understand why there should be any fuss about it:

> **"We are looking for knowledge, it's as simple as that. Bath Rugby Club can develop even more over the next decade or so but there are a number of areas where we need to learn from the experience of others. It doesn't matter whether the people concerned are amateurs or professionals.**
>
> **"All this talk about barriers between Rugby Union and Rugby League is too silly for words. The days when Union players warmed up with a few physical jerks have long gone. We need to know about the science of sport – about physiological and mental preparation. The only way is to broaden our horizons and look elsewhere – we are quite serious in suggesting further coaching study trips to France, New Zealand and Australia."**

It all seems so logical these days but alarm bells sounded at Twickenham where the 'blazers' registered their disapproval, making it clear that there were to be no further contacts of this kind. This came at a time when there was still support for a planned Lions tour of South Africa at the end of the 1985-86 season; Barnes quickly declared his unavailability on grounds of personal principle but the tour was eventually called off.

Meanwhile, Bath had lost their unbeaten record at Aberavon (16-15) where injury problems were exacerbated by the loss of Halliday (hamstring) and Chilcott (trapped nerve). More encouragingly, Hall returned after an absence of six matches with knee ligament problems to score the final try in a 26-12 win over Liverpool. Injuries were not the only factor in player availability in the autumn of 1985. An unusually wet summer and consequently a late harvest had also contrived to delay Somerset farmer Lee's return to the rugby field. Sole had grabbed his opportunity, however, and kept Lee out of the side for the match with Bristol on 9 October.

An 8,000 crowd packed the Rec to see man-of-the-match Sole score one of four tries as Bath won 26-7, a sixth successive derby victory which underlined the gulf in execution, experience and organisation. Others went to Redman, Egerton and Trevaskis with a 70-metre interception while Barnes added two conversions, a penalty and a dropped goal. It was no classic however and Roger Spurrell did not hide his dissatisfaction with Roger Quittenton's strict interpretation of the lawmakers' new directive on refereeing of the breakdown. Skipper John Palmer had to act as peacemaker:

> **"The referee corrected Roger on his method of going into the tackle. Roger said he'd been playing that way for 15 years and if he had to stop now, he might as well give up there and then."**

David Trick displays his phenomenal pace against Bristol on 19 October 1985.

It seems extraordinary now that the fixture list should pit Bath against Bristol on the Saturday and then against Cardiff just four days later. The sense of anticipation was immense and for once the occasion lived up to expectations. Estimates of the crowd vary but it was widely acknowledged at the time as the biggest in the history of the Rec – certainly 8,000, possibly 10,000 or more. They were hanging out of the trees, off buildings and any vantage point.

The contest at half-back – Barnes and Hill versus Gareth Davies and Terry Holmes – was mouthwatering enough but Cardiff also fielded Mike Rayer at full-back, Gerald Cordle and Adrian Hadley on the wings, plus forwards of the calibre of Bob Norster, John Scott and Alun Phillips. Ranged against them were 10 full caps and 3 B internationals. The match itself stands comparison with any in living memory on the Recreation Ground – and that includes those many triumphal occasions of succeeding years.

Cardiff took the lead in the second minute as Holmes launched Cordle in an 80-metre move and then powered over from the resulting scrum. From the restart, Barnes hoisted a Garryowen which was palmed down by Halliday to the onrushing Lee and the prop was swept over the line by his fellow forwards. It was a breathtaking opening. Barnes managed the conversion but then missed a couple of penalties while the more accurate Davies put Cardiff 7-6 ahead.

Bath looked around for inspiration and it came on 35 minutes from Halliday who sliced through on the scissors from his own half before finding Hall on his inside as he reached the Cardiff 22. Pace and determination in equal measure saw him make the line. Fellow flanker Spurrell dived among the boots to add another try in the 51st minute and, despite two more penalties from Davies and a heartstopping scrum on their own line in injury time, Bath held out for a memorable 16-13 victory. Man-of-the-match was Egerton who eclipsed recent England skipper Scott.

> "It was the best club game I played in," says Hall. "I have very vivid memories of it. It was a really tough game – a lot of stuff going on. I can recall scoring the try but the biggest thing I remember was the noise of the crowd. I'm sure the crowds are bigger now but there were 9,000-9,500 people there and in the standing areas they were 10-15 deep. It was just an amazing atmosphere."

It lives just as large in Spurrell's memory: "Yeah, that was when dear old Dave Parsons, three-quarters of an hour before kick-off with huge queues outside the ground, said: 'Oh, sod it. Let's just open the gates.' I scored a try and we got a penalty because their big, ugly second row jumped up and down on me. Halliday made a beautiful break and then Hally cut back the other way to score."

The match represented a high point of the 'Welsh strategy'. "The Welsh thing was huge," continues Spurrell. "Those fixtures were big building blocks for Bath and especially for the second team players, going down to those lovely little Valleys sides in the days where the game was dirtier than it is now. One of my first games for Bath was Pontypool away and we got smashed, completely and utterly turned over up front. I remember going back there later and giving them a good kicking – and winning very easily."

Cardiff were no less formidable opponents and went on to win the Schweppes Welsh Cup for the second time in three years.

It was unreasonable to expect Bath to maintain that level of intensity throughout the campaign and Gloucester became the first English side to lower their colours, winning 15-11 at Kingsholm on 9 November. Although Trick scored two tries, Gloucester's pack was dominant and Barnes was out of sorts with his goalkicking.

Three weeks later and without the injured Spurrell and Hall, Bath surrendered their home record, losing 13-7 to a raw-boned Neath side. The game turned on an interception try by Wales wing Elgan Rees but the outstanding player on the field was the openside with the Devil's Island haircut, Lyn Jones, as Spurrell himself acknowledged at the time:

> "That skinhead won the game for them. All the 50-50 ball that was going, he won. Often he didn't care how he got it but he's a hell of a player ... a bit like me five years ago."

For another of rugby's warriors, however, the match marked something of a sea-change. Chilcott was actually seen walking away from an 11th minute bust-up which resulted in David Sole receiving stitches in a gaping wound under his eye. Had Cooch gone soft? "Not so long ago, I'd have been in there as well, sorting them out," he

Gareth Chilcott: welcomed back into the England fold.

acknowledged to your author at the time. "But I can't get involved now. If I step out of line again it's the end for me."

Restored to the England training squad and with the rare ability to play on both sides of the scrum at international level, he was anxious to show that if the Twickenham authorities were prepared to forgive and forget he would reciprocate. "I sometimes wonder if, by holding back from certain situations, it's taking the edge off my game. But there's no going back to the old ways," he said.

No doubt the 'bad guy' reputation had obscured Chilcott's ability as a footballer but by his 29th birthday on 20 November 1985 he was already an immensely strong and accomplished scrummaging technician. It just took some time for the right people to recognise that fact.

Hall recalls an early England training session at Bisham Abbey: "We were doing some scrummaging; Cooch was on the sidelines and we had John Doubleday and Austin Sheppard from Bristol and Phil Blakeway, of Gloucester, and someone else in the prop positions. They were scrummaging against each other and the second team pack, the Possibles, was getting pushed all over the place. Then Cooch stepped in and the Possibles scrum locked out, completely solid. And I thought, 'Hey, that's something major there.' He just inspired confidence in the people around him. I didn't feel at all intimidated when I went on the pitch and Cooch had a lot to do with that. In the early days he did dish it out but he cleaned up his act.

> "While he didn't have a starring role, he had a very profound effect on the team. He galvanised people – he was also funny, a joker and we always had a laugh. He had a very good relationship with Jack (Rowell) too. Cooch was very influential at Bath – although he never captained the side. It's a shame he didn't but he stepped aside and let others do it."

Chilcott actually spent ten years as vice-captain of the club. But he was no ordinary deputy. They referred to Bath as 'The Family' and not for nothing was Chilcott known as 'the Don'. That was the measure of his authority.

Sheepish departure from Orrell

Peter Hall won the Orrell club raffle on a 50p ticket. As he and his wife, Mollie, were about to depart, they were presented with a whole sheep (thankfully cut up) and an assortment of large sacks containing, potatoes, swedes, cabbages, onions etc. But how to get it all home? Thankfully, friends stepped forward and they all trooped off, each with a sack on their backs like the Seven Dwarfs. A helpful Stones Coaches driver stacked it all in the luggage hold and they were away – 'Happy as Larry!' When th e tired but contented travellers arrived back in Bath in the small hours of the morning, there followed a big share-out in the middle of Great Pulteney Street. Oh what days!

Back in December 1985, however, his main concern was to shake off a groin strain that ended his involvement in the South West's divisional championship campaign after just a couple of minutes of the match with London at Harlequins. The cancellation due to frost of the home game with Northampton meant that Chilcott and Hall – recently returned from knee surgery – were not back in a Bath shirt until New Year's Day at Cardiff. The visitors were in contention until the hour mark but eventually lost 30-12.

The England team named to face Wales at Twickenham on 18 January included Hall, but not Chilcott. For Simon Halliday, however, seeing his name in the line-up for the first time was an especially sweet moment. More than three years earlier, after appearing for an England XV against Canada, he had been denied a full cap against New Zealand by an ankle injury so calamitous that there were fears for his leg, let alone his career.

But the articulate, ambitious stockbroker had fought his way back to fitness and the kind of form that had marked him out as an outstanding talent when still at Oxford University. He was rewarded with a winning start for his country, 21-18, although Wales scored the only try through Bleddyn Bowen. Rob Andrew kicked six penalties and a dropped goal.

A week later, the Bath 'family' gathered in Lancashire for a tricky John Player Cup third round tie at Orrell. Those who may be only vaguely aware of Orrell these days as an amateur outfit in South Lancs & Cheshire Division 2 will have no idea of the serious challenge that Orrell posed in the mid-1980s to the established names in English rugby's top flight.

Bath were therefore more than happy to get away with a 16-16 draw at homely Edge Hall Road. The second row pairing of Morrison and Redman, rubbing out the twin threat posed by the gigantic Bob Kimmins and beanpole Charles Cusani, were at the heart of a prodigious forward effort which negated Orrell's main strength.

"Bath's scrummaging made the difference," said the home coach, Des Seabrook. "Disappointed isn't the word."

The reward for the players was a trip to Moseley, captained by former Gloucester and England second row Steve Boyle. He wasn't exactly overjoyed with the draw, musing: "I would have settled for anyone else. With most teams you can go through the side and pick out the weaknesses – but not with Bath." The 21-year-old Redman duly turned in another outstanding performance on a bitterly cold February afternoon at The Reddings – "sensational" according to Rowell who added: "I have never known a second row forward have such an influence on a game."

Bath reacted to a fourth-minute try by wing John Goodwin and a controversial injury to loose-head Sole, who suffered a smashed nose and cheekbone, to run out 22-4 winners. Hall, Morrison and Hill scored the tries, with Barnes adding two penalties and two conversions.

Then there was barely time to catch a breath before the England squad assembled for the trip to Murrayfield; Hall and Halliday kept their places while Redman and Barnes were among the replacements. For Hall, it promised to be a very special occasion, his 15th cap and the one that took him past the club record held by R A Gerrard. The pre-war skipper was a strapping centre who was first capped as a 19-year-old against Benny Osler's Springboks in 1932 and who rounded off his international career with a 9-8 win against Scotland in 1936.

A true hero to team-mates and supporters, Gerrard had been a Bath architect who joined The Royal Engineers on the outbreak of war. Major Gerrard had only just been decorated in the field for his work in clearing a way through the minefield at Alamein for Montgomery's advance against Rommel when his vehicle hit a mine in the Libyan desert, causing fatal injuries.

Hall's family could trace their own Bath rugby lineage even further back, to his maternal grandfather, Harry Vowles, who was scrum-half and captain (1922-24). His father Peter played for Bath as an RAF serviceman in the early 1950s and John's uncle, the late Tom Smith, was a stalwart front row forward of the same era. As a youngster, Hall remembers being raised in a rugby environment in which the Rec was the nucleus.

> "There was a rugby tradition within my family so I knew a lot about the game. We used to live just around the corner from the Recreation Ground and on a Saturday morning we'd go down to the Rec at 10 o'clock – and I know the kids still do it now – and play rugby all morning right through to lunchtime. I'd waddle over to the clubhouse covered in mud and see my uncle Tom in there and he'd buy me half a cider – I'm now 10 or 11 – and we'd watch the game in the afternoon. I was watching the Glovers and Duckworths and all those people. So I was Bath through and through by that time. That's where I acquired an understanding of the game."

There was no overlooking Hall's gifts as a sportsman. "I was an England Under-16 basketball trialist and at the same age I was an England rugby trialist as well as being a county cricketer at under-15. I played every sport that was available to me. And then when I got to my late teens I went down the route of playing for England Colts although I didn't make it until the second year. Everything at the Bath club led on from there."

By the time he ran out at Murrayfield on 15 February 1986, Hall was a month short of his twenty-fourth birthday, recognised as the perfect example of the modern back row forward. He stood 6ft 3in tall, weighed in at nearly sixteen stones and was blessed with pace and world-class footballing skills. He also had a sharp rugby brain and that essential mental hardness – truly a once-in-a-generation player.

Stuart Barnes affirms that Hall "happens to be one of the greatest players I have played with, against or witnessed." Jeremy Guscott, in his autobiography, regards him as "the greatest player I ever played alongside. Hallie had it all – he was fast enough to train with the backs and matched us stride for stride. He should have been first choice for England for ever and a day ..."

The stage was set therefore for the ex-Beechen Cliff pupil to show the kind of form that singled him out as something rather special on the tour to New Zealand the previous summer. Unfortunately, it all went wrong almost from the kick-off as Hall remembers: "I stupidly threw a punch at Finlay Calder and caught him with the end of my thumb, which disappeared up into my wrist ... which was slightly painful. It happened after five minutes and I actually played on for another 35 minutes with a broken thumb. I wasn't a lot of use and at half-time I went off."

On came Redman for his second cap and his first-ever outing in the back row but England were blown away by the home side's pace around the field. Barnes came off the bench for just four minutes before Kiwi referee Bob Francis blew for no side with the scoreboard reading 'Scotland 33 England 6'.

Chilcott was recalled for the game against Ireland on 1 March 1986. The Twickenham pitch had been protected by a layer of straw but Saturday morning dawned bright and frosty and for some hours the fixture hung in the balance. "It's hard to believe that just 20 years ago the supporters would be invited to turn up early and help clear the straw off the pitch," says Chilcott. "But they got the match on and Gary Pearce and I scrummaged Ireland out of the game, with Dean Richards scoring two push-over tries on his debut.

"I said to myself: 'I'm not a one-cap wonder after all – they've forgiven me.' There was a lot of emotion that day because at one time I thought I'd never play for England again. To get back into the team was fantastic."

Bath captain John Palmer came on as a replacement to earn his third and last cap, an astonishingly meagre return for one of the more gifted players of his generation. But Chilcott stayed in the side for the final game of the 1986 Five Nations Championship in Paris although the formidable French front row of Philippe Marocco, Daniel Dubroca and Jean-Pierre Garuet were not so easily subdued and England lost 29-10.

Sole, still only 23, had also made his Scotland debut against France in the championship and demonstrated his mobility by coming close to scoring at least twice against Wales. The injury at Moseley meant a temporary halt to a promising international career.

Hall's absence solved a selection problem at Bath where Simpson had been vying with Spurrell for a place in the back row. Both had been struggling to lose weight – Spurrell after

Paul Simpson: semi-final Man of the Match.

giving up his 40-a-day habit and Simpson because he had begun the season tipping the scales at 18 stones-plus . But there was no mistaking their intent when both lined up either side of Egerton for the John Player Cup quarter-final at London Welsh on 8 March, as Chris Ducker of the Bristol Evening Post observed: "Simpson, invariably able to ride the first tackle, enjoyed himself immensely in open play with Spurrell snapping at his heels and proving that even with the new laws there is still a role for a ball winner on the ground." Simpson duly claimed the first Bath try and others followed from Egerton and Swift in an 18-10 victory but it was an ill-tempered affair.

Spurrell, who had managed only ten appearances during the season, afterwards declared his enthusiasm and ambition for the cut and thrust of rugby revived ... "but I'm a dying for a fag," he added.

Listeners to the semi-final draw on Radio 2 at midday on the Monday again heard the Bath ball drawn out second ... away to Leicester, who had recovered their poise since the early season humiliation. "Bath will notice the difference this time – it will be a very different game," said Tigers skipper Cusworth.

Bath warmed up with wins over Stroud (28-7), Richmond (30-12) before overcoming Bristol 10-3 on Easter Saturday, a seventh successive win over their neighbours. Swift scored the only try, with Barnes adding two penalties on his return to the Memorial Ground. An Easter Monday victory against Vale of Lune (16-4) featured an all-action performance from a young Loughborough student, Andy Robinson.

The following weekend, 14,000 packed into Welford Road for an eagerly awaited John Player Cup semi-final. The Tigers were protecting a winning run of 17 matches in the cup so it was never going to be a repeat of the September romp. The Bath pack laid down their challenge as early as the fifth minute when they shoved Leicester off their own scrum ball and carried on that ferocious effort into line-out, ruck and maul.

Bath's backs "chased and tackled with destructive efficiency" in the words of the Evening Post's Ducker, who made Simpson Man of the Match for his bludgeoning ball carrying. The decisive try came just before half-time when Halliday made a scything outside break and was driven over the line by Barnes and full-back Martin. Dusty Hare matched Barnes with his second penalty in injury time to pull Leicester back to 10-6 but Bath held on.

The match marked something of a rite of passage for one of Bath's newcomers, 26-year-old Tamar Valley farmer Graham Dawe who had made rapid progress since his arrival from Cornish club Launceston at Christmas. Dawe, a competition sheep shearer and enthusiastic member of the bell ringing team at St Constantine's in the village of Milton Abbot, was to make the hooking role his own for a decade, wearing out a succession of cars on a twice-weekly 300-mile commute, the longest in rugby.

Among the 'hard men' of rugby, he was the hardest of them all and possessed of extraordinary stamina. The old players of Bath and Leicester met for a fund-raising game all of 21 years later and it was no real surprise to find him involved and as fiercely competitive as ever. "When Dawsey played in that 'Grudge Match' at Leicester in April 2007 he was no different, still the player he was – perpetual motion for 80 minutes," says John Hall, almost disbelievingly.

Graham Dawe: champion sheep shearer.

For Egerton, the opportunity to pitch himself against Leicester and England's Dean Richards and to finish on the winning side, was another milestone in a blossoming first season of top-class rugby and it earned him selection as the only No 8 on the England B tour to Italy. Pairing up again at Bath with Richard Hill, his old schoolmate from Salisbury, was an advantage, he acknowledged. "It took me a couple of matches to settle in, but I had been in the Bishop Wordsworth school team and the local club side with Richard and it soon clicked."

Egerton had also contributed 13 tries in 28 appearances for Bath but sadly for the 24-year-old British Aerospace ergonomist, a back problem was to rule him out of the Twickenham final against Wasps on 26 April 1986. He was one of several from the semi-final line-up who missed the rehearsal at home to Llanelli. But Hall was back in harness after his thumb injury and helped guide Bath to a 19-10 victory in which Trick announced his readiness to face Wasps with two electric tries on the right wing. Halliday also crossed for a score and stand-in fly-half Phil Cue brought up 1,000 points for the season with a dropped goal.

So to Twickenham for the third year running. The ritual was now established – frantic ringing round for coaches of the 52-seat variety, lengthy but good-natured

Swift scores against Wasps.

queues for tickets at the Rec, travel plans finalised and orders taken for picnic food and plenty of liquid refreshment, of course.

In the Bath camp the outward signs of confidence disguised unease at a rash of injuries at the end of a long and exhausting season. Redman had needed a cortisone injection in an ankle on the Thursday evening but the main concern was over the fitness of skipper Palmer who had strained his groin against Llanelli. Palmer's value as a peerless reader of the game, as someone whose timing of a pass could unlock the tightest defences, was only really appreciated by his team-mates – and the more discerning of opponents.

BATH: *C Martin; D Trick, S Halliday, J Palmer, A Swift; S Barnes, R Hill;*
G Chilcott, G Dawe, R Lee, J Morrison, N Redman, R Spurrell, P Simpson, J Hall.

WASPS: *N Stringer; S Smith, RCardus (capt), R Pellow, M Bailey; G Rees,*
S Bates (P Balcombe); G Holmes, P Simmons, J Probyn, J Bonner, M Pinnegar,
D Pegler, M Rose, M Rigby.

REFEREE: *F Howard* (Liverpool).

Palmer, who had earned a third cap as a replacement against Ireland the previous month, did lead his side out but began to have second thoughts when Wasps raced into a 13-nil lead after soaking up almost continuous pressure for the first quarter of an hour. Twice the holders were caught napping by counter-attacks and on both occasions tries were gratefully accepted by Nick Stringer and Roger Pellow. Stringer kicked a conversion and then added a 24th minute penalty after Bath were hit on the break yet again, the drift defence struggling to cope. This was definitely not in the script.

The stricken Palmer considered going off but Cue stayed on the bench as Bath calculated that what was really needed in this situation was experience and stability. Slowly they turned things around. Within five minutes, Simpson and Hill worked an opening on the short side of a scrum for left wing Swift and then Trick took over the goal kicking to land a penalty as Wasps lost scrum-half Steve Bates to injury. At half-time, 13-7 suddenly did not look so bad.

After the irrepressible Spurrell took a short pass from Simpson to score a second try – and Trick curled over the conversion – it was one-way traffic. Another ferocious forward assault on the left put Hill in for a try on 56 minutes and Simpson claimed the fourth 20 minutes later after a series of scrums on the Wasps line. Trick, selected for his pace, finished with a priceless tally of three conversions and a penalty and Wasps' final score from replacement scrum-half Balcombe came too late to silence the joyous relief of the West Country supporters. All that mattered was the final scoreline of 25-17.

Rowell said afterwards: "To most teams the game would have been dead with a deficit of 13 points. But we had the sense to play to our strength. It would have been nice to be more expansive – in fact we talked at length about playing the game that way – but it has to be appreciated that our players were under tremendous pressure

This is becoming a habit! Players' bus tour, with John Hall, Roger Spurrell, Jon Morrison, Graham Dawe, Richard Hill and Richard Lee soaking up the adulation.

to win the match. Clinching three John Player Cup titles in a row is still one hell of a performance."

Try-scorer Spurrell added: "The great thing was that no-one panicked. We just looked around, knew something had to be done and got on with it."

Amid the elation, for at least one player there was a feeling of a burden lifted. Trick had decided to take a break from rugby, disillusioned with what he believed was a joyless approach to the game although he had finished second highest scorer with 77 points, including 15 tries, from 26 appearances.

"I didn't enjoy my rugby for most of last season," he said at the end of July when his decision was made public. "I wanted to stop last December but a friend persuaded me that it might seem like sour grapes because I was out of the team. There's not enough enjoyment in it for me. Don't get me wrong, I like competitive rugby but as soon as you become as successful as Bath there is a tendency to tighten up." He did however make a cameo appearance at Leicester in September.

Others, however, seemed to be thriving on it. Hill succeeded Palmer as captain for the 1986-87 season a little more than three years after arriving at the Recreation Ground as a fresh-faced, carrot-topped student. Even though Hill had already led the English Universities and England Students sides, it was re-markable progress; he already had five caps to his name – although no victories in an England shirt.

"There's no gentle introduction at Bath for the new boy," he said in a pre-season interview. "The senior players let you know when you're not doing things the right way. In the end it's a case of sink or swim according to how you take the pressure. I've watched the likes of Nigel Redman and David Egerton put through the same routine since then. It's tough. But those lads have survived to become outstanding members of the side. Perhaps this explains why we breed winners."

It seems that Trick's departure had rung a few alarm bells though. Hill acknowledged the need for the players to pace themselves more effectively than they had the previous season when the combination of a tough pre-season training programme and a congested fixture list had left them 'burned out' even before the Divisional Championship in December.

"It was a real struggle to regain our edge in time for the John Player Cup," he confessed. "And to be honest, we never really performed consistently well. That mustn't happen this time. This year we haven't gone so mad on training. I'm hoping we can build to a peak more gradually. It's also vital that we attempt more of a 15-man game. Last season we played it tight in a lot of matches because of the importance of the occasion. But there's nothing worse than having your centres coming off the field moaning about not seeing the ball."

The opening fixture of the new season could hardly have been tougher – away to Pontypool, who had lost only twice at home in 104 matches. But a leaner looking Chilcott helped shove the much vaunted Ponty pack off their own ball at the first scrum and then took a line-out tap to dive over for the first try. Further tries followed from Trevaskis, Simpson (2) and Swift with Guscott adding a penalty as Bath cruised home with authority to win 23-10.

Sole returned to the fray at Plymouth Albion after seven months recuperation from the collision with Steve Boyle's elbow at Moseley. That most cultured of props had used the time profitably, setting up a wine importing business in Corsham, and looked to have lost none of his dynamism. For front row partner Dawe it was the shortest trip of the season and he made the most of it by scoring two of Bath's six tries in a 41-10 victory. Among the spectators was former Royal Navy and Somerset captain Ray Robinson. Already confined to a wheelchair by multiple sclerosis, which had also robbed him of his sight, he relied on friends to describe

Damian Cronin outstanding in the line-out against Pontypool (3 September 1986).

events on the field – particularly the performances of his son, Andy. An engaging character who never betrayed an ounce of self-pity, Ray was just happy to encourage his son on the rugby field – and to enjoy a pint of Guinness with his friends afterwards.

"Obviously, I like to follow my sons' rugby careers," he confided to your author that evening. "Andy's doing very well at Bath but I also have two other sons playing for Taunton Colts and Cirencester. I'm lucky to have an understanding wife and friends who take me to matches and describe the action to me."

Robinson Jnr, 22, who had just started teaching at Writhlington School near Radstock, affirmed: "Although Dad's registered blind, he's got great spirit and is in tremendous form." Ray continued to attend Bath matches and was 'witness' to many a momentous occasion before the disease finally wore out his body – leaving that indomitable spirit to live on in his sons, not least in Andy.

As Bath followers looked forward to a series of glittering autumn fixtures, the City Council imposed an 8,000 all-ticket limit on attendances at the Recreation Ground, a logical move after the reputed 10,000 crowd for the Cardiff clash a year before. The price of a match programme was increased to 30p.

The first big test was at home to Leicester on 15 September, Bath edging past their old rivals 6-3 but only after a worrying injury to Palmer. The ambulance drove right across the pitch to the North Parade Bridge corner where the centre lay unconscious and play was held up for 18 minutes in a constant downpour. He was given the all-clear after a night in the Royal United Hospital.

Six conversions out of six by Barnes, despite a septic big toe, helped Bath to a 36-nil rout at Moseley with Guscott scoring twice. Spurrell shrugged off a chronic back problem to enjoy his first outing of the season, a 33-6 victory at Newport where Halliday and Swift provided the dash and sparkle. "Performances like that on Welsh soil leave you with such a great feeling," said Spurrell. "People keep saying the Bath bubble will burst. But I'm now virtually the old man of a very young side. We will get even better."

The injury that ended Spurrell's rugby career troubles him even now: "Yes I was getting back problems at that time. I still am." It did not make it any easier to hold off the challenge from Robinson. Their tussles at Lambridge have passed into Bath folklore, proving that training at Bath was harder than playing the matches. "That's how it should be," says Spurrell. "What are you going to do? Train one way and play another? That doesn't make any sense whatsoever. Yeah, training was hard, very hard. People tried to come in and force their way into the group and they had to work their way in." And when Robinson took his place, how did he feel? "Fairly pissed off. I hated it at the time. But no, I don't think I ever thought 'Oh, this is unfair'."

A 9-6 defeat at home to Llanelli on 29 September 1986 came as a rude shock, especially the failure to score a try in front of 6,000 of the Rec faithful. There was more than a hint of complacency and a rather reckless desire to please the crowd rather than subdue a tenacious Scarlets side who did manage a try, courtesy of Wales No 8 Phil Davies.

Management commitee honour Mabel

It was agreed that the Club Flag be flown at half-mast prior to the Wasps game, as a mark of respet to the late Mabel Redwood who had been involved with the Club for 30 years. She had been a splendid servant, helping with the players' teas in her earlier days, but she was best remembered for her individual efforts in running a raffle most weeks on the Rec. Mabel had her own particularly individualistic style and was sadly missed.

A week later the show was back on the road as Graham Dawe celebrated a call-up to the England bench for a non-cap international against Japan with a stirring display in the loose against Welsh hooker Billy James as Aberavon were beaten 26-6. As soon as Dawe received the good news from Twickenham a neighbouring farmer ploughed through the telephone cable!

Despite the absence of seven players on England duty, debutant second row David Churchill and other understudies stepped up to beat South Wales Police 23-12. The real significance of the occasion was not apparent for some weeks or months however – it was Spurrell's last appearance in a

Fred Sagoe: bow-tied barrister.

Bath shirt. In the seven years since the first of his 206 appearances against Seahawks of California, the tousled-haired flanker had been an inspirational figure whose contribution to the Bath rugby phenomenon could not be overstated. Physical wear and tear – and the emergence of Andy Robinson as a loose forward of the highest quality – had finally ended an illustrious career which deserved at least one England cap.

Liverpool St Helens were beaten 29-19 on their own turf and when the main men returned to take on Bristol at the Memorial Ground, they coasted into a 21-6 lead. But again the foot came off the pedal and their neighbours battled to within three points, giving Bath "one hell of a scare" in Chilcott's words.

Flamboyant bow-tied barrister Fred Sagoe ran in four tries and Hall three against United Services Portsmouth (66-14) before the regulation 8,000 crammed into the Rec for the visit of Cardiff on 30 October. The 29-year-old John Palmer, having announced his retirement from representative rugby, was at his creative best in laying on tries Simpson, Halliday and Morrison in a 28-9 victory. It was a virtuoso performance, combining flicked back passes, breathtaking ball handling and sublime dummies.

"I dropped out of this weekend's training trip to Portugal (with England) because quite honestly I was dreading it," he told Chris Ducker, of the Bristol Evening Post. "When you feel like that, it's time to call it a day. But a big club game still offers a huge challenge – particularly against Welsh sides."

After a largely second string side subdued Newbridge 10-6, Wasps came to the Rec a week later but Bath were not in any mood to give them a head start as they had done at Twickenham some six months earlier. Again the Bath scrummage produced two tries, both for Robinson, and Chris Martin completed his recovery from a dislocated shoulder to claim the third in a 22-6 victory.

The winning run continued against Coventry (38-13) and Fiji Barbarians (35-4) only for the wheels to come off under the Rec lights on 27 November against

Gloucester. The 12-9 defeat was hard to bear and even the controversial award of a penalty try by referee Terry Friend, who almost missed the kick-off after travelling up from Devon, could not hide the fact that Bath had played poorly, notwithstanding the selection of a number of United players.

It was hardly ideal preparation for the trip to Neath three days later, billed as the unofficial Club Championship of Great Britain after the men from The Gnoll had accounted for Cardiff, Llanelli, Pontypool, Swansea and Bridgend. It will be remembered as the 'Jonathan Davies Match' for his impeccable performance at fly-half, culminating in a marvellous solo try after shaping to drop for goal. The 26-9 scoreline delighted the 9,000 crowd and did not in the least flatter Neath. It was probably the only time in that era that a full-strength Bath team finished a distant second, unable to match their opponents for intensity and pace.

Back to the bump and grind of the unloved Divisional Championship, the only route into the England team at that time, the stars handed the Bath baton back to the United squad who drew at London Scottish (12-12), lost at Harlequins (9-25) but brushed Clifton aside (38-9) on Boxing Day 1986. Preparations for the new Five Nations Championship season left Bath without five England players for the final match of the year, away to Northampton, and it took an injury time try under the posts from Lee to earn a 12-10 victory.

The New Year's Day fixture at Cardiff, marketed as the British Gas Challenge, also clashed with England's build-up. Second-string players such as hospital doctor Colin Bevan, who scored a try from No 8, rose to the occasion superbly and were in no way disgraced by the 32-21 scoreline.

Much of the entertainment was provided by referee Clive Norling who resolutely refused to award a penalty until four minutes into injury time. The assessors would have had plenty to say these days!

Chapter 7

LOOKING OUT OVER THE WORLD

As 1987 dawned, Bath's domination of the English club game was unanswerable. As many as 14 players had been involved in the Divisional Championship and most of them were serious contenders for places in the national team.

Only this season was different. At the end of it was the first Rugby World Cup, to be played in Australia and New Zealand.

When 24-year-old Richard Hill was confirmed as early as 2 October 1986 as the first Bath player to captain England in the club's 122-year history, their hegemony was complete. The nearest that Bath had come to achieving this honour had been in the period 1952-56 when England's 1951 captain, John Kendall-Carpenter, saw out the last few seasons of a distinguished career on the banks of the Avon.

How appropriate then that the same John McGregor Kendall-Carpenter should be one of the main architects of the Rugby World Cup. As the RFU's representative on the International Rugby Board, he famously broke ranks to side with New Zealand, Australia and South Africa after a voting deadlock in March 1985.

Richard Hill: first Bath player to captain England.

The urbane schoolteacher, headmaster of Wellington College, then assumed the role of organiser as co-chairman with Nick Shehadie, doyen of Wallaby rugby. The story goes that rather late in the day the Englishman rang the Australian to say: "Son, we have a problem – we haven't got a trophy."

So Kendall-Carpenter popped into Garrard's in Regent Street and found what he wanted, a £6,000 gilded silver cup which had been sitting in the crown jeweller's vaults since 1906. Appropriately enough, the honour of presenting The William

Webb Ellis Trophy – known these days as 'Bill' – fell to Kendall-Carpenter a few months later.

Meanwhile, earnest preparations had been under way for months to ensure that the 1987 Five Nations Championship gave England the perfect springboard for the nascent global competition. World Cup pool opponents Japan came to Twickenham on 11 October to face an England XV with six Bath players in the starting line-up – Hill himself, Halliday, Barnes, Chilcott, Redman and Hall – plus Dawe on the bench.

A hastily arranged England Final Trial on 3 January involved all these, plus Lee, Simpson and Egerton – and Bath's representation might have been higher if Palmer had not already removed himself from consideration. With Hill installed as the man to lead England into a 'golden era', he was joined by Dawe, Redman, Hall and Simpson for the opening fixture at Lansdowne Road. A squall blew in from Dublin Bay and Ireland played the appalling conditions perfectly, running out 17-nil winners.

> **One of the main casualties was Paul Simpson whose international career ended on that February afternoon. To rub salt into the wound, he was also overlooked for Bath's John Player Cup tie against London Welsh the following weekend and turned out instead for the United on the equally windswept Kingswood School pitches. "From Lansdowne Road to Lansdown in seven days ... must be some sort of f****** record," he was sometimes heard to mutter, but not without the characteristic grin.**

Barnes had won his seventh cap – his fourth as a fullback replacement – when called on in the 39th minute for Marcus Rose. However Barnes was growing so disillusioned with his role as bench warmer that he was about to cast himself into the international wilderness. He reflected in his 1995 biography: "Before the French game I reached the decision to retire from international rugby, aged 25 with seven caps and a despised reputation as the nearly man, if I was not chosen for Wales away. At no point did I think that England might perform so well that selections could be justified. They did not. On the Thursday morning training session I knew that my planned decision would not be a folly."

England duly lost to France at Twickenham and still Rob Andrew, of Wasps, kept the No 10 shirt. For Barnes, the die was cast. For Chilcott, however, the pendulum seemed to be swinging the other way. An injury as early as the 12th minute to another Wasps player, Paul Rendall, gave the Bath man his chance to show what he could do.

Despite the 19-15 scoreline Chilcott performed creditably against Jean-Pierre Garuet, who formed an unholy trinity with Daniel Dubroca and Pascal Ondarts right through to the World Cup final against New Zealand. In the grand tradition of rugby union combat, a bond of friendship was formed with the fierce men of the South of France.

Some years later Chilcott was in Biarritz and wandered into Ondarts' bar on the harbourside. "I got a tremendous welcome," he recalls. "Pascal was straight on the phone to Jean-Pierre who lived near Lourdes where he was the mayor. He dropped everything, drove over and joined us in a feast of cognac, beef and pate. The party went on for some time," adds Cooch, with a chuckle.

Back in 1987, the real enmity was between England and Wales, however, and the tension before their meeting at Cardiff was almost tangible. "Hilly's team talk was all about fighting fire with fire," recalls Chilcott. "Almost from the kick-off it erupted into a brawl."

Lock Steve Sutton had his nose broken at the first line-out – by a fellow Welshman's elbow – but it was after six minutes that the fun really began. Hall had the best view: "Phil Davies took a swing at me at the back of the line-out, missed, then caught the back of my shirt and pulled me down. It looked like I'd been punched when actually I had just been pulled to the floor. The next thing I know I was looking up to see Wade Dooley stepping over and hitting Davies, caving his cheekbone in. Then the big punch-up started." The 19-12 scoreline in Wales's favour was largely incidental.

Hall adds: "It was a dirty old game – a grudge match – but we weren't going to be physically taken apart. That was the way it was right through the game. Players got singled out, I think unfairly, and Dawsey and Chilcott and Hilly got dropped. I suppose Hilly had to take some of the responsibility as captain but I think it was unfair on the others. That was the way it was then."

Having lost the captaincy almost as soon as he had earned it, Hill did not reappear in an England shirt until the World Cup. Dooley was banned for one match but why Chilcott and Dawe were disciplined too was something of a mystery, although there was a suspicion that they were being made to pay for past misdemeanours. By the time England disposed of Scotland 21-12 on 4 April the only Bath players in the team were Halliday, Redman and Hall, with another of their number, Sole, among the opposition.

Back at Bath, there was at least another John Player Cup campaign to provide a welcome diversion. After disposing of Plymouth Albion 32-10 and London Welsh (30-4), Moseley offered sterner opposition in the quarter-final on 2 March before a penalty try sealed a 12-3 victory. It was stodgy fare and at one stage Jack Rowell left his seat in the stand to deliver a few choice words of advice to his players via replacement scrum-half Steve Knight.

Yet another away draw in the semi-final sent Bath back up to Orrell. Still hurting from all the fall-out over the 'Battle of Cardiff' three weeks earlier, much of the opprobrium having been flung in their direction, the Bath contingent were keen to restore tarnished reputations. The roar of defiance was heard all over the land as Orrell were swatted aside 31-7 on their own ground. Four of Bath's six tries came directly from pushovers as the much-vaunted home pack was demolished. Barnes summed up the mood by saying: "I have never known us quite so determined before a match."

By the time Newport were overcome 34-8 a fortnight later – Bath's 15th win in a row – even Hill was back to his chirpy, confident self, grabbing two tries before his team ran away with the match, scoring 18 points in just three minutes of injury time. He said afterwards: "It's a long time since I got two tries in a match but the 'zip' is definitely back in my game. Losing the England captaincy was the lowest point of my career but then I realised that things could only get better." Having already completed the double over Pontypool, Bridgend were then added to the list of Welsh scalps in an awesome 38-24 performance at the Brewery Field.

Expectations for the Twickenham rematch with Wasps and the prize of a fourth successive John Player Cup triumph were therefore huge. So why did the occasion – and the performance – fall so short?

BATH: *C Martin; A Swift (J Guscott), J Palmer, S Halliday, B Trevaskis; S Barnes, R Hill* (capt); *D Sole, G Dawe (G Bess), G Chilcott, J Morrison, N Redman, J Hall, D Egerton, A Robinson.*

WASPS: *H Davies; S Smith, K Simms, R Lozowski, M Bailey; R Andrew, S Bates; P Rendall, P Simmons, J Probyn, M Pinnegar, J Bonner, D Pegler* (capt)*, M Rose, M Rigby.*

REFEREE: *F Howard* (Liverpool).

As in the previous year's final, Wasps took advantage of a breeze to go 6-nil ahead and even after the excellent Redman went over from a tapped penalty, the Londoners stretched their lead to 12-4 just before half-time with a converted try by Huw Davies. Bath lost Dawe and Swift to injury, with Greg Bess and Guscott coming on as replacements. Wasps tighthead Jeff Probyn was causing problems for Sole throughout but he eventually fell foul of referee Fred Howard and Barnes kicked a 40-metre penalty.

With just six minutes of normal time remaining, Halliday took a fast, flat pass from Hill to score by the posts, leaving Barnes an easy conversion. It was then left to Redman again to force his way over the line in injury time, sparking an exuberant invasion from young Bath fans. When the pitch was cleared, Barnes kicked the conversion – and they all swarmed on again to celebrate the 19-12 victory which brought an unprecedented four-in-a-row.

Richard Hill leads his team out for the 1987 cup final.

*Bath supporters jump for joy as referee Fred Howard awards a try to Nigel Redman,
buried under a pile of bodies.*

It was not the champagne performance everyone had expected and once more it raised questions about Bath's ability to produce their very best form on the big day. Chilcott took a pragmatic view however: "Some of the lads are a bit stunned but I feel on top of the world. OK, we were below form and Wasps played really well. But to win in those circumstances is still a tremendous achievement and it's all that really matters."

More than 20 years later, John Hall makes no bones about the hard-nosed approach adopted on that day and others, explaining: "I played in both finals against Wasps. We could quite easily have lost them but we didn't and that was quite simply down to ruthlessness, the will to win. The second half of one of the finals wasn't too pretty because we just stuck the ball up our jumpers and played a driving game. But we knew what we needed to do in a final – and that was to win. We don't make any apologies for that."

In truth Bath were often exhilarating to watch – the statistics from 1986-87 show just seven defeats in 44 games with 184 tries in a points total of 1,167 – but it was not as much fun for opponents, as Hall acknowledges now.

"People still talk about playing against us," he says with a rueful smile. "Yes, we were probably a pretty unpleasant bunch to face. A friend of mine called Hugh McHardy, who played for London Scottish, called us 'the one-eyes from Bath'. That was the way we were. We played tough, hard rugby and we also played very entertaining rugby. But at the end of the day it was all about winning."

Back in 1987 Hall's dreams of rounding off a successful season at the World Cup were shattered almost immediately he arrived in Australia. The 25-year-old, already with 19 caps, returned home for surgery to repair cartilage damage and told your author at the time: "I'm a big bloke and pretty quick with it. It's not surprising my knees take a battering," he said. "Having needed an operation on the same knee the year before last, I'm not going to push it too hard. But I certainly don't feel that it threatens my career – although the knees may give me some trouble when I'm 40 or 50."

With Hall absent and Halliday unavailable owing to business and domestic commitments, Bath representation at the first Rugby World Cup did not reflect their ascendancy at club level. Redman was the only player to start the opening pool match against Australia (lost 19-6) and, joined by Chilcott, scored a try in a 60-7 rout against Japan. Hill and Dawe, Bath's Player of the Season, got their chance in the third pool match against the USA (34-6). Moving from Sydney to Brisbane for the quarter-final against Wales, Redman was paired with Dooley but Chilcott was on the field from the first minute as a replacement. It was a poor all-round performance, Wales winning 16-3 to reach the semi-finals.

> **Back in Bath, the future could not have looked rosier. At a Management Committee meeting on 9 June, officials were told that Tesco had made an initial offer of £7.25 million for the Lambridge training grounds and that an alternative site had been found for the club at Bathampton. A successful deal was subject to "certain conditions" many of which depended on a degree of co-operation from the city council, but who then announced that they had their own plans for Lambridge – a park-and-ride site. At worst, it was thought, this might take a couple of years to sort out. Little did they know...**

Bath had finished 1986-87 as winners of the national John Smiths Merit Table A, which had been introduced by the RFU two years earlier, and the South West Merit Table. They were also runners-up to Neath in The Sunday Telegraph's unofficial but authoritative Anglo-Welsh Merit Table.

Merit tables were a strange construct of the amateur game, whose more traditional elements had struggled to come to terms with competitive rugby because of its connotations with the 13-man professional code and a fear that 'leagues' would usher in violence and demands for players to be compensated. For 1987-88, however, the clamour for more meaningful competition had led to the introduction of the Courage Club Championship, complete with promotion and relegation to reward the more ambitious clubs held back by the 'old boys network'.

The good news was that you no longer needed a calculator to work out the percentages of wins against matches played in order to determine the positions. But there was a major snag: the RFU had shied away from imposing fixed Saturdays for championship fixtures among the major clubs – although they had done so at junior level.

So Bath and their rivals had to work things out among themselves on an historical or arbitrary basis, knowing that some Courage Championship fixtures would inevitably clash with divisional and international matches. Generally, the first fixture between clubs was to count towards the championship, with four points to be awarded for a win, two for a draw – and one for turning up. Note that they did not call it a 'league'. The only virtue of the system was that it gave clubs a season to sort themselves out before the introduction of leagues proper in 1988-89.

For Rowell, the main concern was how to motivate his players after the extraordinary four-in-a-row in the cup. An opening 59-3 victory at home to South Wales Police on the evening of Wednesday 1 September allayed his fears – for the time being at least.

Arriving straight from a business trip in Holland he watched them run in nine tries, with Barnes contributing 27 points. Rowell observed afterwards: "We've been the best side in England for over five years. The players are young in terms of years but old in terms of experience and success. A number of them have only recently returned from the World Cup so I knew my major problem this year would be one of motivation, in helping them stay at the top. That's why I was pleased with this performance."

Yet a home reverse to Pontypool (12-14) on the Saturday was followed a week later by a comprehensive defeat (24-12) against Leicester at Welford Road in their opening Courage Championship match. Rowell was not so sanguine on this occasion, delivering a 30-minute 'dressing down' behind locked doors before stalking off to a weekend get-together of RFU coaching hierarchy at the University of Leicester. One of the main exercises was a collective video analysis of his team's edgy, ineffectual display.

The level of performance was not significantly higher in a 14-nil victory over Moseley and the feeling of unease was reflected in skipper Hill's post-match comment: "We've some way to go before we get things right again. But it's given us breathing space." Palmer, one of several players hampered by injury, was more forthright: "Against a really top side we could have lost by 30 points," he said.

Fortunately, Simpson and Swift crossed for tries and Hall, despite a leg injury, was in uncompromising mood as Moseley repeatedly tested the blind-side defence. Both Hall and Hill (bruised kidneys) missed the trip to Llanelli where just two minutes had elapsed before Martin was taken off with a dislocated shoulder. Stand-in skipper Chilcott did his best to rally the troops and Robinson had a storming game in the loose but Bath lacked the fire power to seriously trouble the Scarlets and lost 27-14. It had not been a good September.

One notable absentee was Sole who had joined Edinburgh Academicals after collecting his 10th cap in the World Cup quarter-final against eventual winners New Zealand. However, the Scottish connection was to be continued through Damian Cronin who, although born in Germany to an Irish father, was discovered to have maternal grandparents from Lothian.

Cronin had considered himself English – like Palmer he had been educated at Prior Park College in Bath – but Sole's recommendation had been enough to earn the 6ft

6in second row a run-out with the Anglo-Scots against Glasgow the previous season and latterly with a Scottish XV against a French tour side. Now Cronin was looking forward to a B cap against Italy and to pursuing his claims in the Scottish provincial championship, saying: "Scotland have given me a chance and so, whatever happens, I shall stick with them. The game last weekend was enjoyable and I was reasonably satisfied with my performance."

As one player departed, another more familiar face had returned. David Trick, who had taken a sabbatical following his rare display of goal-kicking prowess in the 1986 cup final, landed a touchline conversion after Cue and Barnes missed five between them at Aberavon. But the home side still won 16-13. At Nottingham the following Saturday, much attention was on the hooking battle between Brian Moore and Dawe, but a dropped goal and four penalties from Simon Hodgkinson in a 25-15 scoreline consigned Bath to their fifth defeat in eight games and began to raise doubts about their Courage Championship credentials.

So out of sorts were Bath that the visit of Bristol on 17 October 1987 raised the prospect of a rare derby defeat. In the event, the home side rose to the occasion in front of 7,000 spectators to win 15-9, the decisive early tries coming from Hill and Halliday as Bath scored all their points inside 23 minutes with Cue adding two conversions and a penalty. Even Palmer, deputising ably for the injured Barnes at fly-half, admitted that Bristol should have been awarded a penalty try in the second half but all they had to show for their efforts were a try by skipper Andy Dun, converted by Jon Webb, who also kicked a penalty. For Bristol, a tenth derby defeat in a row was no way to celebrate their centenary.

With the 'show back on the road', Bath showed rather more confidence in winning 24-7 at Newport and then dealt with Cheltenham (46-3) and Vale of Lune (20-16) before negotiating a potentially tricky midweek trip to Newbridge with a 17-6 victory in which Halliday was outstanding.

But back to the serious business of the Courage Championship, they fell short again at Wasps whose tiny Sudbury ground rocked to a 19-15 home win. By the time Egerton barged over from a tapped penalty well into injury time, the Londoners had sewn things up with two tries from Mark Bailey. It was the England wing's first game since the World Cup but he did not look half so rusty as some of the opposition, as Redman conceded.

> "The harder we try, the worse it gets," said the 23-year-old lock. "When we took a tapped penalty, for instance, I ran straight at Gareth Chilcott, which isn't like us at all. Most annoying of all, we won more ball than Wasps." There was intense irritation with the refereeing of Welsh official John Groves but Bath's problems ran deeper than that. Could it get any worse? Yes, it could.

On a dank and dismal Saturday afternoon at Coundon Road, Coventry, the match was only 23 minutes old when Stuart Barnes staggered off the field, dazed and spitting out gobbets of blood after suffering a fractured cheekbone. Knight made a good fist of deputising at fly-half but it was late in the game before Halliday created a try for Swift and Cue's conversion earned a 9-9 draw. After lying unattended in the casualty department at a Coventry hospital for three hours, Barnes was eventually operated on the next day, 22 November – his 25th birthday.

Nine days later, Hill and his squad – minus the injured Barnes and Hall – made the short trip to Gloucester for a severe examination of their credentials. The response was typically cussed and conclusive as they rediscovered the passion and pride to win 16-9 under the Kingsholm floodlights.

Coming back from 9-3 down, Hill's pass first created a try for Halliday who had earlier seen a seemingly good score overruled by the home touch judge. With Redman, Morrison and Egerton in control of the line-out and Dawe and Robinson providing extra impetus in the loose, the platform was established for No 8 Egerton to force his way over from a scrum. Cue added to his earlier penalty by landing the conversion and Palmer, again recalled at fly-half, rounded off a most satisfying victory with an injury-time dropped goal.

Halliday spoke for most when he said: "I must admit I had begun to wonder whether we would ever get it right again. Tonight restored my faith in the side. It is not easy coming into the fairly hostile environment of Kingsholm. But our forwards were tremendous, playing with great commitment and keeping their heads when the pressure was on."

When the Divisional Championship got under way, Bath were left with little more than a United side to negotiate the December fixture schedule. Surprising as it may seem in the light of his subsequent achievements, 22-year-old Jeremy Guscott was not yet in the South West squad although now established as Halliday's partner in the Bath team.

After a 23-10 win over London Scottish, Guscott scoring one of the tries, Bath lost 10-17 at home to Waterloo, collecting one Courage Championship point. Waterloo, then among the top 12 major clubs, were a well-drilled side with the uncompromising Jim Sydall at the heart of a workmanlike pack. Guscott also scored a spectacular try at Saracens, at that time in Division 2, but the home side prevailed 13-10 largely thanks to the all-round efforts of try scorer Sean Robinson, brother of Andy. Clifton were beaten 26-10 in the traditional Boxing Day fixture at the Rec.

With their England contenders required elsewhere by new national coach Geoff Cooke, Bath were far from full strength for the New Year opener at Cardiff, especially after Phil Cue somehow missed the rendezvous on the M4 and Keith Hoskin, a full-back or centre, found himself pressed into service as emergency fly-half. Without even a recognised goalkicker, Bath lost 38-9 in poor conditions but the sight of Hall recovered from knee and hip problems provided a degree of consolation.

Meanwhile, with Halliday stricken by a hamstring strain, not a single Bath name appeared in the starting line-up for England's opening game of the 1988 Five Nations Championship, although Chilcott and Dawe were on the bench. Cronin was selected for his Scotland debut against Ireland having scored a spectacular try in the Scottish trial. Although he had already amassed 12,000 miles travelling to Scottish sessions from his home in Batheaston via Heathrow, Cronin did not yet command a regular place in the Bath side.

Palmer continued his series of occasional performances by returning to guide his club to a 35-11 victory at London Welsh and produced a vintage performance at fly-half in a 45-7 rout of Metropolitan Police, although Guscott raised the biggest cheer with an extravagant break from his own 22 to score in injury time.

Attention then turned to a John Player Cup third round tie at Lichfield – or it would have done if snow had not blanketed Staffordshire. The Rec was playable, however, so Streatham & Croydon gamely agreed to provide some sparring practice, letting in 16 tries in a record total of 84-nil.

A week later the snows had thawed around the cathedral city of Lichfield. The local club had managed to run Harlequins and London Welsh close in the past but on this occasion were given no quarter by an unforgiving Bath pack in which the athletic Redman was again outstanding. The cup holders eventually ran in nine tries to win 43-3, the reward being a trip to Leicester.

It would have proved a worthy final and it drew a record fourth round attendance of 13,000 who were left breathless by an explosive opening. Cue landed a third minute penalty and the visitors set about establishing total dominance of the forward exchanges, mainly through the line-out work of Redman, Hall, Egerton and Cronin, finally given his chance in the absence of the injured Morrison. Behind them, Palmer was in commanding form at fly-half, using the wind intelligently and dropping a goal to extend the lead to 6-nil. After Cue landed his second penalty in the second half and Egerton drove off the back of a scrum to touch down, Bath led 13-nil and rode out the final few minutes following a Nick Youngs try converted by Dusty Hare.

Leicester coach Peter Wheeler was unstinting in his praise: "There's no side in the country can compete on equal terms with this Bath pack. We simply couldn't string any possession together. Bath responded to the occasion superbly but then they're big time players ... and very good ones too." With a fifth cup success beckoning, who could possibly stop them now?

After Gloucester grabbed a 26-26 draw at the Rec on 20 February, Bath travelled to Moseley for the cup quarter-final knowing that if they came anywhere near the quality of performance achieved at Welford Road, then a semi-final spot was theirs.

It could not have been closer – Moseley 4, Bath 3 – but the great cup adventure was over and there was a feeling that the champions could have battered away for a fortnight without ever adding to Phil Cue's penalty, scored after just 90 seconds. Almost unbelievably, it was the only success from 13 attempts at goal; six of them were attempted drop goals by Palmer and David Trick even hit the post with a close range penalty kick on 78 minutes. It was truly bizarre, almost as if they were destined to lose.

While Moseley feted their try scorer, No 8 Peter Shillingford, Rowell told his dejected team: "It's been a pleasure working with such a great bunch of players. Don't think of losing this game … look back and realise what a unique experience it has been."

Reflecting afterwards on the ending of a record sequence of 22 cup-ties unbeaten, he told The Bath Chronicle: "The Bath dressing- room does tend to be a little quiet after a defeat. The first few minutes seemed like hours. After all, the Cup has become a way of life – you are bound to get withdrawal symptoms. Given the territorial advantage, given the chances, we should have won. The run wasn't going to go on forever but for it to end like that was heart-breaking."

Simon Halliday: "we must ensure this experience makes us even stronger."

Halliday summed up the players' mood: "I think we all knew that one day we'd just beat ourselves. And that, of course, is what happened. You haven't seen the last of us though … we must ensure this experience makes us even stronger." And four days later, as if to rub it in, Barnes nonchalantly kicked 16 points at Exeter in his first outing since fracturing a cheekbone at Coventry.

The remaining two months were to be endured rather than enjoyed as Bath resigned themselves to a trophy-less campaign, having also been ruled out of contention for the Courage Championship. They could occasionally recreate the old sparkle and panache, as in winning 28-23 at Swansea where Guscott scored twice to take his try tally to 16, but five days later they plumbed the depths in losing 39-15 at home to Bridgend. Admittedly, the side looked a little threadbare – Camborne's David Rule was drafted in as guest scrum-half – but Barnes said: "With the team we put out I was not particularly surprised to lose to a side of Bridgend's quality. But to go down without offering much of a fight – that's another matter altogether."

Barnes guided his side to a 30-nil win over Liverpool St Helens a few days later. The Rec was a quagmire that afternoon as his opponent on the day, Alan Simpson, recalls. "I can still remember that game as if it was yesterday," he says. "It was a crappy, muddy pitch and I was playing against the 'Barrel' as he was known. I like to think that if we had swapped over, it would have been 50 points! But my abiding memory is of their winger – Fred Sagoe I think his name was – wearing a dicky-bow and going round the bar afterwards with a tray of gin and tonics. Good fun!"

Orrell put up rather more of a fight before going down 23-18. Astonishingly, it was only Redman's fourth appearance on the Rec during the 1987-88 season but that only underlined how difficult it had been to maintain consistency of selection in the face of representative demands and the long list of injuries.

Bath's exit from the John Player Cup had left Bristol to carry the West Country mantle, cruising past Moseley 34-6 at The Reddings while Harlequins won 20-16 in extra time at Wasps to join them at Twickenham. First, however, there was the small matter of a centenary derby match at the Memorial Ground on 2 April 1988. The sides had first met on 27 October 1888 at the newly opened home of Gloucestershire cricket at Nevil Road, Bath winning 5-3 in front of a crowd estimated at 'between 700 and 800'. Fast-forwarding 100 years, there was something of a careworn atmosphere around the Bath camp as they prepared for a rematch against their near-neighbours. With Halliday opting to play for an Oxford University XV and injuries continuing to rule out Hill and Hall, Bristol scented blood and squeezed out a deserved 16-15 victory in front of their ecstatic supporters.

Coincidentally, Bath met the eventual cup winners a week later at the Rec. Jamie Salmon apart, they made no great impression on Bath who won 21-9. It was no surprise that Hall totally eclipsed Skinner, who had taken his place in the England back row, or that Dawe comfortably saw off the challenge of John Olver for the Dublin Millennium match against Ireland and subsequently for the tour of Australia. The decision to name every member of the squad except the reserve hooker was one of the more bizarre decisions of the England selectors – and there were quite a few of those in the 1980s. With Dean Richards suspended, Egerton won a deserved first cap in Dublin on 23 April, England winning the one-off international 21-10. Chilcott again took the field as a replacement

Meanwhile Bath continued to play for pride, accounting for Newport (22-7) but drawing at home to Llanelli (9-9) before outclassing Clifton (43-nil). The final fixture of a long and trophyless season, a 35-7 victory over Bedford, would not normally merit a mention except for the fact that Bath included a guest player – 37-year-old John Horton whose departure from the Rec in the summer of 1985 had left an unpleasant taste. The club had long wanted to make it up to him and this was the opportunity.

> **Horton's response was typically gracious: "The invitation came as a complete surprise and I'm very grateful. I don't mind admitting I was very nervous beforehand. It was nice to drop the goal," he added, referring to his 80th minute score. Horton was later presented with an inscribed tankard marking his outstanding contribution to the club from 1973 to 1985.**

The man who deposed him, Stuart Barnes, was persuaded at around the same time to end his self-imposed exile from international rugby and was named in the party to tour Australia and Fiji. It was a mistake, as he admitted in his autobiography:

"The bitterness that marred my rugby from 1985 to 1987 reappeared and my emotional wranglings dragged my game downward. It was the same old story: I performed well in the first game, did not gain selection and then disintegrated. When an opportunity was presented, England's forwards always appeared to perform so poorly that I had no opportunity to play. That was how it seemed when I was selected for a side that lost badly to New South Wales. I can see now that while my initial treatment was harsh, I constantly failed to help myself, preferring the soft option of self pity."

England, with Rob Andrew in the No 10 shirt, had lost the first Test 22-16 in Brisbane. Barnes was given his chance against a strong New South Wales side the following weekend but was just as quickly shunted back down to the dirt-trackers after a 23-12 defeat. When Andrew hung on to his place for the Sydney Test which England lost 28-8, Barnes made his dissatisfaction plain to Geoff Cooke in no uncertain terms, as they say. He did start against Fiji, with Andrew shifted to full-back, and England won 25-12 but Barnes's reconciliation with England had been brief and toxic.

For Egerton, capped in the first Test, and Robinson, who made his England debut in Sydney and retained his place in Suva, the experience was far more positive. Redman was regarded by most observers as unlucky not to force his way into the side at the expense of skipper John Orwin until the Fiji leg of the tour. Halliday only played in the Brisbane Test while Moore had the hooker position nailed down ahead of Dawe throughout the tour.

For Chilcott, however, a chink of light had appeared after the first Test. It was obvious that England had been out-scrummaged so, like Barnes, he was given his chance against New South Wales, this time at tight-head.

Subsequent events are still vivid in the big man's memory: "Geoff Cooke came up to me and said 'If you can keep the scrum solid you're in the Test team'. So I found myself up against a chap called Peter Kay, who was moderately famous for being 'the hardest man in Australian rugby' – an ex-biker with long hair, a doorman like me and a Pommy-basher.

"It was a particularly rough and rugged game and I did very well, kept the scrum tight and had him all over the place. When the final whistle went and we were all shaking hands, I sensed something was about to happen. Kay swung this huge haymaker; I sort of ducked and it only half-stunned me. Next thing I was on top of him and as I looked to my right I saw this photographer, lying on the ground taking pictures. There was quite a fuss.

"He started it – I finished it. But he was selected for the next Test and the England management threatened to send me home!" Chilcott was picked for the Fiji Test but still bristles at the injustice, although Kay only ever won that solitary cap.

With so many players being blooded as internationals, the old clubhouse at the Rec began to acquire quite a gallery of stars. Ever since Mike Beese in 1972, any player capped for the first time had a date with a kindly old former committeeman called Reg Monk who would set up a makeshift studio in the members' bar and a new framed studio portrait would soon join the others adorning the walls. Sadly, Reg died in April 1988 only a few weeks after adding Damian Cronin to his collection. If you study them all you will see that the portraits of subsequent internationals are not captured with quite the ineffable style of Reg Monk.

As Bath mulled over the failure of the 1987-88 campaign – they managed only fourth in the first season of the Courage Club Championship – there was intense debate among the players over who was to succeed Hill as club captain.

David Egerton: first cap in Dublin Millennium match.

> **The two contenders were Barnes, preferred by Rowell, and Chilcott, who had been nominated by Hill. Chilcott won by some margin but then, in a remarkable gesture of selflessness, withdrew in favour of the fly-half. It was as if the prop forward knew instinctively what his club needed, that to get the very best out of Barnes he needed to be given responsibility. Time and again, Cooch proved himself an astute judge of people and character, which was why he commanded such respect. Barnes not only set about applying some innovative thinking to the business of leadership – but he also knuckled down to the task of preparing himself physically for the challenge of restoring Bath's reputation.**

The springboard was a tour to the Thailand and Malaysia where Chilcott was a forbidding and unforgiving tour judge resplendent in home-made wig. That was followed by a pre-season 'loosener' in the Netherlands with top French side Toulon. In the Far East the matches were inconsequential affairs with scores of 58, 54 and 80 points but the training was a different matter entirely, starting on the dot at 7.30am every morning. Barnes said on his arrival in the Dutch town of Leiden: "I am training harder at the moment than at any time since I was 17, and that goes for all the players. The benefits have been obvious. The high level of fitness means we can concentrate on skills, individually and collectively at club sessions and more importantly, moves can be rehearsed at high speed. We are hungry again and as tough mentally and physically as we were three years ago."

While that was an acknowledgement that standards had slipped in the previous season it was just as much a statement of intent. The poacher had turned gamekeeper and he meant business!

The sea-change in attitude was obvious from the first minute against French champions Toulon who launched a physical attack on their English opponents. "That was the biggest punch-up I've ever been in," recalls Hall. "I won a line-out off them and got clocked. It just went on and on. It was fearsome." While the forwards fought off their assailants, the backs totted up the points and Bath registered a comfortable 28-7 victory.

> **Barnes can also now laugh at the memory of 'the most violent match I have ever played in'. A couple of years later he bumped into the Toulon coach, the flamboyant Daniel Herrero, always resplendent in red bandana, who immediately took him to task over Bath's behaviour on that August afternoon in Leiden. A disbelieving Barnes questioned Herrero's recall and then noticed a twinkle in the Frenchman's eye: "Then he had the cheek to ask me: 'But for sure you appreciated ze beauty of ze violence?' No, I bloody did not."**

The opening to the season proper could hardly have been more daunting – a visit to the Welsh Merit Table champions, Pontypool, who had lost only two games the previous season. The match was covered live by BBC TV Wales and viewers were treated to a Bath performance of the highest quality, far removed from the limited approach seen in recent Twickenham cup finals.

The outcome was unforgettable as Barnes's team ran in nine tries through Swift, Barnes, Audley Lumsden 2, Halliday, Hall, Redman and finally Barnes again to complete a stunning 50-9 scoreline. The skipper also contributed four conversions and two penalties for a personal haul of 22 points. Perhaps the most enduring memory is of thousands of Pontypool supporters crowding on to the pitch to accord the opposition a standing ovation, their initial hostility transformed into admiration by this exposition of 'total rugby'.

One of the first to congratulate Barnes was the late Ray Gravell in his capacity of TV interviewer. Barnes responded: "We've been criticised in the past for not being adventurous. We've worked a lot on our back play pre-season on tour in the Far East and I think today the dividends were shown. At this stage of the season we are in very good shape, a very confident side."

Among the most spectacular of the Bath performers was young full-back Lumsden, who had first made his debut at full-back in December 1986 but whose development had been stifled the following season by also being required to fill in on the wing and in the centre. Bath used nine different fullbacks during 1987-88 and it was only towards the end of the campaign that Lumsden appeared to be first-choice in the No 16 shirt. When Martin again dislocated his troublesome shoulder early in the new campaign, Lumsden made the position his own.

At Pontypool many of the attacking moves brought Lumsden's coruscating pace into play. Combined with Barnes's generalship, Halliday's directness and Guscott's blossoming talents, not to mention the complementary skills of Sagoe and Swift, it

Audley Lumsden sprints away to score at Pontypool Park (3 September 1988).

was a potent mix. Among the spectators was a newcomer to the Bath squad, a young Nigerian-born prop from Oxford University. As he walked back through the park to the Pontypool clubhouse, Victor Ubogu said to John Hall: "Gosh, I'm going to have to play well to get into this side."

It wasn't just in recruitment, fitness and coaching that Bath sought to gain an edge. This book and its predecessor, Before the Lemons, take their titles from the 19th century tradition of offering players lemons at half-time – eventually replaced by oranges. But at Pontypool, they were replaced by Gatorade drinks, already favoured by Olympic athletes and swimmers as a more scientific way of replacing salts and minerals lost through perspiration.

Barnes explained: "We used it on England's tour of Australia where it was particularly hot and it seemed a good idea to introduce it for club games back home. Frankly, a slice of orange is no use at all; it's just a hangover from the past."

The weather was just as pleasant at Harlequins a week later as Bath put the new John Player Cup champions in their place with a 26-9 away win, the first of the fixed dates now set aside for the Courage League campaign. But the match ended under a cloud after Richard Hill was sent off for punching his opposite number, Richard Moon. As the international scrum-half began a 30-day suspension he began to reflect on his attitude to the game. Was he just too combative for his own good – and that of his team-mates?

The unsung Steve Knight filled in ably, scoring a try in the 40-3 demolition of London Welsh, and celebrating a 19-9 home victory over Gloucester whose forwards were systematically taken apart on the Rec. A smartly taken first-half try by Guscott was followed in the second half by a scrum pushover credited to Egerton and a tapped penalty touchdown by the in-form Morrison. Barnes converted two along with a penalty.

Ubogu announced his arrival with a try in a 22-3 win at Clifton and also set up another for young Cornish lock Martin Haag, who had made his debut a year earlier but had then only been given two more outings. Mindful of the importance of the league campaign, Bath again rested players for the visit of Aberavon and scrambled to a 24-13 victory before turning out in strength at Rosslyn Park.

Chilcott, mystifyingly overlooked by the South West selectors, scored the try that secured a 19-6 win but it was unspectacular stuff, not that Rowell was unduly worried. "It must be appreciated that every league game is still like a cup-tie," said the coach. "Training has been going very well but other sides, Rosslyn Park included, are very fit too. At this stage of the season we've got to be satisfied with the win."

Three days later, on 12 October 1988, there was an opportunity to reflect on the astonishing progress the club had made in the decade since Rowell's arrival. Some months earlier your author had mentioned to the coach that with Egerton's elevation to the England senior side, the club could now field an entire XV of internationals, all of them playing in positions in which they had been capped.

Rowell noted the fact and that was why a match was arranged against Public School Wanderers at the Rec on that Tuesday evening. But for the absence of Scotland's Sole – his wife was in hospital – and Egerton, ruled out by a calf injury, the Dream Team would have taken the field together. Richard Lee, a B international, stepped in for

Bath International XV lines up before taking the field against Public School Wanderers (12 October 1988).

127

Sole while Robinson, even more recently capped than Egerton, came into the back row and Simpson moved to No 8, his role as tormentor of the All Blacks in 1983.

BATH (England unless stated): *S Barnes; D Trick, S Halliday, J Palmer, C Martin; J Horton, R Hill; G Chilcott, G Dawe, R Lee (substituting for D Sole, of Scotland), N Redman, D Cronin* (Scotland), *A Robinson, P Simpson, J Hall.*

The biggest cheer was reserved for John Horton as he jinked under the posts for one of 10 tries in a 54-44 victory. A crowd of over 3,000 raised a sizeable sum for the Great Ormond Street Children's Hospital.

After warming up with a 16-10 win against Orwin's Bedford, Bath prepared to face Bristol at the Rec. There were a few flutters among home supporters as Matthew Skuse and Andy Blackmore dominated the line-out but England fullback Jon Webb had an off-day with his kicking and, once Hill had burrowed over for a try early in the second half, Bath did not look back. A 69th minute dropped goal by Barnes to add to his three earlier penalties secured the 16-9 victory.

Even at this stage of the season, people were talking of Bath as an odds-on bet for the Courage Championship. It was entirely in character therefore that the club should already be looking further afield for a stiffer challenge. On Halloween they welcomed Pierre Villepreux's Stade Toulousain to the Rec in a forerunner of the European club fixtures that are so much part of the rugby calendar today. Although missing leading lights such as Denis Charvet and Eric Bonneval, Toulouse earned a 24-24 draw with second-half tries by Didier Codorniou and Jean-Philip Canavy.

Both coaches were enthusiastic about the possibilities opened up by such matches, Rowell saying: "It was tremendous rugby and I'm sure we learned a lot from it." Villepreux, capped 34-times at fullback by France, concurred: "I am very pleased, both with the success of the whole venture and with our performance today."

Within ten years, the tiny seeds sown with the aristocrats of French rugby were to bear fruit in the most spectacular fashion when Bath became the first English team to lift the Heineken Cup.

Chapter 8

A STAR IN THE WEST

Twenty or so years ago, if you wanted an honest, straightforward appraisal of an up-and-coming Bath player it was always worth talking to the lean, athletic looking pensioner who helped park the cars on match day behind the Flowerpots Stand.

Alec Lewis: veteran of El Alamein.

His name? Alec Lewis. When he was their age he was a Desert Rat, already a veteran of El Alamein and preparing to fight his way up through Italy with the Eighth Army. After surviving a brush with an anti-personnel mine, he was eventually demobbed and spent a few seasons playing soccer before arriving at the Rec. A wing forward who was equally comfortable at centre, Alec was 31 before he won his first England cap but he went on to play ten times for his country.

He then embarked on a successful selectorial career and, as mentioned previously in this history, was manager of the England team who pulled off a shock win in South Africa in 1972.

"Of all the players, Jeremy Guscott is the one who really excites me," he told your author one afternoon in October 1988. "It's the poise and pace in his running – much like Carl Lewis – so effortless and deceptive. Yet he can tackle, pass and kick and reads the game well."

Alec's opinion on Guscott was endorsed by the national selectors when a few days later they named the 23-year-old bricklayer in the England B team to face the touring Wallabies at Sale.

Bath-born Guscott had scored a remarkable 21 tries in 37 games during the ill-starred 1987-88 season but his precocious talents had really come to public notice when highlights of the rout at Pontypool were shown on BBC Grandstand. In those days devotees of the game were not well served by TV and were certainly not treated to wall-to-wall coverage as they are now, with expert analysis from every angle, aided by 'slow-mo' and high-definition technology. You were just thankful if you knew what time on a Sunday afternoon (or evening) the BBC would be transmitting dear old Rugby Special.

Slightly embarrassed by the growing level of attention and predictions of a glittering international career, Guscott said at the time: "At the moment my personal ambition is to stay in the South West

Jeremy Guscott: England B call-up against the touring Australians at Sale.

side. Anything else is a bonus and there's no point in building up my hopes only to be disappointed.

"The difference this year is that I've carried on where I left off last season. Until now I've not been that consistent at the start. No one player has particularly influenced me but I watch rugby on television and try to pick things up. Of course, in the Bath set-up with so many good players around you it's not too difficult to play well."

You didn't really need an RFU coaching qualification to appreciate the seemingly effortless way Guscott would drop his shoulder and accelerate through the narrowest of gaps. That was what set him apart – that and his finishing ability – but he confessed that he had not really been regarded as a great sprinter at Batheaston Junior School or at Ralph Allen Comprehensive.

"I wasn't that quick, to be honest. But after moving out of the Bath Youth side to senior rugby I worried a little about having to play against grown men. I wanted to make sure that they never got near me! So I worked on my pace at the time and it developed from there."

Although the gloss was taken off Guscott's England B debut by the 37-9 scoreline, distinguished by a David Campese hat-trick, the newcomer was given an immediate opportunity for revenge when the South West lined up against the Australians at Bristol four days later. There were eight Bath men in a team captained by Guscott's centre partner, Simon Halliday, and the tourists were roundly defeated 26-10 with Barnes contributing 18 points from a try and conversion and four penalties. Other tries went to Halliday and the Gloucester prop, Malcolm Preedy.

Ten days later Halliday crowned a hugely encouraging outing for a new-look England side under Will Carling by coasting in from 40 metres for the last of four tries in a 28-19 victory. Robinson was outstanding against the Australian loose forwards and Egerton played a full part on the blind-side flank.

Meanwhile, Ubogu was on the scoresheet again in Bath's 25-12 win at Llanelli and the squad came together in good heart for the next Courage League match. To say that the Bath players were looking forward to the trip to Moseley – and a chance to wipe out the memory of their cup exit the previous February – was something of an understatement. Sure enough, Guscott scored a hat-trick and other tries flowed at regular intervals from Hall (2), Egerton, Robinson and Lumsden. Three conversions from Guscott completed the vengeful 38-nil scoreline.

And Bath made it six league wins out of six the following weekend when Stuart Barnes returned from ankle trouble to guide the club to a 36-12 win over Orrell on the Rec, making it six league wins out of six. Guscott added two more tries to his growing tally and even if Hall could not get into the South West divisional side he consoled himself after a 16-9 win over Wasps with the thought that "this is the best Bath side in my experience."

Such was the air of invincibility surrounding the Rec that the more ambitious individuals within the club began looking around for bigger fish to fry. Tom Hudson, fitness and conditioning guru, came straight out with it: they wanted to play the All Blacks.

As the man who had helped Carwyn James prepare the Llanelli side which beat Ian Kirkpatrick's tourists in 1972, he did speak with some authority on the subject.

"We need stronger and more varied opposition to develop properly," he insisted. "Taking on the All Blacks here would create tremendous interest. I cannot see the point in English Students or Combined Services playing major tourists. It's a nonsense and serves no useful purpose," added Hudson as he prepared to deliver a presentation at Twickenham on the subject of 'the Bath philosophy'.

Hudson, a member of Britain's Modern Pentathlon team at the 1956 Olympics, had become the University of Bath's first Director of Physical Recreation in 1971. Blessed with an academic's propensity to think the unthinkable – and more to the point 'say the unsayable' – he seemed to delight in upsetting the many traditionalists within rugby union, most notably when he called for the establishment of trust funds for players. At first the Bath committee were a little embarrassed but by New Year 1989 they were saying: "He's just five years ahead of his time."

Already, the sacred principle of amateurism was under threat, undermined by the escalating demands made on senior players. 'Boot money' had been commonplace in South Wales and the game in France and South Africa was awash with cash; New Zealanders and Australians were openly endorsing commercial products.

No doubt there was money for some in the English game – and Bath were at that time negotiating a three-year £155,000 sponsorship deal with the South Western Electricity Board – but it didn't amount to much. Far more significant was the ability to find employment for players. The late Dave Robson, as well as being one of the coaching triumvirate with Rowell and Hudson, used his network of business contacts with increasing energy and ingenuity to ensure that players he recruited were able to lay down roots in Bath.

But this was nothing new in the sport of rugby union – it was just that Bath, being Bath, approached the task of player recruitment and development with a systematic sense of purpose. 'Job search and selection' was part of the package.

What was significantly different was the increase in the number of England squad sessions and on 5 January 1989, Chilcott, Robinson, Egerton and Halliday flew out to Portugal for a training camp in Portugal. As soon as they were back, with the exception of Halliday who was still regaining full fitness after a knee operation, they flew out to the Canaries with the Bath squad.

Meanwhile the self-imposed international exile of Barnes and Hall allowed them to strut their stuff in devastating style against Cardiff on the Rec. On the final whistle, the new electronic scoreboard read 'Bath 35 Cardiff 4' – their biggest win since the first fixture between the sides on Christmas Eve 1924.

On their return from Lanzarote, the club made it eight from eight in the Courage League after a 21-7 victory at Liverpool St Helens, Guscott and Egerton sharing the four tries. Guscott collected four more in a 64-21 rout at Metropolitan Police the following Wednesday afternoon to take his tally to 18 for the season and Bath opened their cup campaign – now sponsored by glass manufacturer Pilkington – with an even bigger score, 82-9, against hapless Oxford. It was another occasion to savour the slashing breaks from full-back of Audley Lumsden who led the 16-try rout with four of his own.

Robson had no hesitation in declaring the youngster the "best fullback in England," before adding: "Of course, he's incredibly quick but the difference is that the timing of his runs into the three-quarter line has improved 500 per cent. I've never known a player so willing to work to improve his game."

The man actually in possession of the England No 15 shirt was Dr Jon Webb, of Bristol and only two Bath players, Halliday and Robinson, faced the Scots at Twickenham on 4 February. After all the promise of the win over Australia, this was a depressing 12-12 draw.

The Bath pair, joined by Chilcott as replacement for the concussed Jeff Probyn, did play their part in a performance of more character than quality in defeating Ireland 16-3 in Dublin however. Two weeks later, on 4 March 1989, all three celebrated an 11-nil win over France at Twickenham, particularly Robinson who scored the clinching try.

Only Wales – without a win – stood in England's way. But on a mucky day in Cardiff, Robert Norster's line-out excellence, Robert Jones's tactical nous at scrum-half and Paul Thorburn's goalkicking eked out a 12-9 victory and France took the title despite losing at Murrayfield.

As a spectacle, the 1989 Five Nations Championship had been tense and unedifying, certainly no grand stage for elegant runners such as Halliday. But for combative forwards such as Robinson and Chilcott it provided the ideal opportunity to promote their match-winning credentials to the men selecting players for the Lions tour of Australia in the summer.

But were the Lions strategists prepared to look beyond national teams? When Bath won 20-4 at Llanelli in the first week of February, Lions selector Derek Quinnell was seen in earnest conversation with Bath officials, far from convinced apparently that England were wise to discard talent of the calibre of Hill, Barnes and Hall. Yet it was Guscott who was to come with a run on the outside.

After a 48-nil defeat of Midlands First Division opponents Hereford in the Pilkington Cup fourth round, Bath's 38-match unbeaten run finally ended at Kingsholm. Bath were without their three England players and Barnes but Gloucester were good value for their 18-12 victory and the visitors, perhaps regretting a decision to prefer Damian Cronin above the stronger-scrummaging Jon Morrison, failed to score a try for the first time in very nearly a year.

As ever, No 8 Egerton accurately summed up their shortcomings. "Rugby is 50 per cent heart and attitude and they certainly seemed more committed," he admitted. "We won little clean ball and they smothered what possession we did manage to obtain. And when we were starting to get into our stride they got an interception which led to the try."

There was no time to dwell on the defeat though – not with the small matter of a home Pilkington Cup quarter-final with Bristol to prepare for. On the day, however, the greatest influence on the contest was the weather – it was simply awful, possibly the worst conditions ever seen at the Rec. Yet in every sense the deluge added to the drama.

Bath wanted a postponement but referee Andrew Mason agreed with Bristol that the Recreation Ground pitch was playable – just. Great lakes of water lay across the pitch, especially in the in-goal areas; elsewhere there were swathes of mud, glutinous in some places, slippery in others. The match was decided 14-12 in Bath's favour by a Richard Hill try three minutes from time, pouncing on the proverbial 'bar of soap' at the back of a Bristol scrum.

Jon Webb, immaculate at full-back for Bristol despite the conditions, scored all Bristol's points from a try and conversion plus two penalties while Jeremy Guscott splashed over for Bath – "like a canoeist shooting the rapids" – and Barnes kicked two penalties immediately after the break.

Mud, glorious mud: relief rather than revelry from Gareth Chilcott and John Hall after the tightest of quarter-final victories over Bristol (25 February 1989).

Even after the final whistle, which prompted wild water-ballet celebrations by the Bath players, Rowell was not convinced the match should have gone ahead. "It was

After the mud bath, the clean-up.

a lottery," he said. "We were lucky to win. Really, it was down to willpower – collective will we call it here at Bath. Rugby playing ability did not come into it. At 12-4 down I had my doubts. When we failed to score from all those put-ins on the Bristol line, I thought it was all over."

A week later an unbeaten home record stretching back more than a year was surrendered to Swansea for whom Robert Jones, in pole position for the Lions scrum-half spot, was the key performer in a 15-13 win. By the end of the game, the Bath XV included no more than four first-teamers as attention began to focus on the visit of Nottingham a week later, a match that was destined to bring the Courage League title to the Roman city.

Player welfare was now becoming a live issue, particularly regarding Andy Robinson who had

134

been involved in a league, cup or international match every Saturday since the New Year. But when Rowell tried to persuade the 23-year-old flanker to sit out the Nottingham match, Robinson was having none of it. Winning matches and trophies was what he lived for.

The RFU blazers turned up in force for the coronation at the Rec on 11 March 1989 and the trophy was there too. Stuart Barnes caught a glimpse of it beforehand and his blood ran cold – it had already been inscribed 'Bath 1988-89'! "Talk about tempting fate ... I'm superstitious enough as it is," he said. "And I had been trying to persuade everyone that this was not the foregone conclusion they imagined it to be."

True enough, Nottingham, well-organised and with an effective back row predator in 17 times-capped Gary Rees, made life uncommonly difficult for the champions-elect before succumbing 22-16. Bath's tries came from Egerton and Lumsden, his 18th of the season, but it was injury time before Barnes dropped the goal that effectively sealed the title. The 'Little General' had also kicked three penalties and a conversion, his 200th of the campaign.

After receiving the trophy from RFU president Sandy Sanders, Barnes led his team on a lap of honour in front of 7,000 ecstatic supporters. The table could not have been more conclusive – nine games played, nine won, 213 points for and just 74 against. The nearest challengers were Orrell who had lost twice and drawn one other game.

But this was a job only half-done. Rowell and his cohorts wanted the 'double' of league and cup and nothing was going to stand in the way, as a dismayed Bristol soon discovered. With a Pilkington Cup semi-final at Gloucester on 25 March, Rowell

The Rec rises to salute the new 1989 Courage League champions – and it's only 11 March.

made it clear to the Management Committee that he was simply not prepared to field a team for the scheduled fixture at the Memorial Ground on 14 March. The match was off!

Bristol, faced with the loss of considerable sponsorship income from their biggest home game of the season, reacted with shock and then with considerable anger. The Bath committee could only shrug their shoulders shamefacedly and offer to forfeit home advantage the following October – but the ill-feeling persisted. Two decades later we can see this break in club solidarity as a warning tremor triggered by the opposing forces of amateurism and professionalism. The two clubs were on opposite sides of the divide.

Absolved of the need to put bodies on the line against Bristol, Bath contented themselves with a fairly gentle 55-nil run-out against Ebbw Vale on the eve of the Wales-England game. With Cronin being tipped in some quarters to earn a second row spot against Gloucester, Redman and Morrison slammed the door on the Scottish international with a definitive combined performance.

Sure enough, they repeated their double-act in the semi-final at Kingsholm where consistent pressure in the scrums, cleaner possession in the line-out and mastery of the loose were the key ingredients for a 6-3 victory which was more conclusive than it sounds. Two penalties from Barnes to one from home full-back Tim Smith accounted for the points as Bath enjoyed 75 per cent territorial possession.

If ever there was a game made for a tight forward prop like Richard Lee, this was it. "That was a real bruiser," said the 29-year-old farmer from Wellington afterwards, "the sort of affair when, even by Monday morning, you wake up knowing instantly you've been in one hell of a game."

Lee added: "We knew after losing our unbeaten record at Kingsholm last month

Richard Lee: 'an unsung hero'.

that it would be necessary to match physically everything they could throw at us. As a result there were twice as many scrums as usual and precious little creative play by the backs. For front row forwards it was like being on a double shift. It was hard going from start to finish ... although the end result was ever so satisfying."

As if to prove it, Lee had to pull out of a Barbarians match at Swansea on the Monday with a strained back. But already, coaching staff and players were looking ahead to meeting Leicester at Twickenham on 29 April.

One of the reasons for publishing a history of this type is the opportunity to acknowledge the value of someone like Lee, who fell short of full international honours but played a crucial role in Bath's success. Titles were rarely decided by

David Egerton moves in as John Hall wraps up John Gadd in the Pilkington Cup semi-final at Gloucester (25 March 1989).

flamboyant displays of running rugby, but more often by lung-bursting graft in the rain and mud when games were decided by the odd score.

> **Lee was part of the folklore of the Rec, as John Hall remembers: "Richard was a fantastic character, who drove a Morris Mini Minor van. Of course we'd have a drink after games. In the early morning I'd wander back to the car park to pick up a kit bag and he'd be asleep in the van, sleeping off the alcohol before he had to get back to the farm and milk the cows. He was an amazing character and as a player he had his moments – he was in the England set-up for a while. Richard was a great player for the club."**

That view is echoed by Rowell today: "Richard Lee was outstanding ... an unsung hero."

By 29 March, only one game mattered – and it was not the visit to Plymouth Albion that evening. Richard Hill was among a handful of first-teamers who made the trip to Beacon Park and there was generally a lack of focus and application about the Bath effort, so much so that they led only 20-19 with a few minutes left.

Cue nudged them further ahead with a dropped goal but no Bath player attempted to claim the restart kick and Lumsden was suddenly left to make a head-on tackle in front of his own posts to deny Plymouth centre Frank Meakin. Bath cleared the danger and pulled away in injury time with a Trick penalty and an interception try by Guscott but by this time Lumsden had been taken off the field, clearly in a bad way and complaining of numbness in his limbs.

At hospital the problem was diagnosed as fractures to two vertebrae. Although it was thought the young fullback would make a full recovery there was absolutely no prospect of him being fit to play in the Pilkington Cup final. Of course, the prognosis could have been even worse but it was a savage blow to a player whose incursions from fullback had given Bath the sharpest of cutting edges in attack. His tally of 20 tries so far that season was a remarkable statistic in itself and it had been only earlier that month that he had won an England B cap against France at Leicester.

Fielding United-strength sides for the next two fixtures, Bath bumbled to defeat at Bridgend (23-3) and also at home to Newport (13-17) whose match winner was their 23-year-old full-back, Jonathan Callard, scoring an opportunist try and three penalties.

Equilibrium was restored on 8 April with a 38-9 win over Waterloo in which Cronin again turned up the heat on the semi-final pairing of Morrison-Redman with two tries, one of them a particularly athletic effort from near half-way. There was also the question of who would replace Lumsden at full-back, so there was more than a little interest in Palmer's outing for a second string at South Wales Police the following Wednesday evening. Despite a 37-4 defeat, the former captain kept the No 16 shirt (still no number 13 in those days) for the visit of Llanelli three days later.

Having already announced his retirement, Palmer was given a rousing reception from the supporters for his final home game; remarkably it was 14 years to the day since he had made his first appearance on the Rec against Cardiff on 15 April 1975. With a more recognisable line-up in front of him, Palmer ended any debate about his fitness with a typically inventive display and Guscott ended a relatively lean spell with four tries to bring his tally for the season to 25. Simpson, Hall and Swift were the other try scorers in a 43-25 victory while Palmer landed a conversion and Barnes kicked two more plus three penalties.

Seven days out from the big occasion at Twickenham, Simon Halliday was insistent that mere victory at Twickenham would not satisfy their hunger for recognition of their achievements. "That would prove nothing," said the England centre. "Not only do we know we're the best side in England – everybody else knows it too. But on the big occasion, and certainly in our last two finals, we have not shown what we are capable of."

It was already known that the Twickenham showdown with Leicester on 29 April would be a sell-out, setting a world record attendance for a club game of 58,000. The club had booked two trains and 31 coaches for supporters and there were countless other excursions organised by local rugby clubs and pubs.

"If we can't do it in those circumstances, will we ever?" asked Halliday. "For our own satisfaction, we must establish such superiority that people will regard us in a different light. We were so far ahead of the other clubs three or four years ago but they learned from us and caught up. Now we have the chance to stretch ahead again, to set new standards."

Having lost Lumsden to such a tragic injury, Halliday conceded that Bath were fortunate in having Palmer to call on, providing the 32-year-old with a grand stage for his retirement. "I played alongside JP for a long time and an understanding has developed," he said. "We know exactly where each other is going to run, although Audley Lumsden's injury is a great loss. He added an extra dimension to our back play."

Bizarrely, the cup finalists were scheduled to complete the Courage League campaign at Welford Road seven days before their Twickenham date. The trophy had been sitting in the Bath clubhouse for more than a month so both sides suggested that the Pilkington final should also count as the now-meaningless league fixture. But the RFU ordered the game to be played – so both sides picked reserve teams, to a chorus of protests from their counterparts within the Senior Clubs Association. Leicester, fielding a promising 19-year-old lock called Martin Johnson, won 15-12 to spoil Bath's unblemished record in the Courage League.

On the big day, however, it was Bath who prevailed – but only just, 10-6. Despite Halliday's fervent hopes for a spectacular display of attacking prowess, both sides became locked in a tense battle of nerves and will. At no stage had Bath been concerned, maintained John Palmer afterwards: "Six-nil down at half-time? No problem ... that's easily the best start we've had on this ground. Leicester shook us in the first half. But it would have been impossible for them to maintain the same commitment for a full 80 minutes."

Here we are again! Jack Rowell, John Hall and Victor Ubogu stride through Twickenham's
West Car Park on 29 April 1989.

Dean Richards looks on as Richard Hill fires out a pass from a scrum.

So it proved. Despite the loss of Egerton with damaged knee ligaments on 53 minutes, the Bath forwards began to crank up the pressure and Barnes kicked two penalties to bring his side level before scampering through a gap on the blindside with two minutes of normal time remaining.

Rowell's decision to play Cronin rather than Redman was vindicated by the Scottish international's mastery of the line-out and high-stepping drives in the loose. Simpson also added vigour to the forward effort when coming on as replacement for Egerton.

"Never in doubt!" growled Chilcott with a huge grin as they prepared to celebrate an historic league and cup 'double'. The contrast in moods was summed up by the two full-backs, Palmer ending his career on the biggest 'high' while Dusty Hare was forced to console himself with a warm ovation from both sets of supporters after bowing out as the world's record points scorer. Then it was back to Bath for the customary civic reception followed by the now obligatory Sunday party at the Rowells' residence on High Bannerdown.

BATH: *J A Palmer; A H Swift, S J Halliday, J C Guscott, F K Sagoe; S Barnes* (capt)*, R J Hill; G J Chilcott, R G R Dawe, M R Lee, J S C Morrison, D F Cronin, R A Robinson, D W Egerton (Simpson 52 mins), J P Hall.*

LEICESTER: *W H Hare; B J Evans, P W Dodge (capt), I Bates, R Underwood; L Cusworth, A Kardooni; S Redfern, T Thacker, W P Richardson, M V Foulkes-Arnold, T Smith, J M Wells, D Richards, I R Smith.*

REFEREE: *F Howard* (Liverpool).

When the Lions squad was named to fly out to Australia on 3 June it included Robinson and Chilcott – the first Bath players to be picked for a post-1910 Lions tour. Injuries and disillusion with the international scene had blunted the claims of others such as Halliday, Barnes, Hill and Hall.

Try scorer Stuart Barnes lifts the trophy to complete Bath's first league and cup 'double'.

Almost immediately came news that England captain Will Carling had pulled out of the tour with shin splints, but what was not generally known was that Lions coach Ian McGeechan had been on the phone to Jack Rowell inquiring about Guscott. Rowell rang Guscott on the Bank Holiday May Day morning to alert him but added: "Don't build your hopes up too high though; they're talking to other players and coaches." So Guscott put down the phone and thought little more about it until he received a call next day from tour manager Clive Rowlands to confirm his selection – the wildest of wild cards.

At that stage, Guscott was still uncapped by England but that was remedied on 13 May when he made his entry on to the international stage with a silky hat-trick against Romania in Bucharest. It was all happening for the bricklayer from Walcot. His finishing ability and sheer star quality had also attracted interest from Rugby League clubs, particularly St Helens and Wigan. Guscott's autobiography recounts in some detail their ultimately unsuccessful efforts to sign him but, even as he was packing his bags for Australia, he acknowledged to your author the dilemma he faced.

"I'm obviously going to be interested in what they say and what price they are coming in with," he said. "I mean, every player's got his price. It really depends on how much you're going to give up to go. I'd have to be offered enough money to buy a house here, buy a house up there and come back with a lot of money." And then he mused: "But I love Bath too much to leave." And so it proved.

There were no such distractions for Robinson or Chilcott, who had worked hard to overcome a calf injury, and when the trio set off to join the party in London on 31 May, they had to hire a mini-bus to accommodate all their kit. Did they know that they were the first Bath players to tour with a joint Home Unions representative team since R J Rogers (Great Britain to Australia & New Zealand 1904) and before that F C Belson (Australia 1899)? Almost certainly not.

Robinson suspected from the outset that his route into the Test team was firmly blocked by the captain, Finlay Calder, but both Chilcott and Guscott found themselves on the bench for the first Test in Sydney on 28 June. A resounding 30-12 defeat exposed any number of shortcomings in that original selection but it was Guscott who profited, receiving the best possible 24th birthday present on 7 July when he was named to partner Scott Hastings in the centre for the Brisbane Test.

The match was finely balanced when a 76th minute Gavin Hastings try put the Lions 13-12 ahead but there was still time for Guscott to deliver the coup de grace in exquisite style. Confronted by a flat Australian defence, Guscott slipped through a little grubber kick which bounced up invitingly on the other side for the Bath man to gather gratefully and score under the posts. Back home in front of their TVs, Bath supporters leapt to their feet in acclamation, the more knowledgeable of them spotting that this was a well-known John Palmer ploy picked up by the young pupil. Retained for the third and final Test, Guscott celebrated with the rest as the Lions won 19-18 to clinch their first series win since 1974. A star had been born.

Meanwhile his club had been planning a pre-season warm-up against Toulouse, only to discover that the French had set them up in a four-team tournament with Brive and Neath. Club secretary Clive Howard made clear to their hosts that they would play only French opposition.

Before leaving for France, however, they took on the Home Office over England Colts flanker Steve Ojomoh who had been threatened with deportation to the country of his birth, Nigeria. Negotiations began to obtain the work permit and visa which would allow him to stay in the UK.

When a makeshift Bath team did make it to France, bolstered by the presence of their new Lion in Robinson, they defeated Brive 16-10 on their home ground. And even though only five first teamers were available on the Sunday for a near midnight kick-off against Toulouse in the agreeably rustic surroundings of Pompadour, Bath won 16-11 against all the odds – especially after wing Steve Walklin was sent off for dissent! Having steered his side expertly through both games, Barnes hoisted the Rugby Tournoi du Bas Limousin trophy.

Even now, Barnes rates that seldom-acknowledged victory over the Toulousain among his most memorable as Bath captain. A glance through the Bath team that took the field that night will tell you why: Mark Westcott; Steve Walklin, Alastair Saverimutto, Keith Hoskin, Peter Blackett; Stuart Barnes, Richard Hill; Victor Ubogu, Graham Dawe, Richard Lee, Jon Morrison, Martin Haag, Adrian Bick, Peter Miles, Kevin Withey. With absolutely no disrespect to loyal members of the United and Spartans, such as Westcott, Hoskin and Miles, they had no right to win with just five first teamers.

The achievement was overshadowed however by the abandonment of the Brive-Neath match earlier in the evening after three dismissals and a petulant walk-off by the Welsh Cup holders. For the 50 or so Bath supporters who had been following their team's progress, however, it just added extra drama to an enjoyable weekend in the Dordogne, fortified by good wine and food, excellent company and some enthusiastic serenading of the locals!

The 1989-90 season proper opened with a 23-8 home win over Pontypool, notable for a promising debut by Jon Callard. The ex-Newport full-back scored a try on his second outing as Harlequins were beaten 32-12 on the Rec – it should have been 34-12 but Barnes rather too nonchalantly struck a close range conversion of his own try under the bar. Man of the match was Hall, scorer of the first try and making none too subtle a point to the England selectors by his domination of Mickey Skinner.

A week later came a visit from the Rumanian army side, Steaua Bucharest, in a fixture brokered by Glyn Maddocks, Bath-based UK adviser to the Romanian Rugby Federation. The visitors had no answer to the speed and intensity set by the half-back pairing of Barnes and Hill and lost 35-12. Steaua fielded 12 internationals including the Rumanian captain, Florica Murariu, who scored both his side's tries from five-metre scrums.

Hampered by injuries, Steaua had asked to borrow a player to fill their replacements' bench. A slightly hesitant David Trick was 'volunteered' and when the centre, Vasile David, was carried off with a leg injury after just 20 minutes, an unmistakably English voice was heard to say plaintively: "But he looks perfectly OK to me!"

The match would have remained an interesting staging post in Bath's efforts to widen their rugby horizons had it not been for events surrounding the extraordinarily rapid break-up of the Soviet-controlled Eastern Bloc.

After Romania lost 32-nil to Scotland at Murrayfield on 9 December – a month after the fall of the Berlin Wall – the young lock, Christian Raducanu, eluded his Securitate minders in a pub run by former Scotland prop Norrie Rowan and applied for political asylum. Back in Romania, the regime of Nicolae Ceausescu eventually collapsed and on Christmas Day the dictator and his wife were arrested, sentenced to death by a hastily convened military court and machine-gunned against a wall. On the same day the aforementioned Murariu, a 34-year-old army officer and veteran of more than 70 Tests including the 1987 World Cup campaign, was shot dead at a road block by a trigger-happy fellow soldier.

His memory and that of another casualty of the uprising, coach Raducu Durbac, are preserved at the Heroes Monument within Steaua's Ghencea stadium in Bucharest.

Meanwhile, Bath set about defending their league and cup titles. By this time Rowell was managing director of Golden Wonder Foods, commuting to Market Harborough in Leicestershire, but he showed no sign of easing off on his rugby responsibilities. In fact during the summer he had added Chairman of Selectors to his role as Head Coach. "To me, it's just like running a business," he said as he prepared the team for the perennially challenging trip to Gloucester. "But the hard work really begins when you have to maintain success. In other words, you have to keep that edge on your competitors."

Twenty years on David Egerton offers an illuminating perspective on the dynamics of 'the team that Jack built': "As a board director, Jack would have understood the dynamics of the social environment within the club as it was evolving and changing. You had to have a flexible framework within which each player is autonomous in his decision-making as an individual. But, most importantly, that player must understand the decisions that other members of the team are making and then support them.

> **"There was no Plan A or Plan B. We would get into a huddle and someone would say: 'Why the hell aren't we winning the ball? The No 7 is killing it.' Or Swifty would say: 'Just get the ball out to us a bit quicker. There's stacks of space out here.' And then we'd agree: 'OK, this is how we are going to do it'. The players were doing the thinking and decision-making but they were doing it with tools and strategy and tactics which had been coached into them and also they'd been bright enough to take on board the need to think for themselves."**

The scale of the task facing Rowell was evident in a 13-6 defeat at Gloucester where Chilcott was sent off two minutes into the second half for a comparatively innocuous punch and an ill-judged fly-hack by Morrison presented hooker Kevin Dunn with the clinching try. Egerton had crossed for Bath.

Two try debut for 18-year-old Adedayo Adebayo.

Spirits were quickly lifted by a two-try debut from an 18-year-old winger called Adedayo Adebayo in a 40-15 midweek romp against South Wales Police. The Nigerian-born youngster then found himself at centre three days later for the trip to The Gnoll where Neath had not lost for 18 months in a sequence of 34 matches. His inclusion was forced by the need to switch Guscott to fly-half in the absence of Barnes but Adebayo produced the goods yet again, jinking past two defenders and enabling Egerton to set up a try for Lee. Swift added another and a penalty and conversion from Callard clinched a 17-14 win.

Adebayo, delighted at being given his head so soon, said: "The great thing about Bath is that they never say, as some clubs do: 'You're not old enough.' That's rubbish. If you are good enough, it doesn't matter how young you are." At Aberavon a week later, Bath fielded Adebayo and three other members of the England Under-21 squad in Saverimutto, Ojomoh and Spencer Bromley and won 32-6.

It was a good job that the young bloods were stepping up because too many of the old hands were dropping out of contention. Following Chilcott's dismissal at Kingsholm – the Lions tourist and unofficial 'folk hero', was relieved to find that his offence merited only a 30-day ban – Hall was sent off in the league match at home to Rosslyn Park. Having already been warned for illegal use of the boot in a ruck he overstepped the mark with a late body check on visiting skipper Tony Brooks. Hall had been an early try scorer and others followed from Halliday, Swift 2, Barnes and Callard with Barnes adding five conversions in a 34-6 victory. As it was his first sending-off Hall received the mandatory 30 days from Somerset RFU disciplinary committee.

Bath set great store by their 'Jeux Sans Frontieres' approach to competition so a tame 26-14 defeat at home to Toulon on 21 October came as something of a shock, prompting a rare public admission of disappointment from Rowell: "I was appalled," he said. "We were so short of desire – which isn't Bath." Despite a well-taken hat-trick from Swift, Bath were undone by Eric Champ's athletic work at the tail of the line-out and the sheer panache of the French back line. It was a taste of tougher challenges to come in Europe.

With a visit to the Memorial Ground to follow and Bristol unbeaten in the Courage League, the onus was suddenly on the 'double champions' to recover some semblance of form. On the kind of horrible, squally afternoon that signals the onset of winter, Bristol were seemingly home and hosed when Jon Webb's third penalty put the home side 13-6 ahead on 57 minutes – Paul Collings had scored their try after nine minutes. But Barnes roused his side with a blind-side break that created the space for a Swift try and seven minutes from time left wing Blackett collected a long pass from his mate, Guscott, to give Bath a 14-13 victory.

Barnes maintained that on a dry day Bath would have won by ten points: "Even today, in a hurricane, we were the only side to show anything outside the scrum. Bristol did compete very well for an hour or so but then they blew up."

As rugby prepared to enter the 1990s, there was much debate about professionalism or, more accurately, allowing players to be compensated for the costly demands made by rugby on time normally committed to work and family. Former Gloucester prop Mike Burton believed that Rugby Union stars were destined to be the marketing man's dream and would soon receive £100,000 or more a year in commercial earnings. "Rugby players are highly articulate – given the odd prop or two," he said. "They fit the bill – no rings in the ears, no tattoos, and by and large they are from the top AB groups."

At Bath, however, club officials were increasingly concerned at the limitations of the Recreation Ground as a major sports venue. Approaches to purchase the land had

It's a forwards' game ... Bath end Bristol's unbeaten Courage League run by squeezing out a 14-13 win at the Memorial Ground (28 October 1989).

been rebuffed by the council but there were plans to construct a new press box to accommodate all the journalists wanting to cover the matches.

The main concern though was with spectator comfort – even safety after Bath beat Moseley 27-9 on the Rec to go to the top of the Courage League. A 69-year-old ex-Royal Navy hooker, Jack Andrews, was treated for cuts and abrasions to his legs after being trapped under an advertising hoarding as players rushed to join a scuffle on the touchline.

"It's a good job I'm a tough old bugger," said the former Bath and Somerset player as he cradled a large, restorative Scotch afterwards. "I could have been killed. There were half a dozen players fighting on top of me and one lady said I was going blue." It transpired that it was Nigel Redman who intervened to avert a possible tragedy. "I saw this elderly man trapped under the board and started pulling players off," said the lock. "The trouble was that a Moseley forward thought I was attacking his team-mates and whacked me from behind. It was very confused."

Moseley centre Chris Spowart was sent off for sparking things off by running 20 metres to punch Robinson and, mindful of the Hillsborough Disaster just six months previously, the Bath club quickly reversed their experiment to bring the advertising hoardings closer to the pitch to accommodate an extra rank of spectators.

The common view of Bath, expressed by Will Carling among others, was that this was very much a forward-orientated side with talented backs who under-achieved. "They win games through their forwards and then release their backs – never the other way round," said the England captain. "It's tragic that our leading club doesn't play more adventurous rugby because they have the most talented squad in the country."

The league table certainly suggested that other sides were closing the gap on Bath but Rowell maintained that his team was in a transitional phase. "What people do not seem to have realised yet – and I am talking about other clubs and the media as well – is that we have changed direction. We are now playing a more expansive game, encouraging our forwards to operate as backs and vice-versa." The statistics – 17 tries and just three penalty goals in five league matches – seemed to bear out his contention but it took a third penalty from Barnes on the final whistle to earn a 9-6 victory at Orrell.

A week later, Bath journeyed to Sudbury to face Wasps, one of the main threats to their league crown. Rowell had cancelled the customary Tuesday training session, preferring to leave the players to discover whether they still had "the desire." It was a master stroke.

While Adebayo deputised for Guscott, who was playing for the Barbarians against the All Blacks less than ten miles down the road at Twickenham, Wasps' Rob Andrew had declined the invitation. The Lions fly-half soon found himself on the end of a devastating Adebayo tackle which knocked the ball loose for Barnes and Hill to set up a try for Swift.

Andrew took some time to shake off the effects and eventually landed all his sides points with a penalty and converted try but with Robinson in top form and Hall an able deputy at No 8 for the injured Egerton, Bath had already squeezed the life out of the Londoners' challenge. Swift snapped up an interception try and Blackett added another before Dawe forced his way over for the fourth try early in the second half. Just as significantly, Saracens full-back Sean Robinson (brother of Andy), scored a try in a 21-21 draw at Kingsholm which dented Gloucester's league ambitions.

Barnes, Swift, Hall and Chilcott had already declared their lack of interest in the unloved Divisional Championship. That signalled the end of Chilcott's international career after 14 caps and just months after the Lions' tour of Australia where he had been a proud member of 'Donal's Donuts', the midweek team led by Donal Lenihan. 'Cooch' had just turned 33.

The Divisional Championship was viewed by the RFU as essential to the task of assembling an England team for the 1990 Five Nations Championship and for the development of a squad capable of winning the 1991 World Cup. So for those who had been capped against Fiji on 4 November – Hill, reinstated as No 1 scrum-half, Guscott, Egerton and Halliday, a replacement – and for Robinson, there was no opportunity to recharge the batteries.

While the England hopefuls were being put through their paces on a training camp in Portugal, Barnes cheerfully accepted the opportunity for rest afforded by a calf strain and Chilcott became the first Bath captain to avoid defeat in Cardiff, although the 10-10 draw felt like an opportunity missed.

Bedford, whipping boys of the Courage League First Division, were hammered a record 76-nil on the Rec and then Bath embarked on their own mid-winter training in Lanzarote, the long week away coinciding with England's opening match of the Five Nations at home to Ireland.

Happily, that marked the final stage in the rehabilitation of Hill, his first International Championship appearance since the 1987 'horror show' in Cardiff. "I just feel very fortunate to have been given another chance," he told the Bristol Evening Post. "Now it's up to me to make a success of it. If I manage a good Championship season, another World Cup would be a realistic target – which for me would be the fulfilment of a great ambition."

On the pugnacious, win-at-all-costs approach that deprived him of so many caps, Hill added: "The problem was that I thought this was the way to climb to the top – and clearly I was wrong. Now I am through the aggressive stage. I have been concentrating on improving my skills and relaxing a lot more. Before the Fiji match I wasn't at all nervous – and that wouldn't have been the case in any of my earlier internationals."

With Guscott scoring one of four England tries, the Irish were beaten 23-nil but Egerton lost his place in the back row to Gloucester's Mike Teague for the visit to Paris a fortnight later. It was a conclusive English victory by 26-7 and Guscott scored again. Hill exorcised the ghosts of Cardiff '87 with the try that completed a 34-6 demolition of Wales at Twickenham and prompted the immediate resignation of the Welsh coach, John Ryan. Geoff Cooke's England appeared unstoppable.

Meanwhile, Bath had enjoyed a Pilkington Cup 'mud bath' in which Carling's Harlequins were beaten 9-nil at the Rec and the cup run continued on 10 February with a 25-3 defeat of Headingley. On the eve of England's win over Wales, four Barnes penalties earned a 12-9 victory over Gloucester at the Rec. It was by common consent a curiously flat affair – but the next meeting between the sides would be rather more memorable.

The 1990 cup campaign moved on to Richmond where Guscott offered a glimpse of his England form with two tries in the last ten minutes. There was even time for Swift to score a fifth try under the posts to round off a 35-3 victory.

But the serene progress was rudely halted after Hall was again sent off, this time in a 38-14 win over Plymouth Albion. Having been dismissed earlier in the season against Rosslyn Park, Hall had every reason to fear he would miss the 'business end' of the season.

Spirits were temporarily lifted by the surprising defection to the Recreation Ground of Bristol full-back Jon Webb, whose loss of confidence and waning appetite for the game had seen his England place surrendered to Simon Hodgkinson, of Nottingham. Webb's first appearance in a Bath shirt was in the 'Spartans' 3rd XV at home to Blackheath on 10 March.

Ironically, the Bath first team was playing in the Courage League at Nottingham that day but Hodgkinson decided to take a rest ahead of England's Grand Slam decider at Murrayfield a week later – as did hooker Brian Moore and Scottish lock Chris Gray. Did that prompt Bath to drop their guard? Nottingham certainly tore up the form guide, scoring the only try late on through lock Chris Hindmarch to snatch a 12-9 victory that left the champions hoping beyond hope that other results might let them back into contention for the title.

It was a traumatic month all round. Ex-Bath prop David Sole slow-marched his side out at Murrayfield to inspire Scotland to a famous Grand Slam victory. Although Guscott scored his seventh international try in that game, he was then dropped for his club's cup semi-final at Moseley; and Hall learned that his ban was to be all of 90 days, even ruling him out of Bath's pre-season tour to the Far East. Fortunately there was no repeat of the 1988 cup debacle at Moseley, Bath winning 21-7 with tries from Swift, Chilcott and Callard. Significantly, Ubogu's ability around the field won him a place ahead of Lee for the first time and he could look ahead with some confidence to facing Gloucester in the final on 5 May.

Conspicuous by his absence, Guscott was still attracting most of the headlines, especially after Second Division Rugby League club Huddersfield made public a £300,000 offer to the 25-year-old centre. His fitful form for Bath had finally exhausted the patience of skipper Barnes but, as Guscott joined the Barbarians for the Hong Kong Sevens, Rowell proffered a more conciliatory view of Guscott's temporary relegation to the Bath second team, saying at the time: "We just felt he needed a break. The majority of people simply do not understand the pressure Jeremy has been under. Suddenly the lad was playing for England, the British Lions and had become a world figure in the game. He was trying to build a new career outside rugby as well.

"At Moseley, we considered it necessary to try something different. But Jeremy is obviously an outstanding performer and will be one of the leaders into the future as far as Bath are concerned."

With Adebayo again deputising for Guscott and Callard filling in at fly-half, Bath's league campaign finally unravelled at Saracens' welcoming little Southgate ground on the last day of March. The Hertfordshire side, with No 8 Ben Clarke particularly prominent and young prop Jason Leonard only four months away from the first of 114 England caps, took advantage of the absence of Barnes and several other regulars to win 9-7. The winning conversion was kicked by Sean Robinson, inflicting a cruel defeat on his brother Andy, captaining Bath for the first time.

Saracens coach Tony Russ, looking ahead with no great enthusiasm to the all-West Country Pilkington Cup final, Bath v Gloucester, declared: "It's going to be the most boring final of all time. Both are so predictable these days – as Bath so clearly demonstrated here... Neither are flexible – they can't change their tactics – so it's just going to be thud and blunder on May 5. The cup final will be decided on penalties." He couldn't have been more wrong.

With a month to prepare, Bath did seem close to resolving one or two issues: Guscott's recall was a 'no brainer'; Adebayo was therefore likely to pip Blackett for the left wing spot; and it was clear that Ubogu was to be loose-head. What nobody expected was for Jon Webb, so recently a forlorn and dispirited figure at Bristol, to rediscover his form by scoring a try and kicking three conversions and a penalty on his first team debut, a 25-3 win at Newport.

But the Frenchay Hospital surgeon had left it too late to dislodge Jon Callard who then landed five conversions in a 42-14 rout of a near full-strength Llanelli on 7 April. David Trick scored two tries in as many minutes but just as eye-catching was the second row partnership of Redman and the young Haag, standing in for Damian Cronin. On Easter Saturday Adebayo confirmed his place with all three tries in a 22-13 victory at Bristol while flanker Kevin Withey ran in four as Cheltenham were hammered 70-10. Webb kicked a record-equalling 11 conversions and the Bank Holiday Monday crowd at the Rec were afforded a first look at Durham University student Philip de Glanville until the centre left the field at half-time with a head injury. The match had added significance as the last fixture between the clubs, breaking an association dating back to 28 January 1892 when Bath won 22-2 at Henrietta Park.

In previous years, the top players had been wrapped up in cotton wool before a final but the need to rediscover rhythm and intensity persuaded Bath to field a near full-strength side for a second meeting with Llanelli in two weeks. As if to underline the dilemma, Simpson was replaced at the break by Withey after injuring his knee but Chilcott proved his fitness after knee surgery just three weeks earlier and Bath scored six tries at Stradey Park to win 31-19, their fifth in a row against the Scarlets.

The final rehearsal was a home match against Leicester, Les Cusworth's farewell appearance for the Tigers but also the last round of the Courage League programme. Bath won 26-15, scoring five tries to one, but that did not soothe Barnes's sense of anger and frustration. "It annoys me when I think how we lost at Saracens recently," he said, after hearing that Wasps had sneaked home by beating their London rivals as favourites Gloucester were ambushed at Nottingham. "There were too many occasions when we just didn't perform as we should."

Somewhere, sometime there just had to be a big performance on a grand stage.

Chapter 9

GLOUCESTER GRILLED ON THE TWICKENHAM BARBECUE

As the Bath team coach inched through the picnicking hordes in Twickenham's West Car Park on 5 May 1990, the weight of expectation was almost oppressive, magnified by the sweltering heat.

No-one felt it more than Simon Halliday, appearing in his fifth Twickenham final. Still a few months short of his 30th birthday, he had decided to give his battered body a rest and to move to London to pursue his stockbroking career in the City. This was his last match in a Bath shirt; although he would play again and with great distinction, it would be as a Harlequin. Sacrilege!

Before the 1989 final against Leicester, Halliday had been more vocal than anyone in the club about the need for Bath to make a big statement, to show what they were really capable of. So for him this was the last chance; but he had been a little more reticent this time, not least because the opponents were Gloucester.

Denied the Courage League title just seven days before, the Cherry and Whites were not going to lack for motivation, especially against their upstart West Country

Bath's 1990 Pilkington Cup contingent pose with the match officials before facing Gloucester at Twickenham.

Kevin Withey: memorable try.

rivals. The 'Shed' was confident, lifting their decibel levels in line with the soaring temperatures.

The occasion was a strange mix of old and new, amateur and professional. Capacity at Twickenham was restricted to 52,000 while the new North Stand was being constructed and the BBC, seemingly caught between two eras, provided live TV coverage of English rugby's cup final for the first time – but only of the second half!

But by that time the match was well and truly over. Even the watching John Hall would have struggled to match Kevin Withey's improbable first try, a 60-metre touchline dash direct from a line-out, leaving a trail of defenders sprawling in his wake. Guscott broke the Gloucester line and exchanged passes with Swift to score the second and Callard chased his own kick-ahead to claim a third. When Swift completed a lung-bursting 80-metre interception on the stroke of half-time and Barnes kicked his third conversion to add to an earlier penalty, Bath were 25-nil ahead.

BATH: *J Callard; A Swift, S Halliday, J Guscott, A Adebayo; S Barnes, R Hill* (capt) *(S Knight); V Ubogu, G Dawe, G Chilcott, N Redman, D Cronin, N Maslen, D Egerton, A Robinson.*

GLOUCESTER: *T Smith; D Morgan, D Caskie, R Mogg, J Breeze; M Hamlin, M Hannaford; M Preedy, K Dunn, R Pascall, N Scrivens, J Brain, J Gadd, M Teague, I Smith.*

REFEREE: *F Howard* (Liverpool).

Tony Swift races away for an interception try against Gloucester in the 1990 Pilkington Cup final.

Gloucester Grilled On The Twickenham Barbecue

It was not that the line-out functioned perfectly or that they had a decided advantage in the scrums but that Robinson, Egerton and Co were utterly in control in the loose, especially on the fringes, and that Hill's immaculate service gave his backs room to use their superior pace and ball skills. Tom Hudson's carefully planned hydration programme in the hours before kick-off also ensured that they were far better equipped to tackle the problems of fluid loss and possible heat exhaustion.

Moreover, Gloucester's discipline was poor and when John Gadd was sent off on 56 minutes for kicking Egerton, there was no way back. Man-of-the-match Swift poached a second try and also created another for Redman and it was no coincidence that the other tries went to the super-fit Dawe and Ubogu as lesser mortals wilted in the heat. Fittingly, Barnes handed the final conversion to Halliday.

Gloucester coach Keith Richardson observed graciously: "We had no answer to what was the best display by a club side on a major occasion. Bath come here every year ... we have yet to get the hang of it." Chilcott said: "We've been waiting to do this in a final for six years."

These days Egerton has is own view of why the Bath side of that era were able to do to Gloucester what they failed to do to other cup final opponents. "It's because it was Gloucester," he says. "You had to pick people who would put their heads where it hurt and If you didn't have that hardness, hitting the rucks and mauls, you'd never be in it – because that was Gloucester.

"In all the other cup finals we knew we would win We weren't scared of Wasps or Leicester – which is why we fell behind and had to fight back. But on this day the players, and the forwards in particular, had that 'snake in the stomach'. They couldn't live with us. That was the one game when we actually did what we always threatened to do to all teams. It was a challenge to produce the goods."

Swift finished the season as top try scorer with 26 in 28 matches while Barnes had contributed 219 of his team's 1,166 points, from seven tries, 61 conversions, 22 penalties and a drop goal. It was no surprise that he was soon elected unopposed for a third season as captain, although he was already looking for a successor.

"Two years is a long time as captain of a club like this and I had hoped one or two people would be interested in taking over," he said. "But that hasn't happened so I am now prepared to carry on. One of my main tasks will be to try to groom someone to take over the following year. That's not as straightforward as is might seem though, because if that person is a current international he won't be available for the first few months of the 1991-92 season when the World Cup is on."

To be played throughout the UK, Ireland and France with the final at Twickenham, the World Cup was already dominating events off the field too. In particular, the RFU was increasingly at odds with the International Rugby Board over the issue of payment to players for commercial activities.

Those issues were of little interest in those parts of the world where qualifiers were already under way. As Bath were demolishing Gloucester at Twickenham, Tunisia were celebrating a 16-12 qualifier victory over Morocco in Harare.

Meanwhile, England manager Geoff Cooke hastily assembled a squad for a short, late summer tour of Argentina, hoping to unearth at least one player who might yet force his way into contention for the World Cup. Ubogu hoped it might be him but after being on the losing side against Banco Nacion and a Buenos Aires Selection it was another prop who forced his way into the Test side. In its digest of a disappointing tour Rothmans Rugby Union Yearbook observed with some prescience: "There was evidence that Jason Leonard would develop into an international prop."

A diplomatic incident

David Egerton made his last appearance for England as a 50th minute replacement for Wade Dooley in the second Test against Argentina on 4 August 1990 but even he would admit that he made rather more impact at the post-match dinner.

The England team's visit was public acknowledgement of the restoration of diplomatic relations a full eight years after the Falklands War so the banquet was a suitably grand affair. Upward of 1,000 guests included the head of state President Carlos Menem, Her Majesty's Ambassador to Argentina Humphrey Maud, Cardinal Basil Hume and bigwigs from the respective rugby unions.

Egerton had arrived in full Batman regalia – cowl, cape and black Y-fronts over his Number Ones – by order of the Players' Court. Late in the evening, egged on by his team-mates, he then proceeded to perform an extravagant table-top rendition of his party piece, Johnny Cash's 'Ring of Fire'.

"It was something of an out-of-body experience in that, after leaping from table to table knocking over bottles of wine and everything else, when I sat down I couldn't believe I'd actually done it," recalls Egerton.

"Up to that point I was in two minds whether to bluff it out, sit tight and take the stick from my mates or just stand up and do it half-heartedly. After all, I'm dressed up as Batman; I'm not in a good mood and I've had enough of it. But really there's only one way out of a situation like that. So as the pressure from the boys got greater and greater, I took a sip of wine and leaped onto the table and off I went.

"President Menem and Cardinal Hume were smiling but I could see the old farts from the RFU, Dudley Wood, Mickey Steele-Bodger and Don Rutherford, with their heads in their hands. That was the first formal diplomatic occasion after the Falklands War … and, funnily enough, I never played for England again!"

Hill and Redman continued their outstanding club form into England's 25-12 First Test victory in Buenos Aires but England lost the return match 15-13.

Scotland's Grand Slam status cut no ice in New Zealand where Damian Cronin and Co lost 31-16 in Dunedin and 21-18 in a closer contest in Auckland. Another face to enter the world stage that summer was a 29-year-old ambulance driver from Longwell Green, Tony Spreadbury, called up at short notice to referee Australia v France in Sydney on 9 June. The match was only three minutes old when a vicious fight broke out and barely 10 minutes later Spreadbury had to send off Abdel Benazzi for stamping on an opponent's head. Welcome to international rugby!

Emotions were also running high back at Bath where the increasingly autonomous playing side of the club had arranged a match against the Romanian national side for the opening day of the season. Billed as a fund raiser for the cash-strapped Romanian rugby union and sanctioned by the RFU, it clashed directly with the scheduled fixture at Pontypool , challenging the authority of the fixtures secretary and the Management Committee. This was certainly not the way that the club hierarchy had intended to mark the club's 125th anniversary.

When they first met to discuss the matter in the second week of July, the committee ruled against the Romanian fixture. Clive Howard, the mild-mannered building society manager reluctantly caught in the middle as club secretary, declined to comment on suggestions that the coaching hierarchy of Rowell, Robson and Hudson had made the issue a resignation matter. But senior players, already preparing for a pre-season tour of Australia, talked of boycotting the Pontypool match, ignoring the damage that would do to the club's reputation .

Within a week, however, a hastily summoned meeting of the club's emergency committee came up with a compromise – play both matches on the same weekend and worry later about the impact of the fixture congestion. Hudson saw this as a fudge however and resigned, citing "disillusionment" with the attitude of the Management Committee.

"The straw that broke the camel's back was the Romania game," he said. "I feel that the club needs some new faces. We have taken Bath as far as we can with the present management structure. We wanted to make the club world-class – but I don't think that is now possible."

Skipper Barnes, embarking on a third season as club captain, tried to persuade Robson not to quit too – but to no avail. Barnes said: "I'm very disappointed at the way things have turned out – especially at the club's reaction to the apparent resignations. Merely to suggest that 'no man is bigger than the club', as the secretary was quoted as saying, is not good enough. That sort of reaction does not do justice to the tremendous contribution of these two men over many years."

And before leaving with his players on a tough tour of Australia to play state side Queensland and leading Sydney club Randwick, Rowell broke his silence to say:

"Regretfully, it's something that's happened … and at a bad time for morale reasons, just before the beginning of the season. Tom and Dave were doing their usual stint with a great deal of zeal and suddenly something like this blows up.

"As far as the Romanian visit was concerned, I got what I was after. It was all sorted out by playing two games in one weekend. It was too far down the line to cancel our scheduled fixture against Pontypool but for me the Romanian game was a big opportunity. They've just emerged from an horrific period – some of their players were killed – so it's a privilege to be able to do a bit to help them."

In the weeks following, Rowell's demeanour betrayed his hurt at the way things had turned out but to neutral observers the spat between the playing side and the committee had been inevitable given the forces at work. Rowell and his players had upped the ante and the committee had too much sense to call their bluff. It became a more equal – and productive – partnership as a result.

It was not as if the committee did not have plenty of other matters to occupy them, not least a continuing debate over whether the club should appoint a paid administrator – and whether that person should have decision-making powers, as the playing side urged.

There was also the continuing saga of Lambridge. After Bath City Council's refusal of permission for a superstore on the Lambridge training ground there had been a five-day inquiry in May, chaired by Planning Inspector Frank Cosgrove. He eventually ruled on 13 October that the scheme could not proceed because of the traffic impact. With a tantalising £18 million windfall at stake the club continued to hold out hope for an appeal by Tesco to the Secretary of State but Wansdyke Council had further complicated matters by turning down plans for a training ground at Bathampton.

> **Clive Howard summed up the situation later in 1990: "… we must persevere at the Rec with the facilities we have. So much needs to be done but you can't spend money you don't have. If we get the £18 million, then things might be different." But they didn't get the £18 million and things didn't change.**

With Redman entering hospital for surgery on his elbows after towering performances in Argentina, only Ubogu of the six-strong Bath contingent in the returning England squad flew on to join the tour in Australia. There, Barnes had inspired his team to a 27-24 win over a Cairns Barbarians XV before a second string line-up drew 19-19 against a Darling Downs Invitation XV in Toowoomba.

In Brisbane on August 14, scrum-half Knight scored two tries and the late-arriving Ubogu another but Bath went down 21-19 to Queensland at Ballymore. The game's dominant figure was a 20-year-old lock who won 17 line-outs. His name: John Eales. The final match of the tour – billed the Unofficial World Club Championship, despite the absence of key figures such as Hill, Robinson, Egerton and the suspended Hall – ended in a 20-3 win for Randwick in front of 6,000 at Coogee Oval, Sydney.

After a stopover in Thailand, the tour party returned to yet more upset as Jon Morrison, rather than settle for second fiddle behind Redman and Cronin, left for Bristol and Withey, a spectacular stand-in for Hall at Twickenham just four months earlier, opted to join Newport. He was not the only one though; the Welsh club also signed up United and Spartans players such as wings Sagoe and Martin Sparkes, utility back Mark Westcott and scrum-half Mark Plummer. The were dark mutterings from the Rec of financial inducements, angrily denied by Newport, but Withey said publicly that he was just fed up with United rugby.

Of course, not everyone was heading for the exit. Fresh faces for the trip to Pontypool included Devon-born wing Jim Fallon and a 6ft 6in lock from Cornwall called Andy Reed. Both scored tries but Pontypool exerted rather more control to win 34-17.

The next day a more familiar looking Bath side provided a stern test for the Romanians ahead of their World Cup qualifiers against the Netherlands, Spain and Italy. They had shocked France at the end of May, winning 12-6 in Auch, but Bath scored six tries to win 38-9 and there were encouraging touches from newcomers such as de Glanville and Haag as well as commanding performances from Robinson and Hall, back from his 60-day ban. The match attracted a crowd of 3,500, paying increased admission prices – up from £3 to £4 (£2 for OAPs and juniors) with a £1 transfer to the stand.

Andy Reed: rapid rise.

Former Beechen Cliff schoolmaster Glyn Maddocks, the UK-based representative of the Romanian Rugby Federation, explained exactly what it meant to his friends:

"Today's match is very significant because this is the first occasion in which a freely elected Romanian Rugby Union has sent a team to this country. There are no 'Security' men this time, just a team of dedicated players and officials who have survived one of the most repressive regimes ever known and whose devotion to the game we all love has carried them through to a new era."

And that put into perspective the bickering behind the scenes at the Rec. There were equally emotional moments the following week as the club paid tribute to Chronicle reporter John Stevens, who had followed his father Bill into the press box at the Recreation Ground but was now being forced into retirement by ill health. 'Scoop', as he was known to his contemporaries within the club, was reckoned to have covered some 2,000 matches since 1959 when he first occupied the press bench at the back of the West Stand. The match programme for a Wednesday fixture with Toulouse carried a tribute by John Mason, of The Daily Telegraph.

"John Stevens has chronicled these events with care and considerable pride. He is a journalist of the old school in that he prefers to report – accurately of course – what people say. You would be surprised how many luminaries do not enjoy reading what they have said. Not surprisingly, John does have opinions (very firm ones at times) but he is not in the habit of ramming them down throats. He allows devoted readers to make up their own minds – and when you are reporting the day-to-day affairs of the most successful rugby club in the United Kingdom, the path remarkably, is not always as rosy as it might be.

"Not the least of John's virtues, which includes a gloriously sardonic view of events, past and present, is that he is not easily impressed. This week after years of faithful service to the Bath & Wilts Chronicle as copy boy, trainee, reporter, sub-editor, rugby and cricket correspondent and, until recently, Sports Editor, John is retiring. Indifferent health has prompted the decision to break the bond with the paper, which has employed him since he left school. Somehow, that crowded, cramped Press Box at the Rec. will seem empty without the comfortable figure of J Stevens, cigarette precariously perched, still guarding that Press Association 'phone. It was moved finally, though, claims John, not before the old stand was demolished and the building of the clubhouse began."

John, whose father and grandfather played for the club, was later honoured as a Patron Member of the Old Players' Association and died peacefully on 8 January 2000.

All the trials and tribulations of the close season began to recede as Toulouse were put to the sword, conceding ten tries. The 44-6 scoreline prompted skipper Barnes to observe: "This display must be our benchmark for the season. Above anything else, our ambition is to regain the Courage League Championship." Although rebuilding his squad, Toulouse coach Pierre Villepreux could not remember his team suffering such a heavy defeat and did not hide his admiration, saying:

"Bath's linking between forwards and backs is done at such speed ... most unusual for an English side."

The 'Rag Doll' match went Llanelli's way, 28-12 at Stradey Park, and Chilcott dislocated and fractured a shoulder, which put him out of the game for three months. But normal service was resumed at the Rec a week later when an experienced Cardiff team conceded eight tries in a 45-23 defeat. Barnes crossed twice himself, adding five conversions and a penalty and Cardiff coach Alan Phillips dismissed his side's effort as "men against boys".

The Courage League campaign opened with a less than fluent 46-3 home victory over Liverpool St Helens but Bath continued to knock over international opposition as Ulster were beaten 25-6 at the Rec. Next up were Neath, boasting a run of 44 consecutive victories since being beaten by the touring All Blacks 11 months earlier. Unfortunately the match clashed with the Wales v Barbarians match, which claimed Barnes, Guscott and Lee as well as half the Neath team.

Sadly, after contributing two tries in a 27-13 victory, the in-form Egerton suffered a fracture-dislocation of his right shoulder in a collision with Neath's 20-stone prop, Jeremy Pugh.

But among the more heartening aspects of Bath's imperious form had been the way two players in particular had begun to look like their old selves. Hall was deservedly recalled to the England team for his 20th cap against Argentina, being preferred to both Teague and Skinner. And Jon Webb, now first choice for Bath at fullback since his move from Bristol seven months earlier, found a place on the bench after a season in the wilderness.

"Today's news is brilliant – and a complete surprise," Hall told the Evening Post. "When I heard that I had been picked I thought it was for the B side. My real goal this year was to try and squeeze into the Five Nations team – and if that didn't work out, to win a World Cup place."

First though, there was the little matter of a local derby with Bristol at the Memorial Ground. Webb returned to his old club to provide the pass for the only try, scored by Adebayo, and also kicked two penalties in a 10-3 win. A week later at Twickenham, Hall marked his return to the international arena with a try from No 8, a switch necessitated by a general reshuffle of the pack after Paul Ackford was laid out by 18-year-old Federico Mendez. Among the other try scorers were Hill and Guscott (2).

With so many internationals in the club, Rowell faced a real challenge to keep his players fresh and mentally attuned to the domestic campaign. Just 72 hours before the Courage League clash with a dangerous-looking Harlequins side, he said a few short words to his players on the Lambridge training ground, got into his car and went home! The message had been simple – go and run the show yourselves from now until Saturday night.

Bristol fall short again as Bath win 10-9 at the Memorial Ground (27 October 1990).

After a conclusive 23-3 victory on the Rec, Rowell explained: "You can employ all the consultants in the world, but as in business, success is not really achieved unless those who do the work feel a sense of ownership. All I said to the players was 'This is your enterprise. You own it, you run it'."

Having eclipsed such a distinguished performer as Peter Winterbottom, Robinson next set his sights on Neil Back as Bath met Leicester in front of a Courage League record attendance of 11,500 at Welford Road. Energised by Robinson's all-action performance on the openside and particularly his Herculean feat in denying Dean Richards a try off the back of an injury-time scrum, Bath triumphed 9-3 with three Webb penalties to one from John Liley.

As luck would have it, the Pilkington Cup draw pitted these two old rivals against each other just seven days later. The tie marked Lee's 350th appearance in eleven seasons, giving the 31-year-old prop a chance to reflect on rugby and farming, with cows rated his most dangerous opponents. "They'll often let fly with a kick. It always seems to get me in the same place. I get more dead legs and bruises in the milking shed than on the field," he said with a chuckle.

Although full international honours eluded Lee and he was overlooked for two cup finals, there was not a hint of bitterness as he ruminated on lost opportunities:

"I've been dropped, like every other player; it's disappointing at the time but I've never held it against anybody." With so many games under his belt, he conceded that retirement was increasingly in his thoughts, mainly because of the travelling commitments. "But ... there's another season in me. I say that every year."

The 23 November cup-tie was a huge anti-climax, however, as the Tigers overturned the form book to win 12-nil, inflicting on Bath their first cup defeat on the Rec in nine years. Barnes, no longer able to conceal the debilitating effects of a long-term groin injury, had a kick charged down by Aadel Kardooni and Brian Smith hacked through to touch down the only try.

While the Divisional Championship got under way with ten Bath players in the South West side to face the Midlands at Moseley, a collection of second and third teamers jetted off to Toulouse for the opening match of the £1.3 million Toulouse Centenary tournament. Lumsden's try clinched a 13-9 victory over the Soviet Union and earned Bath a return match with the hosts just six days before Christmas.

After wins over both London Scottish and London Welsh, United skipper Nick Maslen took his players back to France to face a full-strength Toulouse still smarting from the hiding handed out at the Rec earlier in the season. A 23-6 defeat was no disgrace and left Bath with a play-off against Fiji for third place. Bolstered by the arrival of Chilcott, Webb and Hill, Bath were just 22-15 adrift at the break but were then blitzed by some vintage Fijian rugby and eventually went down 60-19. After a remarkable gala dinner for 2,000 guests, entertained by pop stars and laser light shows, the Bath contingent shared an early morning Christmas Eve flight back to Heathrow with the Queenslanders.

The Toulouse party had been a remarkable glimpse into a money-laden future for rugby union with home players rumoured to be on £1,000 a man to win the final. But amid the extravagance were examples of traditional amateur sacrifice, such as Spartans flanker Julian Olds, a 54th minute replacement against Fiji. He reckoned taking time off as a self-employed carpenter had cost him £650 in earnings.

Even a stellar performer like Guscott, named in 1990 World XV by French rugby magazine Midi Olympique, was yet to benefit from a relaxation in the regulations allowing players to undertake paid promotional work. "I have not noticed any extra income," he said during England's New Year 1991 training camp in Lanzarote, after agreeing to his off-field interests being handled by the RFU's official agents, David and Bob Willis. "I suppose there will be something around in due course but I am not going out looking for it."

He also reiterated his commitment to the 15-a-side game, despite continued overtures from Rugby League. "I enjoy this game so much. I don't care if I don't make a fortune. If I had wanted money for rugby I would have gone north a couple of years ago."

Players or performers? Victor Ubogu, Nigel Redman, Andy Robinson and Jeremy Guscott dress for the occasion.

Other news from the England training camp was not so sunny. Hall, ranked No 1 of the blindside flankers, injured his knee during a practice match and went straight into hospital on his return to Bath. The surgery kept him out of action for only a month but, crucially, he lost his place to Teague for the opening Five Nations match in Cardiff. Hall himself fully understood the significance: "It's a dreadful blow. I have never trained harder than during the last few months." As he feared, Teague made the No 6 shirt his own throughout the 1991 Grand Slam season and right through to the World Cup final ten months later.

Hall even saw his own Bath club record for international caps, 20, eclipsed by Cronin in Scotland's defeat at Twickenham. When England's selectors picked an unchanged line-up for the Triple Crown decider in Dublin, with Guscott and Hill as the Bath representatives, manager Geoff Cooke was sympathetic, but only to a point: "Hall was injured at the wrong time and has not had sufficient rugby since his return," he said. "In the circumstances, we saw no compelling reason for change."

Still waiting for skipper Barnes to recover from his injury woes – finally traced to a trapped sciatic nerve – Bath had stumbled through January, fielding Jon Callard at fly-half for the 11-6 Courage League match at home to Moseley. The side that faced Coventry on a snow-covered Rec on 2 February looked more like the Bath of old, with Barnes, Hall and Chilcott restored to fitness and young de Glanville available again from Oxford University. It was only a friendly but the 52-12 scoreline was invigorating in itself. Friendlies against Barnstaple (68-nil), Ebbw Vale (58-nil) and

Llanelli (34-14), in which Egerton made a welcome return from his shoulder injury, maintained the momentum.

But it was all just a bit too easy, as Wasps proved on 9 March by becoming the first club to win a league match at the Rec. It was close – Bath led into injury time before centre Fran Clough ran a clever angle to snatch a 16-15 victory – but Rowell acknowledged: "They're catching us up. We're still the best but it's perhaps unreasonable to expect to win every league match. It would help though if we kicked our goals," he observed wryly.

Attention then turned to England as they headed for a Grand Slam decider with France . For scrum-half Hill, enjoying the proverbial armchair ride behind a dominant pack, it was the ultimate rehabilitation after the disappointment and disgrace of Cardiff '87. Meanwhile Adebayo, de Glanville, Dawe and Redman were named in an England B squad to face the French at Bristol on the eve of the Twickenham showdown. England won 21-19 to claim the major prize although they were forced to regroup after the French conjured a wonder try through Philippe Saint Andre, finishing off a move begun behind his own posts by Serge Blanco.

With the second Rugby World Cup in the offing, much planning was going on behind the scenes for a more commercial future, perhaps even a fully professional game. Earlier in March Bath had announced plans to upgrade the Recreation Ground, first with a roof over the east terracing and, more ambitiously, a £750,000 stand at the Sports Centre end. Club secretary Clive Howard said it would provide accommodation for spectators and hospitality boxes, adding: "It is something we have been thinking about over the years."

Progress towards so-called professionalism had its darker side. Although normal service was resumed with a 22-9 league win at Nottingham, Barnes followed up his two tries with a very public condemnation of the 'winding up' tactics employed by the home team. "This is the sort of professionalism we can do without," he declared.

The ever voluble Barnes had quite a lot to say that weekend, also ending his self-imposed England exile – although with no guarantee of selection for the July tour of Australia and Fiji – and then reiterating his intention to step down from the Bath captaincy.

Another looking to the future was 34-year-old Chilcott, named by ITV as one of their broadcasting panel for the World Cup, which immediately raised questions over interpretation of RFU rules on payment to players. Chilcott, insisting that his immediate priority was helping Bath to win the Courage League, said: "As far as I am concerned, you are allowed to take money for communications work."

RFU secretary Dudley Wood, while noting that the arrangement had not been looked at in detail, added helpfully and without a hint of irony: "One of the great things about Gareth is that he has always been concerned not to overstep the bounds. If there are any difficulties, we will look at the situation when the time comes."

Gloucester Grilled On The Twickenham Barbecue

Bath entered the run-in with a 17-15 win at Gloucester to maintain a four-point lead at the top of the table. It was Webb's first appearance at Kingsholm in a Bath shirt and he obliged with two tries, a conversion and a penalty while Chilcott was true to his word, diving over from a ruck in the 48th minute.

And the championship was theirs just a week later on 13 April as Rosslyn Park were trounced 45-21 at the Rec, although no-one had really expected the title race to be settled until the end of the month. News of second-placed Orrell's surprise home defeat by Wasps filtered around the ground just before the final whistle and was finally relayed to the players by the public address system. Skipper Barnes, scorer of the last of seven tries, punched the air in delight – and Rosslyn Park promptly pinched their third try. With no trophy to present – the Courage representatives had neglected to bring it with them – the players had to make do with parading champagne bottles.

A more discordant note was the sight of Egerton being led off the pitch in agony with a dislocated shoulder, the same injury that had required surgery back in October.

The line-up was a mix of old faces and some new ones, particularly try-scorers such as Haag, who had claimed a second row spot ahead of Cronin, and Mark Crane, standing toe-to-toe with his brother Geoff at the line-out. "We had quite a lot to say to each other," grinned Mark.

Rowell, who had earlier quashed fears that he might step down because of commitments as managing director of the Golden Wonder foods group and a new role as coach to England Students, was already turning his thoughts to the 1991-92 campaign. "We are looking to add a new dimension to our play next season," he said, without betraying any more details.

> Looking further ahead, he did voice concerns about Bath's ability to compete for playing talent if rugby union became an open sport. "Ultimately, we depend for our success on having world-class players. Without them we won't win anything. But I have been very pleased that some of the younger members of our squad have emerged this season – Martin Haag, of course, Mark Crane and Phil de Glanville." On his own contribution, he tapped his forehead and said: "Look, when this stops working we're in trouble – and there are plenty of ideas in this brain yet."

The title won, Bath could afford to field a mix-and-match line-up for a home 'friendly' with Gloucester, a largely unsatisfying affair which they won 32-19.

So to Southgate where they were finally presented with the league trophy after an unanswerable 49-6 win against Saracens. Barnes had dislocated and fractured a finger against Gloucester but no-one was going to deny the little fly-half this sweet moment: "There were several attempts to put it back, including under a local anaesthetic on Monday," he said cheerfully. "That didn't work either so they had to take me into hospital on Wednesday and put me under. I was still a bit groggy next day so I couldn't train but I wasn't going to miss this match, my last as captain."

Gloucester Grilled On The Twickenham Barbecue

The beer flows as Barnes & Co celebrate a second Courage League title in three years after winning at Saracens on the last day of the 1990-91 season.

A devastating rush of 24 points in just seven minutes around the hour mark put paid to any Saracens resistance, particularly after Ubogu outpaced fullback Sean Robinson and England centre John Buckton from inside his own half. Barnes then collected the restart, combining with Webb and de Glanville to create a try for Guscott. Other try scorers were Hall, Barnes, Redman, Fallon, Guscott again and de Glanville with Webb contributing seven conversions and a penalty.

The final league table saw Bath finish three points clear of Wasps after just one defeat in 12 games with more points scored and fewer conceded – 280 against 104 – than any side in the top two divisions. Just 24 hours later, Bath hosted the first national sevens tournament and, with Martin Haag making a remarkably effective appearance after all the celebrations, Bath actually lifted a second trophy in 24 hours.

Of course, the cup defeat at home to Leicester still rankled among supporters, denied their annual trip to Twickenham for only the second time in eight years. It did not make it any easier when they saw Simon Halliday in Harlequins colours score one of the tries that broke Northampton resistance to lift the Pilkington Cup.

After his Bath swansong against Gloucester a year earlier, the stockbroker's rugby career was enjoying a remarkable resurrection. First he underwent major surgery on a chronic ankle condition, the legacy of that awful injury at Bridgwater in 1983; he had then trained alone for several months, unsure whether he would ever be able to play again. He made a tentative return with Harlequins during December and after just six games had been called back into the England fold as a replacement against

A second trophy in 24 hours after Bath win the Worthington National Club Sevens on the Recreation Ground (28 April 1991).

Scotland. "If at any time I had broken down, I would have given up," he admitted at the time.

Back at Bath where Barnes was preparing to hand over the captaincy to Robinson, the outgoing skipper did not share the sense of supporters' emptiness at the lack of cup success. "Last season (1989-90) was a disappointment and the cup win over Gloucester, great occasion that it was, was only compensation for throwing away the league," he declared. "This time we came top of the First Division and that to me is the sole criterion for a successful season." Reflecting on his three-year tenure, he said:

> "In retrospect, four major trophies out of six is an acceptable return. But I must stress from the outset that we set out to do the 'double' in every season. The really pleasing thing about it is the team have continued to evolve. I wouldn't be satisfied now, even with the league won, if it had been achieved with no thought for the club's future.
>
> "It has been said that I'm giving up the captaincy because I'm sick of it. That's not true at all – I have really enjoyed the job, notwithstanding the less pleasant tasks like ringing up one of your mates on a Monday morning to tell him he's been dropped."

As Barnes pointed out, he continued to wield considerable influence on the field as playmaker and within a few months he had secured for himself a place on the Management Committee together with Chilcott and Egerton. In taking three of the five elected places at the annual meeting on 19 July, in addition to Robinson as first team skipper and the captains of the United and Spartans team, the players enjoyed a powerful say in the club's decision making along with Rowell.

Meanwhile Webb, Guscott, Hill, Redman and Hall were pressing their World Cup credentials on England's tour of Australia and Fiji. For Webb, inclusion ahead of Hodgkinson for the Test against Australia represented a remarkable turnaround in his rugby fortunes because it had been barely a year since his wife, Amanda, persuaded him not to give up the sport entirely, so disillusioned had he become while at Bristol. England lost 40-15, Guscott scoring the only try.

But the tour ended disappointingly for Hall as his troublesome knee again reacted badly to the hard grounds and he flew home before the Sydney Test. When a fairly routine clean-out operation led to a debilitating post-operative infection, it soon became clear that a place in the World Cup squad was out of the question. It was 1987 all over again.

"I soon realised that I had to reinvent myself," he says now. "Once I got fit again, I had to become a different type of player, playing closer to the set piece. I'd lost that extra yard of pace."

As Hall knuckled down to yet another rehab regime, Bath announced a significant signing in Saracens' England B forward, Ben Clarke. Apart from Hall's problems, there were continuing doubts about the future of No 8 Egerton because of his recurring shoulder injury and Clarke's arrival allowed Ojomoh to cover for Hall on the blindside.

Egerton was not to return to action until February 1992 but he fully understood the significance of Clarke's recruitment. He reflects now: "Ben arrived as soon as I got injured. They weren't stupid! The one thing about Jack was that he was very cut-throat like that. And fair enough, you'd do exactly the same if you were running the show."

In a season dominated by representative rugby – October would not only accommodate the second Rugby World Cup but also the

Ben Clarke: recruited from Saracens.

divisional and county programmes – Robinson refused to be distracted from his task of ensuring Bath stayed at the top.

"We're pretty well covered in most positions and we certainly won't be hanging around for the World Cup players," he declared during pre-season training in July. "They'll have to fight for their places as much as anyone."

Clarke made an impressive debut as Bath beat Pontypool 28-12 on the first weekend of the season but collected a rib injury so Bath were soon having to dig deep among dwindling resources. Yet, with Mark Crane moving from prop to lock and Iestyn Lewis and Alastair Saverimutto forming a youthful centre partnership, they defeated Llanelli 25-9.

On 21 September they even managed what no other Bath side had done – achieve an away win at Cardiff after 67 years of fixtures. They made particularly hard work of a 10-9 victory, not helped by the officiating of Les Peard, who disallowed a try by Clarke for a non-existent knock-on by Barnes and five minutes later sent off the rangy No 8 for stamping on home scrum-half Matthew de Maid.

While a puzzled Clarke trudged off to begin a harsh 60-day ban, the remaining 14 players kept their shape and composure to leave their own mark on the club's records. That did not satisfy Chilcott who sounded off in the changing room about the fall-off in scrummaging effort in the final 20 minutes. It then dawned on the rest that Cooch had been entirely unaware of Clarke's dismissal. "And him a World Cup TV commentator," said one wag.

Bath finished a testing September programme with a 13-3 home win against Irish league champions Cork Constitution, also celebrating their centenary. England Students prop John Mallett made his debut but Adebayo suffered a knee injury in the slippery conditions and went under the knife soon after. Something had to give but Newport were far from impressed when Bath announced they could not raise a side for their fixture at Rodney Parade on 5 October after injuries, World Cup and divisional calls stretched resources beyond breaking point. Rowell, soon to be confirmed as the new coach of the England B side, was unrepentant: "We were about to play one of the leading sides in Wales. With what? It's not really on."

While Webb cemented his place in the England line-up alongside Guscott and Hill for the crunch games with France and Scotland – and the anticlimactic final against Australia, Bath did not return to action until 26 October. Second row Reed scored a try against his old team-mates in a 34-3 scoreline against Plymouth Albion and Barnes was in superlative form in guiding Bath to a 21-14 win at Neath in the showdown between the Welsh and English champions.

With eight wins out of eight under his belt Robinson was persuaded to take a breather for the derby friendly with Gloucester at Kingsholm only for the home team to squeeze out a 14-12 victory. Left wing Fallon, having reinforced his growing reputation with a try, also played a starring role in the opening Courage League fixture at London Irish a week later; he outshone Ireland's Simon Geoghegan to lay on tries for third-choice fullback Laurie Heatherley and Swift as well as scoring another himself in a 26-21 win.

Unfortunately, a rather well informed BBC Rugby Special viewer reported to the RFU that Heatherley had not been properly registered. Bath insisted it was an innocent oversight but that cut no ice with the Senior Clubs' Executive Committee. Their decision to deduct one league point from the defending champions, upheld on appeal by a nine-man RFU committee, drew a characteristic response from skipper Robinson: "We will just have to win the league with 23 points instead of 24... But this has certainly strengthened our resolve."

Like many sides before and since, Bath found their best form when nursing a sense of grievance. If there was no love for Bath outside of the city , there was at least admiration from those without an axe to grind. After witnessing the ten-try, 52-nil demolition of Nottingham in the Pilkington Cup on 31 November, England coach Dick Best was back at the Rec just seven days later for the league fixture with Northampton, as if he could not get enough of it. "Some of the moves they've worked out are unstoppable if done properly," he observed.

Elaboration on that point from Barnes was not exactly designed to offer any comfort to their rivals: "Sides will find they just cannot defend against us," he said. "Nobody is playing the game we are at the moment, not even England. The basic principle is fairly simple but you have to have the players to put it into operation. We do everything very close to the opposition – not 20 metres away where they can see exactly what's happening and then counter it."

And Barnes, who had developed a number of moves in concert with South African full-back Andre Joubert while on the Barbarians' tour of Scotland earlier in the season, was dismissive of any notion that rival clubs would be able to unlock Bath's secrets by studying videotape.

"I can assure them it won't do any good because we have so many different moves and even more variations. That's because we involve everybody, especially our wingers , and opponents cannot really guess who is going to make the breach."

Perversely, they then failed to cross the Northampton line at all, relying entirely on the boot of Jon Webb for a 15-6 victory which degenerated into a battle of the front rows. There had been much interest beforehand in whether the Saints' 6ft 10in Martin Bayfield would rule the roost over 6ft 4in Redman in the line-out. Bayfield won only two clean balls off his own hooker, John Olver, and although he pinched two off the Bath throw, he was generally nullified.

With Redman in possession of the middle jumper position – Haag's mobility and appetite for hard work had secured his place at the front of the line-out – Cronin had increasingly found himself on the sidelines. Lack of first team rugby was also hampering his chances of adding to his 22 Scotland caps after losing his place to Doddie Weir during the World Cup. But it was still a shock when he announced that he was quitting to join London Scottish. The club discounted a move for a big-name replacement, preferring to pin their hopes on developing young Andy Reed.

As one departed, however, there was the comforting sight of Hall back in training after a five-month lay-off. "I feel much better now," he said. "I'm back to near my normal weight of 16 stones-plus and hope to be back in contention for the Pilkington Cup tie at Northampton next month."

The confidence was misplaced however because he played no part in the 1991-92 season and his power and experience was sorely missed as Bath suffered a 10-9 defeat at Orrell on 14 December, a bitterly cold day when the country was blanketed in freezing fog. With just three points to their name from three league games, your author wrote at the time: "Bath have an uphill task to retain the Courage League title – but perhaps they are the only side who could contemplate achieving it."

Normal service was resumed with a 9-4 win over Bristol, courtesy of two Webb penalties and a dropped goal from Guscott, as Barnes controlled things expertly from fly-half. His compelling form had only just been rewarded with inclusion in a 33-strong England squad for the 1992 Five Nations Championship, along with Webb, Guscott, Hill, Redman, Dawe and Clarke. Redman and Dawe had absented themselves from the Bristol match in favour of a skiing holiday – Rowell made no attempt to hide his displeasure.

Following England's hosting of the second Rugby World Cup, marketing of the game was moving into a different gear. The BBC, having again lost out to ITV for the right to televise the World Cup, was now pressing to show a live Courage League match on a Sunday – but the RFU was having none of it. Competitions committee spokesman David Robinson explained the ruling body's thinking: "High level, competitive rugby on a Sunday would mean a complete cultural change for our game. It could be the thin end of the wedge." But in the same breath he said that they might consider a feasibility study.

Bath, so much the innovators in other ways, were firmly in the 'No' camp, as club secretary Clive Howard made clear: "We do not object on religious grounds although there are some people attached to the club who might feel strongly for that reason," he said.

"Bath have never been keen on Sunday rugby. For a start, it would make the organisation of games extraordinarily difficult – we need stewards, people to work in the clubhouse and others to help with the car parking. And how many fans would want to come along on a Sunday? We believe it far better to stick to traditional Saturday afternoon sport and will make that clear if asked."

Chapter 10

'NEVER IN DOUBT'

The phrase 'Never in doubt!' has become part of Bath folklore. Whether or not it was actually coined by Gareth Chilcott, his was always the definitive version – delivered with a wide grin, an air of improbable innocence and not a little relief.

The Bath team of two decades ago often made Harry Houdini look like Norman Wisdom. It was in the knock-out cup that their talent for escapology was practised and perfected, particularly against their unfortunate neighbours, Bristol and Gloucester.

The first half of the 1991-92 season had been frustrating in the extreme ... wholesale disruption by injuries, an October World Cup, a defeat at Orrell and a point deducted for fielding an unregistered player. Everything was in the balance.

Having stolen a march in the early years of truly competitive club rugby, Bath soon discovered that other clubs had learnt the lessons and upped their game – on and off the field.

The first match of 1992 involved a trip to second-placed Harlequins, who were celebrating their 125th anniversary and also the award of an OBE to England captain Will Carling in the New Year's Honours. This was no soft-centred London side to be routinely rolled over however – Quins paraded six of the England team that had so narrowly lost the World Cup final nine weeks earlier, including one Simon John Halliday, late of this Bath parish. Bath fielded Webb and Hill but Guscott was away in the USA on a business trip.

> **Harlequins programme notes, welcoming Bath to the Stoop for the first time since September 1988: "Since then, apart from seeing our team lose every encounter at the Recreation Ground, many Harlequins have built up an encyclopaedic knowledge of the parking possibilities offered by the City of Bath – so all has not been in vain"**

Halliday lasted until just before half-time, his eye split entirely accidentally by a wayward boot. But by that time Peter Winterbottom had seen his side build a seemingly unassailable 18-nil lead. First Mickey Skinner laid on a try for Carling, David Pears added a penalty when Dawe elbowed Brian Moore off the ball and then Bath conceded a penalty try after sustained pressure from the home front row. Pears' second penalty on 34 minutes seemed to support some pundits' contention that the Stoop was becoming the new powerhouse of English rugby.

Whether Quins took their foot off the gas or they were unsettled by Halliday's departure is not clear but having lock Troy Coker sent off in the 54th minute for punching did not help. Bath had been awarded a penalty try themselves by that time and the revival continued with two Webb penalties. At 18-12, with the game moving into injury time, Bath summoned up every ounce of belief and team spirit and finally Barnes sent de Glanville through the tightest of gaps. Webb's conversion attempt, a fiendishly difficult one from the left touchline, was the last kick of the game.

Never in doubt … and England hooker Moore wore a look of utter dejection and disbelief as he dragged his body off the field. Yet Hill lost his place to Orrell's Dewi Morris when the England team to face Scotland was announced two days later and Bayfield beat Redman to the second row position left vacant by Ackford's retirement.

So there was a dangerous whiff of grievance about Bath when they entertained Leicester on 11 January. For the first time ever at the Rec the gates were bolted on a record crowd of 8,200, with dozens of unhappy spectators left outside. It was compelling stuff as Bath ran in seven tries to win 37-6, with Swift running in a hat-trick, Fallon adding two and other tries following from replacement forward John Mallett and centre Iestyn Lewis. Webb kicked three conversions and a penalty. Star of the show however was Victor Ubogu who, when switched to flanker after Andy Robinson went off with a rib injury in the 22nd minute, rampaged with devastating effect. "Even if we had played well, we wouldn't have won," said Leicester skipper John Wells.

Webb was faultless in England's Championship opener, a 25-7 win at Murrayfield and five Bath players – Barnes as skipper, Fallon, de Glanville, Dawe, Haag and

Clive Book, take a bow

The match day programme for the 11 January 1992 meeting with Leicester profiled one of the unsung heroes of the Bath club. Clive Book had notched 400 appearances in the blue, black and white and has been captain of the Spartans hird team for six consecutive seasons. He had had 19 outings for the first team.

Clarke – gave Rowell the best possible start as England B coach with a 34-3 victory over Spain in Madrid. They followed up a fortnight later with an impressive 47-15 scoreline against the Irish second string at Richmond, a joyful Haag among the try scorers. Not that it did him much good because he later lost his place to Leicester's 21-year-old Martin Johnson who had been the original selection against Spain but was then ruled out with concussion.

As the internationals did their thing the Bath squad spent the best part of a week during January 1992 in mid-winter training in Lanzarote. Andy Robinson was looking forward to getting some expert treatment on a rib cartilage injury from physiotherapist Julie Bardner, a popular and experienced member of the back room team, ahead of the tough Pilkington Cup tie at Northampton. Bizarrely however she slipped on the poolside and joined the skipper on the casualty list with a fractured tibia and fibula and it was 48 hours before a second physio could be flown out to take over.

While Leicester had been rolled over at the Rec, there was no chance of their East Midlands neighbours surrendering so meekly in the fourth round Pilkington Cup tie on 8 February, not with former All Black skipper Wayne Shelford in the Northampton back row. The Saints had got to the final the previous summer before losing to Harlequins in extra time and had assembled a powerful pack around Shelford, including England's Tim Rodber and Martin Bayfield, not to mention skipper John Olver at hooker, veteran prop Gary Pearce and flanker Rob Tebbut. Strong-running fullback Ian Hunter was pressing hard for promotion from Rowell's B team.

With a full house of 7,000 packed into the Franklins Gardens, the tension was tangible. The tone was set from the very first minute when Barnes was late tackled, leaving Webb to kick a 45-metre penalty. It was bruising, cut-and-thrust stuff throughout the first half and John Steele replied with two penalties to give the home team a 6-3 lead as half-time neared. With a full five and a half minutes of injury time played Bath were penalised by Fred Howard for killing a ruck in a very kickable position, only for the decision to be reversed when a touch judge intervened.

Just after the break, Bath were awarded a penalty wide out on the left just short of half-way; Webb prepared to kick to the corner, far from confident that it was within goal-kicking range. But Barnes rushed forward to grab the ball, planted it on the mark and struck it unerringly between the posts. Olver protested that the Bath man had stolen a vital yard or two – but with such vehemence that referee Howard awarded a second penalty from halfway. And of course Barnes rubbed it in by repeating the feat.

The crowd seethed … Barnes smiled. He then nearly threw it all away by having a pass intercepted but Fallon got back to save the day and the game went into extra time. And it was the burly left wing who settled matters two minutes into injury time by sprinting on to Guscott's sweetly timed pass and racing 40 metres to the corner. After Steele missed a straightforward penalty kick, Bath held out with increasing confidence to win 13-9.

When the quarter-final draw threw up another potentially dramatic tie against Bristol at the Memorial Ground, to be played a fortnight later, relative newcomers like 23-year-old de Glanville were beginning to understand what cup rugby meant to Bath.

> **"There are quite a lot of young players like me and the side has changed quite a bit over the last couple of years," said the Oxford Blue, a marketing assistant at Cow & Gate at Trowbridge. "But we are still managing to do it – hang on when it's really tight. It's a question of attitude and you quickly discover that it's what is expected of you."**

Talking of players with 'attitude', the home side introduced 20-year-old Mark Regan for his Pilkington Cup debut following a neck injury to regular hooker Dave Palmer. Even in the early days of his career 'Ronnie' did not lack for confidence, as his pre-match interview with Chris Hewett, of the Bristol Evening Post, showed. "It's the biggest game I've ever played, by a mile," he said. "But now I'm in the side I want to stay there. While I've never played against any of the Bath blokes I know a fair bit about them. Dawe is very quick and very physical. He's a very good player – his record shows that. I'll have to be on my toes, that's for sure. But the Bristol props are pretty useful too. They'll help me get through."

It was a predictably tense affair – "grim and uninspiring" according to Bath's genial Past President, the late Jack Arnold. Webb kicked a penalty and converted a try at the posts by de Glanville before Barnes landed two superb penalties to kill off Bristol's challenge by 15pts-6.

In all their cup campaigns, Bath had never had a home semi-final draw – and 1992 was no different, throwing up a trip to Kingsholm on 4 April. But that was more than a month away so attention quickly turned back to the Courage League and a home match against ... Gloucester, of course.

With Egerton finally fit after a long and frustrating rehab from shoulder surgery to partner Robinson and Clarke in the back row, Bath soaked up fairly constant Gloucester pressure in the first quarter. They then struck with a slick Swift try before de Glanville followed up good work by Guscott and Fallon to claim another shortly before half-time. Barnes charged down a Marcus Hannaford clearance to grab a third and ended with 17 points after converting not only his own try but also one from Guscott in addition to kicking three penalties in a comprehensive 29-9 victory.

It was Gloucester's first league defeat in six matches and left Bath handily positioned behind leaders Orrell and second-placed Northampton. The defending champions appeared to have the easiest run-in – but there could be no slip-ups.

Andy Robinson, Steve Ojomoh, Victor Ubogu and Ben Clarke attempt to spoil Bristol's possession in the Pilkington Cup quarter-final at the Memorial Ground (22 February 1992).

Wasps, their opponents on 14 March, represented the biggest obstacle but with England's Jeff Probyn feeling the effects of England's successful Grand Slam campaign and injuries ruling out Steve Bates and Fran Clough, a trip to the suburban Repton Avenue ground at Sudbury posed no great fears, despite the absence of Webb with a bruised calf. Bath ran in unconverted tries by Hill, Fallon, Clarke and Swift, plus two Barnes penalties, to win 24-12. A week later Bath finally went top of the table with a 32-nil win at Rugby where de Glanville, Redman, Swift, Fallon and skipper Robinson crossed the line and Barnes kicked the rest of the points on a bare, wind-blown pitch.

"We missed out on three or four tries but the Rugby forwards played well in the close exchanges," said coach Rowell, acutely aware that having played one game more than Orrell and Northampton, Bath still needed to build an unassailable points difference advantage and for their rivals to slip up somewhere along the line if the Courage League trophy was to stay at the Rec.

Rowell's nervousness was even more evident after the following week's 25-15 victory at home to a spirited Nottingham side, who had led 9-7 just before the break. While Guy Gregory kicked five penalties for the visitors, tries by Hill and Egerton edged Bath ahead before Robinson settled matters from a five-metre scrum and Barnes kicked his second conversion.

Afterwards Rowell tried to reopen debate over the one-point deduction earlier in the season, saying: "It was a heavy penalty – a lot of people around the country agree. If it has an effect on the championship – and I stress IF because Orrell, who just have to keep winning, do not look like slipping up – it would be a shame for the Bath players." Robinson saw it slightly differently: "If Orrell win the title, good luck to them. They are the only side to have beaten us. But if Northampton sneak the championship when we have a far superior points difference, it will be a total travesty."

For the time being however attention had to switch back to the cup and the small matter of a semi-final in the cauldron of Kingsholm – the third such meeting of the sides at this stage of the national knock-out competition. Bath had squeezed through 12-11 in 1985, outscored two tries to one; four years later Stuart Barnes kicked two penalties in a 6-3 nailbiter.

But on 4 April 1992, with 14,000 squeezed into Kingsholm and the Shed at its most raucous and irreverent, a peculiarly West Country rivalry stretching back 110 years reached heights of drama beyond all expectation. For all the world like two 19th century prizefighters, they went toe-to-toe, taking everything the other side could throw at them – and then coming back for more.

Bath's back line employed every ounce of their guile and power to create a try for Fallon for a try on 28 minutes but this time it was no knock-out blow and with 79 minutes gone Gloucester had clawed their way back to 15-15 with a drop goal and three penalties from fullback Tim Smith and another drop goal from Neil Matthews. Then Bath somehow lost control of a line-out, allowing hooker Kevin Dunn to swoop on to the loose ball and send lock Kevin Sims steaming into the Bath 22. All it needed was quick ball, another accurate drop kick and Bath's cup dream would have been over. But Robinson raced back to perform an impossible act of pilfering at the ruck and Hill cleared to touch.

Into extra time and Gloucester fullback Tim Smith edged his side ahead with his fourth penalty; deep into the second period, the home side hung on to that three-point lead with increasing confidence that they could avenge to some degree the humiliation of Twickenham 1990.

But in the 98th minute, playing his last big hand of the match, Barnes called a miss-move going left off a rather shaky scrum on the Gloucester 22 and right wing Swift ghosted outside Fallon to run in a try on the left. As thousands of hearts sank to their boots in the Shed, Barnes converted from the touchline. Moments later, Webb fielded a loose kick from Matthews and set off with Guscott on his shoulder. It was then a simple matter for the England Grand Slam winner to put Fallon away for his second try. Barnes added a third conversion to his earlier three penalties to complete the 27-18 scoreline. "Never in doubt," he chuckled afterwards, not at all convincingly and totally unaware that a month later he would trump even this extraordinary finale.

Graham Dawe offered his own more considered assessment of a rugby phenomenon. "There is a spirit in this side that doesn't exist elsewhere," said the granite-like Tamar Valley farmer. "Teams might think they have us on the ropes but when it really matters we find something extra."

Bath supporters beginning to feel a tinge of sympathy for their Gloucester counterparts then headed for the bars in the confident expectation that the feeling would wear off after a few pints. And then they began to plan their trip to Twickenham and a meeting with the cup holders, Harlequins, on 2 May.

That something of a hangover could be detected in a insipid display at Rosslyn Park the following weekend was not surprising. Bath won 21-13 after a deceptively smooth opening in which Barnes dropped a goal and Fallon then scored his fifth try in as many games. Barnes added the conversion and a couple of penalties but Park clawed their way back to within five points by the hour mark. After Bath were twice held up on the home line, Barnes eventually settled for a penalty and two league points.

The travelling Bath support had little to cheer about until news came through that, joy of joys, both Orrell and Northampton had lost – and so the toasts were to Wasps and Nottingham. The stage was set for another 'double', only ever achieved by Barnes in his first season as captain three years before.

Ready to rumble ... Graham Dawe sets off with ball in hand.

Rosslyn Park skipper Richard Moon was seen making a bee-line for the Bath dressing room after his forehead had been split open by Fallon's knee in the second half of their Courage League match at Roehampton. But he was not about to let rip – it had been a complete accident. "I had read that Jon Webb was now extending his skills to plastic surgery," said the 29-year-old solicitor. "And he very kindly put nine stitches in my head, a grand job."

The playing side's unquenchable thirst for success encouraged them to establish links with equally progressive rugby minds wherever they could find them. One such was former France fullback Pierre Villepreux, now to be found coaching at Treviso in north-eastern Italy, so Bath invited this rugby philosopher to bring his side to the Rec on Easter Saturday. In building bridges in one direction, however, they burnt others behind them. Bristol, originally scheduled to host Bath in a friendly that day, had been less than pleased to be told earlier in the season that their guests would not be turning up and, still smarting over a similar spat in 1989, angrily suspended all future friendlies between the clubs.

Not for the first time, there was distinct unease among the more traditional committee members at what they regarded as rather shabby treatment of their friends over at the Memorial Ground. But the decidedly unsentimental Rowell and his coaching team, in which Bruton schoolmaster Brian Ashton was taking an increasingly influential role, had their eyes firmly fixed on the future, not the sepia-toned past.

They were not looking too far ahead though and skipper Robinson told his players in no uncertain terms to forget all about Twickenham on 2 May. "We rate the League as our main target and that's what I want the team to focus on," he said on the eve of their meeting with Saracens at the Rec. "We want the cup as well, but tomorrow's game is the crucial one. There will be no freezing from us. We faced losing the title because of our defeat at Orrell and that maddening deducted point. But it's up to us now. I expect us to succeed."

And succeed they did. Even when Saracens had flanker Justin Cassell sent off just after half-time – for stamping on Robinson – it disrupted Bath's rhythm as much as

Doug launches 2000 Club draw

The BFC 2000 CLUB was launched by Fund-raising Chairman Doug Ryder as a members only scheme involving a monthly standing order of £6 and a monthly draw. Prizes were distributed according to the number of members, with a maximum of 2,000. TVs were a regular and popular prize and one lucky winner was presented with a car.

Courage League hat-trick ... cue celebrations in the home dressing room (25 April 1992).

their opponents. But they were already 17-nil ahead at this stage thanks to the goal-kicking of Webb and Barnes and a try by Clarke. Although Ben Rudling replied with two penalties for the visitors, Barnes (2) and Fallon eased the home side to a 32-12 victory. Orrell finished level on 20 points but lost out on match points difference.

After first offering to speak up for Cassell at his disciplinary hearing, Robinson reflected on an eventful first season of captaincy:

> **"They said we were just a side for the 1980s; we have now won the league twice in the 90s. We are improving all the time, bringing in young players like Ben Clarke and Steve Ojomoh, who have been outstanding this year. Although people said the bubble would burst after certain players retired, we have managed to keep the ball rolling."**

So they prepared for a seventh Twickenham final in nine years and, on the face of it, in rather better fettle than Harlequins who were rocked by a double sending-off in their final game, both Mickey Skinner and the late Richard Langhorn being dismissed for stamping on Gloucester scrum-half Marcus Hannaford. Despite being afforded a special disciplinary hearing on the Thursday evening, the mandatory suspensions were confirmed.

The big surprise was the news that Ackford had agreed to come out of retirement to fill the hole left at lock by the return to Australia of Troy Coker. In the Bath camp, the desperately unlucky Egerton lost out to Ojomoh because of a rib injury while

Guscott returned from duty with a World XV in New Zealand to line up against his former centre partner, Simon Halliday.

BATH: *J Webb; A Swift, P de Glanville, J Guscott, J Fallon; S Barnes, R Hill; G Chilcott, G Dawe, V Ubogu, M Haag, N Redman, S Ojomoh, B Clarke, A Robinson* (capt).

HARLEQUINS: *D Pears; M Wedderburn, S Halliday, W Carling, E Davis; P Challinor, T Luxton; M Hobley, B Moore, N Mullins, N Edwards, P Ackford, M Russell, C Sheasby, P Winterbottom.*

REFEREE: *F Howard* (Liverpool)

Hill and Chilcott were the only players to have appeared in all six previous visits to Twickenham but it was the first cup final for five of the team – Fallon, de Glanville, Haag, Ojomoh and Clarke. Bath had got there without conceding a try, a remarkable statistic considering that their opposition had been drawn entirely from the Courage League First Division and that after beating Nottingham 52-nil at the Rec they had been the away side in the other three ties.

Despite the disruption to the Londoners' team selection, Rowell insisted he was not underestimating their opponents or their coach, Dick Best. "Quins will build themselves up for this," said the Bath maestro. "They said from the beginning that they weren't too interested in the league but certainly, for the cup, they get in the mood. They could score a lot of points – but then again so could we."

By the time trains, coaches, mini-buses and picnic-laden cars set out from towns and villages all over the West of England, 17,500 tickets had been sold through the Bath club. It was estimated however that their fans had snapped up another 10,000 of Quins' allocation. The total attendance was 62,000.

The 80 minutes of normal time in this final do not figure strongly in the memory, perhaps because Bath made little impact in the first half as the cup holders established a 12-3 lead with a Winterbottom try, converted by fullback David Pears, who also kicked two penalties. If there is an abiding image it is of Ackford, in his first game since a Christmas run-out with the Barbarians, confounding all expectations by dominating the line-out in concert with Neil Edwards.

Quins began to relax their grip, however, and Robinson's tireless work in the loose helped haul Bath back into the game. Gradually they built momentum and intensity and Webb kicked a penalty before de Glanville stretched through a tackle to score in the 70th minute. Webb calmly added the conversion and the match moved into extra time.

Nerves were being shredded on all sides of the ground – and in the middle – as Pears and fly-half Paul Challinor fired despairing drop-kicks at the posts in a vain effort to hang on to the trophy. With seconds remaining and everyone wondering

Harlequins players turn away in stunned disbelief as Stuart Barnes is mobbed by teammates after dropping the last-gasp goal that won the 1992 Pilkington Cup final.

when the title had last been shared (Gloucester v Moseley ten years earlier) a long kick out of defence was sliced into touch just short of the Harlequins' 10-metre line by wing Mike Wedderburn. It was the fifth minute of injury time and the 'countdown clock' in everyone's heads told them that the next time Fred Howard blew his whistle it would be for 'no side'.

Redman remembers an exchange with Hill as they made their way to the line-out. "Hilly asked me 'What are we going to do.' 'Two man line-out,' I said. 'But you've not won f* all, all afternoon,' replied Hilly. And I hadn't – but it worked."**

For perhaps the first time in the game, Redman outmanoeuvred the exhausted Ackford at the short line-out and directed Dawe's throw unerringly into Hill's hands; in a flash of his wrists the ball was on its way to half-back partner Stuart Barnes, still some 40 metres from the posts. Time stood still.

"I thought about an up-and-under," said the fly-half, who had been in bed with a flu-like virus during the week. "But when I looked at the other players I saw they were as knackered as I was. And since I had fired a 22 drop-out straight into touch a minute or two before, I knew I was still striking the ball pretty well. It went off the boot OK. From where I was I couldn't be sure that it went over but Fred

Howard eventually raised his arm." The match was over before they could update the scoreboard to read Bath 15, Harlequins 12.

'Never in doubt' somehow seemed rather inadequate on this occasion, for in a season of Great Escapes this was the greatest of them all. It all seemed a little unreal in the aftermath and even Rowell wore a slightly bemused, if satisfied, smile as he acknowledged how fiercely competitive a season it had been.

"Other clubs have been trying very hard and really going for it this year. That's what makes this achievement even better." And he added: "As I said to the players, when you're sweating it out on the training ground in mid-winter, ankle-deep in mud, this makes it all worthwhile."

As Stuart Barnes has since acknowledged, the Bath forwards had not had things so much their own way during the season. After so many humiliating afternoons at the hands – or more often the boots – of the Bath pack in previous seasons, First Division rivals had set about redressing the balance. After some judicious recruitment and smarter focus on the set-piece essentials, Orrell, Northampton, Gloucester, Leicester, Wasps and Harlequins no longer appeared out-gunned up front. The fact that Hall was unfit for the whole season evened things up even more – that's how influential he was.

All of which placed a huge onus on those behind the scrum to deliver the goods. And how they delivered. Fallon on the left wing had been a revelation, thriving on 1,000 press-ups a day to blast his way past and through defences and finishing with 16 tries in 24 appearances.

Jon Webb and Steve Ojomoh battle through joyous crowds outside Bath's Guildhall.

That sort of form had earned him four 'B' caps and a place on the England second string's summer tour to New Zealand. With Rory Underwood retiring, Fallon was favourite to inherit the England No 11 shirt. But he had also attracted attention from Leeds Rugby League club who made the 27-year-old trainee accountant an offer he could not refuse – £200,000 over five years, including a £45,000 signing-on fee, a sponsored car and further employment if he wanted it.

Fallon therefore turned his back on Rugby Union to go 'North' – the first Bath player of note to do so since 1905 when Tom White accepted a signing-on fee of £110 from Oldham, plus a weekly wage of £2 10s. Fallon left with everyone's best wishes but at the cost of a likely England cap.

Jim Fallon: lured away by Rugby League.

Led by Barnes and coached by Rowell, the England B side left for New Zealand a month later, without Fallon of course. A New Zealand XV captained by Warren Gatland took the honours in both Tests but the tourists won their other six fixtures. The first Test was sullied by a gratuitous stamping which left Ubogu with a badly torn ear while the main talking point after the second Test in Pukekohe was the refereeing of Colin Hawke who, ignoring a host of knock-ons and other infringements by his compatriots, also disallowed a good try by Barnes and awarded a dubious try to the home team.

Barnes, in whose lexicon diplomacy was a dirty word, did most of the talking: "It looked to me like the guy was bent," he told Steve Bale, of The Independent. Hardly pausing for breath he went on: "You don't come across the world to have a referee do that to you. There's the old stiff-upper-lip British attitude but sometimes when there's a performance like that I think you've got to speak out... It was noticeable that as soon as we got two scores ahead there was penalty after penalty after penalty."

There were those back home who thought Barnes should have been a little more circumspect but even in his autobiography he remained unrepentant, merely conceding: "It was another example of my brutish rugby manners."

With no other major Home Union tours there was a decent cooling off period before the start of the 1992-93 season, Bath beginning gently with a trip to Northern Italy to play Casale and Benetton Treviso. Alan Pearey, of The Bath Chronicle, reported: "While Bath's 'potenze e dinamismo' (power and dynamism) won many admirers, the tourists could only envy the outstanding facilities at Treviso, whose training ground – La Ghirada – included eight pristine pitches, a restaurant and a magnificent array of merchandise in the lavish club shop."

In April 1992 Bath had announced that its unwieldy 28-man Management Committee structure was being overhauled, to be replaced by an eight-man Executive with power to make day-to-day decisions. Underlying tensions between the traditional and progressive elements within the club finally surfaced during the summer over the construction of the new Press Box in the roof of the West Stand.

At an eventful management meeting on 15 September, Grounds Committee chairman John Roberts, also fixtures secretary, advised that an extra £3,000-4,000 would be needed to strengthen the foundations of the steelwork. This took the costs to over £60,000, which came as something of a shock, especially as a new electricity sub-station was also required at a cost of £17,000. Roberts, a distinguished former captain who amassed 354 appearances before retiring in 1958, tendered his resignation shortly afterwards as did club chairman Roger Berry, who was succeeded by local solicitor and long-time supporter John Gaynor.

At least John Roberts had bequeathed in his fixture list a peach of a game to open the season – a re-run of that epic Pilkington Cup final four months earlier.

The Club Shop had been moved to a portable building and there was a marked increase in sale of club memorabilia, replica jerseys, sweatshirts, T-shirts etc.

On the field there was a new face in the pack in rangy second row Sean O'Leary, recruited from Wasps, but the main interest was in the return of Hall after missing the whole of the 1991-92 season following the knee surgery. His inclusion alongside Clarke, with Ojomoh filling in for injured skipper Robinson at open side, made for a decidedly muscular back row. With the new 'turnover' experimental law variation in operation at ruck and maul, that was where Bath laid the foundations for a 22-6 victory. Hall acknowledged he was not operating at full throttle, saying: "I'm not quite there yet. The knee is fine but I was a bit off the pace. Luckily it wasn't a very fast game."

Sad farewell to second row Mark

The match programme against Orrell on 24 October 1992 included a memorial tribute to former second row forward Mark Jones, who died earlier in the month aged just 29. He played 36 times for the 1st XV, scoring six tries, his last appearance being at Leicester in the Courage League on 22 April 1989. He was a quiet unassuming lad and at the same time a friend to everybody.

Bath were leading 12-6 seven minutes into the second half when Barnes spied a gap down the blindside of a scrum, drew two defenders and put Guscott over with a well-timed inside pass – the first five-point try on the Rec following changes to the points scoring laws. Webb converted and later added his fifth penalty.

Newly promoted London Irish were the visitors a week later and found the champions – particularly Ubogu – in irrepressible mood. The England B prop burrowed through for the first try inside five minutes and added another on 20 minutes, storming 25 metres to touch down after latching on to a loose Irish line-out tap. The Exiles kept in touch up to half time, notably when Geoghegan read the bounce correctly to score, but Bath ran out 42-19 winners. De Glanville, Clarke and Barnes, profiting from a 40-metre burst by Ubogu, scored second half tries.

David Hilton, a recent recruit from Bristol where his family ran a butchery business, made his debut at prop a week later at Blackheath. Fielding a formidable back row in Hall, Egerton and Robinson, now recovered from a hamstring injury, Bath could afford to introduce a few fresher faces and still win 51-nil. It was the last fixture between two clubs, both of whom pre-dated the founding of the Rugby Football Union 121 years earlier.

Dave Hilton: debut at Blackheath.

Rowell was on business in Spain in the lead-up to the Courage League trip to Northampton on 10 October but that was no excuse for an error-strewn display which saw the Saints edge an 11-8 victory. Nor could Bath really make much of the blatant knock-on by Nick Beal that earned the right wing a breakaway try to establish an 11-nil lead on the half-hour.

Too many experienced players made too many errors and Rodber, shunted into the second row after the late withdrawal of Bayfield, made life distinctly uncomfortable for O'Leary in the line-out. Barnes kicked a penalty and Clarke scored a fine individual try in the second half but time ran out on Bath and they experienced defeat in the league for the first time since losing at Orrell ten months earlier. "It's like losing a member of the family," said skipper Robinson, with feeling.

The only Bath player entitled to walk around with a big smile on his face was Ubogu, selected for his England debut against Canada at Wembley Stadium a week later. Guscott scored a try as England won 26-13, with Webb at full-back and Barnes and de Glanville on the bench.

The raft of experimental law variations had included changes to the refereeing of line-outs, with the gap between the two lines doubled to one metre; the requirement for a one-metre gap between players in the line was dropped. A player jumping for the ball could no longer use his outside arm to catch or tap the ball but once he

Victor Ubogu: Wembley debut for England.

had touched the ball others could move to bind on to or support him.

What this meant, of course, was that clubs were suddenly casting around for even taller and supposedly more athletic men who could be held up – not lifted, mind you, although that distinction was eventually quietly dropped. This radical reappraisal of what it took to be an international class second row forward was largely responsible for the extraordinarily rapid emergence of a player who began the season facing opponents of the calibre of Casale and Blackheath yet nine months later was running out at Okara Park, Whangerei, in the opening match of the Lions' tour of New Zealand.

Andy Reed, a 23-year-old, 6ft 7in Cornishman, had played just 19 matches for Bath since joining from Plymouth Albion two years earlier. But, after O'Leary's uncomfortable afternoon at Franklins Gardens and having featured in a 63-6 thrashing of Coventry, Reed was given the No 5 shirt for the visit of Orrell on 24 October, paired with Redman.

Ranged against the even taller Charles Cusani, Reed began nervously but once the line-out began to operate more smoothly, Bath pulled away to win 39-3. Hall was the pick of the forwards with two of the five tries and Hill had the satisfaction of touching down when Dewi Morris, who had nicked his England place, dropped the ball at a scrum on the line. Webb scored 19 points.

Continuing their recovery from the shock of Franklins Gardens, Bath made the short trip to the Memorial Ground where they defeated a dogged Bristol 31-8, purely by dint of their superior attacking skills. Just three minutes had elapsed before Webb combined with Adebayo and Clarke scored at the corner flag. Bristol battered away at line-out, scrum, ruck and maul but made absolutely no headway. Swift added another before half-time and although Bristol finally got over the line through Johnston, Webb scored on his former home ground and Swift crossed for his second try.

November 1992 was historic month in rugby because it marked the return of the Springboks to Britain, offering a final glimpse of one of the game's truly great players, Danie Gerber. Barnes skippered the England B side that faced the tourists at Bristol on 7 November, joined by de Glanville, Clarke and Redman, with Hill and Ojomoh on the bench. Back at the Rec, a scratch side defeated Cardiff 31-22 but it was a pale imitation of the great contests of the previous decade.

Clarke continued his inexorable development from raw-boned prospect to world-class performer with an England debut at Twickenham seven days later; de Glanville's all-round excellence also earned him a first cap off the bench as England won 33-16.

Ubogu had kept his place on the tight-head and Guscott scored one of four tries while Webb contributed three penalties and two conversions. Stuck firmly to the replacements' bench however was Barnes, still waiting to add to his measly tally of eight caps after more than four years of occasionally self-imposed exile.

Bath got back to the serious stuff on 21 November – and it didn't come much more serious than a Courage League trip to Welford Road. There was a punch-up at the very first scrum, prompting a warning for Darren Garforth, and Webb kicked a penalty from 30 metres, later cancelled out by John Liley. It became a duel between the two packs and the fullbacks until home scrum-half Aadel Kardooni made an ill-advised break from a scrum inside his own 22 – "criminal, just criminal," was the unforgiving verdict from his coach Tony Russ – and was robbed of the ball. Barnes sniped, Guscott supported and his overhead pass put Adebayo away in the 68th minute.

Five minutes later Bath scored a second try through Redman, who provided the power and technique from lock to win the scrum and was then up in support of Guscott when the centre danced through the cover. Both conversions by Barnes were off target but 13-3 at Welford Road was satisfactory enough, thank you.

There was unfinished business at an extraordinary meeting of the club the following week when the disagreements of the recent months – and even recent years – came to a head. It was a painful, if ultimately cathartic experience, in which the resignations of Roger Berry and John Roberts were aired, the £60,000 press box chewed over and even the question of an agent's fee for the sponsorship deals laid open to public scrutiny. In the end it was generally agreed that the old Management Committee system that had served the club for a century or more was no longer up to the job of overseeing a club with the ambitions of Bath Football Club (RFU) in the 1990s.

That was the nub of the matter. A new structure had to be devised to meet those demands, as Barnes made clear in one of the last speeches of a long evening. His call for an end to cliques, better communication between the playing and management functions of the club and for easier executive decision-making was heartily supported, not least by Life Member and Past President, Jack Arnold. Still a contributor to the match programme, Jack's allegiance to the club stretched back more than half a century as a team-mate of the legendary R A Gerrard.

While the Bath squad travelled up to Blundellsands to begin their defence of the Pilkington Cup against Waterloo, Barnes and Clarke were excused in order to turn out for the Barbarians against the Wallabies at Twickenham.

Waterloo posed no great threat, on paper at least, but they had a 19-year-old Austin Healey on the left wing and England Under-21 fly-half Paul Grayson opposed Barnes's deputy, Craig Raymond.

Bath had not lost an away cup-tie for five seasons but it was Moseley all over again. The absence of Ubogu and Reed, replaced by Mallett and O'Leary, seemed hardly to weaken the front five and Egerton was as capable a deputy for Clarke as anyone could have wished for. Unfortunately, Raymond was not on the same wavelength as his three-quarter line and the teamwork around him fell apart as Waterloo seized their opportunity.

Grayson and Webb swapped penalties at the end of the first quarter and when Swift scored an unconverted try two minutes into the second half, it looked as if Bath would pull away. Yet Grayson added a second penalty and suddenly nerves were beginning to affect the champions' touch finding and ball handling. All they could do was hoof the ball into the air and hope to cash in on an error; that's how it happened, only the other way round. Grayson kicked ahead, was obstructed and gratefully landed the penalty from 25 metres to put his side 9-8 ahead.

Panic-stricken Bath began to run everything and Guscott found himself with a two man overlap. Why he then attempted a dropped goal, no-one will know. It was nowhere near the target and Waterloo held out to celebrate long into the night as the Bath coach set out on a 200-mile trip home, a "funereal" journey according to Rowell. It was only their third cup defeat in ten years.

It was little consolation that Gloucester and Bristol also exited the competition at such an early stage or that Waterloo also accounted for Orrell in the next round and gave Harlequins a run for their money after that.

Suddenly, the Divisional Championship offered a rather more attractive diversion to Bath players who had previously shunned the competition and ten of their number featured in the South West team that beat the North. On successive weekends, a below-strength Bath accounted for Nottingham, Richmond and London Welsh.

A 21-year-old South African-born player by the name of Mike Catt made the quietest of debuts in a 24-17 win at Nottingham on 5 December 1992. He was on holiday from Port Elizabeth, visiting his uncle in Stroud.

Having spent a season at fly-half for Eastern Province he naturally fancied a spell of rugby to liven up his globetrotting and had first rung Gloucester. But no-one at Kingsholm answered the phone – so he had called the Rec instead and was put in touch with Chilcott.

Simon Jones takes up the story: "Catty rang Cooch and he gave him my number. I told him to come down to Lambridge – and we could tell straight away that he 'had it'."

The youngster also featured in the 38-22 victory at Richmond but then had to wait five weeks for his next outing,

Having performed his duties as 'go-between', Chilcott began a two-month run in the pantomime Cinderella at Bath's Theatre Royal, cast as the dastardly 'broker's man' alongside Rolf Harris, Lesley Joseph and Sylvester McCoy. Resplendent in Regency frock coat, breeches and buckled shoes, Chilcott was able to give free rein to a comical version of the character he had chiselled out for himself on the rugby field – mellowed but still slightly menacing.

The sabbatical was a salutary reminder that Bath must contemplate a future without Cooch. Now 36, he had acquired all the experience and technique to play on either side of the scrum at the highest level but he relied on his nous rather than his legs to ensure he was in the right place at the right time.

Although he was missing for three months in total, Chilcott missed only two significant matches, such was the fragmented nature of the fixture list in 1992-93. He was certainly not missed when Rugby were thrashed 61-7 at the

Mike Catt: 'stopover' in Bath.

Rec on 9 January. Skipper Robinson and Redman scored two and the others were shared by Barnes (2), Adebayo (2), Guscott and Webb who added five conversions and a penalty.

The following Friday night, Clifton were brushed aside 43-3 on the eve of England's Five Nations opener against France. Webb kicked three penalties at Twickenham, also converting Hunter's try in a 16-15 victory notable for the debut of Martin Johnson; Guscott won his 25th cap and Clarke his second while Barnes, de Glanville and Ubogu stayed on the bench. Hall continued his comeback by earning a B cap against the French second string that weekend and perhaps most significantly, Reed made his debut for Scotland against Ireland, having discovered the obligatory Scottish grandparent.

London Irish came to the Rec a week later for a non-League fixture and Catt celebrated the arrival in the post that morning of a British passport by scoring his first tries in a 47-5 victory. "I was going back to South Africa next month but my rugby future is with Bath now," he said. "The passport is the key to everything because I don't need to worry about visas and I should have automatic league registration."

The youngster's Courage League debut came rather more quickly than anyone had expected, least of all Catt himself. After a 63-13 run-out at Plymouth Albion, Barnes picked up a calf injury which ruled him out of the trip to Gloucester on 13 February. With Hill sidelined by an ankle problem, Bath were left with no option but to field an untried half-back combination of Catt and Ian Sanders.

If Kingsholm was still an intimidating venue, then Gloucester themselves were anything but. Catt slipped effortlessly into the playmaking role alongside his half-

Every Time Ref, Every Time

It was in 1991 that a six-page A4 printed fanzine, lovingly put together by Clive Banks and Glen Leat, first grabbed the attention of fellow Bath supporters. Not so much 'desktop' as 'kitchen tabletop' publishing, it immediately struck a chord with the denizens of the Rec, for its freshness and for its ability to connect with the ordinary supporter and player alike.

Just 100 copies of Issue 1 were distributed, containing "some embarrassingly sad l ittle articles which at the time we clearly thought were good," according to Leat, rather too modestly, in a 2006 retrospective on the www.bathrugbyere.co.uk website i nto which ERE morphed.

Issue 3, a Christmas edition, saw the introduction of the hand drawn salmon, which surfaced improbably in a variety of stories for several seasons.

It owed its surreal existence to the all too real fresh salmon awarded at every home game to the winner of the 'Lucky Programme Number'. "Take it from me, it was a bloody big fish," said Leat. "If the fish wasn't collected by the winner the players took it; not to eat but to lark around with in the changing rooms. Can you imagine the mess and of course the smell?"

The 300 copies of Issue 3 sold out in 45 minutes and so its successor was bumped up to 450, "no mean feat when one should remember we were copying the thing by hand at the time," added Leat.

Issue 5, "a bumper 16-pager," featured the first interview with a player, Victor Ubogu. By that time, some eight years on, ERE had spawned its own website, which continues to provide an independent soapbox for Bath rugby supporters.

back partner, creating a try for Swift with a 'bomb', while Webb added five penalties in a routine 20-nil victory.

In the month leading to the next league fixture, a potentially decisive visit from table-topping Wasps, Bath faced all-Welsh opposition. The first game against Swansea was extraordinary – a 79-3 Friday night try-fest with 13 touchdowns of which four were scored by Clarke. Wings Swift and Adebayo nabbed two each and the others went to Catt, Ubogu, Robinson and Callard, who kicked seven conversions. Ojomoh, although not on the scoresheet, was as impressive as anyone. A near full-strength side went to Cardiff on 27 February but came up short, losing 27-17 at the Arms Park, while it was very much a United/Spartans line-up that lost 19-13 at Newbridge the following week.

Attention was very much focused on Twickenham that weekend though because Barnes had finally been picked ahead of Andrew following England's sterile 10-9 defeat in Cardiff. Trust the Bath man to put his money where his mouth was – it was a stunning break from his 22 that laid on a try for Rory Underwood and set England up for a 26-12 victory over the Scots. Barnes suddenly found himself in the unusual position of being everyone's favourite fly-half and could look forward with some confidence to a place on the Lions tour.

Sandwiched between that uplifting performance and England's final match in Dublin, the meeting of the country's top clubs never lived up to expectations. It was a niggly affair in which Wasps had Fran Clough sent off in the 15th minute after a clash with Guscott and it went downhill from there. Andrew, reacting to his demotion to the England bench, banged over his kicks, including one from five metres inside his own half and laid on a try for Phil Hopley, while Webb struggled to find his range. Eventually, however, the one-man advantage told and the England fullback put his side 12-11 ahead on the hour. On 77 minutes Barnes dropped a goal after de Glanville set up a ruck and Guscott's injury time try, converted by Webb, confirmed a 22-11 victory.

After missing five kicks at goal Webb was critical of his own performance, saying: "It was a poor game and I kicked badly. Mentally I was spot on but it got to the stage where I was perhaps trying too hard. If I had kicked those goals we'd have been 15-20 points ahead and they would have had to play catch-up rugby, which they weren't strong enough to do."

Looking back, however, it was nothing short of miraculous that Webb was able to play at this level at all. There had been occasions when he would have to travel to away matches after a night in the operating theatre and his growing responsibilities as a surgeon at Princess Margaret Hospital in Swindon were making it increasingly difficult to pursue a first-class rugby career.

As it became clear that he would miss out on selection for the Lions tour, Webb made his farewell to international rugby in Dublin the following weekend. It was not an auspicious occasion because the Lions-laden English team was overwhelmed 17-3. Webb kicked his side's only points. It soon became known that he would be retiring from the game altogether at the end of the season and indeed medical duties forced him to miss Bath's Courage League matches at West Hartlepool and at home to London Scottish.

That opened the door to Callard who had been patiently waiting in Webb's shadow for three seasons. Any anxieties were settled at Brierton Lane where the 27-year-old Downside schoolmaster scored two tries in the 38-10 victory. Barnes, having been confirmed in the Lions tour party to New Zealand along with Guscott, Clarke and

Reed, ran in a hat-trick and added a conversion and three penalties. Rowell, back in his home town, was suitably impressed: "That's the best we've played in weeks. Some of it was breathtaking."

With an unassailable points difference of 218, all Bath needed to do to retain their league title was to beat London Scottish at the Rec and then account for Saracens at Southgate. Callard scored a try and a conversion as the final scoreline of 40-6 sent the Exiles down to the Second Division. On an usually wet and windy day for the first week of April, Clarke and Ubogu were the heavy cavalry clearing the way for the backs to run through the remnants of the Scottish defence. Both were among the try scorers as were Swift, Barnes, Callard and de Glanville. The other points came from Barnes's boot – two penalties and a conversion.

There were two friendlies before the deciding league match – an 81-8 drubbing of Newbury with Catt scoring three tries and eight conversions and an anti-climactic farewell for Webb at the Rec when Gloucester nicked a 17-16 win. Chairman John Gaynor made a presentation on the final whistle to the unassuming 29-year-old, who reflected afterwards: "The reason I gave it one more season was to make absolutely sure it was the right decision. I know now it is, but I've had such good fun that it was always going to be sad to turn my back on it. I've had a lot of support from team-mates, club officials, friends and the ordinary supporters, which was important whenever things got difficult."

It was no surprise that Webb was handed the No 16 shirt – there was still no No 13 in the Bath team numbering – for the trip to Saracens. What did come as something of a shock, not least to Callard, was his selection on the left wing after an injury to Adebayo earlier in the week.

With only one and a half training sessions to learn the ropes, he had no desire to extend the experiment beyond that match but ended up winning the title with his two tries. Just eight minutes from time, Bath were trailing 13-11 but Barnes struck a penalty goal from 35 metres to snatch a one point lead and then sent up a high kick which was spilled by home fullback Andy Tunningley under pressure from Guscott. In a replay of the first half score, de Glanville swooped on the loose ball and flicked up a pass to Callard who had just enough momentum to make the corner. Barnes's conversion was wide but Bath saw out the remaining minute or two to grab the spoils.

At the final whistle, amid all the noisy jubilation, there was a quiet, almost poignant moment as Chilcott walked over to Rowell and shook his hand. It was recognition by the old warrior that this would be the last time he would savour such an occasion. The 'old guard' were preparing to enter the pantheon reserved for heroes.

Chapter 11

'UPS AND DOWNS'
OF A LINE-OUT JUMPER

As the Bath players savoured a hat-trick of Courage League title successes on 24 April 1993 an unfamiliar face appeared around the door of the Away dressing room at Saracens.

It belonged to an enterprising character who had seized the opportunity of a bumper crowd to set up a bungee-jump attraction suspended from a huge crane behind the Saracens clubhouse. "As reward for winning the league I'm offering you a free jump," he said. "Who's up for it?"

Guscott was first to take up the challenge, to be followed by Clarke and Barnes, who insisted on being launched backwards on the oversized elastic band – whether through bravado or because he could not bear to look down at the drop, it was not entirely clear.

Nigel Redman: topsy-turvy season.

Second row Redman was the fourth player to be launched into the air 165ft above Southgate Park and the experience is still vivid: "All I remember was that there were hundreds of people watching from the ground and that the inflatable on the ground looked very, very small."

It was an oddly appropriate way to round off a topsy-turvy season but the human yo-yo experience also served as a neat metaphor for Redman's career at the time.

While second row partner Reed prepared to join Guscott, Barnes and Clarke and the rest of the Lions' tour party to tour New Zealand, Redman's reward was a short five-match tour of Canada with an under-strength England squad. Also involved were Adebayo, de Glanville, Ubogu, Hall and Ojomoh.

At 6ft 3in, not the widely quoted 6ft 4in – as he freely acknowledges now – Redman was then regarded as too short for an international class line-out jumper. He did not even merit a place in the side for the two-Test series against the Canadians, which was squared 1-1. As skipper of the midweek team, he found himself ranked a distant fifth in the second row pecking order, behind Wade Dooley, Martin Bayfield and his rivals on tour, Martin Johnson and Bristol's Andy Blackmore.

Almost ten years out from the 2003 World Cup, the Canada tour provided valuable experience for uncapped youngsters such as Matt Dawson, Graham Rowntree and Neil Back. An Under-21 tour to Australia that summer also blooded Catt, Mark Regan and Simon Shaw. Meanwhile Johnson, called up by the Lions as replacement for Dooley, fully justified his selection for the second and third Tests in New Zealand.

So Redman prepared for an 11th season as a Bath player, this time under the captaincy of John Hall. Both were at a time of their careers where they had been forced to reinvent themselves, one because of persistent knee injuries which had limited his mobility, the other because of changes in the law book.

"All of a sudden the change in the laws brought about a situation where there was more space and no lifting," says Redman. "Up to that point it was toe-to-toe, 'hand in the pocket', using the outside arm to win the ball, elbows and the rest. Because those days were over it became an aerial contest rather than a physical battle.

"The way I adapted was to move and think differently, to look at different places to stand in the line-out, to move forward and back using footwork and to time the jump. My attitude also was not to get too wound up about whether you were or weren't going to win line-out. You win games by scoring more points. So what could I do to contribute around the park?

> **"I had to be fit and to be strong, so I trained differently. I needed to have the skills of a back row forward, so I had to work on my hands, on my ability to win ball on the floor, on my defence; I worked on everything I could, not just the line-out, but all facets of the game."**

It was a strategy that Redman pursued with a relentless ambition – a quality shared with many of his Bath team-mates – and if the England selectors did not always seem to appreciate his worth, opponents of the quality of the All Blacks and the French certainly did.

On the other side of the world the tour had ended ignominiously for the Lions 'dirt trackers' with a 38-10 loss to Waikato. A developing knee problem also meant it was Reed's last match for four months so newcomer Pat McCoy joined Redman in the second row for the opening match of the 1993-94 season – a trip to Ireland to mark the opening of Garryowen's new clubhouse at Dooradoyle in Limerick.

A sore groin ruled out Guscott too but Bath did their hosts the honour of including both Barnes and Clarke, who showed something of his Lions Test form as Bath scored six tries to none in a commanding 38-8 victory.

Newly appointed Garryowen coach David Leslie, the former All Black captain, professed himself a card-carrying member of the Clarke fan club, saying: "He's the kind of honest-to-goodness forward we appreciate in New Zealand but he has a rare quality about him." He was just as impressed with Bath, saying: "I would say that there are only two or three club sides back home who can play the game the way Bath do. It's an approach that seems sadly lacking in the British Isles but at least our players know now exactly what I'm aiming for."

Bath returned to beat Bristol 18-10 on the Memorial Ground in a dour opening league fixture which appeared to turn on a collective half-time 'bollocking' delivered by Chilcott. "We'd started terribly slowly and Bristol were getting right in there amongst us," he said. "We weren't giving it anything like enough. I called everyone together and said: `You look as though you don't want this one. Remember who you're playing. I don't want to lose to this lot and I don't think you do either. But we will if we don't get stuck in.'

"It seemed to do the trick. I think we were well on top come the end – when the Bristol forwards called a big scrum, we didn't go anywhere. In fact, we put them up in the air at one point."

It was an open secret that this was going to be Chilcott's last appearance at the Memorial Ground and already people were preparing their valedictions. Graham Dawe viewed him as "almost irreplaceable," adding:

"I don't suppose even Cooch would claim he gets around the field as much as he did, but he'll always be the first name on my team sheet. He makes my life so easy. We knew they were talking about coming at us in the front row, but they were never going to get the better of us in that department. Cooch told us what he wanted in the dressing room and, after a ropey start, we gave it to him on the pitch."

Mike Catt was the match winner with two tries but it was also an important game for young Haag who stole a crucial line-out one-handed from Shaw and proceeded to take a string of clean catches in important positions. He partnered Redman again for the home match with Northampton whose line-up included 6ft 10in Martin Bayfield as well as Paul Grayson, recruited from Waterloo to fill the fly-half spot. In the lead-up Saints had made it known that they viewed Bath as very beatable but after being trounced 37-9 their skipper, John Olver, said rather soberly: "It's back to the drawing board I suppose."

Audley Lumsden, back in harness after a cruel succession of injuries – a broken neck and a twice-fractured leg – scored two tries on the left wing and offered some sharp advice: "Sides coming down here should never make the mistake of shouting their mouths off beforehand. They should keep quiet and do it on the field." The other points, scored in devastating 20-minute spells at the start of each half, came from a Clarke try plus another by Callard who converted all four and added three penalties.

Hall wisely made no brave predictions ahead of the visit to Orrell on 25 September and was relieved to come away with an 18-15 victory. With its celebrated meat pies and local ales, Edgehall Road was always a wonderfully welcome venue – until you ran down the steps on to the pitch. Leicester had come a cropper there the previous weekend but Bath got off to an encouraging start with tries by Callard and Guscott until injuries to Swift and Callard left Robinson filling in on the blindside wing. Coming down the slope in the second half with the wind at their backs and with Dewi Morris chivvying effectively from scrum-half, Orrell punished Bath's indiscipline with two more Simon Langford penalties but that was a close as they got.

Gloucester arrived at the Rec on the back of draws against Wasps and Newcastle-Gosforth and a defeat at home to Leicester. Even without Barnes to run the show, Bath showed no mercy, running

Martin Haag: new partner for Redman.

in six tries to win 46-17. Five conversions and four penalties from Callard, his head swathed in a turban-like bandage to protect the gashed scalp he suffered at Orrell, complemented tries from Clarke, Guscott, Ubogu 2, Adebayo and Hill. A tendency to 'switch off' during periods of the game and a penalty count of 20 against were matters of concern, however.

New man in the secretary's chair

The match programme for the visit of Harlequins introduced a new Honorary Club Secretary in John Quin following the death of Clive Howard three months earlier. There was also a collection in his memory, which raised the remarkable sum of £1,474 for cancer research, care and special equipment both for the medical practice at Beckington near his home and at Ward 7 of the RUH where Clive spent his final days.

Later in the year came news that former chairman George Brown, a stalwart of the club in almost every capacity, had died in Spain.

'Ups And Downs Of A Lineout Jumper'

The 1993-94 season was the first to feature home-and-away fixtures – 18 matches in a 10-team National Division 1 – but the programme was about to take a break before the Divisional Championship, itself brought forward to accommodate the All Blacks' tour.

The first four fixtures had established a clear pecking order, with Bath just ahead of Leicester, closely followed by Northampton and Wasps, the leaders' next opponents. Bath squeezed through 19-13 on the tight little ground at Sudbury thanks to three first-half penalties by Callard and tries after the break by Catt and Clarke. Visiting Irish referee Gordon Black obligingly declared Clarke's try good, although the big flanker emerged from under a pile of bodies with a sheepish grin. Wasps skipper Dean Ryan, who had been robbed by Hall at the preceding line-out, protested in vain that the ball had been grounded short and was even more indignant when Mr Black ruled against his own claim for a try in the closing seconds.

Hall was more than happy to take a fifth straight Courage League win. "The message I've tried to get over to the team – and they keep joking about it – is that we are trying to break the season down into digestible chunks," he said. "This was the first chunk. We've bitten that off and swallowed it," he added.

Attention then turned to the Divisionals, more for the pointers towards selection to face the All Blacks than for any indication as to the respective strengths of England's regions. But the South West, now with Hall as skipper, took control from the first game with a 31-3 win against the Midlands at Bath and followed up by defeating the North 29-16 at Gloucester. Rowell claimed the divisional selectors were raiding Bath for replacements and "bleeding us dry" but his makeshift team then beat Nottingham 77-34 on the Rec!

In restructuring the competitive season, the RFU had bizarrely earmarked the final divisional championship round on the same day – 6 November – as England A were due to meet the New Zealanders at Gateshead. It therefore had to be rearranged for 3 January when, with Dawe as skipper, the South West took the title by beating London 25-17 in front of 7,000 at Twickenham.

Their big game however was on 30 October when Hall led the South West against Sean Fitzpatrick's All Blacks at the other Recreation Ground in Redruth. With 10 Bath players selected, it was an odd choice of venue, influenced very much by rugby politics and a desire to placate the Cornish constituency. A Jamie Joseph try turned a close game in favour of the All Blacks, who edged it 19-15, but the main talking point was the sight of 15 ugly stitches around Phil de Glanville's left eye after yet another unsavoury raking incident.

When Hall led England A against the tourists at Gateshead's International Stadium a fortnight later he was joined by five other Bath men – Callard, Catt, Dawe, Redman and a fit-again Barnes – while Ojomoh was a temporary replacement. But the All Blacks again took the honours, 26-12, with Callard kicking all the home points. Clarke, nailed on for a Test spot, scored a try when he turned out for the club in a bruising encounter with the South African Barbarians, who won 34-23 on the Rec despite having 'Toks' van der Linde sent off for stamping on Hilton.

Guscott also tested out his troublesome groin but to no avail and that was his last appearance of the season for club or country, proving that even his supremely athletic frame was not immune to the rigours of the modern game. His only meaningful period of rest since his spectacular emergence on the world scene a four and a half years earlier had been in the summer of 1992.

While the All Blacks headed north over the border for the Scottish leg of their tour, Bath's England hopefuls switched back into Courage League mode. Callard kicked five penalties and converted tries by Clarke and Hill in the 46-3 demolition of Newcastle-Gosforth on the Rec. Other tries followed from Jon Bamsey, Dawe and Lumsden but the score that earned the biggest cheer was undoubtedly a conversion by Chilcott. It was Cooch's final game on the Rec, his 373rd in a Bath career that had begun way back on 28 September 1977 when he lined up against Sir Leonard Cheshire's International XV.

The programme for his final home game was therefore a 'Chilcott special', incorporating tributes from all quarters, including Rowell who said: "What a great stalwart he has been, not only an outstanding player but an enduring enthusiast," and also in the regular feature by 'Bill and Ben, The Flowerpot Men': "Not only does

Cooch, the Grand Master

Gareth Chilcott has long been held as one particular image of Bath, the West Country tough-nut, the snarling prop with the bristling bonce, the streetfighter you hate to face but always want close by in the trenches.

Imagine, therefore, the size of the peg I was taken down during the 1988 England tour of Australia and Fiji when, having bored the backside off my colleagues with an increasingly detested chess set, I turned my attentions on the squad.

Is it not amazing how quickly a packed bar can clear when someone issues the immortal opening line: "Any of you chaps play chess?" What I found utterly amazing was seeing the Bath legend of biff, 'Coochie' Chilcott, approaching and hearing his Bristolian burr reply: "I'll give you a game Rochey, but you'll have to show me the finer moves."

Suffice to say the only fine moves I made were towards the Irish whiskey bottle. Coochie won what became a tour-long series either 5-4 or 6-5 and has not stopped baiting me since.

Tony Roche
Praetorian order of Bath, Pilkington Cup final programme notes – 7 May 1994

Gareth Chilcott fashions a new life outside of rugby, given a stylish send-off
by Martin Haag and John Hall.

he hold up (or down) the opposition when their heads are locked in the scrum but he manages to tie in three opposing players at the line-out without going anywhere near the ball – poetry in motion."

Stuart Barnes offered an equally fond tribute under the title 'Cooch – a Sort of Obituary'. Here are some extracts:

> **"When I first met Cooch he was not the same animal. A cocky eighteen-year-old full back from Newport, I fielded a teasing John Horton cross-kick and refused to release the ball when in touch. A second later I was displaying the closest ever interest in an advertising hoarding as a large man with a crop of black hair, headband and snarl, drove me head-first into semi-oblivion...**

> **"While he may have disarmed himself as a nuclear force he has remained one of the most fearsome opponents in the game. Nobody slips in a sly, but sweet, reminder like Cooch; Richard Hill and myself still rate a slow-motion flying butt aimed at Bob Kimmins as one of the funniest sporting moments we have witnessed and, by God, he still 'hates they Waspies'...**

> **"We will all miss the fat old bastard and the question on every player's lips is 'Who will fill his seat at the card table?' May his runs never dry up."**

Chilcott was still needed for two away matches, however, beginning with a trip to title rivals Leicester. The build-up began inauspiciously for his mate Barnes when he was again overlooked by England for the New Zealand Test. Bath lost 9-6, the winning score coming from a John Liley penalty in the last minute after Barnes, on the eve of his 31st birthday, was ruled offside charging down a Jez Harris drop goal attempt. He still had time to attempt a long-range penalty to level the scores – but the ball dropped short.

"It's not been a very good week for me," said Barnes, after having 12 stitches in a gash behind his ear. "Things often seem to go wrong around my birthday – even the electrics on my car froze this morning so my wife couldn't get my present. But things are more often good than bad at Bath. We've just got to be man about it and come back even stronger. Good luck to Leicester but they've got to come to us yet and with our points difference I reckon we've effectively got a three-point lead on the rest."

While Barnes had lost out to Rob Andrew for selection against the All Blacks a week later, Redman earned his first cap for two years in the continuing absence of Bayfield, injured during the Lions tour. The durable lock was joined by Callard, making his debut, as well as de Glanville, Ubogu and Clarke.

Looking back, Redman emphasises how valuable it had been to play for both the South West and England A against those same All Blacks, who flexed their muscles by running seven tries past a hapless Scotland. "We had experienced two defeats against the All Blacks but you learn so much about teams when you play against them," he observes. "So before the game against New Zealand we were encouraged to share that information – Geoff Cooke (England's manager) was good that way. The players all pooled their knowledge and we came up with a plan. It was like playing chess. We just knew what to do when they did certain things; the players worked out most of it beforehand."

Callard kicked four penalties in an epic 15-9 victory but it was just as much a personal triumph for Redman, who exerted a remarkable influence on the game from the moment he soared above the All Black forwards to field Rob Andrew's kick-off.

Bath enter the 'branding' market

The home match against London Irish on 11 December 1993 marked the official 'branding' of the new South Stand housing the hospitality boxes and additional low-level seating. It thus became known as The Teacher's Stand after drinks group Hiram Walker won the naming rights, choosing one of their main spirits brands.

Thanks to astute marketing by Peter Downey, take-up of hospitality boxes had been brisk and with continuing support from the main club sponsor SWEB, Bath's financial position was as strong as it had ever been.

'Ups And Downs Of A Lineout Jumper'

"In running the 10 metres or so to jump in front of Ian Jones I set the tempo straight from the kick-off," he recalls with some satisfaction. "I won line-out, disrupted theirs, got through to make a tackle on the No 9 a couple of times, carried the ball and made my tackles. Everything worked. It was just one of those games – and I was dropped for the next match!"

As luck would have it – or what passed for luck in Redman's career – he played one more game for Bath, at Harlequins, before picking up an injury which ruled him out until after Christmas. Desperate to prove his fitness before the opening Five Nations match against Scotland, he was told that Bayfield would play anyway.

Chilcott played his 375th and final game in that 14-12 victory at the Stoop before retiring, as he famously said, "to enjoy a quiet pint … followed by fifteen noisy ones." His team-mates organised a post-match 'Farewell to Cooch party' on a 'This is Your Life' theme, compered by Egerton who had donned a fetching purple velvet jacket for the occasion.

Both sides had been disrupted by late withdrawals but after Robinson wheeled off a scrum to score a seventh minute try, Barnes kept Quins at bay with an impressive display of tactical and defensive kicks, also landing two penalties. It was the gutsiest of performances from the fly-half, who played on after injuring his knee making a tackle on a 17-stone forward and was having treatment when the decisive third penalty was kicked by Catt.

Within days of Chilcott's departure it became known that Richard Hill too would be gone at the end of the season, heightening the sense that a great team was beginning to break up. Hill could afford to take a rest against London Irish, who would be relegated at the end of the season; he came on as a replacement centre, taking a pass from understudy Sanders to score a try as Bath won 28-8.

"I said to him in the dressing room `Have a good game but don't go scoring four or five tries!'. That wouldn't have been so good for me," joked Hill. "It wasn't the ideal game because there wasn't a lot of good ruck ball and we were pretty static at times, but he did well."

Each of Hall's predecessors, Barnes and Robinson, had led Bath to the league and cup double in their first seasons but the draw for the fourth round of the Pilkington Cup had left them with a tricky tie at home to Wasps just seven days before Christmas. Bath took the field in appalling weather without 'big game players' in Guscott, Swift, Hill, Redman and, of course, Chilcott.

Oxford Blue Chris Clark, a member of the South West team, was drafted in at prop for his debut while McCoy kept his place alongside Haag in the second row. But the weak link was on the Wasps side in the unlikely shape of Rob Andrew. The Lions and England fly-half kicked a penalty and dropped a goal in the first quarter but then saw his normally secure game go to pieces; a heavy collision then ended his involvement. Meanwhile, Catt squeezed in at the corner for the first of three Bath tries, all converted by Callard. The others went to Sanders and Lumsden, with Barnes also scooping a drop goal out of the mud.

Hall could afford to be mildly scornful of suggestions that Bath had been at all vulnerable. "I've been reading all these things about Bath being under pressure, with so many players out," he said. "It's rather foolhardy to dismiss us like that, especially here where we are so difficult to beat. We're a good cup side; we've proved that over the last ten years and we are looking to put our name on it again. Even if some of

Of spongemen and surgeons

From the early 1920s, the team relied on Honorary Surgeon Dr R Scott-Reid and perhaps, one or two St. John's Ambulance men. On-field cuts and bruises were remedied by the faithful 'bucket and sponge' man. W B S Crawford joined Scott-Reid in 1950 and J R Kirkup in the 1960-70 season. Dr David Protheroe, whose wife helped to start up Mini Rugby, joined the medical team in the 1976-77 season. Mr Phillip Bliss and David Protheroe were in tandem from the 1986-87 season and by 1994, a, organised team of Medical Officers was in place, including Dr Keith Gruffydd-Jones, Mr Cledwyn Jones, Dr Ian Grandison, Dr Robin While and Dr Simon Burrell

It was January 1976 when Bath's first chartered physiotherapist, Gareth George, ran on to the pitch to tend to the wounded. It was about the time that Phil Hall was winding up his long playing career. Gareth was eventually succeeded by Mrs Julie Bardner as Senior Physiotherapist. Her arrival was heralded with a few wolf whistles, but soon the talk was about other clubs: "They've got one at London Welsh you know!"

Things had certainly moved on since 'early sponge-man,' as the Club had to match medical support with the ever increasing wear and tear on players' bodies and also in compliance with strict RFU regulations relating to treatment of wounds. Hard knocks and intensive levels of play had brought inevitable bruises and strains, which demanded to be remedied within ever shortening recovery spans.

A succession of dedicated female 'physios' tended to refer to player patients in terms of Andy's back, John Hall's knee, Ollie's shoulder, and just about every appendage of United/ Spartans (mega outpatient) Paul Cosgrove! Ever more power to their elbows, we say. But John Donne (1571-1631) said it better:

> *"License my roving hands, and let them go,*
> *Before, behind, between, above, below"*

Peter Hall

the players have not experienced anything like this before, they have played in league matches and it's all credit to the coaching staff and the players themselves that they can slot in so that it causes very little disruption."

The drive for success in the cup and in an expanded league programme, not to mention the international ambitions of so many players, left very little room for other fixtures, however significant either from a historical or strategic perspective. For instance Clifton had been on the fixture list for 121 years but found themselves bumped off to make way for Toulouse, only for Bath to field a team largely comprising United players skippered by Richard Hill.

Both clubs recognised the need to foster truly competitive pan-European rugby but for the time being it was only talk. Before a crowd of just 2,000, Toulouse ran out 23-9 winners thanks to tries from France centre Christophe Deylaud and the Carbonneau brothers, Olivier (2) and Philippe. Andy Webber and Haydn Long (2) kicked penalties for Bath.

Hill also turned out against Cardiff on 30 December, one of the better games of the season despite the liquid mud that glistened under the Rec lights. Catt turned up demanding to play, which was just as well because Adebayo's train from Paddington was late. Tries from prop Darren Crompton, centre Ed Rayner and wing Mark Woodman saw Bath to a 24-20 victory.

The unrelenting weather forced the cancellation of the New Year's Day home match with Richmond and made it difficult to find anywhere to train, Lambridge being under water, so it was indoor five-a-side football or the rowing machine. Swift and Adebayo played for the Spartans in a 25-17 win over Frome and both Reed and Redman were back in training.

Still it rained and as the derby match with Bristol loomed, Bath officials could see no way in which the Rec would be fit to play. Bristol, of course, took the view that that Bath just did not fancy taking on their forwards in unfavourable conditions. Finally, as late as Friday at 5.10pm, a call arrived from RFU Honorary Secretary Dudley Wood ordering Bath to play the game or forfeit the league points.

That was no choice at all. So willing volunteers behind the scenes swung into action to get the game on. A 16-page programme – less than half the normal size – was printed overnight while the bank was persuaded to provide change for the ticket sellers on the gate. Losses on sponsorship, programme advertising and TV fees meant it was going to be an expensive exercise. It took Hall three hours to phone around his team to tell them the game was on after all. "We're a bit unhappy about it – it's such short notice. But by 3pm tomorrow we'll be ready. There'll be some steam coming out of their ears, I expect," he added darkly.

Actually, Bath looked anything but 'up for it' as they fended off a mighty Bristol forward effort to squeeze out a 9-nil victory through three Callard penalties. With Clarke outstanding in defence and Catt incisive on a gluepot pitch, the league leaders just about deserved it, for their resilience as much as anything. It certainly whetted the appetite for the sides' Pilkington Cup fifth round tie a fortnight later.

But Bath travelled to Northampton on 15 January knowing that they had to rediscover the 'bite' that would deliver one trophy, if not two. A 30-9 win and a degree of 'niggle' showed there was plenty of appetite after all. The scrummage, under scrutiny after the derby match, earned a penalty try as early as the 14th minute and a brace of tries from Swift took his Bath tally to 147. The other try went to de Glanville and Callard kicked ten points.

The match marked a return to action for Reed, pitted against Bayfield who flapped and flicked so much poor ball to youngster Matt Dawson that the scrum-half eventually found Dawe and Ubogu on the end of one particularly reckless tap and disappeared on a stretcher for hospital checks on his ribs. It was the Saints' heaviest home defeat since their return to the top flight in 1990.

Yet Bristol were still confident that their pack could more than match Bath up front and secure them a place in the Pilkington Cup quarter-finals. They managed the first bit but again lacked firepower to progress further. The home team stole a 14-nil lead in little more than half an hour with tries by Ojomoh and Catt, both converted by the inventive Barnes, before Bristol clawed their way back into contention through their pack, and particularly the line-out. Lumsden, deputising for Callard at full-back, took everything that was chucked at him and the visitors could only muster three Mark Tainton penalties.

Bath did not play that much better when they returned to league action at home to Orrell a week later. Swift scored the only try in a 13-7 victory but the delightful Joan

Yet another cup-tie against Bristol ... and still the near-neighbours cannot shake off that Bath hoodoo (22 January 1994).

204

Budge, who assisted the club's energetic press officer Ken Johnstone, probably summed it up best with a pithy: "A really awful game. Probably Bath's worst performance this year. Lucky to get by really." Joan also featured in the match programme as the latest winner of the Bath 2000 Club monthly prize, collecting a colour TV.

Extraordinarily, it was all of seven years since Hall had featured in a Five Nations campaign but if some of Bath's midwinter performances had been below-par, that criticism could not be aimed at their captain whose forthright leadership of the South West had also laid the foundation for their winning of the divisional title. Now reinvented as a bulwark of the blindside rather than the supremely dynamic back row who had so impressed the All Blacks in 1983 and on tour in 1985, Hall was recalled to the England side to face Scotland at Murrayfield.

The Bath captain hauled Gary Armstrong down in the first half when the nuggety scrum-half looked certain to score but the Scots did cross the line through Rob Wainwright and at the death Gregor Townsend snatched a 14-12 lead with a drop goal. But there were still a few seconds left on Kiwi referee Lindsay McLachlan's watch when he spotted a hand in the ruck and Callard kicked his fifth penalty from near half-way to break Scottish hearts. Closer examination by TV replay suggested that the hand belonged to England's Rob Andrew but his team-mates, who included de Glanville, Ubogu and Clarke, were not complaining.

It was a disjointed England performance, however, and Hall found himself surplus to requirements when the Irish came to Twickenham a fortnight later. Ojomoh, a late inclusion for Clarke, cut an impressive figure on his debut but Ireland snatched an unlikely victory through left wing Geoghegan, whose electrifying pace would be seen in Bath colours before too long.

Ojomoh's appearances for Bath had been limited by the presence of Hall, Clarke and Robinson and it was only a week earlier that he quashed rumours that he was to leave the club. "I wasn't a happy man, it's true," the 23-year-old admitted after scoring the only try in a 16-6 victory at Gloucester. "I was playing a lot of second team rugby but being picked for the South West as well – still performing but not getting a chance to show what I could do for Bath. It crossed my mind that I should leave. But there's no chance of that now."

Clarke's injury meant that Ojomoh lined up with Hall and Robinson for the Pilkington Cup quarter-final at Saracens on 26 February. An even newer face was that of 23-year-old loosehead prop Hilton, who had seen off the challenge of Clark and Crompton after his 'defection' from Bristol.

Second Division Saracens proved obdurate opponents for an hour or so despite conceding a 12th minute try to de Glanville and more than an hour had passed before Adebayo carried on his England A form by finishing off a slick set move orchestrated by Barnes and Catt. Both tries were converted by Callard who also kicked three penalties and while Saracens finished strongly with Tony Diprose and their own Richard Hill prominent, they looked no more likely to score a try than any of Bath's cup opponents that season. Remarkably, for the eighth time in ten years, the semi-final draw again denied them a home tie. They would have to fight their way past Harlequins.

Among the spectators at Southgate was England coach Dick Best who had identified two particular problems against Ireland: difficulty in securing line-out ball, despite the presence of Bayfield, and a reluctance to attack the restarts. Despite his perceived lack of inches, Redman met the requirements on both counts and was recalled as one of five changes to face France in Paris. Callard who had struck the posts with two penalties, missing four kicks out of eight in total, was one of the casualties but Clarke joined Ojomoh in the back row and, with de Glanville and Ubogu also in the XV, Bath's representation rose to five.

Not for the first time – or the last – nerves beset the French and England's pragmatic approach paid off with an 18-14 win, their fourth in succession at Parc des Princes. Andrew dropped a goal and kicked five penalties.

Ojomoh was unlucky to lose out to the fit-again Dean Richards for the finale at Twickenham, particularly as they needed to win by 16 points to deny Wales the championship. The Leicester No 8's presence guaranteed England a rock-solid forward platform and a 15-8 win but denied them the pace and mobility they needed to score more than the two tries from Rory Underwood and Tim Rodber. Deprived of the Grand Slam but still champions, Wales's celebrations were understandably muted, rather more so in fact than Catt's elation at winning his first England cap off the bench.

Not that everyone in the England camp was cock-a-hoop, as Redman reflects: "We dominated the game so much we should have won by those 16 points. I reckon

Jon Callard: scored 21 points in a 24-8 win over Wasps on 12 March 1994.

Ken so proud of his best-seller

Ken Johnstone, Bath's ebullient press officer and editor of the match programme, announced record sales during the 1993-94 season of 45,000 – more than double the figure for the previous year.

The last programme of the season for the visit of Harlequins featured Richard Hill on the cover and a detailed breakdown of his exploits over 12 seasons with the club. He had made 245 appearances since making his debut in 1983 and was already coach of the Emerging England team having served as assistant coach to England A for their match against the All Blacks on 6 November 1993.

Stuart Barnes offered a tribute to his half-back partner and "the club's most dedicated trainer", observing: "Of all the scrum-halves with whom I have played it has been Hill who has coped easiest with my infuriating late choice of direction."

And on a more serious note: "On the pitch nobody has wanted to win more than Richard; off it nobody has been more courteous."

we could have done it but the focus was beating Wales rather than winning the championship. I was disappointed by it."

In the interim, Callard had enjoyed some degree of compensation for his removal from the national squad by scoring two tries in a haul of 21 points as Wasps were beaten 24-8 at the Rec on 12 March.

> **But it was a dreadful spectacle, perhaps the poorest competitive match seen on the ground, punctuated by 48 penalties and free-kicks. Referee Geraint Davies was in no mood to apologise, saying afterwards: "The laws are there and the players break them. I don't give away penalties – they do."**

Then word began to filter through of Leicester's 66-5 win at Newcastle-Gosforth, a result which cut Bath's points differential to just five as well as consigning the North East club to the drop. When the Courage League programme resumed a fortnight later, Leicester kept up the pressure with a 25-13 victory at Harlequins while Bath won 29-5 to end Newcastle's last mathematical hopes.

The player who caught the eye was home flanker Martin Corry, who had captained Northumbria Students to victory in the UAU final just three days earlier. He crossed in the left corner to open the scoring early on but Bath eventually took control and Martin Haag, called up at short notice for the sick Andy Reed, scored two of Bath's four tries, the others going to Catt and Ian Sanders.

The Leicester showdown for the Courage League title loomed on 9 April but first Bath had to switch into 'cup mode' for an Easter Saturday semi-final at Harlequins. The last time the two sides had met in the Pilkington Cup the final had been settled in the last seconds of extra time by that extraordinary drop goal from Barnes. Surely nothing could top that?

As the Stoop was swept with hail and sleet borne on a freezing wind, Bath roared into a 19-nil lead. It is worth detailing that the first try, after three minutes, was the product of nine phases and 32 passes involving 13 different players – fairly commonplace these days but remarkable under the laws at that time. It was Swift who finished things off, a full minute and 23 seconds after Redman's original line-out catch. Ten minutes later Barnes was quickest to react when Robinson charged down an attempted Garryowen by Challinor and the fly-half scurried away to score at the other end of the field.

They don't make pitches like that any more: Dave Hilton and Graham Dawe come off the field wearing the obligatory mid-winter Rec 'mudpack'.

Callard converted and then supported Catt's break in midfield to score a third try, again converted by the full-back. With 23 minutes gone, it was becoming a rout but the half-time interval broke the spell.

Although Quins lost centre Adrian Thompson with an ankle injury and back row Chris Sheasby with a dislocated kneecap, their fortunes turned once they had the wind at their backs. Challinor's kicks pinned Bath back and the points began to flow – a penalty from the fly-half, a try from flanker Martin Pepper, a farcical penalty try as Callard was 'nutmegged' by a charge-down from Catt's attempted clearance and then hauled down Challinor before he could ground the ball. The fly-half added the conversion and then kicked another to put his side ahead after Cassell scored from a rolling maul. When man-of-the-moment Challinor then dropped a goal to give Quins a six-point lead with eight minutes left on the clock Bath looked down and out.

These days the impression is sometimes gained that the Bath side of 80s and 90s, apart from the odd hiccup at places like Moseley and Waterloo, strode effortlessly from one title to another. But this history attempts to show that, as often as not, victories were eked out in extremis. This was such a day.

With just four minutes remaining, Catt knifed down the short side close to the old East Stand and linked with Callard who cut infield, supported by the ageless Swift. In his path stood Kent Bray but the full-back failed to hold the Bath right wing who somehow wriggled out of the tackle, leaving the anguished Australian sprawling in his wake. Swift still had the presence of mind to get as close to the posts as he could, leaving Callard with a more straightforward conversion to win the tie.

It was Swift's 150th try for the club and, although just two weeks short of his 35th birthday with 18 years of first-class rugby under his belt with Fylde, Swansea and Bath, he could not remember a more dramatic one. "Once I was through I knew I had to get near the posts," he said afterwards. "But in a situation like that you can't let people come across and knock the ball out of your grasp. I had more kisses today than in my whole life – which wasn't a terribly pleasant experience. I think the first came from Graham Dawe."

He then added: "When the emotion of the day disappears we will be analysing how we can play so well for 25-30 minutes and then let it go like that. In terms of rugby ability, this is the best Bath side I've ever played in but we seem to have trouble in focusing in on the game for 80 minutes."

They soon learned that their opponents in the final were to be Leicester, 31-18 victors at Orrell. But that was more than a month away – first the country's top two clubs must meet at Bath to decide the Courage League championship. This was personal and everyone knew it. The Tigers were hungry and confident, their pack mixing the energy and ambition of youngsters like Rowntree, Cockerill and Johnson with the hard-nosed, streetwise grunt of Garforth, Richards and Wells.

The visitors' rolling maul had been particularly effective in previous weeks and one look at the grey skies, a waterlogged Rec and the torrential showers suggested that conditions suited them down to the ground ... literally. So that is just where Hall and Co attacked them – at their point of strength. It was unexpected, merciless and so characteristically Bath. In fact the 14-6 scoreline did not really reflect the home team's superiority, established by Swift's first half try and three penalties by Callard.

"Expansive rugby was not on the cards but there was only one team in it," declared Hall, who had stationed himself at the front of the line-out to nullify the threat posed by Johnson. "It was a superb pack performance – and for the full 80 minutes. There was a lot of talk about their rolling maul and how dangerous it was, but it really didn't come into play. We proved that we are the boys in that department."

Not that Hall had in any sense underestimated the threat posed by their nearest challengers. "The way I was billing it in the changing room, this was one of the biggest games we've ever had," he said. "This could have been a massive turning point for the club. If we had lost, we could have lost the league too and gone into the cup final feeling down and psychologically on the back foot. I have played with these guys for so long, you just want the team to do well and that's why we have been so successful over the last ten years."

It left Bath four points ahead of Leicester with two games left and an advantage in points differential of 32. It was a situation they had often found themselves in before and no-one, least of all Leicester, expected them to slip up. Yet the atmosphere in the final few weeks of the 1993-94 season was different. This was a club that always maintained that no-one was irreplaceable – but the final home game against Harlequins on 23rd April, St George's Day, was awash with emotion. Not only would it be the last time that Richard Hill would run out on to the Rec but, almost unbelievably, Jack Rowell was leaving Bath after 16 years to succeed Geoff Cooke as England team manager.

In the end there was never any danger that Harlequins would spoil the party to deprive Bath of a fourth successive Courage League title. Clarke crossed unopposed inside nine minutes and when the pack took a scrum against the head, Hill fired out a reverse pass to Barnes who sent de Glanville over for a try. Callard added the conversion to an earlier penalty and Bath led 15-3 at the break. The all-powerful scrum provided a popular score for Hall early in the second half and the fourth try went to prop Hilton, finishing off a remarkable rolling maul which had started with a line-out take by Redman a full 35 metres up the touchline. Gavin Thompson registered a late try converted by Bray but at the final whistle the scoreboard read 32-13.

Some 8,000 supporters flooded on to the pitch in the sunshine to acclaim their heroes and to cheer a jubilant Hall as he paraded the trophy. It had been a tough campaign, briefly knocked off course by defeat at Leicester but in the end it was their Midland rivals who failed to stay the distance. Hall's leadership had been crucial in maintaining focus amid the distractions of the All Blacks tour and England commitments, not to mention the absence of Guscott and the retirement mid-season of Chilcott.

Suddenly, the focus was on the figures of Hill and Rowell, one the scrum-half whose absolute commitment to improving his skills had earned him 29 England caps and, standing a good foot taller, the intensely ambitious rugby strategist with an approach to man management which was invariably as effective as it was idiosyncratic.

Rowell's voice welled with emotion as he took his leave of the Rec, in body if not in spirit. Picking up the microphone a little reluctantly and struggling at times to articulate exactly what he felt, he called Bath "the Rolls-Royce of rugby clubs" and paid tribute to all those who had contributed to "the sensation that has gone on here for ten, 15 years or more."Gathering his thoughts, he added: "This has great momentum. We have an outstanding squad of players and what I want to say, with no arrogance at all, is that what we've seen and are celebrating today is but a milestone in the best journey of any rugby club at any time." His parting "Thank you" was drowned in applause.

Jack Rowell: an emotional farewell.

Typical of Bath, the club was already looking to the future and it was soon common knowledge that they had recruited one of the most exciting wingers in world rugby, Ireland's Simon Geoghegan. Unfortunately his club, London Irish, were due to host the newly crowned champions the following weekend, their last match before relegation.

It led to an unseemly row behind the scenes at Sunbury when Geoghegan was dropped from the team to face Bath, prompting fellow-internationals Jim Staples and Gary Halpin to withdraw in protest. Skipper Paul Collins then pulled out with a mystery 'flu virus'. Geoghegan was diplomatic about it all saying: "There are no hard feelings," he said. "I would have liked to play in this game but now I can only wish the lads all the best for next season."

Bath could afford to field a second team with Egerton the only capped player on show and he scored one of the tries, along with Kevin Yates and Mark Woodman. They had built up a 32-24 lead before the Exiles claimed a last-minute try and conversion. With 34 points gained from 18 matches and for-and-against

Callard's boys in Sevens heaven

The insatiable quest for trophies in 1994 did not end with the Pilkington Cup final. Jon Callard returned to Twickenham a week later with a hastily assembled squad to contest the Middlesex Sevens.

"We had a one-hour training session during the week, and that was it," said Callard, who stole away for the winning try in the final against Orrell. The other try scorers in a 19-12 win were Ed Rayner and Audley Lumsden while the skipper kicked two conversions. Ian Sanders, Eric Peters Gareth Adams and Martin Haag made up the winning Seven who had accounted for London Scottish, Loughborough Students and Saracens.

Three months later the club also carried off the Snelling Trophy at the Welsh Worthington Sevens on Cardiff Arms Park, where new recruit Simon Geoghegan was the stand-out performer.

The rush for cup final tickets: Phil de Glanville can be spotted in the queue (seventh from left).

totals reading 431 to 181, Bath's dominance of the league could hardly have been more conclusive.

Having won 12 of the 17 domestic trophies on offer over ten seasons, there was just one more for Bath to claim and a record 68,000 crowd flocked to Twickenham a week later for a rematch between English rugby's heavyweights. If there were any neutrals naively expecting a feast of flowing rugby they would have been disappointed. This was strictly reserved for 'two tribes going to war'. Even the match programme's 'Welcome from the President of the Rugby Football Union' was from a former Bath player, Ian Beer CBE JP.

BATH: *J Callard; A Swift, P de Glanville, M Catt, A Adebayo; S Barnes, R Hill; D Hilton, G Dawe, V Ubogu, N Redman, A Reed, A Robinson (S Ojomoh, 46 mins), B Clarke, J Hall.*

LEICESTER: *W Kilford; T Underwood, S Potter, L Boyle, R Underwood; J Harris, A Kardooni; G Rowntree, R Cockerill, D Garforth, M Johnson, M Poole, J Wells, D Richards, N Back.*

REFEREE: *E Morrison* (Bristol/RFU).

Fittingly, Hill rounded off an illustrious career by collecting an eighth cup winner's medal after Bath's 21-9 victory. For Hall however, emulating Barnes and Robinson as the third Bath captain to lead his side to the league and cup double, the overwhelming feeling was one of relief. "I'm mentally drained and, if I'm honest, glad it's all over," he said after the game. The weight of expectation had already been huge but the burden had been heavier with the introduction of home and away matches, not to mention his own commitments to the South West and to England. He was also facing a possible challenge to his captaincy from Clarke but that fizzled out over the summer.

As for the match, an intensely attritional affair played out in heavy drizzle, Callard and Harris kicked three penalties apiece in the first half and Bath pulled away after the break with tries by Swift and Catt, Callard rounding things off with a conversion.

Defending cup holders Leicester offered limited ambition but plenty of aggression, playing right into the shovel-like hands of opponents like Graham Dawe, who met the challenge head on. "They'll never beat us in a million years with those tactics," he said. "Yes it was niggly. But speaking personally, I thoroughly enjoyed it."

And Hilton, playing in his first cup final, added: "I'm just so happy to have been involved in something like this. There were some antics up front, but I thought we scrummaged pretty well. The most important thing from my point of view is that I've finally justified my move from Bristol."

Not so happy was Ubogu who tested referee Ed Morrison's patience by throwing a haymaker at Johnson, although the Leicester lock was shown by TV replays to have repeatedly punched the Bath prop: "It was provoked by Leicester, quite frankly," said Ubogu. "They came out and got quite niggly. It's not in Bath's nature to go out to niggle; we go out to play and win. They just provoked us. Why? You'd better ask Leicester about that. There was just an undercurrent throughout the whole game."

Barnes offered his own typically acerbic opinion: "All that talk about the Tigers being the team of the 90s has been confirmed as precisely that – talk. They showed us nothing out there. All they tried to do was work us into the corners and beat us on penalties. You might label them a very English side, in the worst sense of that."

That was largely true but Bath were more than capable of slugging it out if required. When it came down to the nitty-gritty, it was all about winning. That was the Rowell way and that is how an extraordinary era ended, with yet another Twickenham success and a 13th trophy in ten seasons. They had missed out on just five – the cup in 1988, 1991 and 1993 and the Courage League in 1987 and 1990.

After one last obligatory post-Twickenham celebration at 'Rowell Towers' the new England team manager prepared to fly out with his national squad to South Africa on the Wednesday evening.

Among those selected was Redman, one of ten Bath players in the party for the two-Test series. On the Monday morning he took a call from the RFU asking him if he was coming to their awards dinner that night. "I said I couldn't because I had so much to do," he recalls. "They said they'd really like me to be there because I had been nominated for an award. Sorry, still couldn't be there. Then they told me I'd won it ... 'OK,' I said, 'What time do you want me there?' I was up against Brian Moore and Rob Andrew, as I recall, all televised. I still have a big bronze statue in my office."

After a less than impressive build-up which saw England win just one of five matches, Redman was joined in the team for the first Test in Pretoria by de Glanville, Ubogu and Clarke. England owed their surprise 32-15 victory to a purple patch in the first half in which Clarke scored a try but the Springboks came back to square the series in Cape Town a week later.

In addition to picking up the RFU Player of the Year award, Redman's 'never say die' spirit earned him a place alongside clubmate Clarke, Philippe Sella, Phil Davies and Tim Horan in the illustrious Rothmans Rugby Yearbook 'Five Players of the Year' accolade. That did not cut any ice with Rowell though. Redman was dropped for the autumn internationals against Romania and Canada and it was another three years before he pulled on an England shirt.

Today he can laugh about his record of being dropped more often than any other England player and the legacy of injuries from 15 years of top flight rugby with club and country. "My left knee needs replacing. My buttock basically strangulates my sciatic nerve. I can't lift my left arm properly because I have no rotator cuff. Apart from that I'm fine! But I wouldn't have had it any other way – I wouldn't have changed a thing."

David Gay: the Bath No 8 was only 19 when he forced his way into the England team to face Wales on 20 January 1968.

ABOVE: John Palmer is feted by supporters after leading his side to victory in the 1986 John Player Cup final.

RIGHT: David Egerton works the ball away from a maul against Gloucester in the 1990 Pilkington Cup final.

BELOW: The morning after ... Stuart Barnes 'crowns' replacement full-back Jon Webb, watched by Simon Halliday (left), Andy Robinson, David Egerton, Damian Cronin, Nick Maslen and Gareth Chilcott.

ABOVE: skipper John Hall lifts the cup after the 21-9 victory over Leicester in the 1994 Pilkington Cup final.

LEFT: Jon Callard puts boot to ball against the Tigers, watched by Dave Hilton and Ben Clarke.

BELOW: Jeremy Guscott completes his hat-trick in a 52-19 win over Bristol on a sunny October afternoon in 1995.

ABOVE: ten finals, ten victories … the 1996 vintage celebrate with skipper Phil de Glanville after their 16-15 victory over Leicester at Twickenham (Photo: David Rogers/Getty Images).

BELOW: Victor Ubogu on the burst in the 44-19 win against Wigan under Rugby Union laws at Twickenham on 25 May 1996 (Photo: Mike Hewitt/Allsport).

Chapter 12

MONEY, MONEY, MONEY

When Jack Rowell handed over the reins to his assistant, Brian Ashton, in the summer of 1994 Bath were at the pinnacle of achievement.

Admittedly, the loss of Rowell and Hill at the end of the season had been compounded by Stuart Barnes's sudden retirement after returning from the tour to South Africa, again without adding to his meagre total of 10 caps, but for the moment there was plenty to celebrate.

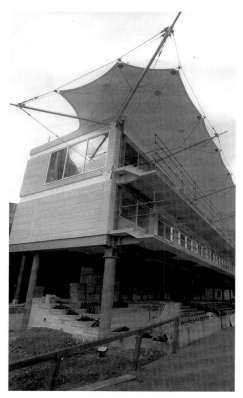

A new South Stand to mark 100 years at the Recreation Ground.

Firstly, it was 100 years since the club had first made the Recreation Ground their home, establishing a productive alliance as tenants of The Bath & County Recreation Ground Company Ltd. (In the light of subsequent events it needs to be pointed out that this company was strictly a commercial enterprise, which had purchased what was then known as Pulteney Meadows for development and subsequent renting out of various sporting and leisure facilities).

Secondly, the centenary of the ground was marked by the emergence of a magnificent new stand at the South end, boasting 25 hospitality suites plus 1,000 extra seats and also neatly obscuring the ugly bare facade of the municipal sports centre. Meanwhile the middle section of the old 'flowerpots' terrace on the east side had been replaced by temporary seating.

To celebrate these improvements, the club extended an invitation to one of the few teams with the drawing power of

The Maestro leaves the stage

To a new generation of rugby watchers Stuart Barnes is a TV pundit, extravagant in his vocabulary and highly visible – except for Cheltenham Festival week when his absence from the Sky Sports studio is all too conspicuous.

To Bath followers of an older vintage, however, Barnes is still the 'maestro', the little man in the No 10 shirt whose uncanny tactical vision was reinforced by extraordinary self-belief. But other qualities were just as important – footballing skills of the highest order, bravery, a cast-iron cussedness and a surprising turn of pace over 20 metres. As an Arsenal fan, his hero was Liam Brady but in his early Bohemian days at Bristol the physique was occasionally more reminiscent of the Magical Magyar, Ferenc Puskas, hence the nickname 'Barrel'.

His triumphs and tribulations have been well documented here and elsewhere but Barnes's outstanding contribution to the Bath success story is seen even more starkly in how seldom he experienced the pain of defeat.

Consider for a moment how many times he was on the losing side in cup or league matches for Bath in those eight seasons from 1985 to 1994. Nine, just nine – with an average losing margin of just five points – and in at least one of those he should not have taken the field. That was the 12-nil home defeat by Leicester in the 1990-91 Pilkington Cup third round. Bath were by no means a one-man team but when they were knocked out of the cup in 1988 and 1993, Barnes was missing on those occasions too.

If Gareth Chilcott represented the soul of the club and John Hall the heart, then 'Barrel' was the brain on the field.

Barnes's formidable rugby intellect would have made him a supremely innovative coach but he had long ruled out the possibility in an interview given to Glen Leat and Clive Banks of the ERE' fanzine (Every time Ref, Every time): "I never had any intentions of doing any coaching at Bath, it's too close and I know the people too well. It would also be very difficult as I was not the best of trainers and I could not go back and give people a lot of stick for not putting in enough effort. Also coaching would have meant turning up on Mondays and Wednesdays and a bit extra. If I had been prepared to put up with that I would have carried on playing."

the home club, if that were possible. And who better than the Barbarians, particularly as they had provided the 'star' opposition in that very first season at the Rec in 1894?

It was not the most star-studded Barbarians line-up, it has to be said, and their second-half replacements included home players Rayner and Yates. Bath, in comparison, brought Ireland's Geoghegan off their bench at half-time with the score 6-6 and he scored two tries to provide the impetus for a 23-18 victory. Ubogu had crossed for the other Bath score, converted by Callard, who also kicked two penalties. Bristol's Paul Hull was prominent at fly-half for the invitation side, laying on one of two tries for Scotland's Graham Shiel.

Hull, who had impressed not only on his Test debut in South Africa but also in England's subsequent defeat in

Simon Geoghegan: try-scoring debut against the Barbarians (Photo: C W Sports).

Capetown, returned to Bath in his customary club position of full-back a week later as Sky launched their rugby union club coverage in the UK with the opening Courage League fixture.

This was Ashton's first big test as Head Coach and Bristol must have hoped that the 48-year-old schoolmaster, renowned as a backs coach, might have neglected the basics of forward play. Not a chance. The match turned on a 61st minute scrum feed by Kyran Bracken under his own posts; Bath piled on an eight-man shove and the Bristol scrum-half conceded a penalty try when he dived in to prevent a more conventional touchdown by Clarke.

It was a sweet moment for Dave Hilton, late of Bristol, who said: "We had worked so hard on our scrummaging during the week. It was serious stuff. Robbo said to us tight forwards: `You know what happened last time. If you're not going to scrummage, we might as well give Bristol the two points now.' The position was right for a pushover. We have two different eight-man calls but I won't say any more than that because it's a trade secret." Bath wrapped up an 18-9 victory shortly before the end with a second try by Lumsden after Catt broke clear from fly-half and Swift provided the link.

Bath were then in the middle of an unbeaten run which was remarkable even by their own lofty standards, carrying them right through to the first week of March.

In fact when they were finally beaten at Cardiff on St Patrick's Day 1995, it had been more than a year since they had lost at Rugby on 3 March 1994 with a United-Spartans line-up.

With the peculiar pressures of the Bristol derby behind them, Bath's Courage League campaign gathered pace with a commanding 32-16 victory at Franklins Gardens where Callard made light of a sore knee by punishing Northampton transgressions at the breakdown with five penalties, including one from six metres inside his own half, plus a conversion. Two tries came from Swift and left wing Adebayo grabbed the other.

With Geoghegan eligible for league duty in October and another promising young wing in Jon Sleightholme awaiting his chance after moving from the Wakefield club, retirement finally beckoned for Swift – but not quite yet. The way he subtly deceived England's

Brian Ashton: 'no kicking' policy
(Photo: Val Cooper).

Ian Hunter to score in the corner just before half-time fully supported Brian Ashton's view that his fellow-Lancastrian was "the best striking winger within 20 metres of the line in the country."

His coach added: "One-on-one you've always got to back Swifty. I know he was delighted to beat an England full-back but he's looking very sharp this season. He's got the knack of peaking for Saturdays – at 35 you have to. We are quite happy, provided he does the technical work with us, that he just turns up and plays like that every Saturday afternoon."

England Under-21 wing Sleightholme was unleashed against Orrell the following weekend and began his Bath career in spectacular style with a try inside three minutes. With Catt again paired with Sanders at half-back and skipper Hall sidelined with a sprung rib, the average age of the side was just 25. Hooker Gareth Adams, de Glanville and Clarke scored further tries and Catt kicked 12 points in a 32-13 win.

At Kingsholm a week later, it was again the turn of 'old heads' like Dawe and Robinson to exert their influence. It was typically abrasive stuff, no doubt hugely entertaining for the Shed, until Robinson and Sanders scored tries in quick succession just short of the hour. Catt's conversion made it 15-3 and a converted try by Tim Smith came too late to seriously trouble the visitors.

There were no tries when Bath met Wasps at the Rec on 8 October but that hardly detracted from the entertainment value as the home side prevailed 12-9 with four Callard penalties. Hall, who had made a rapid recovery from a rib injury to lead his side, admitted: "They don't come any harder than that. When we have to dog it out, we dog it out. We got the result we wanted, if not in the style we wanted."

That win set a record of 16 consecutive league victories but the sequence was sorely tested at West Hartlepool a week later. It was Jeremy Guscott's comeback match after being out for a year with a deep-seated groin injury and Dawe's 200th appearance but there was little to celebrate in the 20-18 win where the star performer was West Hartlepool's No 8, Army captain Mick Watson. "At times it was a shambles – there was a lack of commitment tackling-wise," said Hall, scorer of both Bath tries. "Just how badly do we have to play to lose?" asked Tony Swift.

Leicester came to the Rec on 22 October as league leaders on points difference and left the field much the happier after a 20-20 draw, becoming the first side to take a point from the Rec for two and a half years.

Unbeaten or not, it was clear that Bath were out-of-sorts, an impression reinforced by their surrendering a 17-8 lead. Swift finished off a 23rd minute move and Catt sliced through to score at the posts just after the break but the Tigers pack, with Richards and Johnson prominent, forced Bath to concede penalties and Harris filled his boots. Jamie Hamilton, only on the field because Tony Underwood had been caught in traffic, scored the equalising try ten minutes from time.

An oversized task in the boot room

Bath's backroom staff had been in touch with boot manufacturers to solve a sizeable problem for 19-year-old flanker Ed Pearce.

The ex-Clifton College captain had been blessed with size 16 feet but made his fourth senior appearance at Nottingham, still squeezed into a pair of size 15s. "My feet are particularly broad too," said the 6ft 5in Pearce. "And the problem is the boots last hardly any time at all because there's so much stress on them."

In the meantime Pearce was making of the most of an unexpected promotion to first team rugby: "These players are really amazing, so you listen to what they are saying," said Pearce, who won four caps the previous season at Schools 18-Group. "Everyone is really helpful and wants you to succeed. Training's been brilliant."

Minister of Sport Iain Sproat was in attendance to perform the official opening of the Teacher's Stand as Harlequins rolled up at the Rec on a wet afternoon. Geoghegan scored a 70-metre interception try on his debut but the 22-11 scoreline did little to suggest that the process of rebuilding was going very smoothly. Fortunately, Callard's goalkicking was spot-on and Harlequins were no great threat until Will Greenwood scored in injury time.

A glowering Hall summed up the general mood of dissatisfaction: "Whatever people say about modern rugby players, we still play for enjoyment and I didn't enjoy that at all."

It was all the more surprising then that Bath found themselves back on top of the Courage League on Bonfire Night after labouring to a 19-3 victory at Sale. A chargedown try by de Glanville and a second-half effort by Adebayo, latching on to Guscott's grubber kick, made the difference but the most encouraging aspect was the performance of No 8 Eric Peters, making the most of his chance as Clarke was rested. Word then came through of Bristol's unexpected 31-22 win over Leicester.

It had been a hard slog over nine consecutive weekends so to be able to play some 'fun' rugby against Oxford University (33-26) and Coventry (45-10) while the leading lights answered international calls or just enjoyed some rest and recuperation came as a blessed relief. Sadly, the home game against the Dark Blues proved

Eric Peters: took his chance when Ben Clarke was rested.

to be the last of Egerton's 168 club appearances, scoring a remarkable 68 tries. Now 33, he had won seven England caps, the last as a replacement against Argentina in Buenos Aires in 1990, and had also featured in the British Lions XV brought together in Paris on 4 October 1989 to commemorate the Bicentennial of the French Revolution.

Meanwhile Guscott made his England comeback against Romania at Twickenham, Rowell's first home game in charge of the national team, and Ubogu, Clarke and Ojomoh also featured. Although de Glanville lost his place to Guscott he won his tenth cap as a replacement in an even heavier defeat of Canada a month later. Catt did even better, scoring two tries off the bench as England won 60-19 to raise expectations of a new free-running era under Rowell.

The Divisional Championship continued, but as a proving ground for 'Emerging Players', and although the South West finished bottom of the table, Saracens' Richard Hill scored a total of five tries including a hat-trick against the North.

Back on the club front, the innovative Ashton instituted a 'no kicking' policy for the trip to Pontypool on 23 November. With Robinson fit again to play after his rib injury and spearheading the forward effort, the young backs responded to their coach's invitation by creating tries for wing Woodman (2) and centre Lewis, a summer recruit from Swansea. Another newcomer, fly-half Rich Butland, impressed with his running and distribution. He also also kicked two conversions and in spite of Ashton's edict, dropped a goal and landed a late penalty to clinch a 25-13 victory.

Andy Robinson: return to fitness.

Robinson continued his build-up to the Pilkington Cup fourth round tie at London Scottish on 17 December by turning out in a 65-7 thrashing of his alma mater, Loughborough. The winning run continued with victories at Nottingham (22-10) and at Exeter (53-14) where hooker Gary French dislocated his shoulder ten minutes into his debut. Hall was among a number of first-teamers who returned after a month away from the action.

The only unfamiliar face in the cup-tie at Richmond Park was Marcus Olsen who impressed with a quick, clean service from scrum-half. Once Hilton had forced Lions tourist Paul Burnell into conceding a penalty try, Bath eased away with further tries by Callard and Swift, the full back also kicking 16 points.

Although Hilton's Scottish antecedents were later brought into question by the 'Grannygate' saga, he had performed well for Scotland A against the South African tourists six weeks earlier. Burnell endorsed the Bristol butcher's credentials, saying: "Hilts is a David Sole-type prop in that he's good with the ball in his hands. He's not just in there for his scrummaging or his line-out support work. He's a good player and he's only 24. I would say he's almost certainly next in line."

As a sign of 'progress', the curtain came down on 122 years of rugby history on Boxing Day when Clifton, now of National Division 3, made their final visit to the Recreation Ground. Bath fielded more a third choice line-up than even a United team but won 17-3 nonetheless. Time had run out on such quaint tradition.

The Clifton fixture pre-dated matches with Bristol by some 16 years but that particular derby now loomed large on 7 January. Having seen off Leicester, Bristol fancied their chances now more than ever. The front five – Alan Sharp, Mark Regan, David Hinkins, Simon Shaw and Andy Blackmore – were a formidable unit, spearheaded by all-action flanker Derek Eves and bossed from scrum-half by England's Bracken. Mark Tainton posed a considerable threat as a goal-kicker, as was clear from his haul of seven penalties, a dropped goal and a conversion against the Tigers.

Some 11,000 packed into the Memorial Ground, mostly Bristol supporters who had convinced themselves that this was finally to be the day, especially as they had now seen the back of Chilcott, Barnes and Hill. It made the 10-9 defeat all the harder to bear.

It was ferocious, intense and nerve-shredding, as only a local derby can be. Bristol were 9-nil up in 20 minutes through Tainton's boot and starting to believe.

Chris Hewett, now of The Independent, wrote in the Bristol Evening Post: "Bath were rattled to the core and a combination of their frustration and Bristol's over-eagerness led to countless flare-ups. At times it was more like an afternoon at the Roman Coliseum, although no-one could quite work out who the Christians were."

All Bath could do was hang in there and when a penalty was reversed right on their line for a retaliatory punch by Blackmore, they roused themselves to create a try at the other end for Geoghegan, converted by Callard. The full-back knocked over a 64th minute penalty to claim the lead for the first time and although Tainton peppered the Bath posts with three penalty attempts in the last 11 minutes, it was to no avail. "I can't tell you how disappointed I feel," said Bracken. "I honestly felt that this one had our name on it."

Northampton were heading for Division 2 but looked rather better than that when they lost 26-6 at the Rec on 14 January. Tries in the last 12 minutes by Swift and Geoghegan, both converted by Callard, swung the game after Bath had butchered a succession of scoring opportunities.

The league programme did not resume for another month with a trip to Orrell but first came the fifth round of the cup – also at Orrell. The match was notable for a hat-trick of dropped goals by Catt which eased Bath into a 17-16 lead on the hour mark. Callard and Simon Langford swapped penalties and Guscott confirmed a place in the quarter-finals for the ninth time in 12 seasons with a last-minute try.

Orrell gained revenge of sorts a fortnight later on 11 February when they held Bath to a 6-6 draw on the same afternoon that Leicester lost to Gloucester. Granted the visitors were without England representatives Guscott, Ubogu and Clarke plus the injured Hall, but there were far too many basic errors. Callard's equalising penalty came just five minutes from time.

It was deja vu all over again, as they say, when cup quarter-final opponents Northampton arrived at the Rec on 25 Feb – even down to a reprise of the 26-6 scoreline in the January league fixture. Callard kicked six out of six including conversions of tries by de Glanville and Clarke and the draw for the last four sent Bath to Harlequins for the second year running. But that was six weeks away. Meanwhile, their league campaign was faltering, the players energy levels sapped by the demands of a game which required a professional commitment of amateurs, even more so in World Cup year.

After scoring all Bath's points in a disappointing 19-19 draw at home to Gloucester, Callard spoke for all when he said: "The players have had a hard slog but we know better than anyone that we have very high standards to follow. The trouble is that when things don't go well some people jump on our backs.

"But we are still winning – or drawing. I know it's not good enough but the pressure is immense, even more so these days with international and World Cup demands. This last week we have had training sessions with Bath on Monday, Wednesday with England and again here on Thursday – and this is supposed to be an amateur game. I'd be very disappointed if anybody questions our commitment. If things don't go right out on the pitch so be it, but it's certainly not through lack of commitment."

A hastily arranged friendly with Orrell – their fourth meeting of the season – yielded a 5-5 draw and the year-long unbeaten record finally fell at Cardiff before a Spartans-strength line-up lost 29-5 at home to The Army. The spell broken, Bath travelled to Wasps on 25 March without the injured Hall as well as Hilton, Ubogu, Dawe, Guscott and Swift. Youngsters such as fly-half Butland, scorer of the only try, and prop Yates acquitted themselves well and the quality of performance was an improvement on the drawn games with Orrell and Gloucester but the Londoners deserved the 11-10 win. It left Bath trailing leaders Leicester on points difference and still with the prospect of a visit to Welford Road on 16 April.

Not for the first time, the cup provided a welcome distraction from the rigours of league rugby and the semi-final at The Stoop on April Fool's Day put smiles on people's faces at last. On a warm, sunny afternoon Catt typified the new-found confidence with a classy display at fly-half, creating a dazzling try for de Glanville on 16 minutes and keeping the Quins back row busy throughout. The master finisher Swift ran in two tries either side of a Catt dropped goal in the second half and Bath's place at Twickenham was booked long before Challinor's late try made the scoreline a little more respectable at 31-13.

Swift confirmed afterwards that he would be retiring after the final against Wasps on 6 May. "After scoring two tries in last season's semi-final and then another in the final, I thought I had another year left in me. I'm not going to make the same mistake again," he said. "This is definitely the

Kevin Yates: new face in the front row.

swansong. I'm still fairly sharp over the first 20 yards but I can't be as quick as I was 15 years ago. The important thing is to be in the final once again. The semis are such important games because there are 20,000 people back in Bath looking forward to their day out at Twickenham."

Supporters were relieved to see Bath carry that cup form into their next league match at home to West Hartlepool, scoring seven tries in a free-running game, all without eight of their World Cup contingent, including Geoghegan. Fly-half Butland kicked six conversions and two penalties in an impeccable all-round performance and the 53-17 scoreline put them back on top of the table. But with Leicester lying in wait there was no margin for error.

So it proved in front of a full house of 14,000 at Welford Road on 15 April. Without offering any threat beyond a suffocating forward effort, the Tigers built a 21-9 lead on the hour through the kicking of John Liley and Jez Harris. Bath fought their way back into contention with well-worked tries for Adebayo and Catt but at 24-21 the comeback was killed off when Adams' 'quarterback pass' was intercepted by England's Rory Underwood. "Rory certainly wasn't going to get a pass from

John Hall resigns himself to missing the cup final.

his own side," observed Brian Ashton as Bath reflected on a 31-21 defeat which, as far as a fifth successive league title was concerned, took matters out of their hands.

When Bath trailed 19-3 at half-time at Harlequins a week later, reports came through of Leicester players popping champagne corks at Sale, where they had kicked off at lunchtime. But a remarkable spell of 19 points in eight minutes involving tries by Guscott, Yates and Sleightholme earned a stay of execution and Butland wrapped up a 25-19 victory with a late penalty.

It was only putting off the inevitable, however, and Bath's season petered it out in an inept 18-13 defeat at home to Sale. Skipper Hall had confirmed that he would join Swift in retirement after the cup final against Wasps so this was their farewell to the Rec. Hall's swansong lasted 34 minutes as he trudged off with a badly bruised shoulder. It was a cruel anti-climax and it was hardly believable that he would also miss out on the opportunity of leading his side out at Twickenham. That was confirmed in an impromptu fitness test a few days later. It was a simple exercise involving the skipper running

*Steve Ojomoh: powerful performance against Wasps at Twickenham in the 1995
Pilkington Cup final.*

into a tackle bag held by Chilcott. The searing pain that accompanied the first 'hit'
ended any doubt.

With Hall ruled out and Catt, Hilton and Geoghegan also unavailable, neutrals
fully expected a resurgent Wasps to end Bath's run of eight winning finals. Perversely,
Hall's absence did not weaken the side as much as some expected – in fact, on a
sweltering afternoon the forced inclusion of Ojomoh was a major factor in a stunning
36-16 victory in front of 60,000.

> **The losers' coach, Rob Smith, certainly thought so. "We're all grown-ups and
> we have to accept the fact that we were seriously second-best on the day,"
> he said. "The crucial spell was early in the second half, when we had all the
> territory and pressure we could ever wish for. We set the big runners at them
> and they stopped us. All credit to them. To be honest, I was not at all happy
> when John Hall pulled out and Ojomoh came in. We were always looking to
> play a fast, wide game and Ojomoh makes the big hits far wider than Hall,
> whose strength is very much at close quarters."**

Haag sets things rolling after just four minutes, slipping undetected from a maul to
score a try converted by Callard and 20 minutes later finishing off a move down the
short side carried on by Clarke, Callard and Robinson. "For once, we gave ourselves
a decent start," said the lock. "I was quite surprised my first try came in the way
it did – it was a planned move from the set scrum but it was also one that hadn't
worked for ages!"

Clarke galloped on to a Swift pass for the third try but there was just time for Wasps to pull back to 19-11 with a Dunston try on the stroke of half-time. Wasps summoned up a huge effort after the break but with Robinson at his obdurate best and de Glanville looking every inch a captain-in-waiting, the defence won out.

After Callard added a penalty and the Wasps storm blew itself out, Swift bowed out in inimitable style by leaving Jon Ufton and Nick Greenstock for dead to score the fourth try. That would have been enough in itself but Butland, growing in confidence at fly-half, put Guscott through a gap and Callard was on his shoulder for the score. The full-back's conversion brought his match tally to 16 points, which was all that Wasps managed after Damian Hopley's late try.

BATH: *J Callard; A Swift, P de Glanville, J Guscott, A Adebayo; R Butland, I Sanders; K Yates, G Adams, V Ubogu (Mallett), M Haag, N Redman, S Ojomoh, B Clarke, A Robinson.*

WASPS: J *Ufton; P Hopley, D Hopley, G Childs, N Greenstock; R Andrew, S Bates; D Molloy, K Dunn, I Dunston, M Greenwood, N Hadley, L Dallaglio, D Ryan, M White.*

REFEREE: *John Pearson* (Durham)

While it had been a remarkable team effort, highlighted by the efforts of the back row, everyone was delighted that Swift had finished his career with a flourish. "The whole day was absolutely fabulous," said the 36-year-old chartered accountant: "The thing that pleased me most out there was the performance of the younger lads. They are the ones who have to take Bath forward now. We've all had our day and we have great memories but they've got everything to play for and I think they'll do it for us.

"It was one of the great Bath displays. We had a lot of injuries and we had to soak up a tremendous amount of pressure, so to win in that style is a dream come true..."

Fittingly, de Glanville sought out John Hall at the final whistle and sent him up the steps to accept the trophy. "I told Phil he should go up, but he wasn't having any of it," said Hall. "It was a wonderful thing for him to have done and I thank him for it. Phil did one hell of a job out there. He was in a difficult situation and handled things magnificently. For my part, I was quiet all day. I never liked outsiders getting involved in the dressing room side of things when I was playing and I thought Phil would probably want to do it in his style, so I kept out of the way."

For nine of Bath's England players, there was little time to savour the triumph as they immediately turned their attention to the third Rugby World Cup in South Africa. Rowell had named an unchanged team throughout in steering England to a third Grand Slam in five years. Catt, at full-back, Guscott, Ubogu and Clarke had been among that select group while Ojomoh won his sixth cap as a replacement in the deciding victory over Scotland.

For the World Cup adventure, they were joined by Callard, de Glanville, Dawe and Mallett. Progress through the Pool B matches against Argentina, Italy and Western Samoa was unspectacular but a last-minute drop-goal by Rob Andrew to beat Australia in the quarter-final brought the competition to life before Jonah Lomu's rampage in the semi.

On 23 June 1995, the eve of the World Cup final between South Africa and New Zealand, Rupert Murdoch's News Corporation announced in Johannesburg that it was willing to pay $550 million for broadcast rights to a new Tri-Nations competition between the finalists and Australia. The inevitable decision to declare Rugby Union an 'open' sport and therefore to sanction payment of players under professional contracts was taken at a meeting of the International Rugby Board in Paris two months later. A working party had already identified 'wholesale' breaches of amateur regulations when it reported to the IRB earlier in the year.

While the Southern Hemisphere unions were mapping out at a future based on a centrally-contracted franchise model, the Rugby Football Union's response was to declare a year's moratorium on payment of players. In adopting a policy of 'wait and see' they were acting true-to-type but a club like Bath could hardly be expected to sit on their hands and see a squad of internationals raided by their rivals.

Realising that their destiny was in their own hands, English clubs had to come up with their own business models. But where was the money to come from? Bath and others began to look around for a 'sugar daddy'. The first rich benefactor to emerge was Sir John Hall, who followed up his takeover of Newcastle-Gosforth in September 1995 with the aggressive recruitment from Wasps of Rob Andrew, Dean Ryan and Steve Bates.

By comparison with most clubs, Bath were financially in good heart. The shortfall of £20,000 associated with the costs of building the new press box, the focus of so much discussion three years earlier, had been met first by a brewery loan, negotiated by club treasurer Colin Gale, a regional bank director.

Colin recalls: "We had a long relationship with Bass and the loan was very advantageous, based on barrelage. We built up our cash from our cup runs and paid it off early. By the end of the 1995-96 season we had a clean sheet, £1.5 million of assets, no debts at all and cash in the bank. The new Teachers stand was a commercial success thanks to good work by Peter Downey in selling 10-year agreements to holders of hospitality boxes and there had also been an excellent fund-raising effort by Doug Ryder with his 200 Club."

But quite what the financial commitment would be in terms of contracting a squad almost entirely composed of international players was another matter entirely. Without significant investment it was clearly more than the club could afford as it was currently constituted.

The new season opened with a new face in the Bath team, although he had been technically part of the playing squad since his registration 17 months earlier. Andy Nicol had joined Bath from Dundee High School Former Pupils as the heir to Richard Hill but a second serious knee injury and the consequent rehabilitation programme had delayed his debut for a full year. The 24-year-old, who had won eight Scotland caps and been a replacement on the Lions tour to New Zealand – but without actually taking the field – scored within 11 minutes of his first appearance on the Rec and Bath went on to win 62-19 against Garryowen.

Andy Nicol: belated first appearance.

Only the continuing absence of Geoghegan with a groin strain prevented Bath travelling at full-strength to West Hartlepool on 9 September but left wing Sleightholme turned in one of his more convincing displays, crossing for the only try in a 20-15 victory to kick off the Courage League campaign.

Lumsden scored with a clever change of pace to complete a 37-11 rout of Gloucester a week later and other tries went to Nicol and Sleightholme. Callard kicked 19 points and Catt a dropped goal but the damage was really done up front where the Gloucester pack were ruthlessly dismantled and were driven nearly half the length of the field from one second-half line-out.

Ben Clarke charges into the West Hartlepool defence as Bath get their 1995-96 league campaign off to a winning start.

Even with Swift retired and Geoghegan seemingly injury-prone, there was more jockeying for the wing places than in other areas of the team. For the trip to Leicester a week later – then as now a potential tipping point in the league season – Ashton sprang a surprise by naming Adebayo on the left, little more than a week since his return from New Zealand where he had been playing for Southland.

The gamble, if it was such, paid off handsomely as Adebayo poached a 61st minute try to punish a wild pass by Neil Back. The England flanker also came second to Robinson in the loose where Clarke and Ojomoh played a full part in establishing Bath's superiority despite the wealth of first phase possession that came Leicester's way.

Their frustration was reflected in a yellow card for Dean Richards, flagged for foul play, and although John Liley eventually cut Bath's lead to 11-9 with his third penalty, Callard replied in similar fashion in injury time. As 16,000 fans filed out of Welford Road, the Tigers' dressing room door remained firmly shut on a first home league defeat in two years.

One of the big plusses for Bath was the quality of Guscott's performance, particularly his defensive work in the last 10 minutes. Against Orrell seven days later, the Lions centre showed off his peerless attacking skills too as signs emerged that the players were beginning to tune in fully to Ashton's coaching philosophy.

Guscott, who was already looking ahead to a third Lions tour in 1997, ran in the fourth of eight tries at the end of a 90-metre move and said: "I'm trying to build a little more into the season, in terms of my fitness, pace and power. I'm looking to be at my peak, hopefully, in readiness for South Africa."

For de Glanville, who had declared that one of his aims as captain would be to get "big games from the big names", to help his centre partner display international form at club level was a critical factor in winning trophies – yet it directly harmed his own prospects of splitting the Carling-Guscott partnership. "It's frustrating – it has been for two years. I've got used to it but that doesn't mean it's any less frustrating," he said. "But if Bath win the double, I'll be happy." The other try scorers included de Glanville himself as well as Adebayo (2), Callard (2), Ubogu and Catt. Callard's kicking left him with a match total of 25 points.

As the season moved into October, England tighthead Ubogu was given a sharp reminder that no-one was indispensable as he gave way to Hilton for the trip to Wasps. The outstanding individuals in a 15-6 victory were de Glanville, on his 100th appearance, and Robinson whose man-and-ball tackle on Rob Andrew led to a second of two tries for Adebayo, taking the wing's tally to five in three games.

It was not a great spectacle but Robinson was not unduly bothered: "Playing up here is not the same as at the Rec," he said. "All the same, we've gone to Wasps and Leicester in recent weeks and won, whereas last year we lost. That's two good results."

John Hall, now installed as team manager, condemned the first-half showing as "inept" and accused players of operating "in the comfort zone." That was despite the fact that Bath had been training without tackle bags in an effort to find that competitive 'edge'. It was an approach that certainly found favour with a seasoned campaigner like Robinson. "The training's been tremendous this year," said the 31-year-old flanker. "Because people are more body-hardened in the training sessions, you get used to the knocks and there seem to be fewer injuries."

It all came together in spectacular fashion a week later when Bristol arrived at the Rec seeking a first league win over their rivals. The gulf in ambition and execution was embarrassing as Bath inflicted a record 52-19 defeat. With Sanders' slicker service earning him a place ahead of Nicol, Ubogu restored at tight-head and Hilton displacing Yates, the home side let rip in glorious weather. Chief beneficiary was Guscott who scored three tries inside 46 minutes before others were added by Ojomoh, Clarke, Catt and Geoghegan, making his first appearance of the season. Two of the scores came from restarts as Bath rattled up 19 points in one devastating four-minute spell, Callard contributing three penalties and four conversions.

On occasions such as this, the most accurate view of a performance of this quality often came from the opposition. A shell-shocked Kyran Bracken, preparing to inherit the England No 9 shirt following the retirement of Dewi Morris, was able to offer his perspective: "That's the way I hope to see England playing this year. It's the way I like to play. They were just out of this world.

"It was almost like playing sevens. We were kicking off, losing possession, and they weren't giving it back. They don't kick for line-outs. They just try to keep possession, nicking any ball they can, rucking and running, rucking and running – and there's nothing you can do. Obviously it was very difficult for Bristol but Bath are playing the sort of rugby the All Blacks have been playing."

England manager Jack Rowell was back on his old stamping to witness the carnage – but his successor was not. Unbelievably, even with the game preparing to go professional, as master-in-charge of rugby at King's Bruton school, Brian Ashton could not get Saturdays off until the half-term break allowed him to attend the away match at Harlequins. The only try in the 19-13 win came on 27 minutes when Haag won a line-out and Guscott made a telling break before de Glanville put Lumsden over.

Glad that he could make an assessment at first hand rather than on video but concerned that the performance tailed off in the second half, Ashton said: "We do set ourselves very high standards and it's disappointing, especially after last week's performance against Bristol, to feel that we couldn't actually repeat it on a similar sort of day 100 miles east. But we're going to have to do that, have the patience and the will to play the same sort of game – for 80 minutes, not 20 – away from home as we do at home."

It has to be said however that the 1995-96 team scaled heights seldom seen in club rugby, even on the Rec. In running eight tries past Saracens on 28 October de Glanville's side took their try total to 32 in eight games – five more than Leicester managed in winning the title over 18 matches.

The 52-16 scoreline represented their third 50-pointer in a row at home and included Guscott's 100th try for the club. The first score was a penalty try after just 50 seconds as Clarke was tackled off the ball in an offside position; Geoghegan 2, de Glanville, Lumsden and Sanders 2 grabbed the others and Callard weighed in with six conversions. Saracens spent two thirds of the game in the Bath half and won plenty of ball, as coach Rob Cunningham, the former Bath hooker, observed ruefully: "It's not as if we did much wrong from our point of view – our forwards went particularly well and we had our chances – but once they've got the ball, look out!"

With their rivals making little impression, Bath's coruscating form was bound to have some influence on Rowell's planning for the visit of world champions South Africa on 18 November. Making an unanswerable case for inclusion since September had been Robinson, even though his last cap had been fully 50 Tests previously, against Wales at Cardiff on 18 March 1989. So was Callard whose goal-kicking form left Rowell with the attractive option of switching Catt to fly-half against the country of his birth.

So it proved. Rowell named his side three days before Bath's league trip to Sale on 4 November and there was a double celebration for Callard as his

Victor Ubogu, Graham Dawe and Kevin Yates take a breather against Saracens (28 October 1995).

wife, Gail, gave birth to daughter Georgia on the Friday. Joining his team-mates after four hours sleep and a long drive up the M6, Callard shanked the first penalty but settled down to collect a try, three penalties and three conversions. Lumsden crossed for the other tries in a 30-18 victory which left Bath with a 100 per cent record from the first half of the league programme.

After a glorious autumn, the weather finally broke for the visit of West Hartlepool a week later. Robinson and Ubogu were rested ahead of the international while Catt, who had been injured late in the game at Harlequins, was still missing. But the other three England men all took the field, Callard passing 1,000 points for the club and Guscott and Clarke both scoring tries in a 34-22 win.

> **The big No 8, who was also denied a pushover score by the award of a penalty try, said: "It's always at the back of your mind before you play a game that there is a prospect of getting injured. But I wouldn't be an international if it wasn't for Bath Rugby Club and the players here, so I don't have any problem whatsoever about playing the week before South Africa."**

Lumsden scored the other Bath try and Callard kicked 14 points on a heavy pitch. Unfortunately for Robinson, apart from occupying the bench against Western Samoa a month later, England never called again. The dominant back row forward at Twickenham was not Robinson but the Springboks' Ruben Kruger, sadly lost to cancer in January 2010. The World Cup winners prevailed 24-14, scoring three tries to one. England's try scorer was de Glanville, who had come on as replacement for Carling, while Callard kicked three penalties. Lawrence Dallaglio also won his first cap off the bench.

Back at the Rec, a squad of second and third-teamers stepped up to the plate for a series of friendlies. After stretching the winning run to 12 matches by defeating Coventry 28-23 in front of a small crowd at the Rec, they then found Loughborough Students just a little too lively, losing 17-19.

> **Back came some of the 'big guns' for the visit of Nottingham on the first Saturday of December and the ferocity of the barrage was beyond all expectations as Bath won 99-12, scoring 15 tries. Callard landed 12 conversions and would have brought up the century had his final effort not struck the post – but that came as something of a relief to the those operating the digital scoreboard which could not cope with three figures!**

The only member of the back line not to get on the score sheet was 18-year-old debutant Matt Perry, son of Brendan Perry, Bath's fly-half of the 1960s and 70s. Although his first appearance was in the centre alongside de Glanville, Perry Jnr was to forge a reputation as one of the finest full-backs the club ever produced and at the time of writing was still England's most capped player in the No 15 shirt with 36 appearances, plus three Test outings for the 2001 Lions.

Perry did score a try the following week, dummying his way over in a 33-24 victory at London Scottish where flanker Adam Vander made an impressive debut in both attack and defence. John Palmer, who had been coaching the United, provided some background: "He's an ex-Bath University lad and was with Rosslyn Park. They gave him a car ... I think he's been living in it. He was everywhere today, quite outstanding, the best prospect I've seen for a long time."

Hall, newly appointed as the club's first Director of Rugby, issued a 'no kicking' edict for the home date with Exeter on a cold, windy night at the Rec on 15 December 1995. Fraser Waters, a 19-year-old Bristol University economics student, made his debut, having already been recognised at divisional level and with a place on the England A bench against Western Samoa a few days previously. Crompton crossed for a try within a minute and Bath eventually won 36-29, at times appearing to mistake 'no kicking' for 'no tackling'.

Just five first-teamers featured in that game but a full complement, including Geoghegan, returned from the mid-winter training camp in Almancil on the Algarve to line up against runaway Second Division leaders Northampton in the Pilkington Cup fourth round. It was two days before Christmas. Cold, drenching rain fell all day on the Rec and a 12-3 scoreline – four Callard penalties to one by Paul Grayson – seemed to say it all. Only it didn't, not by a long way. Bath's line-out and a ruthlessly efficient driving maul gave them the edge and forced the crucial decisions from referee Ed Morrison but on another day Northampton's adventurous approach and extraordinary defensive effort might have done enough. It was one of the most enjoyable, absorbing games of the season.

The Gloucester match was lost to the weather and when Leicester arrived on 6 January the conditions were not much better, blustery with driving rain and a sticky pitch. But Bath struck within 35 seconds as Adebayo ran in from 60 metres after Haag collected the kick-off and Clarke and Ubogu set up rucks for skipper de Glanville and Guscott to release the left wing. Callard missed the conversion but added a penalty after five minutes when Graham Rowntree pulled down a scrum, Clarke tried to wrest the ball from scrum-half Aadel Kardooni and Martin Johnson added his two penn'orth.

Leicester take revenge at the Rec, winning 15-14 on 6 January 1996.

Leicester's tactics were clear enough: to ensure the ball never ventured more than arm's length from Dean Richards' grasp. As ever, the front row contest provided the flashpoint and it became a dogfight, decided by the kickers. Four successful shots from John Liley earned the visitors a 12-11 lead and, as the weather deteriorated, all the second half produced was a penalty apiece for the two full-backs.

It left the Tigers just two points behind Bath in the league with seven games to play. For de Glanville, the failure to break the forward stranglehold, even in those conditions, was a source of frustration. "We played into their hands," he said afterwards. "We needed a killer blow and it didn't come. It's a big setback but not a disaster – it depends how we react. The test of the side is how we bounce back." Leicester's Director of Rugby Tony Russ was pragmatism personified: "It wasn't pretty, but that's how we planned to play."

It was clear that Bath had been unable to adapt their tactics when conditions militated against the ambitious, athletic style that had seen them storm through the first two months of the season under sunny skies and on firm pitches. But Ashton, whose philosophy was diametrically opposed to that of Russ, was in no mood to compromise.

He even persisted with the 'no kicking' rule when Bath sent a youthful side up to Northampton for a friendly fixture the following week. Reflecting on a 21-12 defeat, Ashton was not in the least apologetic, saying: "In some ways – and this might seem strange coming from a Bath coach – it's more important for me that I learn which players look as though they can handle the type of game we want to take into the future, as opposed to actually winning. If they can't, then I'm afraid they've either got to improve fairly smartly or …" his voice trailed off.

> "We know exactly how we want to play the game in the next five years and we now need to look at some of these younger players and say: 'Are you going to be able to cope with it?' So I'm forcing ambition on them at the moment. If you want to blame anyone for this defeat, blame me, because we could have kicked umpteen penalties at goal and probably won the game. I'm quite happy to take the blame from that point of view but I'm much more interested in the future of these younger players and the way Bath want to take the game forward."

A 21-11 win against Moseley gave an opportunity for Robinson and a few others to sharpen up before the scheduled fifth round Pilkington Cup match at Wakefield on 27 January but snow, freezing rain and hail across England caused the tie to be postponed. So was the visit from Cardiff on the Tuesday following but a young side travelled to Swansea four days later. Scrum-half Charlie Harrison made his debut as Bath lost 27-10.

One had the sense that it was not only the weather that had disrupted Bath's serene progress. The RFU's moratorium on a truly 'open' game had only months to run and there was concern around the Rec at the apparent lack of progress in keeping the squad together for 1996-97. Actually , as club chairman Richard Mawditt confided to your author in the Swansea clubhouse, there had been much planning and number crunching behind the scenes.

> **"We've gone through every aspect of things very thoroughly. I will lay it all before the committee on Thursday. The proposals will include a business plan and a development plan for the ground. We haven't been shouting our mouths off but that's been a deliberate policy. We've just got on with the job of planning a successful and prosperous future for Bath Rugby Club.**

And was he aware of concerns among the players?

> **"Yes, but we have been talking to them. I am confident their interests will be properly looked after."**

But when it eventually came to playing Wakefield on 10 February, that same star-studded group of internationals looked seriously undercooked. How Second Division Wakefield did not add their name to those of Moseley and Waterloo in capturing the most prized scalp in cup rugby is still a mystery.

With remarkable timing, Sleightholme returned to his former club as England's newest cap, having made his debut on the right wing against France on 20 January. Thomas Casteignede snatched victory for the home team with a late dropped goal but Sleightholme was on the winning side against Wales at Twickenham a fortnight later, when Guscott scored his nineteenth England try in a 21-15 victory.

Wakefield president Alan Birkinshaw wrote in the match day programme: "I am sure that we shall see some good attacking rugby from both sides to make this game worthy of the Pilkington Cup and who knows what might happen, the Cup does have this habit of throwing up the odd surprise now and again."

One notable absentee when the Bath team coach arrived at the Yorkshiremen's College Grove ground was Catt, the England full-back. Anxious to cement his place in the national team in that position ahead of the 1995 World Cup, he had told Bath that he would only consider playing at full-back. Hall was in no mood at that point to drop Jon Callard so Catt played in the United that day.

It was not the best preparation for a cup-tie but Butland, the young aeronautical engineering student, was happy to find himself officially first-choice fly-half. In fact, he was one of few players to shine on the day, along with first-half try scorer Guscott, Sleightholme and Haag, and it was Butland's try that stole an improbable win for the cup holders with just 35 seconds of normal time remaining. Agonisingly for Wakefield, it came after their inspiring hooker, Terry Garnett, was penalised by Ashley Rowden for delaying a line-out throw. When the whistle blew shortly afterwards and the scoreboard read Wakefield 12, Bath 16, Garnett sank to his knees in utter despair.

Sleightholme went straight into the home dressing room to commiserate with his former team-mates but there were no celebrations in the Bath camp. It had been a 'horror show', as Butland admitted afterwards: "We like to try to hit the line quickly but we hadn't had much opportunity to do it for most of the game. It just happened to come in the last minute or so. We were shocking but we got through it. To be fair to Wakefield, they played very well and came at us with all cylinders firing. But we kept our heads, stuck at it and in the end our experience told."

As often happened, normal service was resumed at the Rec a week later when a dangerous-looking Wasps side came to the Rec. The Catt issue was temporarily resolved when Guscott was forced to pull out at the eleventh hour with a shoulder injury, leaving his England colleague to pair up with skipper de Glanville, while Butland continued at fly-half. Catt nearly scored in the first minute but Dawe crossed from the resulting 22 drop-out and, after Catt accelerated through a gap to send Sleightholme sprinting 50 metres to the line five minutes later, Bath were unstoppable. Wasps found themselves trailing 26-nil on the half-hour and although Dallaglio and his pack hauled the Londoners back into the game, Bath eventually won 36-12, having scored further tries through Yates, de Glanville and Nicol, with Callard contributing four conversions and a penalty.

> Coach Ashton was more than satisfied with the quality of performance, saying: "It's a joy to watch a match like that, where both sides are prepared to play the game the way it was devised to be played. For 20-25 minutes, we played some of the best rugby I've ever seen on the Rec. We tore the opposition apart. We weren't going to carry on like that, for a variety of reasons, but that's the standard we set ourselves now."

Reflecting on the Catt dilemma, your author reported at the time: "Catt, for all his desire to turn out for Bath in his England position of full-back, may eventually discover that centre is his best position." Sometimes we did get it right.

Yet Callard was dropped the following week for the Pilkington Cup quarter-final at Bristol, a fairly routine 19-12 victory to Bath. With Butland slotting his four penalties and converting Clarke's try, it was an uncomfortable time for Callard who was also having to play second fiddle to Catt in the England squad. But his combative spirit endeared him to Bath supporters and his demotion was brief.

Two years later he would gain immortality in the annals of Bath rugby by scoring all 19 points in the Heineken Cup final as Bath became champions of Europe.

Chapter 13

THE RIGHT MAN AT THE RIGHT TIME

John Hall's declaration in late February 1996 that Bath were going to build "the most formidable club in Europe," was a characteristically powerful statement of intent from Bath's Director of Rugby. But where was the money to come from?

As an amateur concern, the finances of Bath Football Club (RFU) were in rude health but there was simply not enough cash to sign up on professional contracts a squad packed with internationals.

Without a major injection of funds, the worry behind the scenes was that other clubs who had already found their 'sugar daddies' would pillage the Rec and that it might induce a 'domino effect' as the squad broke up.

So Hall's bold statement after the cup quarter-final win at Bristol also served as a 'hands off' warning to their rivals. "I keep reading stories about cash-strapped Bath but the amount of interest in terms of investment is phenomenal," he said. "I accept that as a club we were probably a bit slow to react when rugby turned professional, yet everything has now been looked at in great detail."

To say at that time that interest from potential investors was 'phenomenal' might have been stretching it somewhat but it was essential that the integrity of the Bath squad was preserved. For the time being the 'Bath family' was prepared to hold together but the players had written collectively to club chairman Richard Mawditt as early as 4 December to voice their fears and that had prompted Mawditt to write each one a 'personal and confidential letter' as the squad prepared to fly out to Portugal. The letter, dated 15 December 1995, ran to some 3,000 words over four A4 pages and began in emollient tone:

> **First, let me say that I do not wish to quarrel with your point of view or make excuses for any shortcomings which you feel that I or the Management Committee have in moving forward as rapidly as you might have liked. Much as though these last three or four months have been frantic and I believe that we have moved on with so many issues which have taken a considerable amount of time and energy, I would openly admit that a number of other avenues could well have been taken in our way forward.**

Richard Mawditt: letter to players.

Ahead of a special general meeting of the RFU on 14 January, Mawditt summarised the wider situation and assured the players that despite all the the talk about contracts elsewhere, the moratorium declared by the RFU had left all clubs in the same state of limbo, unable to contract with their players. He did reveal however that the Bath management committee had agreed the establishment of a trust fund into which the club could deposit a sum of money for the benefit of the players when the moratorium was eventually lifted – "and that is somewhat against the current rules," he confided, before continuing: "The form of players' contracts for 1996/97 onwards is as advanced here in Bath as it is elsewhere, I can assure you. We have those draft contracts in place and I hope that we can successfully negotiate to our mutual benefit in these coming weeks."

Mawditt pointed out that, notwithstanding recent successes, he had a duty to take into account 130 years of history as a members' club with 'shared ownership'.

It would have been all too easy for me to make a simple proposal that the Club becomes an incorporated body and the Trustees relinquish their responsibility and liability to such a new form. I know that has been the firm proposal of a number of people who feel that should be the way forward. Whilst my own views would not be so far from that, I would like to ensure that we give every opportunity for our members to share in the future prosperity of the Club and to feel part of that ownership, albeit recognizing that unless they are prepared to put significant sums of money into the Club, we shall have to look outside for such investment. I have to say, however, that it is not my view that I should move in the direction of a Northampton or a Saracens whereby we totally abandon, it would seem, the membership from the future of the Club. However, in more recent weeks we have set up a Bath Commission to look at issues such as this and there has been wisdom in the proposal that we should take independent and external advice on the alternative ways in which we could construct the Club and that is now well in place.

Even with the benefit of 15 years' hindsight, Mawditt is sure that the management of the club were right to take a considered view of the options available. He says now: "Our players were putting a hell of a lot of pressure on me – in the nicest sort of way. They were asking me why I wasn't coming up with a deal straight away. But while I had Plans A, B and C, I wasn't going to go beyond Plan A with the players, many of whom did not really know what they were going to do. That was understandable,

Phil de Glanville with John Mallett, just embarking on a teaching career when the game prepared to go professional.

especially for young men like John Mallett, who had started a teaching job at Marlborough College. They were really at the cross-roads, trying desperately to get on board in one sense but having to be cautious as well."

The pressure was coming from Hall himself and the skipper, de Glanville, who remembers it as a fraught time. "Because we were the top club in the land, we had individual players or groups of players being picked off," he says. "John and I knew that and we could see that quite possibly we could lose half the squad before anything had been done on the Bath side. So that's why we tried to put the pressure on Richard. Obviously there was all the due process to go through, with the risks to the members and all that; those are all proper things for the chairman to consider but when you are a player you know very little about them."

"From our point of view it was the pace at which things moved and the realisation that, well, the horse could have bolted and half these guys might have gone."

Then came what de Glanville describes as "a huge kick in the guts", when Ben Clarke revealed to him that he had decided to leave for Richmond at the end of the season. The star of the 1993 Lions tour to New Zealand had been lured by the extravagant plans of Monaco tax exile Ashley Levett and a reputed £1 million contract.

"It went from a reasonably planned, systematic process where there were wider issues for the club and the membership to be sorted out to, very suddenly, individual players being picked off by other clubs," says de Glanville. "Ben Clarke's Richmond offer was the first in a line. There were quite incredible sums of money being offered at that stage. That caused huge anxiety for John and myself because, if you were an individual player in that position, why wouldn't you take it? There were people like

Mike Catt, in particular, and others were getting these offers too. And I don't think Richard and the others realised that."

Meanwhile, Mawditt was in a unique position of influence having been invited to represent the clubs on an RFU Commission set up in September 1995 and chaired by the RFU Honorary Secretary, Tony Hallett. An RFU statement had laid out the Commission's terms of reference:

> '... to conduct a full review of the regulations, rules and structures to be applied to rugby union following the Paris IB declaration. The principal considerations are international and national competitive structures; regulations applicable to participation in open rugby; a professional code of conduct; finance and marketing; preparation of legal documentation and amended rules. The commission is authorised to consult as widely within the game as is practicable. Essentially, its work is fast-track and is to be unencumbered by the normal process of committee-work. It has exceptional authority and its findings will form the foundation for the Rugby Union in England and England's participation in international rugby in the future.'

"I did find it useful to be on the inner circle," Mawditt remembers. "Clubs didn't know what was going on at Twickenham. The First Division clubs, who met monthly on Sunday mornings at Moseley, rebelled very quickly against the indecisiveness of the RFU, because they would not make a decision one way or another on when the moratorium might be lifted.

"Everything revolved around the players' contracts. It wasn't really a matter of what recognition do we give to professionalism," explains Mawditt. "It was: 'How on earth do we deal with contracts?' The RFU wanted to have central contracts but the players were being wooed by all sorts of people."

The main distraction was a proposal for a 'World Rugby Competition', funded by Kerry Packer, the man whose 'World Series Cricket' had transformed that sport two decades earlier. De Glanville was one of the English players targeted by Packer's front man, Ross Turnbull and he confirms: "Their world club competition proposal was very close to getting off the ground. There was all the to-ing and fro-ing and deciding whether we should sign or not. Was it right or wrong? Who would be involved? The pressure was on from all sides."

And de Glanville, newly married and having moved from his job with Cow & Gate in Trowbridge to a marketing post with an IT consultancy, also had to consider where his own best interests might lie. "Within the wider responsibility as captain of the club, you were also trying to decide what to do as an individual. Lots of people were trying to weigh up how secure it all was. Could you afford to give up a job you already had, especially those who were in professions? It was a very risky thing to do because there was really very little guarantee. It could all have gone pear shaped after a year. And, of course, after three years or so Richmond did go into administration.

"But there was mild – or more than mild – panic caused by these people suddenly coming into the market quite aggressively. Unless you were one of the individuals concerned, you didn't see all this. That was why we were pressurising or harassing Richard. It was because we could see the player base disintegrating before the club could even have a chance of contracting them."

Did it come closer to 'meltdown' than people appreciated at the time? "I think so," says de Glanville. "Obviously they went for the top players first. Who knew what would have happened after that? It was just that feeling that things were out of control. All of a sudden there was a market and people were putting figures in front of players that they would be stupid to say 'No' to. It was a very strange time."

There should have been some clarity achieved at a special general meeting of the RFU in Birmingham on 14 January 1996 but it broke up in chaos and acrimony when Staffordshire representative Cliff Brittle led a revolt of the game's 'backwoodsmen'. Astonishingly, having already voted acceptance of amended RFU regulations following the International Board decisions, they successfully demanded another special general meeting at which they would vote on whether to abandon the principle of amateurism.

It was a farcical situation and one which was not resolved until 24 March when the second meeting bowed to the inevitable in approving an 'open' game. Brittle's main ally, former England and Lions prop Fran Cotton, pressed for the retention of divisional rugby and for those regional teams to represent England in European competition – a clear challenge to the First Division clubs – but the notion of 'central contracts' was now a dead issue. In retrospect, the hiatus worked in the major clubs' favour because they were able to develop a collective strategy while the RFU dithered and squabbled.

So Bath and their big league rivals had won that battle, although 'a club-based' structure was only what the RFU Commission had recommended when it reported back to the RFU on 30 October 1995. The lifting of the moratorium was confirmed for 6 May.

That was a huge relief to all at Bath, not least to Mawditt, who recalls: "Once that was decided, it was much easier to go forward in all sorts of ways, with the players' contracts, with looking for investment. Bear in mind that most of us as clubs had to face the reality of how to deal with players' contracts. Even Bath, which was one of the clubs in the 'black', couldn't negotiate with players. I could not say to our captain, Phil de Glanville, or John Hall, who badgered me consistently and quite properly: 'Yes, we can give you contracts.' The club did not have the asset base to offer half a million pounds of contracts. It would have been criminally negligent of us to do so. That's the law of the land.

"I said to them: 'You are members of the club as I am and you know perfectly that unless we do actually have a million pounds in the pocket, we can't do that.' But Phil was a very sharp young man and understood that and John was very astute too. He may not have had an Oxbridge education but he was no mug."

Mawditt's attention had already turned to finding Bath's 'white knight' and he had enlisted professional help in tracking down a target list of ten 'high net worth' individuals. During February 1996 the second draft of a 'strictly confidential' Information Memorandum, effectively a business prospectus, was circulated to the committee.

"The players were free agents, of course.," says Mawditt "We couldn't hold them because we did not have a contract with them. And we couldn't offer a contract until we had the wherewithal, the backing from someone to put the money in. So we put together this memorandum and business plan, together with two external advisers, chiefly with Richard Smerdon, senior partner with Osborne Clarke, the Bristol law firm; he was my guru. We also employed Graham Robinson of Ernst & Young Corporate Finance." The purpose of the Information Memorandum was:

> **"... to enable BFC to plan the financial management of the business, accommodating the requirements related to the 'open' game and if appropriate attract funding. Additionally, the Information Memorandum summarises the proposed management structure of the Club that will be put in place in order to facilitate the changes required resulting from professionalism."**

The document noted that in the most recent annual accounts, for the year to 31 May 1995, revenues totalled £1.2 million, of which £450,000 was derived from gate takings. Commercial activities provided the balance with the most significant contribution being £300,000 from debentures, hospitality boxes and branding of the Teacher's Stand. The club's main sponsorship deal was with international drinks group Hiram Walker (Allied Domecq) and worth £100,000. Teacher's Whisky was one of their best known brands

Overheads for the entire 1994-95 season had been £875,000, with the salaries of administrative staff running to just £166,000. The scale of the task facing the management of the club was outlined by the estimated increase in operating costs that would follow the introduction of professionalism – a hefty £1.5 million. Not only would players salaries have to be paid, at a projected cost of £1.13 million in the first full year, but the club's administrative functions would need to be placed on a professional, full-time basis.

Extra income of around £200,000 was expected from participation in the European Cup and TV revenues were forecast to rise from £430,000 in 1996-97 to £650,000 (1997-98) and £800,000 (1998-99). Commercial activities were said to increase by £250,000 in 1996-97 following the earlier opening of the club shop in Argyll Street and the appointment of a professional Commercial/Marketing Director. The members were also expected to dip their hands deeper into their pockets, with membership fees planned to rise by 75 per cent.

Interestingly, the club's Honorary Treasurer, Colin Gale, considered the revenue projections prepared for the Information Memorandum to be far too optimistic.

Marketing and merchandise: Mike Catt (left), Eric Peters, Jon Sleightholme and Phil de Glanville turn out to promote the newly opened club shop on Argyle Street.

"They were over-hyped," he says. "So I said 'No', I wouldn't put my name to the final draft of the projections. It didn't make me very popular at the time with some people within the club but it didn't mean I wasn't supportive of the agreement. Far from it."

As with all small businesses, the concern was cash flow. The club calculated that it needed short term funding of £500,000 to support the proposed new operating structure of the club and to enable a start on the first tranche of a development plan for the Recreation Ground, which would take the capacity from the current 8,305 to an eventual 14,905. The cost of replacing the West Stand was estimated at £6 million. Without the commitment to developing the Rec, the absolute minimum funding requirement was £255,000.

For three men in particular – Len Hughes, Angus Meek and Reg Hillman – this was all rather perturbing because 'ownership' of the club was vested in them as trustees of Bath Football Club (RFU).

"They were hopping from one foot to the other, never expecting that they would have to deal with anything like this," says Mawditt. The lawyer Smerdon therefore advised the creation of a trust company, Bath Football Club Trustees Ltd, so that ownership of the assets – and the liabilities – could be transferred from the three club trustees. Half a dozen directors, including Mawditt, were

Colin Gale: sceptical of revenue projections.

then empowered to get on with the legal formalities and negotiate with a potential investor, although the trust company did not come into being formally until July 1996.

"Next step was to find some investment," he says, "so I went to ten different people and I think seven of them said straight away: 'Thanks, but no thanks'." Among the remaining suitors was Malcolm Pearce, a longstanding 'friend' of the club.

Many young players had been working for businesses run by Pearce, a convivial entrepreneur with interests in dairy farming and newspaper and magazine distribution. At one time he employed ten of the Bath squad, as Mike Catt recorded in his autobiography, 'Landing On My Feet':

> **"I was involved in his newspaper business, going into work at two o'clock in the morning and stacking papers for six hours before climbing into a van and going round the city delivering them. Later I was 'promoted' to working behind the till at his newsagents. I had it relatively easy. Ben Clarke worked at Malcolm's dairy and had to go and milk the cows at five o'clock every morning.**
>
> **"Malcolm paid me £8,000 a year at a time when money was hard to come by. He made my life a lot easier at a critical stage of my career. I was able to train and devote myself to rugby, knowing that I had his full support. He gave us all so much time off. He was the heart and soul of Bath, so passionate about the club."**

But it was another individual who eventually met all the criteria – not a 'rugby man' like Pearce but clearly someone with a love of the city and with even deeper pockets, the greetings card entrepreneur Andrew Brownsword. Mawditt describes him as "the right man at the right time – because he had the money, the resources." But he also appeared something of a contradiction to the Bath chairman and his colleagues: "He wanted to be high profile and low profile at the same time in that he wanted to do his bit for Bath but he didn't want to expose himself to public attention," says Mawditt

Cauliflowers on the catwalk

The 'Bath Players' Ladies' organised 'A Charity Fashion Show', in aid of Cancer & Leukaemia in Children' (CLIC) and Dorothy House Hospice' on Thursday 4 April 1996. Many of the Bath team turned out to 'strut their stuff.' In his foreword Phil de Glanville, while attributing selection of most of the "beautiful" female models to Andy Robinson, said: "I am not sure the same can be said about the cauliflower-eared brigade of male models."

"He had not long sold his company and had arrived 'big time' in a financial sense. Once we had approached him, we had to keep John Hall and Phil de Glanville out of things because they were getting very excited. We had to be very careful; there were other people who were possibilities and the other consideration was that Brownsword wanted anonymity. He said that if it got out that he was an interested party he would walk away, so soon as he came into the frame he appointed Tom Sheppard, a lawyer with a local firm, Things & Co, to act for him.

Andrew Brownsword: a love of the city.

"It was tough negotiating. In fairness to Brownsword, he wasn't the mercenary type but he was a hard businessman. We had to negotiate because we did have assets, not just the Rec lease but also Lambridge. I was not prepared in any way to give up the freehold of Lambridge. It was the only real asset that the club owned – and still owns. And that asset of the land – 11 acres of freehold property – was what I was not prepared to relinquish. Time and time again, Tom Sheppard would come back to me and say: 'Brownsword wants the freehold.' And I wasn't prepared to give him that.

"There were other wonderful things that we did possess, however, things that I fought tooth and nail for, the memorabilia, for example. I felt we should own that so that came into the Trust and – all the paintings, the pictures, the trophies."

De Glanville did eventually meet his soon-to-be employer: "I can remember walking into the meeting with Andrew Brownsword, who I knew relatively little about as a man. I was trying to gauge him, to get a sense of what he was in it for. And it was clear that he was in it for Bath as a city. That came through very strongly and indeed in everything he did afterwards. He loves the place and knew how important the rugby club was to the place. That's why he invested."

While Hall tried to keep his squad intact, others were busily spending their new investors' money on some real 'crowd pullers'. Saracens, backed by City entrepreneur Nigel Wray, pulled the biggest rabbit out of the hat by announcing the recruitment of record-breaking Australian fly-half Michael Lynagh and followed that up by signing France's most capped centre, Philippe Sella and England scrum-half Kyran Bracken. They were soon to be joined by South Africa's World Cup winning captain, Francois Pienaar.

In spring 1996 however, there was only one challenger to Bath, their old rivals Leicester. The question was whether de Glanville's team would round off the amateur era by again hogging the silverware. The Rec hosted its first major cup semi-final on 23 March, as Bath faced a Gloucester side now coached by Richard Hill, making his first visit to Bath since resigning as chairman of selectors six months previously, ending a 13-year association with the Rec. Having won all nine of their previous semi-finals away from home, there was a degree of concern among the more superstitious souls and, to be sure, it was a less than assured performance. But a sparkling try by Adebayo immediately after half-time, converted by Callard, opened up a 16-point lead and they held out to win 19-10.

Hill tipped Bath's 15-man game to beat Leicester in the final but Gloucester had exposed a clear ring-rustiness, particularly in the scrummage. Redman, looking to beat Hill's record of eight Twickenham finals, admitted: "It is very difficult to restart our season after so many players have been away on international duty. We probably didn't do enough to prepare properly but we needed this game to get back into our rhythm and give us a launch-pad for six remaining league matches and a cup final."

But Hall, never one to mince his words, said: "That kind of display won't be good enough to beat Leicester. I am not satisfied, coach Brian Ashton is not satisfied and neither are the players. There is a lot of work to be done but we are still firmly on course for the double and will look to regroup in training this week."

Not for the first time it was poor Bristol who copped it a week later at the Memorial Ground, overwhelmed 43-5. The Bath pack was in total control of the set-piece, especially the scrum, and they faced little opposition at the breakdown. Catt was in faultless form at fly-half despite playing the entire Five Nations Championship at full-back and de Glanville, Guscott and Co ran with deadly purpose. Geoghegan kicked it all off with a try inside the first minute and others followed through Callard, Guscott 2, Geoghegan again, Lumsden and Hilton, enjoying himself hugely against his old club. Callard kicked four conversions as the visitors registered 116 points from the three derby matches of the season, including 16 tries. If Bath had concerns about their own transition to professionalism they were nothing compared to the trepidation felt by their neighbours.

When Harlequins were despatched at the Rec the following weekend it seemed nothing could stop Bath's march to the Courage League title. It was not as one-sided as the 41-15 scoreline suggests however, and the Londoners actually led until the 54th minute, thanks to tries by half-backs Rob Kitchin and Paul Challinor. Bath's points had come from five Callard penalties but then his forwards 'flicked the switch' and, after Redman won a restart, six more pairs of hands created a try for England wing Sleightholme. A sixth Callard penalty and a Catt dropped goal stretched the lead to 26-15 and Harlequins were run off their feet in the final minutes as Bath added a de Glanville try, a Nicol dropped goal and a Guscott try, converted by Callard. Hall was beaming for once – "probably the best we've played all season" – while opposite number Dick Best was philosophical, saying: "It was interesting for us to pitch ourselves in against the best – and they are the best, by a long way."

That left Bath with a run of three away matches in the league, the first being only four days later at Kingsholm, a rearranged fixture after the weather having forced a postponement of the original Christmas date. With more than 10,000 packed into the historic old ground and Richard Hill leaving the home players in no doubt what it would mean to him to put one over on his old club, Bath walked straight into an ambush.

Gloucester's miserable form and lengthy injury list were suddenly forgotten after Scott Benton set up a try for wing Peter Holford inside four minutes. Veteran full-back Tim Smith kicked the conversion and added three penalties as his pack, splendidly roused by skipper Dave Sims, reduced the visitors to rabble. De Glanville did his utmost to rally his troops, scoring a 67th minute try, but Bath's customary poise and control deserted them and they finished well beaten 16-10.

To make matters worse, Ben Clarke ended up in hospital for X-rays on his ankle. Not only did ligament damage rule him out of the trip to Saracens three days later but it finished his season and signalled an ignominious end to his first spell at Bath.

Less than three years later Richmond's backer, Levett, who had made a fortune trading copper on the commodities markets, cut the purse strings and sent the club into administration. Clarke, always popular and approachable, was welcomed back to the Rec for two more seasons.

As already indicated, his old club Saracens were undergoing a radical transformation and preparing to leave their home of more than 50 years for the more prosaic surroundings of Enfield Football Club. You could say that the trip to Bramley Road Municipal Sports Ground should have been a walk in the park – because that's just what the Southgate venue was – but Saracens were deceptively awkward opponents, no matter where

Jon Callard: injury time penalty.

they stood in the league. Bath had come unstuck there in 1990 and six years later they very nearly came a cropper again.

Callard, restored at full-back after being 'rested' for the Kingsholm debacle, settled early nerves with a couple of penalties and also converted an Adedayo try created by Catt's alertness to a loose clearance and eye for a break. The home side came out for the second half having hardly visited the Bath 22 but fly-half Gareth Hughes eventually pulled back three points as Saracens clawed their way back into the game, thanks to the line-out work of Tony Diprose and Tony Copsey. First Diprose scored from a tapped penalty and when Irish back row Eddie Halvey pounced from a close-range scrum, Hughes put his side 15-13 ahead with the conversion.

Fortunately Catt came to the rescue by chipping ahead, regathering and sending Dawe scampering to the line. The durable hooker, shown a yellow card in the first half, had not been a prolific try scorer in recent seasons but this one was worth a hatful. Callard missed the conversion but landed an injury time penalty to secure the 21-15 victory.

Catt was outstanding again a week later against Orrell in a match played at Central Park, the home of Wigan Rugby League Club. Bath won 44-11, maintaining their 30 points a game average, but only 2,600 spectators came through the turnstiles, leaving the ground barely a sixth full. It suggested that locals were suspicious of a second professional code, although there was plenty of interest in the cross-code challenge between Wigan and Bath, scheduled for May.

Haag and Sleightholme scored two tries apiece and others followed from Nicol and de Glanville, providing the leadership and direction behind the scrum. In Clarke's continued absence, Ojomoh's muscular driving play in the loose was the perfect foil for Robinson's extraordinary work rate in providing continuity. Orrell scrum-half Austin Healey scored a try and penalty in his last 'home' game before a move to Leicester.

Going into the 18th and final game at home to Sale on 27 April, Bath were equal on points with Leicester but with the decided advantage of a comfortable match points difference of 63. It was hot and sunny, the pitch was bone hard and mid-table Sale were guaranteed to provide attractive – but not unduly dangerous – opposition.

> The last 'match magazine' of the amateur era featured Catt on the cover and carried the obligatory Welcome to Sale as well as 'Captain's Call by Glanville', a message of thanks from president Brendan Perry, 'Views from the Pulteney Muse', an invitation to vote for Player of the Year, a review of the United/ Spartans' season (for the last time) and a look ahead to the Pilkington Cup fiinal against Leicester – all for £1.20.

And with the game in England due to go 'open' just nine days hence, 'Club Call' involved a Q&A between Honorary Secretary John Quin and programme editor Jim Clipson, mainly examining the issues around a professional game and the likely scenarios. So the exchange reflected excitement about a planned European Cup competition, commitment to a top-class club league structure, concern about raids on the Bath squad from wealthy investors at rival clubs – and provided an update on plans for a new, redeveloped Rec.

On the field everything went to plan – but only for the first 40 minutes. Bath went in at the break 32-12 up after tries by Nicol, Catt, Sleightholme, Lumsden and Waters, who had come on as replacement for Guscott. Sale had crossed twice themselves but even without the injured de Glanville, Clarke and Dawe, a home win seemed just a formality. Then Nicol failed to appear for the second half while the visitors introduced veteran playmaker Paul Turner off the bench. Bath were suddenly on the back foot, seemingly mesmerised by the Welshman's array of tactical kicks and deft passes and increasingly reliant on Callard's goalkicking. Neil Ashurst pounced for a try and centre Jos Baxendell grabbed his second before Rob Liley's third penalty brought them within range at 38-32.

Then, almost unbelievably, word came through from Welford Road that Leicester had lost to Harlequins, handing a sixth Courage League title on a plate to Bath. The result had hinged on a late penalty miss by Rob Liley's brother John. A party atmosphere broke out on the sun-drenched stands and spread to the home players, who switched off completely. Sale sent left wing Chris Yates over in injury time for their fifth try and Rob Liley's conversion earned the draw.

Skipper de Glanville, stuck in the stand nursing a sore hamstring, did not know whether to laugh or cry. "At 32-12, I thought 'I'm really enjoying this'," he said. "Then it all came unstuck. It's a long time since we played as poorly as that in the second half. Sale played very well but we really made some very bad mistakes – a lot of turnovers. We ended up with a centre and scrum-half both making their league debuts and the organisation wasn't quite there. But over the season we've played some great rugby and I've really enjoyed playing for Bath. That's what it's all about."

Once the champagne began to flow, the air of anti-climax gave way to a more familiar sense of relief and satisfaction but the job was not done yet, not by half. And while the 'Bath family' could not even begin to imagine the anguish felt at Welford Road at gifting the league title to their bitterest rivals in such a fashion, they knew full well that the cup final would be an even more intense affair as a consequence.

Leicester-born Jon Callard was already preparing himself mentally for the big occasion: "The boys would have been better off going shopping in the second half. That's something that won't happen again. We learn by our mistakes... We're used to coming off the back of hard seasons and if we can't muster another 80 minutes of rugby at Twickenham then we shouldn't be there."

Bath's Pilkington Cup line-up against Leicester at Twickenham (4 May 1996) (Photo: C W Sports).

The two Martins, Johnson and Haag,
contest the line-out (Photo: C W Sports).

So a tenth cup final in 13 years. As a record it was beyond remarkable, especially since every one of the previous nine had seen Bath lift the trophy, four with a cigarette manufacturer's name on it and five with a glassmaker's logo.

With de Glanville's hamstring loosened up and Dawe's 36-year-old body fit for the fray once again, Guscott and Clarke were the main absentees on a cold, bright day. The atmosphere was more tense than expectant because the two previous finals between the sides had been 'smile free' sport, more arm wrestling than rugby. And the manner in which the Tigers had surrendered their Courage League crown to Bath seven days earlier had only served to raise the stakes. No-one among the 75,000 spectators imagined in their wildest dreams that this was going to be carefree try fest. But even though most of the play was unremarkable their attention never wandered from the action. This was not an afternoon for Mexican Waves.

BATH: *J Callard; A Lumsden, P de Glanville* (capt), *A Adebayo, J Sleightholme; M Catt, A Nicol; D Hilton, G Dawe, J Mallett, M Haag, N Redman, S Ojomoh, E Peters, A Robinson.*

LEICESTER: *J Liley; S Hackney, S Potter, R Robinson, R Underwood; N Malone, A Kardooni; G Rowntree, R Cockerill, D Garforth, M Johnson, M Poole, J Wells, D Richards, N Back.*

REFEREE: *S Lander* (Liverpool).

A Callard penalty on six minutes opened the scoring but Leicester responded almost immediately when prop Darren Garforth burst through into open space and the ball was recycled for fly-half Niall Malone to cross for a try converted by John Liley. Bath put their best rugby together in a 15-minute spell before half-time and were rewarded with another Callard penalty and a Catt dropped goal.

Liley inched Leicester 10-9 in front with a penalty soon after the break but the second half only came to life in the last five minutes. That was when Leicester's monopoly of possession was finally rewarded with a close range try from lock Matt Poole.

Behind the posts, de Glanville seized the moment: "I told the guys we just had to stay cool, keep our discipline and get up into their half as quickly as possible," he said afterwards "At the same time, I was willing him to miss the kick. And when he did, I knew we could still sneak it."

Liley's miss, compounding a miserable eight days for the full-back, had left Bath with the slenderest of lifelines, a six-point deficit. Nigel Redman remembers how Poole's score had the effect of breaking the spell. "It was weird," he says. "Although they had scored, it relieved the pressure. As we kicked off into their half, we knew we were good enough to score if we could get within range."

Even today de Glanville says: "There was an inevitability about it. Either we were going to score or we'd get a penalty try. Leicester had a very big pack of forwards and were having a good year. It was about how we could compete – although we had a good set of forwards ourselves. I don't think it was a very pretty final ... pretty ugly maybe. We didn't approach any game in a straitjacket. It was literally a few pointers about what to do and what not to do. You want to give the players all the armoury and let them call the battle plan."

Like Jack Rowell in the very first final against Bristol in 1984, John Hall could not bear to watch the final minutes and therefore missed the most dramatic of finales. As the clock ticked towards stoppage time Bath probed for openings, hanging on to the ball and forcing Leicester to kill the ball at ruck after ruck, to the increasing irritation of referee Steve Lander.

Redman recalls: "Steve Lander had warned Leicester repeatedly and said: 'Right, the next one is a penalty try.' They went over the top and he went behind the posts. They went ballistic. At the final whistle, Backy (Neil Back) pushed Lander over; then they went into the changing rooms and smashed up their trophies." The Tigers flanker served a six month suspension but the pain of defeat hung over Leicester for far longer.

Afterwards Hall was in no mood to let his opponents down lightly: "It was almost criminal that Leicester wasted that amount of possession," he said, after emerging from the dressing room where he had taken refuge. "I regard Leicester as a negative force. I don't believe they are going in the right direction – they must look to play a more expansive game."

For de Glanville, emulating Barnes, Robinson and Hall by leading Bath to the league and cup 'double' in his first season as captain, it was just reward for his astute

Leicester players in despair as referee Steve Lander awards the penalty try that decides the 1996 Pilkington Cup final (Photography: Dave Rogers/Getty Images).

leadership and consistently excellent performances. To maintain those standards amid the distractions of the professional revolution and development of his own international career spoke volumes.

Looking back, he talks about a "massive period of change," adding: "It was an odd season. It was fairly full on, I have to say. Evenings, weekends obviously, and doing all the international stuff, with Sunday sessions and the occasional Tuesday night up at Marlow. So it was good fun – but busy! You just felt so out of control at times."

The final act of Bath Football Club (RFU) as an amateur sporting organisation was perhaps the most ambitious of its 130-year history, a cross-code challenge with the champions of Rugby League, Wigan. The idea of a double-header – first under Rugby League rules and then Rugby Union laws – had been mooted many months earlier by sports agent Mark McCombe in discussion with the Bath players, but John Hall decided it would be better handled by the club. The man he approached was the youngest member of the management committee, Danny Sacco, chairman of the club's junior section and then, as now, owner of a successful car dealership in the city.

"Don't forget, I'd never organised a match of any size," says Sacco. "The nearest thing I'd done to this was a Minis' Festival! So it was quite a daunting experience. But I could see that this had huge potential from a business point of view and I just mixed my love of the sport with my commercial sense and came up with some simple principles."

The obvious place to stage the Rugby Union game was Twickenham but when the players had sounded out the RFU the ruling body had not been at all receptive. Sacco went back to Twickenham and suggested that they could not afford to turn down in excess of £100,000 for one day's rugby in a stadium which would otherwise lie unused." And this was at a time when the RFU's pre-tax profits were only around £6 million.

"The RFU told me that we'd be lucky to get 15,000 people in," says Sacco. Determined to prove them wrong, he had extra phone lines installed in a makeshift ticket office at the Teacher's Stand, manned daily by his wife Shirley, sister-in-law Jane and Colin Gale's wife, Liz. It soon became obvious that the Twickenham match on 25 May would attract an attendance of 40,000 or more.

"All of a sudden the RFU got nervous," Sacco recalls. "They just didn't anticipate this volume of people so they were going to close the railway station on us because they would need the Met Police to control traffic in the area. I got the feeling that they didn't want the game to happen. People forget that for one hundred years these two codes didn't drink together, didn't speak to each other – and now there was every prospect that players could swap between the codes. And this match was the catalyst.

"It was a huge success. Even the RFU eventually bought their way into the idea. With the top tier closed we ended up at 46,000. I even sold the TV rights to Australia, the Middle East and Europe, never having negotiated anything like this before."

When it came to merchandising – scarves, flags and memorabilia – Sacco was more than happy to pick the brains of Bath's opponents: "I became quite friendly with the Wigan people. Their commercial director, David Bradshaw, was a great help because he was used to dealing with the merchandising side."

The first match came just four days after Bath had completed their league and cup double, and it would hardly be exaggerating to say that the drinking sessions outnumbered the Rugby League training sessions.

Arriving at Maine Road in the heart of Manchester's grim, gang-ridden Moss Side, the Bath committee coach was immediately surrounded by mounted police and a riot squad. "I don't know what they were expecting but I didn't think we were going to cause them any trouble," says Liz Gale.

In the Bath dressing room, the sheer enormity of taking on one of the most successful club sides in Rugby League history at their own game was beginning to dawn on the 'Rah-rahs' as Union players were known in the North. "I have been involved with Bath for a long time and had been in the dressing room before games as part of my committee duties, but I had never seen our players so scared as before the Maine Road game," says Sacco.

"Scared" is no exaggeration, admits de Glanville. Their only warm-up game had been on the Monday night against a South Wales XIII, assembled by Wales Rugby League coach Clive Griffiths and only equivalent to a Third Division side. "We did end up scoring three or four tries in the end – but only after they had scored eight. We were saying to ourselves: 'Oh my God, and now we're going

to be playing the best team in the world.' That's where the fear came from, that we were so under-prepared, that we still didn't know what we were doing. It's a kind of tough place to learn in front of all those people when you've got the best team in the country against you. Danny was very popular at this time, as you might imagine – almost as popular as Jerry (Guscott)!"

Much had been made of the absence of Guscott, the Bath player who had been most coveted by Rugby League clubs when Union remained determinedly amateur. Having missed the cup final through injury perhaps he needed the rest, but he had made no secret of his antipathy to the cross-code challenge.

Sacco recalls: "The only person I couldn't win over was Jeremy Guscott, the only one I couldn't convince to turn out. I think we'd have had another 5-6,000 at Twickenham because he was the hot property. But he told me: 'I'm not going to be part of this circus. This is just a money-making exercise,' to which I replied: 'Of course it is!' We made £395,000 out of the two games." The surplus accounted for a significant portion of the Trustees' 24 per cent stake in the Plc.

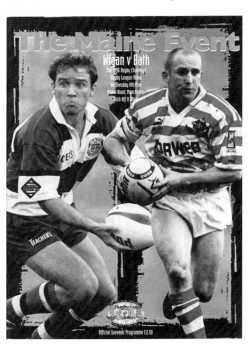

The Maine Event programme.

But the 82-6 scoreline told everyone what they must have known already – that when it came to playing the professional 13-a-side game the most successful Rugby Union club of the amateur era was no match for the world's top Rugby League club. Martin Offiah, who had turned out against Bath when a youngster at Rosslyn Park, scored hat-tricks in each half, crossing twice in the first six minutes. Further tries came in the next 17 minutes from Henry Paul, Jason Robinson, Terry O'Connor and Andy Johnson, with Andy Farrell and Martin Hall kicking all six conversions. By half-time it was 52-nil as Scott Quinnell, Craig Murdock and Offiah added two more tries.

In the second half, after conceding another try to O'Connor, Bath began to play with greater purpose and collective understanding. One player who had cottoned on rather quicker than some of his team-mates and even impressed the opposition, was Sanders, playing at hooker as the closest approximation of his Union position of scrum-half. Ojomoh's tackling was immense and once another huge 'hit' on Neil Cowie forced a penalty within striking range the amateurs battered away through Pearce, Redman and Robinson until the ever-combative Callard nipped through for an historic score. As the Bath player converted his own try Wigan skipper Shaun Edwards raged at his team behind the posts.

Wigan upped the intensity in response and Offiah scored twice in quick succession, followed by Johnson, and Robinson, before the winger rounded things off with another treble.

The result was greeted with glee by Rugby League polemicists, fuelled by 101 years of perceived hurt, but Edwards was genuinely appreciative of the Bath efforts: "Their lads never gave in and you have to give them credit," he said. "Lots of teams would have put their heads down after that first half, but full credit to them." De Glanville was full of admiration for Wigan's skills. "They're a fantastic side," he said. "They're so hard to stop with their lines of running, in particular in the pack. They come on at pace."

Teams for 'The Maine Event':

WIGAN: *K Radlinski; J Robinson, V Tuigamala, G Connolly, M Offiah;*
H Paul, S Edwards (capt); *N Cowie, M Hall, T O'Connor, S Houghton,*
M Cassidy, A Farrell. Substitutes used: *Smyth, Murdock, Quinnell, Johnson.*

BATH: *A Lumsden; J Sleightholme, P de Glanville* (capt), *F Waters, A Adebayo;*
M Catt, J Callard; K Yates, I Sanders, M Haag, A Vander, S Ojomoh,
A Robinson. Substitutes used: *R Butland, N Redman, N McCarthy, E Pearce.*

REFEREE: *R Smith* (Castleford).

When Wigan carried off the Middlesex Sevens title the following weekend, beating Wasps 38-15 in the final at Twickenham, otherwise sensible observers began to harbour a belief that the Northerners' superior fitness and running and passing skills would even eclipse Bath in the 15-a-side game.

Sacco was not averse to stealing a few off-field ideas from the opposition. "The one thing they had at Maine Road and I wanted at Twickenham was fireworks, which they'd never had before at HQ. I warned the pyrotechnics guy before the demo at Twickenham with the Fire Brigade, RFU, health and safety people that I didn't want it too loud. So it just went 'bang, pfff...' On the day though, we had the real thing and the bang was incredible." Even the Sky TV camera shook as the operator flinched in surprise. Richmond Borough Council summonsed Sacco for noise abatement offences but the action was eventually dropped.

Once the smoke had cleared, the Bath forwards tore into the Wigan eight, subjecting them to a torrid introduction to the delights of rucking, mauling and especially scrummaging. Ex-Wales No 8 Quinnell, who was about to return to Union with Clarke at Richmond, had warned his team-mates what to expect but some things in life can only be truly experienced at first hand.

The Right Man At The Right Time

Teams for the Save & Prosper Rugby Challenge at Twickenham

BATH: *J Callard; J Sleightholme, P de Glanville* (capt), *A Adebayo, A Lumsden; M Catt, I Sanders; K Yates, G Dawe, V Ubogu, M Haag, N Redman, A Robinson, E Pearce, S Ojomoh.*

WIGAN: *K Radlinski; J Robinson, H Paul, G Connolly, M Offiah; J Lydon, C Murdock; T O'Connor, M Hall, N Cowie, A Farrell* (capt), *G West, S Tatupu, V Tuigamala, S Quinnell.*

REFEREE: *B Campsall* (Yorkshire).

It was in no way illegal and the onslaught was no more lacking in science or technique than Wigan's angles of running in the 13-a-side game but referee Brian Campsall eventually suggested to de Glanville that they had made their point. Nobody in the ground, least of all the players, wanted to see a stretcher on the field. De Glanville recalls: "We were aware of the scrummaging safety issues. We did talk about that beforehand, getting a nudge on but not completely munching people because they weren't built for it and that would have been dangerous."

A penalty try, awarded as Wigan's makeshift scrum splintered under the posts, quickly took the score to 10-nil. Gaps began to appear in the midfield defence at the end of the first quarter and Adebayo latched on to a flat pass from Catt to score

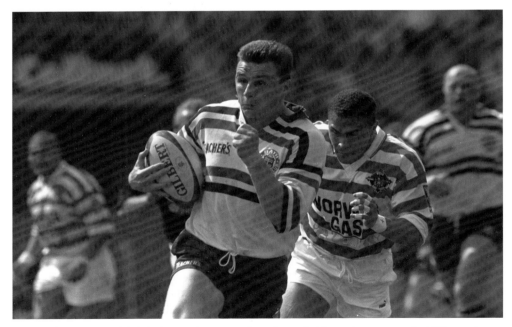

Bath wing Jon Sleightholme sprints away from Jason Robinson to score against Wigan at Twickenham (Photography: Mike Hewitt/Getty Images).

before Sleightholme rounded Robinson to add a third and take the score to 20-nil. It was half an hour before Wigan had an attacking position inside the Bath half but five minutes before the break Adebayo collected his second try, courtesy of a wicked bounce from Catt's chip. A 50-metre rolling maul at the start of the second half nearly presented Adebayo with his hat-trick but Catt carved through for a try and de Glanville then made it 39-nil with only 46 minutes gone.

Wigan's riposte was spectacular as Radlinski, Paul and Offiah conjured the try of the match for Murdock after a break-out from their own line. Ex-All Black Tuigamala quickly added another, converted by Farrell, before the Bath pack reasserted itself with a pushover try for Sanders. Wigan had the final word though as Murdock finished off a 70-metre move to complete the scoring at 44-19.

> De Glanville says: "We did have a very good night afterwards with all the Wigan boys. At the end there was a healthy respect for each others' code and there was always a bit of a debate about which game was harder. Neither side would give way on that though."

Sacco was understandably delighted with the outcome on all fronts: "It was uncharted territory – this had never been done before. People were talking in pubs before these games about what would happen if a Rugby Union and a Rugby League team actually faced each other on the field – but nobody really knew until it happened."

Maurice Lindsay, chief executive of the Rugby Football League, voiced the opinion that there could be a merging of the codes within five years, a view that Sacco says even he shared at one point.

Danny Sacco: 'it was unchartered territory'.

"It was such an exciting time that we could foresee one game of rugby emerging from the two codes," he admits. "That never happened and now we are past that point I don't think it will. There wasn't enough money to sustain it. But it was a revolution – or evolution, if you like."

Over the next six weeks, negotiations progressed with Brownsword's team of advisers, to the point that both sides were happy with the creation of a Bath Rugby plc backed by his investment.

Eventually, on Friday 12 July 1996, Brownsword was ready to 'go public' as the club's proposed new investor, subject to ratification by the annual general meeting of the club six days later. The written and broadcast media, assembled in the HMS Illustrious Suite of the Teacher's Stand waited … and waited. Still no Brownsword.

More than an hour went by before he appeared, posed rather self-consciously with a rugby ball and for a 'grip and grin' handshake picture with Mawditt, read out a statement and left.

Mawditt now reveals that the hold-up was not, as everyone supposed, due to Brownsword's reluctance to meet the media. "He came back again at the 11th hour with a renewed demand that the freehold of Lambridge be included in the deal. I wouldn't budge and eventually he gave way," says Mawditt.

The final act was played out a couple of days later on Thursday 18 July in the nearby Pavilion when an extraordinary general meeting of the club agreed to consign the amateur Bath Football Club (RFU) to history. The membership – comprising some 3,600 individuals who were registered members on 1 October 1995 – would retain a minority share in the new Bath Rugby plc through Bath Football Club Trustees Ltd. Of the 459 members who attended the EGM, seven voted against the proposals while nine abstained.

The fine detail of the transfer of assets, commercial agreements, licences, documents relating to employment and other mundane but essential matters took another year to finalise. The big change, however, was that the players, who had become accustomed to wielding considerable influence over the running of the club during the 1990s, were now mere employees, albeit well paid.

De Glanville concedes that this change of status took quite some time to sink in. "Culturally, that took a long time for everyone to get used to. And that was in the whole of rugby, not just Bath. It was very different, dealing with it as a job. When it was your passion, you could do it whenever you wanted and if you wanted to walk away, you could do so with no real ramifications.

"Also just dealing with the fact that you are doing it every single day – the repetition and the issues with trying to stay fresh and stimulated. I don't think anyone knew what that would be like."

The wholesale break-up of the team had been avoided, however. Eighteen months later de Glanville and nine others of the 'old guard', plus a handful of newcomers, squeaked past Brive to become champions of Europe on that famous weekend in Bordeaux. It was the 'Bath family' fighting its last battle.

Season 1965-66 (Captain: G F Margretts)

Date	H/A	Opponent	Result	F	A
2 Sep 1965	H	Zummerzet Barbarians	W	15	5
04 Sep	A	Devonport Services	W	13	6
06 Sep	A	Penzance & Newlyn	W	5	3
07 Sep	A	Redruth	L	5	8
09 Sep	H	Bridgwater	W	14	3
11 Sep	A	Leicester	L	3	9
16 Sep	H	International XV	L	8	12
18 Sep	A	Ebbw Vale	L	8	17
23 Sep	H	Clifton	W	26	3
25 Sep	H	Royal Navy	W	11	0
28 Sep	A	Weston-super-Mare	L	9	12
02 Oct	A	Aberavon	L	11	12
06 Oct	H	London Hospitals	W	27	3
09 Oct	H	Llanelli	L	14	17
16 Oct	H	Bristol	L	3	8
23 Oct	H	St. Mary's Hospital	W	12	6
30 Oct	H	Bridgend	L	3	6
06 Nov	A	Neath	L	0	11
13 Nov	A	Saracens	L	0	6
20 Nov	H	Royal Air Force.	D	0	0
27 Nov	A	United Services Portsmouth	W	8	6
04 Dec	H	London Scottish	L	6	16
11 Dec	A	Gloucester (Rec. flooded, moved to Kingsholm)	L	9	12
18 Dec	H	London Irish (Rec flooded)	C	C	
27 Dec	H	Old Blues	W	25	5
1 Jan 1966	H	Leicester	L	3	9
08 Jan	A	London Welsh	L	0	17
15 Jan	H	Met Police	C	C	
29 Jan	H	Northampton	L	11	12
05 Feb	A	Rosslyn Park	L	3	8
11 Feb	A	Cambridge University	L	6	9
19 Feb	H	Cheltenham	L	3	8
23 Feb	H	Oxford University (abandoned 65 mins)	W	3	0
26 Feb	A	Wasps	W	6	0
05 Mar	H	Bristol	L	8	12
12 Mar	A	Swansea	L	3	21
19 Mar	H	Newbridge	L	8	12
23 Mar	H	Gloucester	W	19	13
26 Mar	A	Richmond	L	11	32
29 Mar	H	G P Frankcom's XV	W	27	11
02 Apr	H	Coventry	L	3	25
07 Apr	H	Harlequins	W	8	5
09 Apr	H	Liverpool	L	9	22
10 Apr	A	Chateau Renard	W	15	3
11 Apr	A	Nice	L	9	17
16 Apr	H	Old Merchant Taylors	W	14	11
23 Apr	A	Exeter	L	0	19
28 Apr	A	Moseley	L	13	19
29 Apr	A	Taunton	W	11	9
30 Apr	H	Bedford	W	51	3

Played 48   Won 19   Lost 28   Drawn 1.   479   483

Season 1966-67 (Captain: P Sibley)

Date	H/A	Opponent	Result	F	A
1 Sep 1966	H	Zummerzet Barbarians	W	25	8
03 Sep	A	Llanelli	L	0	14
05 Sep	H	Broughton Park	L	3	6
10 Sep	A	Leicester	W	14	8
15 Sep	H	Weston-super-Mare	W	13	6
17 Sep	A	Ebbw Vale	L	8	24
22 Sep	A	Clifton	W	19	3
24 Sep	H	St Mary's Hospital	W	15	13
29 Sep	A	Bridgwater	W	21	6
01 Oct	H	Aberavon	L	11	18
08 Oct	A	Newbridge	D	16	16
15 Oct	A	Bristol	L	3	6
22 Oct	H	Devonport Services	W	24	8
29 Oct	A	Bridgend	L	0	21
05 Nov	H	Neath	L	5	19
12 Nov	H	Saracens	W	6	0
19 Nov	A	Pontypool	W	3	0
26 Nov	H	United Services Portsmouth	W	14	0
03 Dec	A	London Scottish	L	9	10
10 Dec	H	Gloucester	L	11	16
17 Dec	H	London Irish	W	14	6
24 Dec	H	Rugby	W	17	6
26 Dec	H	Old Blues	W	30	3
31 Dec	A	Northampton	L	6	11
14 Jan 1967	H	London Welsh	L	13	20
19 Jan	H	Royal Air Force	W	6	5
21 Jan	H	Metropolitan Police	L	18	21
28 Jan	A	St Mary's Hospital	W	20	0
04 Feb	A	Rosslyn Park	W	8	6
11 Feb	A	Gloucester	W	19	14
18 Feb	A	Cheltenham	W	9	6
25 Feb	H	Wasps	L	0	3
01 Mar	A	Leicester	L	3	11
04 Mar	H	Bristol	L	6	24
18 Mar	A	Moseley	L	9	19
23 Mar	H	Harlequins	L	5	13
25 Mar	H	Liverpool	W	11	6
27 Mar	H	Old Merchant Taylors	W	25	0
28 Mar	H	Sheffield	W	14	9
30 Mar	A	Sale	W	16	3
04 Apr	H	Llanelli	W	11	3
06 Apr	H	Stroud	W	24	3
08 Apr	H	Exeter	W	14	3
11 Apr	H	Weston-super-Mare	W	11	5
14 Apr	A	Combined Services XV	W	52	3
15 Apr	A	West Germany	L	5	9
16 Apr	H	Victoria Club (Hanover).	W	9	3
22 Apr	A	Coventry	L	3	32
27 Apr	A	Taunton	W	24	8
29 Apr	H	Bedford	L	6	9

Played 50   Won 29   Lost 20   Drawn 1   628   466

Season 1967-68 (Captain: P Sibley)

Date		Opponent	Result	F	A
2 Sep 1967	H	Streatham & Croydon	W	17	3
09 Sep	A	Leicester	L	8	17
11 Sep	A	Liverpool	W	9	0
12 Sep	A	New Brighton	D	14	14
16 Sep	H	Ebbw Vale	L	13	16
21 Sep	H	Bridgwater	W	16	11
23 Sep	A	St Mary's Hospital	W	34	3
26 Sep	H	Clifton	W	17	0
30 Sep	H	Old Wesley	W	11	6
07 Oct	H	Aberavon	D	6	6
14 Oct	A	London Irish	W	12	8
21 Oct	H	Bristol	W	6	5
28 Oct	H	Bridgend	L	3	11
03 Nov	H	Neath	L	0	3
11 Nov	A	Saracens	L	3	28
18 Nov	H	Devonport Services	W	20	3
25 Nov	A	United Services Portsmouth	W	17	8
02 Dec	H	London Scottish	L	0	6
15 Dec	A	Llanelli	L	3	6
23 Dec	A	Rugby	L	6	12
26 Dec	H	Old Blues	W	34	0
30 Dec	H	Northampton	W	8	3
6 Jan 1968	H	Leicester	W	8	0
20 Jan	A	Metropolitan Police	L	11	19
27 Jan	H	St Mary's Hospital	W	36	3
03 Feb	H	Rosslyn Park	W	22	15
10 Feb	A	Gloucester	L	0	11
17 Feb	H	Cheltenham	W	13	3
24 Feb	A	Wasps	D	0	0
02 Mar	A	Bristol	D	8	8
05 Mar	A	Gloucester	W	18	6
09 Mar	A	Swansea	D	6	6
16 Mar	H	Newbridge	W	14	6
23 Mar	A	Richmond	W	8	6
30 Mar	H	Sale	L	12	16
06 Apr	H	Moseley	W	12	11
11 Apr	H	Harlequins	W	21	8
13 Apr	H	Percy Park	W	31	16
15 Apr	H	Old Merchant Taylors	W	16	10
16 Apr	H	Llanelli	W	17	9
18 Apr	H	Taunton	W	13	0
20 Apr	A	Exeter	L	11	19
27 Apr	H	Bedford	L	3	9
Played 43			**Won 24**	**Lost 14**	**Drawn 5**	540	368

Season 1968-69 (Captain: P Sibley)

Date		Opponent	Result	F	A
5 Sep 1968	H	Roma (Italy)	W	13	9
07 Sep	A	Pontypool	L	15	25
14 Sep	H	Leicester	L	6	12
21 Sep	A	Ebbw Vale	L	14	16
26 Sep	A	Clifton	W	14	9
28 Sep	A	Old Wesley (Ireland)	L	8	22
29 Sep	A	Blackrock College (Ireland)	W	9	5
30 Sep	A	Armagh (N Ireland)	W	10	3
03 Oct	A	Bridgwater	W	12	6
05 Oct	H	Aberavon	W	14	6
09 Oct	A	Cheltenham	W	10	8
12 Oct	A	London Irish	W	17	9
19 Oct	A	Bristol	W	14	6
26 Oct	H	St Mary's Hospital	W	31	6
02 Nov	H	Neath	D	8	8
09 Nov	H	Saracens	W	21	6
16 Nov	A	Pontypool	W	8	6
23 Nov	H	United Services Portsmouth	W	20	3
30 Nov	A	Bridgend	L	11	17
07 Dec	A	London Scottish	L	6	10
21 Dec	A	Llanelli	D	8	8
26 Dec	H	Public School Wanderers	W	10	9
4 Jan 1969	A	Leicester	L	13	14
11 Jan	H	London Welsh	L	14	23
18 Jan	H	Metropolitan Police	D	14	14
25 Jan	H	St Mary's Hospital	W	26	6
01 Feb	A	Rosslyn Park	W	15	5
01 Mar	H	Bristol	L	8	9
05 Mar	A	Gloucester	L	6	24
08 Mar	H	Swansea	L	8	14
15 Mar	H	Cheltenham	W	18	14
20 Mar	A	Royal Air Force	W	18	13
22 Mar	H	Richmond	D	6	6
29 Mar	A	Sale	W	15	11
30 Mar	H	Harlequins	W	26	8
05 Apr	H	London Hospital	W	28	12
07 Apr	A	Old Merchant Taylors	L	0	11
11 Apr	A	Llanelli	W	31	14
15 Apr	A	Exeter	L	6	26
19 Apr	H	Newbridge	W	13	6
21 Apr	H	Gloucester	L	6	19
24 Apr	H	Taunton	W	33	3
26 Apr	A	Bedford	L	12	31
03 May	H	Rugby	W	29	11
Played 44			**Won 24**	**Lost 17**	**Drawn 3**	540	368

Season 1969-70 (Captain: T Martland)

Date	H/A	Opponent	Result	F	A
3 Sep 1969	H	La Rochelle (France)	W	12	5
04 Sep	H	Broughton Park	W	22	11
06 Sep	H	Pontypool	W	14	9
13 Sep	A	Leicester	L	11	14
18 Sep	H	Clifton	W	14	3
20 Sep	H	Moseley	L	11	12
24 Sep	A	Newport	L	13	14
27 Sep	A	Devonport Services	W	40	3
02 Oct	H	Bridgwater	W	25	5
04 Oct	A	Aberavon	W	17	10
11 Oct	A	London Irish	W	11	9
18 Oct	H	Bristol	D	11	11
25 Oct	H	St Mary's Hospital	W	34	8
01 Nov	H	Bridgend	L	9	14
08 Nov	A	Saracens	W	11	6
15 Nov	A	Pontypool	W	35	14
22 Nov	A	United Services Portsmouth	W	14	3
06 Dec	H	London Scottish	W	32	11
13 Dec	A	Gloucester	L	13	39
20 Dec		Llanelli (flu outbreak)		P	P
26 Dec	H	Oxford	W	27	9
27 Dec	H	Newbridge	W	24	16
3 Jan 1970	A	Leicester	W	13	9
10 Jan	A	London Welsh	L	5	27
17 Jan	A	Metropolitan Police	W	21	19
24 Jan	A	St Mary's Hospital	W	20	9
26 Jan	A	Llanelli	L	6	17
31 Jan	H	Northampton	L	11	30
07 Feb	H	Rosslyn Park	L	9	19
21 Feb	A	Cheltenham	L	0	3
28 Feb	A	Wasps	L	17	22
07 Mar	A	Bristol	L	6	14
14 Mar	H	Swansea	W	11	9
21 Mar	H	Ebbw Vale	W	9	6
27 Mar	H	Harlequins	W	27	6
28 Mar	H	Cheltenham	W	12	6
30 Mar	H	Old Merchant Taylors	W	35	0
04 Apr	H	Sale	W	16	6
07 Apr	A	Neath	L	8	17
11 Apr	H	Llanelli	W	16	8
16 Apr	A	Taunton	W	12	6
18 Apr	H	Rugby	W	20	5
25 Apr	H	Bedford	W	20	6
30 Apr	H	Exeter	W	16	10

Played 43   Won 29   Lost 13   Drawn 1   710   480

Season 1970-71 (Captain: P Heindorff)

Date	H/A	Opponent	Result	F	A
1 Sep 1970	H	New Brighton	W	18	11
05 Sep	A	Pontypool	W	17	9
12 Sep	H	Leicester	W	11	9
17 Sep	A	Clifton	W	22	6
19 Sep	H	Moseley	W	17	13
24 Sep	H	Taunton	W	23	8
26 Sep	H	Cheltenham	W	15	6
01 Oct	A	Bridgwater	W	19	6
03 Oct	H	Streatham & Croydon	W	11	9
10 Oct	H	London Irish	L	17	18
17 Oct	A	Bristol	W	16	15
24 Oct	H	St Mary's Hospital	W	25	5
31 Oct	H	Neath	W	14	11
07 Nov	H	Bridgend	W	9	3
14 Nov	H	Saracens	W	9	6
21 Nov	A	Newbridge	L	3	11
28 Nov	H	United Services Portsmouth	W	22	6
05 Dec	A	London Scottish	L	14	16
12 Dec	H	Gloucester	D	0	0
19 Dec	A	Llanelli	L	6	20
26 Dec	H	South Wales Police	W	17	8
28 Dec	A	Cardiff	L	11	26
9 Jan 1971	H	London Welsh	L	6	14
16 Jan	H	Metropolitan Police	W	6	0
23 Jan	H	Aberavon	W	9	6
30 Jan	A	Rugby	W	11	9
06 Feb	A	Rosslyn Park	W	22	20
15 Feb	A	Gloucester	D	9	9
20 Feb	A	Cheltenham	L	11	16
27 Feb	H	Wasps	W	22	14
13 Mar	H	Swansea	L	13	14
25 Mar	H	Royal Air Force	L	8	14
27 Mar	H	Richmond	W	22	14
30 Mar	H	Newport	W	12	8
05 Apr	H	*Stothert & Pitt (Somerset Cup)	W	19	6
07 Apr	H	Bristol	L	6	32
09 Apr	H	Harlequins	W	20	6
10 Apr	H	Broughton Park	W	17	3
12 Apr	H	Old Merchant Taylors	W	24	6
16 Apr	H	Llanelli	L	18	29
20 Apr	A	Exeter	L	3	37
24 Apr	A	Bedford	L	8	11
01 May	A	*Angouleme (France)	L	12	33
02 May	A	*La Rochelle (France)	L	6	17
08 May	H	*Bath & Somerset Police (Somerset Cup Final)	W	13	8

Played 41   Won 26   Lost 13   Drawn 2   563   478

* matches not included in the official statistics below:

Season 1971-72 (Captain: R Walkey)

Date		Opponent	Result	F	A
1 Sep 1971	H	Pontypool	W	12	6
04 Sep	H	Cheltenham	L	0	20
06 Sep	H	Somerset XV	W	16	8
11 Sep	A	Leicester	L	10	22
16 Sep	A	Clifton	W	39	14
18 Sep	H	Moseley	W	23	13
22 Sep	H	Newport	L	6	40
25 Sep	A	Exeter	L	21	26
30 Sep	H	Gloucester	L	3	12
02 Oct	H	Saracens	L	12	30
09 Oct	H	London Irish	L	7	13
16 Oct	A	Bristol	L	3	15
23 Oct	H	St Mary's Hospital	L	12	24
30 Oct	A	Neath	L	23	15
06 Nov	H	Bridgend	L	3	34
13 Nov	A	South Wales Police	W	23	6
17 Nov	H	Newbridge	W	7	16
20 Nov	H	United Services Portsmouth	W	22	6
27 Nov	A	London Scottish	L	15	16
04 Dec	H	Gloucester	W	20	20
11 Dec	A	Llanelli	L	13	10
18 Dec	H	Streatham & Croydon	W	23	14
27 Dec	H	Leicester	L	16	24
1 Jan 1972	H	London Welsh	W	20	0
08 Jan	H	Royal Navy	W	13	3
12 Jan	H	Metropolitan Police	L	6	29
15 Jan	A	Aberavon	L	16	10
22 Jan	A	Old Wesley (Ireland)	L	13	21
29 Jan	A	London Scottish	L	10	28
05 Feb	A	Rosslyn Park (switched from Rec – flooded)	L	21	15
10 Feb	H	Royal Air Force	W	22	7
12 Feb	H	Gloucester	L	12	15
19 Feb	A	Cheltenham	L	3	9
26 Feb	A	Wasps	W	20	27
11 Mar	A	Swansea	W	12	6
18 Mar	A	Ebbw Vale	W	19	16
21 Mar	H	Stothert & Pitt	L	27	23
23 Mar	A	Cardiff	L	6	12
25 Mar	H	Richmond	W	15	15
31 Mar	H	Harlequins	W	7	10
30 Dec	H	Halifax	W	52	0
30 Mar	H	Old Merchant Taylors	W	20	6
08 Apr	H	Sale	W	34	8
10 Apr	H	Hornets	W	6	3
13 Apr	H	Taunton	W	15	0
15 Apr	A	Llanelli	L	13	33
19 Apr	A	Somerset & Bath Police (Bridgwater)	W	15	8
22 Apr	A	Northampton	W	4	6
26 Apr	H	Bristol	L	12	24
29 Apr	A	Bedford	L	4	10

Played 50; won 23; lost 27. 745 817

Season 1972-73 (Captain: P R Hall)

Date		Opponent	Result	F	A
4 Sep 1972	A	Pontypool	L	15	25
05 Sep	H	Taunton	W	36	8
09 Sep	A	Leicester	L	4	34
11 Sep	A	Hawick	L	6	30
12 Sep	A	Langholm	W	8	6
16 Sep	A	Moseley	L	4	59
19 Sep	H	MATSON (RFU Knock-out Cup)	W	18	6
21 Sep	A	Old Belvedere (Ireland)	W	18	4
23 Sep	H	Exeter	L	6	19
30 Sep	H	President's XV	L	15	30
30 Sep	A	Cheltenham	W	28	0
07 Oct	A	Clifton	W	18	6
04 Oct	A	Aberavon	L	10	18
14 Oct	H	London Irish	W	9	7
23 Oct	H	Bristol	W	12	10
28 Oct	A	St Mary's Hospital	L	7	18
31 Oct	A	Bridgend	W	28	16
11 Nov	H	GLOUCESTER (RFU Knock-out Cup)	L	0	22
18 Nov	H	St Luke's College	L	10	16
25 Nov	A	Newbridge	L	6	16
02 Dec	H	United Services Portsmouth	W	34	3
09 Dec	A	London Scottish	L	9	20
16 Dec	H	Llanelli	L	10	41
23 Dec	H	Neath	L	16	22
26 Dec	A	Clifton	L	16	22
30 Dec	H	Northampton	L	18	23
6 Jan 1973	A	Wasps	W	14	0
13 Jan	H	Bristol	W	25	3
20 Jan	H	Royal Air Force	L	13	13
27 Jan	H	Cheltenham	W	24	7
03 Feb	H	Gloucester	L	16	18
10 Feb	A	South Wales Police	L	14	22
16 Feb	H	Saracens	D	4	11
24 Feb	A	Metropolitan Police	W	4	15
03 Mar	H	London Welsh	L	10	30
08 Mar	A	Leicester	L	10	10
10 Mar	H	Ebbw Vale	W	22	21
16 Mar	H	Richmond	W	31	12
24 Mar	H	Bridgend	W	21	0
31 Mar	H	Bridgwater	W	48	3
05 Apr	H	Sale	W	16	16
07 Apr	A	Newport	L	11	12
10 Apr	A	Llanelli	D	3	17
14 Apr	H	Harlequins	W	37	10
20/Apr	H	Otley	W	38	10
21 Apr	H	Old Merchant Taylors	W	37	6
23 Apr	H	Gloucester	W	16	7
28 Apr	A	Bedford	L	0	4

Played 49; won 24; lost 23; drawn 2. 875 723

Season 1973-74 (Captain: P R Hall)

Date	H/A	Opponent	Result	F	A
1 Sep 1973	H	Pontypool	L	0	7
08 Sep	A	Leicester	L	3	16
13 Sep	H	Taunton	W	34	16
15 Sep	H	Moseley	W	43	7
19 Sep	A	Newport	L	4	10
22 Sep	A	Exeter	L	4	22
26 Sep	H	Bristol	L	9	18
29 Sep	A	Terenure (Ireland)	L	9	12
03 Oct	A	Clifton	W	15	6
05 Oct	A	Aberavon	L	7	17
13 Oct	A	London Irish	L	6	14
20 Oct	A	St Luke's College	L	12	15
25 Oct	A	Cheltenham	W	4	3
28 Oct	A	Midsomer Norton (Somerset Cup, 1st rd)	W	33	0
03 Nov	H	Bridgend	L	13	23
10 Nov	H	Streatham & Croydon	L	16	28
17 Nov	H	Newbridge	W	20	3
18 Nov	A	Stothert & Pitt (Somerset Cup, 2nd rd)	W	23	3
24 Nov	A	United Services Portsmouth	W	19	7
01 Dec	H	London Scottish	L	0	6
05 Dec	H	RMCS SHRIVENHAM (RFU Knock-out Cup, 1st rd)	W	27	6
08 Dec	A	Gloucester	L	8	18
15 Dec	H	Llanelli	L	3	12
22 Dec	H	South Wales Police	W	17	10
26 Dec	H	Clifton	W	19	4
29 Dec	H	Northampton	L	3	10
1 Jan 1974	H	Cheddar Valley (Somerset Cup, 3rd rd)	W	53	6
05 Jan	A	Leicester	W	20	3
12 Jan	H	London Welsh	L	9	21
16 Jan	H	Royal Navy	W	6	4
19 Jan	A	Metropolitan Police	L	3	13
26 Jan	A	Saracens	L	3	4
02 Feb	H	Rosslyn Park	W	19	3
05 Feb	A	Royal Air Force	W	10	4
09 Feb	H	WILMSLOW (RFU KO Cup) Kingswood School .	L	6	17
17 Feb	A	Cheltenham	W	6	4
23 Feb	A	Wasps	W	16	15
03 Mar	A	Bristol	L	7	18
09 Mar	H	Swansea	L	10	36
10 Mar	H	St. Brendan's (Somerset Cup, 4th rd)	W	18	3
15 Mar	H	Ebbw Vale	L	6	13
23 Mar	A	Richmond	D	14	14
28 Mar	H	Neath	W	21	18
30 Mar	H	Bridgend	L	22	33
30 Dec	H	Hawick	L	3	16
02 Apr	A	Gloucester	L	15	19
06 Apr	H	Sale	W	26	6
08 Apr	H	Bridgwater (Somerset Cup, semi-final)	W	31	0
12 Apr	H	Harlequins	W	20	6
13 Apr	H	Broughton Park	W	15	12
15 Apr	H	Old Merchant Taylors	W	42	9
20 Apr	A	Llanelli	L	19	43
25 Apr	A	Weston-super-Mare (Somerset Cup Final)	W	22	3
27 Apr	H	Bedford	L	19	32
29 Apr	A	Stroud	L	11	15
				823	693

Played 55; won 26; lost 28; drawn 1.

Season 1974-75 (Captain: C Perry)

Date	H/A	Opponent	Result	F	A
7 Sep 1974	A	Pontypool	L	6	16
14 Sep	A	Leicester	W	15	9
18 Sep	A	Clifton	W	41	8
21 Sep	A	Moseley	L	13	31
28 Sep	H	FALMOUTH (RFU Knock-out Cup, qualifying rd)	W	13	11
03 Oct	A	Taunton	W	7	0
05 Oct	H	Aberavon	L	4	16
12 Oct	H	London Irish	W	18	3
19 Oct	A	Bristol	W	10	9
26 Oct	H	St Mary's Hospital	W	30	12
02 Nov	H	Bridgend	L	10	23
09 Nov	A	Nottingham	L	6	17
16 Nov	A	FALMOUTH (RFU Knock-out Cup, 1st rd)	D	9	9
23 Nov	H	United Services Portsmouth	W	12	4
30 Nov	A	Neath	L	6	11
07 Dec	A	London Scottish	L	4	49
12 Dec	H	Royal Air Force	W	26	6
14 Dec	H	Gloucester	W	12	7
21 Dec	A	Llanelli	L	0	30
26 Dec	H	Clifton	W	15	6
1 Jan 1975	H	South Wales Police	W	25	6
04 Jan	A	Leicester	L	3	14
11 Jan	H	London Welsh	W	13	8
15 Jan	H	Royal Navy	W	10	6
18 Jan	H	Metropolitan Police	W	15	3
25 Jan	H	Saracens	W	16	10
30 Dec	A	Rosslyn Park	L	0	21
08 Feb	A	LIVERPOOL (RFU Knock-out Cup, 2nd rd)	W	12	6
11 Feb	H	Newport	W	12	4
14 Feb	H	Cheltenham	W	4	0
20 Feb	H	Newbridge	L	14	15
22 Feb	H	Wasps	W	12	6
25 Feb	A	Gloucester	L	3	28
28 Feb	A	Bristol	W	13	4
08 Mar	H	MORPETH (RFU Knock-out Cup, quarter final)	L	9	13
19 Mar	A	Weston-super-Mare (Somerset Cup, semi-final)	W	15	7
22 Mar	H	Richmond	L	9	10
27 Mar	H	Harlequins	W	10	0
29 Mar	H	Plymouth Albion	W	34	4
31 Mar	H	Rugby	W	19	6
05 Apr	A	Sale	L	13	15
09 Apr	A	Northampton	L	3	15
12 Apr	H	Armagh	W	29	19
15 Apr	A	Cardiff	L	12	30
19 Apr	H	Llanelli	W	16	15
23 Apr	H	Old Redcliffians (Somerset Cup final)	W	41	3
				619	539

Played 46; won 28; lost 17; drawn 1.

Season 1975-76 (Captain: J S Waterman)

Date		Opponent	Result	F	A
3 Sep 1975	H	Taunton	W	35	3
06 Sep	A	Pontypool	W	30	15
10 Sep	A	Newport	L	12	30
3 Sep	A	Leicester	L	7	37
17 Sep	A	Clifton	W	25	9
20 Sep	H	Moseley	L	18	40
22 Sep	H	Begles (France)	L	15	22
27 Sep	H	Exeter	W	16	0
04 Oct	A	Aberavon	L	16	14
11 Oct	H	London Irish	L	10	21
18 Oct	H	BRISTOL (John Player Cup, 1st rd)	L	13	24
25 Oct	H	St Mary's Hospital	W	10	22
01 Nov	A	Bridgend	W	19	14
08 Nov	A	Birmingham	W	12	6
12 Nov	H	Bristol	W	6	14
15 Nov	A	Newbridge	L	18	3
22 Nov	H	United Services Portsmouth	W	15	0
29 Nov	H	Neath	W	20	6
06 Dec	H	London Scottish	W	6	9
13 Dec	H	Gloucester	L	4	36
22 Dec	H	Llanelli	L	40	16
26 Dec	H	Clifton	W	16	22
27 Dec	H	Northampton	W	7	12
2 Jan 1976	H	Leicester	L	12	12
10 Jan	A	London Welsh	L	3	29
14 Jan	A	Royal Navy	W	37	3
17 Jan	A	Metropolitan Police	W	30	11
24 Jan	H	Saracens	D	6	6
31 Jan	H	South Wales Police	W	22	15
04 Feb	H	Royal Air Force	W	24	0
07 Feb	H	Rosslyn Park	W	24	6
12 Feb	H	Keynsham (Somerset Knock-out Cup)	W	23	0
14 Feb	H	Cardiff	W	9	4
17 Feb	A	Gloucester	L	3	12
19 Feb	A	Cheltenham	W	29	4
28 Feb	A	Wasps	W	13	12
05 Mar	A	Bristol	L	10	13
13 Mar	A	Swansea	W	15	21
19 Mar	H	Ebbw Vale	W	15	6
23 Mar	A	Bridgwater (Somerset Cup, semi-final)	W	12	7
27 Mar	H	Richmond	L	6	8
30 Mar	H	Newport	W	9	4
07 Apr	H	Weston-super-Mare (Somerset Cup final)	W	22	7
10 Apr	H	Llanelli	L	3	15
15 Apr	H	Harlequins	W	39	9
17 Apr	H	Broughton Park	W	16	13
19 Apr	H	Morley	W	18	9
24 Apr	H	Bedford	W	35	7
26 Apr	H	British Forces West Germany	W	23	14
28 Apr	H	Exeter	W	37	6
01 May	H	Nottingham	W	10	6
				877	648

Played 51; won 32; lost 18; drawn 1.

Season 1976-77 (Captain: J P Horton)

Date		Opponent	Result	F	A
1 Sep 1976	H	Taunton	W	33	3
04 Sep	A	Pontypool	L	6	46
08 Sep	A	Newport	L	3	22
11 Sep	A	Leicester	W	19	10
15 Sep	H	Clifton	W	44	7
18 Sep	A	Moseley	L	3	14
21 Sep	H	Weston-super-Mare	W	32	0
25 Sep	H	Exeter	W	14	0
30 Sep	H	Plymouth Albion	W	20	13
02 Oct	A	Aberavon	W	12	9
09 Oct	A	London Irish	L	15	26
16 Oct	A	Bristol	L	10	35
23 Oct	H	St Mary's Hospital	W	18	0
30 Oct	H	Neath	W	9	7
06 Nov	H	Bridgend	W	9	3
13 Nov	H	Streatham & Croydon	W	10	6
22 Nov	A	Newbridge	L	6	10
27 Nov	H	United Services Portsmouth	W	20	4
30 Nov	A	Llanelli	L	0	36
18 Dec	H	Harlequins	W	10	4
27 Dec	H	Clifton	W	25	4
1 Jan 1977	A	Leicester	L	4	20
08 Jan	A	London Welsh (John Player Cup, 1st rd)	L	3	18
12 Jan	H	Royal Navy	W	15	11
15 Jan	A	Metropolitan Police	W	42	10
22 Jan	A	Saracens	W	21	19
29 Jan	H	Rugby	D	24	24
02 Feb	H	Royal Air Force	W	12	6
04 Feb	H	Rosslyn Park	W	38	9
12 Feb	A	St Luke's College	D	6	6
18 Feb	H	Cheltenham	W	35	6
23 Feb	A	Coventry	W	0	4
26 Feb	H	Wasps	W	24	18
04 Mar	H	Bristol	D	3	3
12 Mar	A	Swansea	L	6	12
18 Mar	A	Ebbw Vale	L	12	24
23 Mar	A	Gloucester	L	7	51
26 Mar	H	Richmond	W	25	4
02 Apr	H	Newport	L	7	32
08 Apr	H	Oxford	L	32	0
09 Apr	H	Roundhay	W	22	9
11 Apr	H	Cheltenham	W	50	7
16 Apr	H	Llanelli	L	3	21
23 Apr	A	Northampton	L	12	14
30 Apr	A	Bedford	L	15	44
07 May	A	Libourne (France)	W	19	10
08 May	A	Begles (France)	L	6	52
				774	721

Played 47; won 27; lost 18; drawn 2.

Season 1977-78 (Captain: J S Waterman)

Date		Opponent	Result	F	A
3 Sep 1977	H	Pontypool	W	27	9
07 Sep	A	Newport	L	6	19
10 Sep	A	Leicester	L	26	39
14 Sep	A	Clifton	W	27	7
17 Sep	H	Moseley	L	19	25
24 Sep	A	Exeter	W	25	16
28 Sep	H	International XV	L	18	24
01 Oct	A	Aberavon	L	12	29
04 Oct	H	Plymouth Albion	W	15	3
08 Oct	A	London Irish	L	6	18
15 Oct	H	Bristol	L	10	16
22 Oct	A	St Mary's Hospital	W	28	13
29 Oct	H	Neath	W	25	9
05 Nov	A	Harlequins	L	6	14
12 Nov	H	St Luke's College	W	18	9
19 Nov	A	Coventry	L	4	42
26 Nov	A	United Services Portsmouth	W	26	0
03 Dec	H	London Scottish	L	16	25
10 Dec	A	Gloucester	L	13	24
17 Dec	H	Harlequins	L	12	19
24 Dec	H	Rugby	W	58	13
26 Dec	H	Clifton	W	37	12
27 Dec	A	Llanelli	L	7	10
31 Dec	H	Northampton	W	16	3
2 Jan 1978	H	Nuneaton	W	57	3
07 Jan	H	Leicester	W	28	16
14 Jan	A	London Welsh	L	0	46
19 Jan	H	Royal Air Force	W	17	12
21 Jan	H	Metropolitan Police	W	11	10
28 Jan	A	EXETER (John Player Cup, 1st rd)	L	6	20
03 Feb	A	Rosslyn Park	L	10	31
17 Feb	H	Bridgend	D	0	0
24 Feb	H	Birkenhead Park	W	34	4
03 Mar	A	Bristol	W	17	11
08 Mar	H	Cheltenham	W	10	6
11 Mar	A	Swansea	L	7	45
17 Mar	H	Ebbw Vale	W	19	14
21 Mar	H	Coventry	W	21	13
24 Mar	H	South Wales Police	W	32	11
25 Mar	H	Morley	W	8	0
27 Mar	H	Bradford	W	27	9
30 Mar	A	Falmouth	W	35	3
08 Apr	A	Richmond	W	38	9
15 Apr	H	Llanelli	L	10	19
17 Apr	A	Newbridge	L	14	25
19 Apr	H	Gloucester	L	10	12
22 Apr	H	Newport	W	15	9
25 Apr	A	Taunton	W	56	0
27 Apr	H	Bedford	W	45	28
				984	754

Played 49; won 28; lost 20; drawn 1.

Season 1978-79 (Captain: M C Beese)

Date		Opponent	Result	F	A
2 Sep 1978	A	Pontypool	W	26	10
06 Sep	A	Newport	D	4	4
09 Sep	H	Leicester	L	6	25
13 Sep	A	Clifton	W	18	3
16 Sep	A	Moseley	W	10	6
20 Sep	H	Cheltenham	W	26	3
23 Sep	H	Exeter	W	15	9
30 Sep	A	Neath	W	12	8
04 Oct	H	Bucharest Select XV	W	18	6
06 Oct	A	Aberavon	W	30	15
10 Oct	A	Plymouth Albion	W	13	12
14 Oct	H	London Irish	L	9	15
21 Oct	A	Bristol	L	16	24
28 Oct	H	St Mary's Hospital	W	44	4
04 Nov	A	Harlequins	W	15	4
10 Nov	H	Newbridge	L	3	6
18 Nov	H	Coventry	W	23	3
25 Nov	H	United Services Portsmouth	W	25	10
29 Nov	A	Llanelli	D	7	7
02 Dec	A	London Scottish	L	12	18
11 Dec	H	Gloucester	W	20	10
16 Dec	H	Harlequins	W	21	10
23 Dec	A	Rugby	W	13	3
26 Dec	H	Clifton	W	35	6
30 Dec	A	Northampton	D	10	10
10 Jan 1979	H	Royal Navy	W	13	6
20 Jan	H	Metropolitan Police	W	16	7
03 Feb	A	Rosslyn Park	L	14	25
07 Feb	H	Royal Air Force	W	16	4
10 Feb	A	LONDON WELSH (John Player Cup, 1st rd)	L	18	28
21 Feb	H	Exeter University	W	68	4
24 Feb	H	Bristol	L	7	23
27 Feb	A	Bridgend	L	6	15
02 Mar	A	Cross Keys	W	22	0
10 Mar	H	Swansea	W	18	6
24 Mar	H	Tiverton	W	69	3
26 Mar	H	Bath XV v English Students (abandoned 50 mins)	L	0	6
31 Mar	A	Nottingham	W	11	6
02 Apr	A	Gloucester	L	3	11
07 Apr	H	Newport	W	15	6
11 Apr	H	Pontypridd	W	20	18
14 Apr	H	West Hartlepool	W	26	12
16 Apr	H	South Wales Police	W	36	16
21 Apr	H	Llanelli	W	23	6
28 Apr	A	Bedford	W	21	13
				853	440

Played 44; won 31; lost 10; drawn 3.

Season 1979-80 (Captain: J P Horton)

Date	H/A	Opponent	Result	F	A
1 Sep 1979	H	Pontypool	W	16	9
05 Sep	A	Newport	W	6	3
08 Sep	A	Leicester	W	10	9
15 Sep	A	Moseley	W	22	11
18 Sep	H	Seahawks (San Jose, California)	W	58	0
22 Sep	A	Llanelli	L	6	14
25 Sep	A	Clifton	W	33	13
29 Sep	H	Neath	D	22	22
03 Oct	H	South Wales Police	W	13	4
05 Oct	A	Aberavon	L	15	17
20 Oct	H	Bristol	W	38	17
27 Oct	A	St Mary's Hospital	W	28	6
31 Oct	A	Cheltenham	W	16	9
03 Nov	A	Harlequins	W	17	17
10 Nov	H	Newbridge	W	41	16
17 Nov	A	Coventry	W	21	16
24 Nov	H	United Services Portsmouth	W	3	0
01 Dec	H	London Scottish	W	29	12
10 Dec	H	Gloucester	L	36	7
15 Dec	A	Harlequins	W	3	12
22 Dec	H	Plymouth Albion	W	13	4
26 Dec	H	Clifton	W	27	10
1 Jan 1980	A	Cardiff	L	16	12
05 Jan	H	Leicester	W	15	4
09 Jan	H	Royal Navy	W	4	16
12 Jan	A	London Welsh	L	22	0
19 Jan	A	Metropolitan Police	W	25	10
26 Jan	H	Marlow	W	22	10
30 Jan	H	Rosslyn Park	L	3	37
06 Feb	H	Royal Air Force	W	7	12
09 Feb	H	Cheltenham (on Civil Service Ground)	W	20	6
15 Feb	A	LIVERPOOL (John Player Cup, 2nd rd)	W	30	10
23 Feb	H	Bridgend	W	6	12
28 Feb	H	LONDON IRISH (John Player Cup, quarter-final)	L	22	10
08 Mar	A	Exeter University	W	19	10
14 Mar	H	Nuneaton	W	27	9
17 Mar	A	Ebbw Vale	W	3	6
22 Mar	H	Richmond	W	6	3
26 Mar	H	Gloucester	W	24	6
29 Mar	H	Exeter	W	27	15
30 Mar	A	Glamorgan Wanderers	L	24	9
05 Apr	H	Bristol	W	19	12
07 Apr	H	Wimslow	W	28	15
12 Apr	A	Birkenhead Park	W	46	7
16 Apr	H	Newport	W	17	3
19 Apr	H	Llanelli	W	13	6
26 Apr	H	Bedford	W	22	16
30 Apr	A	Pontypridd	L	3	49

Played 48; won 37; lost 10; drawn 1.   962   557

Season 1980-81 (Captain: R Lye)

Date	H/A	Opponent	Result	F	A
3 Sep 1980	H	Bridgwater	W	39	0
06 Sep	A	Pontypool	L	13	23
10 Sep	A	Newport	L	7	13
13 Sep	A	Leicester	W	13	4
20 Sep	A	Moseley	W	7	4
27 Sep	A	Llanelli	L	4	17
01 Oct	A	Clifton	W	22	3
04 Oct	A	Aberavon	W	19	13
11 Oct	H	Maesteg	W	25	22
18 Oct	A	Bristol	L	3	16
25 Oct	A	United Services Portsmouth	W	51	0
28 Oct	A	Plymouth Albion	W	13	9
01 Nov	H	Harlequins	L	20	25
08 Nov	A	Newbridge	W	3	23
15 Nov	H	Coventry	W	19	14
22 Nov	A	Exeter	W	6	12
28 Nov	H	Neath	D	13	3
06 Dec	A	London Scottish	W	6	15
15 Dec	H	Gloucester	L	0	19
20 Dec	H	Harlequins	W	16	0
26 Dec	H	Clifton	W	22	4
1 Jan 1981	A	Northampton	L	6	12
03 Jan	H	Nuneaton	W	26	3
07 Jan	A	Leicester	L	11	13
10 Jan	H	Royal Navy	W	21	13
16 Jan	H	London Welsh	W	24	10
24 Jan	H	Metropolitan Police	W	34	6
31 Jan	A	RICHMOND (John Player Cup 3rd round)	W	12	6
06 Feb	H	Ebbw Vale	L	9	13
11 Feb	H	Rosslyn Park	W	17	10
14 Feb	H	Royal Air Force	W	28	6
18 Feb	A	Gloucester	L	10	15
20 Feb	A	Exeter University	W	24	6
28 Feb	H	Bridgend	W	13	29
07 Mar	H	NOTTINGHAM (John Player Cup 4th round)	L	3	4
14 Mar	A	Pontypridd	L	3	12
20 Mar	H	Camborne	W	52	12
24 Mar	H	Wasps	L	12	27
28 Mar	H	London Irish	L	13	4
04 Apr	H	Cheltenham	W	22	14
11 Apr	A	Richmond	L	13	25
15 Apr	H	Newport	W	9	3
18 Apr	H	Llanelli	W	16	3
20 Apr	H	South Wales Police	W	21	3
23 Apr	H	Bristol	W	12	3
25 Apr	A	New Brighton	W	44	13
23 Apr	H	Cardiff	W	18	11
25 Apr	A	Bedford	W	6	3
28 Apr	H	RFU President's XV	L	13	43

Played 50   Won 30   Lost 18   Draw 2   819   549

Date	H/A	Opponent	Result	F	A
2 Sep 1981	H	Weston-super-Mare	W	29	0
05 Sep	H	Pontypool	L	19	22
09 Sep	A	Newport	L	10	24
12 Sep	A	Leicester	L	6	44
15 Sep	H	Plymouth Albion	W	20	0
19 Sep	H	Moseley	W	27	16
26 Sep	H	Terenure (Ireland)	W	19	18
30 Sep	H	Llanelli	L	9	17
03 Oct	A	Aberavon	L	9	46
05 Oct	H	'Bath XV v Salisbury (not in club statistics)			
10 Oct	H	Liverpool	L	8	16
17 Oct	A	Cardiff	W	7	6
17 Oct	H	Bristol	L	3	32
24 Oct	A	United Services Portsmouth	L	6	19
28 Oct	A	Clifton	L	10	23
31 Oct	H	Neath	W	15	6
07 Nov	H	Harlequins	W	21	18
16 Nov	A	Newbridge	W	17	10
21 Nov	A	Coventry	L	6	22
28 Nov	A	Exeter	W	22	18
02 Dec	H	Cheltenham	W	13	3
05 Dec	A	London Scottish	W	22	7
28 Dec	H	Clifton	W	19	10
2 Jan 1982	H	Leicester	W	31	0
16 Jan	A	Havant	D	9	9
18 Jan	A	Marlow	W	36	9
23 Jan	H	ROSSLYN PARK (John Player Cup, 3rd round)	W	24	4
30 Jan	H	Northampton	L	9	11
03 Feb	H	Royal Air Force	W	27	0
05 Feb	A	Rosslyn Park	W	47	4
13 Feb	H	Gloucester	L	3	7
17 Feb	H	Bridgend	L	6	12
20 Feb	A	Maesteg	W	9	4
27 Feb	A	Wasps	L	3	20
03 Mar	H	Ebbw Vale	W	20	13
06 Mar	A	Camborne	L	12	14
13 Mar	A	Swansea	W	16	0
20 Mar	A	London Irish	L	0	41
25 Mar	A	Exeter University	W	7	0
27 Mar	H	Richmond	W	10	6
31 Mar	A	Cheltenham	W	29	14
30 Mar	H	Newport	W	33	3
07 Apr	A	Metropolitan Police	W	21	6
10 Apr	A	Bristol	L	11	28
12 Apr	H	Otley	W	14	8
17 Apr	A	Llanelli	L	14	57
21 Apr	A	Gloucester	L	15	33
24 Apr	A	Bedford	W	15	14
28 Apr	H	South Wales Police	W	28	13
01 May	A	New Brighton	W	24	22
				801	**719**

Played 49; won 29; lost 19; drawn 1.

Date	H/A	Opponent	Result	F	A
1 Sep 1982	H	Cheltenham	W	38	11
04 Sep	A	Pontypool	L	16	37
11 Sep	H	Leicester	W	24	15
18 Sep	A	Moseley	L	11	13
22 Sep	A	Newport	W	12	3
25 Sep	A	Llanelli	L	10	15
29 Sep	H	Havant	W	21	9
02 Oct	H	Aberavon	W	17	16
06 Oct	A	Wyvern (Somerset Cup, 1st round)	W	76	3
09 Oct	A	Liverpool	L	4	12
16 Oct	A	Bristol	L	4	6
23 Oct	A	United Services Portsmouth	L	16	18
30 Oct	A	Neath	L	21	22
03 Nov	H	Bath XV v Marlow (Not in club statistics)	W	16	10
06 Nov	A	Harlequins	W	21	7
10 Nov	A	Clifton	W	20	6
15 Nov	H	Newbridge	L	3	12
20 Nov	H	Coventry	W	19	15
01 Dec	H	Southampton Wales Police	W	28	0
04 Dec	A	London Scottish	W	21	9
11 Dec	H	Gloucester	W	21	12
12 Dec	A	Frome (Somerset Cup, 2nd round)	W	46	6
18 Dec	H	Harlequins	D	13	13
27 Dec	H	Clifton	W	53	4
1 Jan 1983	A	Leicester	L	9	21
08 Jan	H	London Welsh	W	16	11
15 Jan	A	Metropolitan Police	W	34	15
19 Jan	H	Royal Navy	W	27	13
22 Jan	H	Exeter	W	74	3
29 Jan	A	Northampton	W	19	16
02 Feb	H	Royal Air Force.	W	43	4
05 Feb	H	Rosslyn Park	W	35	12
09 Feb	H	Weston-super-Mare (Somerset Cup, quarter-final)	W	43	7
12 Feb	A	Gloucester	D	7	7
26 Feb	H	Fylde	W	31	12
02 Mar	A	Cheltenham	W	31	9
05 Mar	A	Gordano (Somerset Cup, semi-final)	W	10	6
07 Mar	H	Pontypridd	W	19	6
12 Mar	H	Swansea	W	30	14
15 Mar	A	Ebbw Vale	W	7	3
23 Mar	H	Exeter University	D	6	6
26 Mar	H	Richmond	W	32	18
02 Apr	H	Bristol	W	21	16
04 Apr	H	New Brighton	W	53	10
09 Apr	A	Newport	W	13	7
12 Apr	A	Plymouth	W	30	3
16 Apr	H	Llanelli	W	31	28
20 Apr	H	Maesteg	W	45	10
23 Apr	–	Cardiff	W	28	9
27 Apr	–	Old Redcliffians (Som. Cup final, Weston-s-Mare)	W	39	10
30 Apr	A	Bedford	W	30	15
				1278	**555**

Played 50; won 38; lost 9; drawn 3.

Season 1983-84 (Captain: R Spurrell)

Date	H/A	Opponent	Result	F	A
3 Sep 1983	H	Plymouth Albion	W	41	3
10 Sep	A	Leicester	L	15	18
17 Sep	H	Moseley	W	44	9
24 Sep	A	Llanelli	L	13	19
01 Oct	A	Aberavon	L	16	25
04 Oct	H	Cheltenham	W	24	6
07 Oct	H	Liverpool	W	13	6
15 Oct	H	Bristol	W	12	10
22 Oct	A	United Services Portsmouth	W	20	15
26 Oct	A	Clifton	W	29	9
29 Oct	H	Neath	W	67	0
05 Nov	A	Newbridge	W	22	12
12 Nov	A	Wakefield	L	16	19
18 Nov	A	Coventry	L	10	19
25 Nov	H	Camborne	W	17	3
03 Dec	H	London Scottish	W	17	6
10 Dec	A	Gloucester	L	8	16
17 Dec	H	Harlequins	W	13	15
23 Dec	H	Pontypool	L	6	23
26 Dec	H	Clifton	W	26	10
31 Dec	H	Northampton	W	16	6
7 Jan 1984	H	Leicester	W	14	0
14 Jan	A	London Welsh	W	40	9
18 Jan	H	Royal Navy	W	42	8
28 Jan	H	HEADINGLEY (John Player Cup 3rd round)	W	17	0
03 Feb	A	Rosslyn Park	W	13	6
11 Feb	A	Gloucester	W	13	6
15 Feb	H	Royal Air Force	W	35	4
17 Feb	H	Bridgend	W	25	19
25 Feb	A	BLACKHEATH (John Player Cup 4th round)	W	41	12
28 Feb	A	Exeter	W	27	12
03 Mar	H	Launceston	W	50	24
10 Mar	H	WASPS (John Player Cup quarter-final)	W	26	12
14 Mar	H	Ebbw Vale	W	25	18
07 Apr	A	NOTTINGHAM (John Player Cup semi-final)	W	12	3
14 Apr	H	Llanelli	W	22	19
23 Apr	H	Glamorgan Wanderers	L	6	9
28 Apr	–	BRISTOL (John Player Cup final)	W	10	9
30 Apr	A	Newport	L	7	52

Played 39; won 29; lost 10. 870 468

Season 1984-85 (Captain: R Spurrell)

Date	H/A	Opponent	Result	F	A
1 Sep 1984	A	Plymouth	W	26	10
05 Sep	H	South Wales Police	D	10	10
08 Sep	H	Leicester	W	17	6
15 Sep	A	Moseley	W	19	6
22 Sep	A	Llanelli	W	27	9
29 Sep	A	Neath	L	13	28
06 Oct	H	Aberavon	W	37	16
13 Oct	H	Liverpool	L	16	22
20 Oct	A	Bristol	W	18	16
26 Oct	A	United Services Portsmouth	W	46	0
31 Oct	H	Clifton	W	22	9
03 Nov	A	Maesteg	L	9	16
17 Nov	H	Newbridge	W	32	6
01 Dec	H	Coventry	W	23	6
05 Dec	A	London Scottish	W	21	3
08 Dec	H	Exeter	W	64	3
15 Dec	H	Gloucester	W	19	9
22 Dec	A	Harlequins	W	21	12
22 Dec	A	Pontypool	L	10	18
26 Dec	H	Sale	L	7	25
26 Dec	H	Clifton	W	22	9
29 Dec	A	Northampton	W	20	9
5 Jan 1985	A	Waterloo	W	23	13
22 Jan	H	Royal Navy	W	49	0
26 Jan	H	BERRY HILL (John Player Cup 3rd round)	W	24	3
30 Dec	H	Rosslyn Park	W	28	9
16 Feb	A	Bath XV v Brixham (not in first XV statistics)	L	6	9
23 Feb	A	BLACKHEATH (John Player Cup 4th round)	W	37	3
27 Feb	H	Exeter University	W	17	3
02 Mar	A	Redruth	W	67	0
09 Mar	H	SALE (John Player Cup quarter-final)	W	25	15
13 Mar	A	Ebbw Vale	W	15	10
23 Mar	A	GLOUCESTER (John Player Cup semi-final)	L	12	21
27 Mar	A	Cheltenham	W	10	11
30 Mar	A	London Irish	W	35	3
06 Apr	H	Bristol	W	25	3
08 Apr	H	West Hartlepool	W	23	16
13 Apr	A	Newport	W	0	11
17 Apr	A	Clifton	L	11	12
19 Apr	H	Llanelli	W	21	10
27 Apr	–	LONDON WELSH (John Player Cup Final)	W	24	15

Played 39; won 30; lost 8; drawn 1. 923 400

Season 1985-86 (Captain: J Palmer)

Date		Opponent	Result	F	A
7 Sep 1985	H	Plymouth Albion	W	40	0
11 Sep	H	Alberta Province (Canada)	W	36	10
14 Sep	A	Leicester	W	40	15
18 Sep	H	Pontypridd	W	45	19
25 Sep	H	Moseley	W	50	10
25 Sep	A	Newport	D	16	16
28 Sep	A	Llanelli	W	18	15
02 Oct	H	South Wales Police	W	29	18
05 Oct	A	Aberavon	L	15	16
12 Oct	A	Liverpool	W	26	12
19 Oct	H	Bristol	W	26	7
23 Oct	H	Cardiff	W	16	13
26 Oct	A	United Services Portsmouth	W	29	13
30 Oct	H	Maesteg	W	30	9
02 Nov	A	Newbridge	W	23	15
09 Nov	A	Gloucester	L	11	15
16 Nov	A	Coventry	W	22	16
26 Nov	A	Exeter	W	57	0
30 Nov	H	Neath	L	7	13
07 Dec	H	London Scottish	L	8	10
11 Dec	H	Cheltenham	W	19	18
21 Dec	H	Harlequins	L	7	16
1 Jan 1986	A	Cardiff	L	12	30
04 Jan	H	Waterloo	W	16	6
11 Jan	A	London Welsh	L	9	26
17 Jan	H	Metropolitan Police	W	42	12
21 Jan	H	Royal Navy	W	63	10
25 Jan	A	ORRELL (John Player Cup 3rd round)	D	16	16
31 Jan	H	Rosslyn Park	W	35	3
05 Feb	H	Royal Air Force	W	26	6
08 Feb	A	MOSELEY (John Player Cup 4th round)	W	22	4
08 Mar	A	LONDON WELSH (John Player Cup, 5th round)	W	18	10
18 Mar	H	Stroud	W	28	7
20 Mar	H	Exeter University	W	39	18
22 Mar	H	Richmond	W	30	13
29 Mar	A	Bristol	W	10	3
31 Mar	H	Vale of Lune	W	16	4
05 Apr	A	LEICESTER (John Player Cup semi-final)	W	10	6
09 Apr	A	Clifton	D	3	3
12 Apr	H	Newport	W	24	18
19 Apr	H	Llanelli	W	19	10
26 Apr	-	WASPS (John Player Cup final)	W	25	17
03 May	H	Gloucester	W	22	9

Played 43; won 33; lost 7; drawn 3.   1055   507

Season 1986-87 (Captain: R Hill)

Date		Opponent	Result	F	A
3 Sep 1986	A	Pontypool	W	23	10
06 Sep	A	Plymouth Albion	W	41	10
13 Sep	H	Leicester	W	6	3
20 Sep	A	Moseley	W	36	0
24 Sep	A	Newport	W	33	6
27 Sep	H	Llanelli	L	6	9
04 Oct	H	Aberavon	W	26	6
08 Oct	H	South Wales Police	W	23	12
11 Oct	A	Liverpool	W	29	19
18 Oct	A	Bristol	W	21	18
25 Oct	H	United Services Portsmouth	W	66	14
29 Oct	H	Cardiff	W	28	9
01 Nov	H	Newbridge	W	10	6
08 Nov	H	Wasps	W	22	6
15 Nov	H	Coventry	W	38	13
20 Nov	H	Fiji Barbarians	W	35	4
26 Nov	H	Gloucester	L	9	12
29 Nov	A	Neath	L	9	26
06 Dec	A	London Scottish	D	12	12
20 Dec	A	Harlequins	L	9	25
26 Dec	H	Clifton	W	38	9
27 Dec	A	Northampton	W	12	10
1 Jan 1987	A	Cardiff	L	21	32
03 Jan	A	Waterloo	L	26	28
10 Jan	H	London Welsh	W	53	16
24 Jan	H	PLYMOUTH ALBION (John Player Cup 3rd round)	W	32	10
31 Jan	H	Sale	W	46	13
03 Feb	H	Royal Air Force	W	38	6
06 Feb	A	Rosslyn Park	W	25	9
14 Feb	H	LONDON WELSH (John Player Cup 4th round)	W	30	4
28 Feb	H	MOSELEY (John Player Cup, quarter-final)	W	12	3
06 Mar	H	Nottingham	W	15	6
14 Mar	H	Swansea	W	30	8
20 Mar	A	Cheltenham	W	43	3
28 Mar	A	ORRELL (John Player Cup semi-final)	W	31	7
30 Mar	H	Pontypool	W	28	13
04 Apr	A	London Irish	W	36	13
08 Apr	A	Clifton	W	23	6
11 Apr	H	Newport	W	34	8
15 Apr	A	Bridgend	W	38	24
18 Apr	H	Bristol	W	30	8
20 Apr	H	North Devon	W	19	4
25 Apr	A	Bedford	L	6	47
02 May	-	WASPS (John Player Cup final)	W	19	12

Played 44; won 36; lost 7; drawn 1.   1167   519

Season 1987-88 (Captain: R Hill)

Date	H/A	Opponent	Result	F	A
2 Sep 1987	H	South Wales Police	W	59	3
05 Sep	H	Pontypool	L	12	14
12 Sep	A	LEICESTER (Courage League)	L	13	24
19 Sep	H	MOSELEY (Courage League)	W	14	0
26 Sep	A	Llanelli	L	14	27
30 Sep	H	London Irish	W	32	15
03 Oct	A	Aberavon	L	13	16
10 Oct	A	NOTTINGHAM (Courage League)	L	15	25
17 Oct	H	BRISTOL (Courage League)	W	15	9
24 Oct	H	Newport	W	24	7
28 Oct	H	Cheltenham	W	46	16
31 Oct	A	Vale of Lune	W	20	16
06 Nov	H	Newbridge	W	17	6
14 Nov	A	WASPS	L	15	19
21 Nov	A	COVENTRY (Courage League)	D	9	9
28 Nov	H	Exeter University	W	45	6
01 Dec	H	GLOUCESTER (Courage League)	W	16	9
05 Dec	H	London Scottish	W	23	13
12 Dec	H	WATERLOO (Courage League)	L	10	17
19 Dec	H	Saracens	L	10	13
26 Dec	H	Clifton	W	26	10
2 Jan 1988	A	Cardiff	L	9	38
09 Jan	A	London Welsh	W	35	11
15 Jan	H	Metropolitan Police	W	45	7
23 Jan	H	Streatham & Croydon	W	43	0
30 Jan	H	LICHFIELD (John Player Cup 3rd round)	W	84	0
05 Feb	H	Rosslyn Park	W	19	15
13 Feb	A	LEICESTER (John Player Cup 4th round)	W	13	6
20 Feb	H	Gloucester	D	26	26
27 Feb	H	MOSELEY (John Player Cup quarter final)	L	3	4
01 Mar	A	Exeter	W	32	3
04 Mar	H	Plymouth Albion	W	36	10
12 Mar	A	Swansea	W	28	23
16 Mar	H	Bridgend	L	15	39
18 Mar	H	Liverpool	W	30	0
26 Mar	A	ORRELL (Courage League)	W	23	18
02 Apr	A	Bristol	L	15	16
04 Apr	H	North Devon	D	18	18
09 Apr	H	HARLEQUINS (Courage League)	W	21	9
13 Apr	H	Newport	W	22	7
16 Apr	H	Llanelli	D	9	9
20 Apr	A	Clifton	W	43	0
23 Apr	H	Bedford	W	35	9
30 Apr	A	SALE (Courage League)	W	46	17
				1098	549

Played 44; won 28; lost 12; drawn 4.

Courage League Division 1: **4th**

Season 1988-89 (Captain: S Barnes)

Date	H/A	Opponent	Result	F	A
3 Sep 1988	A	Pontypool	W	50	9
10 Sep	A	HARLEQUINS (Courage League)	W	26	9
17 Sep	A	London Welsh	W	40	3
24 Sep	H	GLOUCESTER (Courage League)	W	19	9
28 Sep	A	Clifton	W	22	6
01 Oct	H	Aberavon	W	24	13
08 Oct	A	ROSSLYN PARK (Courage League)	W	19	6
15 Oct	A	Public School Wanderers	W	54	44
22 Oct	H	Bedford	W	16	10
29 Oct	A	BRISTOL (Courage League)	W	16	9
02 Nov	A	Stade Toulousain (France)	D	24	24
05 Nov	H	Combined Services	W	20	7
12 Nov	A	Llanelli	W	25	12
19 Nov	H	MOSELEY (Courage League)	W	38	0
26 Nov	H	WASPS (Courage League)	W	16	6
30 Nov	A	Exeter University	W	30	4
03 Dec	A	London Scottish	W	27	19
10 Dec	A	Newport	D	21	21
17 Dec	H	Saracens	W	24	6
23 Dec	H	Newbridge	W	22	18
26 Dec	H	Clifton	W	57	6
31 Dec	H	Northampton	W	58	3
4 Jan 1989	A	Cheltenham	W	31	6
07 Jan	A	Cardiff	W	35	4
14 Jan	A	LIVERPOOL ST HELENS (Courage League)	W	21	7
18 Jan	H	ORRELL (Courage League)	W	64	21
28 Jan	H	Metropolitan Police	W	82	9
28 Jan	H	OXFORD (Pilkington Cup 3rd round)	W	36	12
03 Feb	A	Llanelli	W	20	4
11 Feb	H	HEREFORD (Pilkington Cup 4th round)	W	48	6
17 Feb	A	Gloucester	W	21	19
25 Feb	H	BRISTOL (Pilkington Cup quarter-final)	L	12	18
04 Mar	H	Swansea	W	14	12
11 Mar	H	NOTTINGHAM (Courage League)	L	13	15
17 Mar	A	Ebbw Vale	L	15	17
25 Mar	A	GLOUCESTER (Pilkington Cup semi-final)	W	6	3
29 Mar	A	Plymouth Albion	W	32	19
30 Mar	A	Bridgend	L	3	23
05 Apr	H	Newport	W	13	9
08 Apr	A	WATERLOO (Courage League)	W	38	9
12 Apr	H	South Wales Police	L	4	37
15 Apr	H	Llanelli	W	43	25
22 Apr	A	LEICESTER (Courage League)	L	12	15
29 Apr	–	LEICESTER (Pilkington Cup final)	W	10	6
				1262	521

Played 44; won 36; lost 6; drawn 2.

Courage League Division 1: **Champions**

Date	H/A	Opponent	Result	F	A
2 Sep 1989	H	Pontypool	W	23	3
09 Sep	H	HARLEQUINS (Courage League)	W	32	12
16 Sep	H	Steaua Bucharest	W	35	12
23 Sep	A	GLOUCESTER (Courage League)	L	6	13
27 Sep	H	South Wales Police	W	40	15
30 Sep	A	Neath	W	17	13
04 Oct	H	Royal Navy	W	43	3
07 Oct	A	Aberavon	W	32	6
14 Oct	H	ROSSLYN PARK (Courage League)	W	34	6
18 Oct	H	Exeter University	W	56	3
21 Oct	A	Toulon (France)	L	14	26
28 Oct	A	BRISTOL (Courage League)	W	14	13
11 Nov	H	MOSELEY (Courage League)	W	27	9
18 Nov	A	ORRELL (Courage League)	W	9	6
25 Nov	A	WASPS (Courage League)	W	18	9
02 Dec	H	London Scottish	W	40	4
09 Dec	H	Richmond	W	16	10
16 Dec	A	London Welsh	W	35	10
23 Dec	H	Blackheath	W	65	3
26 Dec	H	CLIFTON	W	12	9
30 Dec	A	Swansea	L	9	17
6 Jan 1990	A	Cardiff	D	10	10
13 Jan	H	BEDFORD (Courage League)	W	76	0
17 Jan	H	Metropolitan Police	W	36	7
27 Jan	H	HARLEQUINS (Pilkington Cup 3rd round)	W	9	0
10 Feb	H	HEADINGLEY (Pilkington Cup 4th round)	W	25	3
16 Feb	H	Gloucester	W	12	9
24 Feb	A	RICHMOND (Pilkington Cup quarter-final)	W	35	3
02 Mar	H	Plymouth Albion	W	38	14
10 Mar	A	NOTTINGHAM (Courage League)	L	9	12
14 Mar	A	Ebbw Vale	W	26	7
16 Mar	H	Newbridge	W	21	13
24 Mar	A	MOSELEY (Pilkington Cup semi-final)	W	21	7
31 Mar	A	SARACENS (Courage League)	L	7	9
04 Apr	A	Newport	W	25	6
07 Apr	H	Llanelli	W	42	14
14 Apr	A	Bristol	W	22	13
16 Apr	H	Cheltenham	W	70	10
21 Apr	A	Llanelli	W	31	19
28 Apr	H	LEICESTER	W	26	15
05 May	–	GLOUCESTER (Pilkington Cup final)	W	48	6
Played 41; won 35; lost 5; drawn 1.				**1166**	**379**

Courage League Division 1: **3rd**

Date	H/A	Opponent	Result	F	A
1 Sep 1990	A	Pontypool	L	17	34
02 Sep	H	Romania XV	W	38	9
05 Sep	A	Stade Toulousain (France)	W	44	9
08 Sep	A	Llanelli	L	12	28
15 Sep	H	Cardiff	W	45	23
22 Sep	H	LIVERPOOL ST HELENS (Courage League)	W	46	3
26 Sep	A	Clifton	W	30	7
29 Sep	H	Ulster	W	25	6
06 Oct	A	Neath	W	27	13
13 Oct	A	NORTHAMPTON (Courage League)	W	16	10
20 Oct	H	ORRELL (Courage League)	W	17	9
27 Oct	A	BRISTOL (Courage League)	W	10	3
10 Nov	H	HARLEQUINS (Courage League)	W	23	3
17 Nov	A	LEICESTER (Courage League)	W	9	3
24 Nov	H	LEICESTER (Pilkington Cup 3rd round)	L	0	12
01 Dec	A	London Scottish	W	33	19
15 Dec	H	London Welsh	W	42	6
19 Dec	A	*Stade Toulousain (Toulouse Centenary)	L	6	23
23 Dec	A	*Fiji XV (Toulouse Centenary, 3rd place play-off)	L	19	60
29 Dec	H	Swansea	W	29	4
5 Jan 1991	A	Plymouth Albion	W	14	9
12 Jan	H	MOSELEY (Courage League)	W	11	6
16 Jan	A	Metropolitan Police	W	27	19
26 Jan	H	London Scottish	W	22	15
02 Feb	H	Coventry	W	52	12
23 Feb	H	Barnstaple	W	68	0
27 Feb	H	Ebbw Vale	W	58	0
01 Mar	H	Llanelli	W	34	14
09 Mar	H	WASPS (Courage League)	L	15	16
15 Mar	A	Newport	D	15	15
23 Mar	A	NOTTINGHAM (Courage League)	W	22	9
30 Mar	H	Thurrock	W	38	15
06 Apr	A	GLOUCESTER (Courage League)	W	17	15
13 Apr	H	ROSSLYN PARK (Courage League)	W	45	21
20 Apr	H	Gloucester	W	32	19
27 Apr	A	SARACENS (Courage League)	W	49	6
Played 34; won 29; lost 4; drawn 1.				**984**	**392**

Courage League Division 1: **Champions**

*Not included in statistics

Season 1991-92 (Captain: A Robinson)

Date		Opponent	Result	F	A
7 Sep 1991	H	Pontypool	W	28	12
14 Sep	H	Llanelli	W	25	9
21 Sep	A	Cardiff	W	10	9
23 Sep	A	Cullompton	W	56	4
28 Sep	A	Cork Constitution (Ireland)	W	13	3
12 Oct	H	Richmond	W	10	9
18 Oct	H	London Scottish	W	9	6
26 Oct	H	Plymouth Albion	W	34	3
01 Nov	A	Neath	W	21	14
09 Nov	A	Gloucester	L	12	14
16 Nov	H	LONDON IRISH (Courage League)	W	26	21
23 Nov	H	Oxford University	W	19	3
30 Nov	H	NOTTINGHAM (Pilkington Cup 3rd round)	W	52	0
07 Dec	H	NORTHAMPTON (Pilkington Cup 4th round)	W	15	6
14 Dec	A	ORRELL (Courage League)	L	9	10
21 Dec	H	BRISTOL (Courage League)	W	9	4
28 Dec	A	Swansea	L	19	48
4 Jan 1992	A	HARLEQUINS (Courage League)	D	18	18
11 Jan	H	LEICESTER (Courage League)	W	37	6
30 Jan	A	Coventry	W	18	13
08 Feb	A	NORTHAMPTON (Courage League)	W	13	9
14 Feb	A	Blackheath	W	28	7
22 Feb	H	BRISTOL (Pilkington Cup quarter-final)	W	15	6
29 Feb	H	GLOUCESTER (Courage League)	W	29	9
06 Mar	H	Newbridge	W	50	7
14 Mar	A	WASPS (Courage League)	W	24	12
21 Mar	A	RUGBY (Courage League)	W	32	0
28 Mar	H	NOTTINGHAM (Courage League)	W	25	15
04 Apr	A	GLOUCESTER (Pilkington Cup semi-final)	W	27	18
11 Apr	A	ROSSLYN PARK (Courage League)	W	21	13
18 Apr	H	Treviso (Italy)	L	23	31
25 Apr	H	SARACENS (Courage League)	W	32	12
02 May	-	HARLEQUINS (Pilkington Cup final)	W	15	12
				774	363

Played 33; won 28; lost 4; drawn 1.

Courage League Division 1: **Champions**

Season 1992-93 (Captain: A Robinson)

Date		Opponent	Result	F	A
5 Sep 1992	A	Casale (Italy)	W	62	15
12 Sep	A	Treviso (Italy)	W	18	15
19 Sep	H	HARLEQUINS (Courage League)	W	22	6
26 Sep	H	**LONDON IRISH (Courage League)	W	42	19
03 Oct	A	Blackheath	W	51	0
10 Oct	A	NORTHAMPTON (Courage League)	L	8	11
17 Oct	H	Coventry	W	63	6
24 Oct	A	ORRELL (Courage League)	W	8	3
31 Oct	H	BRISTOL (Courage League)	W	39	3
21 Nov	A	Cardiff	W	31	6
28 Nov	H	LEICESTER (Courage League)	W	31	22
05 Dec	A	WATERLOO (Pilkington Cup 3rd round)	L	8	13
12 Dec	H	Nottingham	W	24	9
19 Dec	A	Richmond	W	38	7
26 Dec	H	London Welsh	W	37	22
2 Jan 1993	H	Clifton	W	28	0
09 Jan	H	Sale	W	26	6
15 Jan	A	RUGBY (Courage League)	W	61	7
23 Jan	H	Clifton	W	17	3
30 Jan	A	London Irish	W	43	5
13 Feb	H	Plymouth Albion	W	47	13
19 Feb	A	GLOUCESTER (Courage League)	W	20	0
26 Feb	H	Swansea	W	63	27
05 Mar	A	Cardiff	W	79	7
13 Mar	H	Newbridge	W	22	11
19 Mar	A	WASPS (Courage League)	W	13	19
27 Mar	A	Pontypool	W	12	10
30 Mar	A	WEST HARTLEPOOL (Courage League)	W	38	10
10 Apr	H	LONDON SCOTTISH (Courage League)	W	40	6
17 Apr	H	Newbury	W	81	8
24 Apr	H	Gloucester	L	16	17
	A	SARACENS (Courage League)	W	19	13
				1112	321

Played 32   Won 27   Lost 5

Courage League Division 1: **Champions**

**point deducted for fielding ineligible player

Season 1993-94 (Captain: J P Hall)

Date		Opponent	Result	F	A
4 Sep 1993	A	Garryowen	W	38	8
11 Sep	A	BRISTOL (Courage League)	W	18	10
18 Sep	H	NORTHAMPTON (Courage League)	W	37	9
25 Sep	A	ORRELL (Courage League)	W	18	15
02 Oct	H	GLOUCESTER (Courage League)	W	46	17
09 Oct	A	WASPS (Courage League)	W	19	13
15 Oct	A	Llanelli	L	19	27
19 Oct	A	Oxford University	W	21	8
23 Oct	H	Nottingham	W	77	34
30 Oct	H	Loughborough Students	W	48	8
06 Nov	H	South African Barbarians	L	23	34
09 Nov	H	Combined Services	L	3	20
13 Nov	H	NEWCASTLE GOSFORTH (Courage League)	W	46	3
20 Nov	A	LEICESTER (Courage League)	L	6	9
26 Nov	H	London Scottish	W	35	8
04 Dec	A	HARLEQUINS (Courage League)	W	14	12
11 Dec	H	LONDON IRISH (Courage League)	W	28	8
18 Dec	H	WASPS (Pilkington Cup 4th round)	W	24	11
22 Dec	H	Stade Toulousain	L	9	24
30 Dec	H	Cardiff	W	24	20
8 Jan 1994	H	BRISTOL (Courage League)	W	9	0
15 Jan	A	NORTHAMPTON (Courage League)	W	30	9
22 Jan	H	BRISTOL (Pilkington Cup 5th round)	W	14	9
29 Jan	H	ORRELL (Courage League)	W	13	7
04 Feb	H	Newbridge	W	20	18
12 Feb	A	GLOUCESTER (Courage League)	W	16	6
18 Feb	H	Pontypool	L	6	15
26 Feb	A	SARACENS (Pilkington Cup quarter-final)	W	23	6
05 Mar	A	Rugby	L	11	21
12 Mar	H	WASPS (Courage League)	W	24	8
26 Mar	A	NEWCASTLE GOSFORTH (Courage League)	W	29	5
02 Apr	A	HARLEQUINS (Pilkington Cup semi-final)	W	26	25
09 Apr	H	LEICESTER (Courage League)	W	14	6
16 Apr	A	Bedford	W	18	13
23 Apr	H	HARLEQUINS (Courage League)	W	32	13
30 Apr	A	LONDON IRISH (Courage League)	W	32	31
07 May	–	LEICESTER (Pilkington Cup final)	W	21	9
				891	499

Played 37; won 30; drawn 0; lost 7.

Courage League Division 1: **Champions**

Season 1994-95 (Captain: J P Hall)

Date		Opponent	Result	F	A
3 Sep 1994	A	Barbarians	W	23	18
10 Sep	H	BRISTOL (Courage League)	W	18	9
17 Sep	A	NORTHAMPTON (Courage League)	W	32	16
24 Sep	H	ORRELL (Courage League)	W	32	13
01 Oct	A	GLOUCESTER (Courage League)	W	15	10
08 Oct	H	WASPS (Courage League)	W	12	9
15 Oct	A	WEST HARTLEPOOL (Courage League)	W	20	18
22 Oct	H	LEICESTER (Courage League)	D	20	20
29 Oct	H	HARLEQUINS (Courage League)	W	22	11
05 Nov	A	SALE (Courage League)	W	19	3
12 Nov	H	Oxford University	W	33	26
19 Nov	A	Coventry	W	45	10
23 Nov	A	Pontypool	W	25	13
26 Nov	H	Loughborough Students	W	65	7
03 Dec	A	Nottingham	W	22	10
09 Dec	A	Exeter	W	53	14
17 Dec	A	LONDONSCOTTISH (Pilkington Cup 4th round)	W	31	6
26 Dec	H	Clifton	W	17	3
7 Jan 1995	A	BRISTOL (Courage League)	W	10	9
14 Jan	H	NORTHAMPTON (Courage League)	W	26	6
28 Jan	A	ORRELL (Pilkington Cup 5th round)	W	25	19
11 Feb	A	ORRELL (Courage League)	D	6	6
25 Feb	H	NORTHAMPTON (Pilkington Cup quarter-final)	W	26	6
04 Mar	H	GLOUCESTER (Courage League)	D	19	19
11 Mar	H	Orrell	D	5	5
17 Mar	A	Cardiff	L	24	34
21 Mar	A	The Army	L	5	29
25 Mar	A	WASPS (Courage League)	L	10	11
01/04/10	A	HARLEQUINS (Courage League)	W	31	13
08 Apr	A	WEST HARTLEPOOL (Courage League)	W	53	17
15 Apr	A	LEICESTER (Courage League)	L	21	31
22 Apr	A	HARLEQUINS (Courage League)	W	25	19
29 Apr	H	SALE (Courage League)	L	13	18
06 May	–	WASPS (Pilkington Cup final)	W	36	16
				839	474

Played 34; won 25; drawn 4; lost 5.

Courage League Division 1: runners-up

Season 1995-96 (Captain: P de Glanville)

Date		Opponent	Result	F	A
2 Sep 1995	H	Garryowen	W	62	19
09 Sep	A	WEST HARTLEPOOL (Courage League)	W	20	15
16 Sep	A	GLOUCESTER (Courage League)	W	37	11
23 Sep	A	LEICESTER (Courage League)	W	14	9
30 Sep	H	ORRELL (Courage League)	W	55	20
07 Oct	A	WASPS (Courage League)	W	15	6
14 Oct	A	BRISTOL (Courage League)	W	52	19
21 Oct	H	HARLEQUINS (Courage League)	W	19	13
28 Oct	A	SARACENS (Courage League)	W	52	16
04 Nov	A	SALE (Courage League)	W	30	18
11 Nov	H	WEST HARTLEPOOL (Courage League)	W	34	22
18 Nov	H	Coventry	W	28	23
25 Nov	H	Loughborough Students	L	17	19
02 Dec	H	Nottingham	W	99	12
09 Dec	A	London Scottish	W	33	24
15 Dec	H	Exeter	W	36	29
23 Dec	H	NORTHAMPTON (Pilkington Cup 4th round)	W	12	3
6 Jan 1996	H	LEICESTER (Courage League)	L	14	15
13 Jan	A	Northampton	L	12	21
19 Jan	H	Moseley	W	21	11
02 Feb	A	Swansea	L	10	27
10 Feb	H	WAKEFIELD (Pilkington Cup 5th round)	W	16	12
17 Feb	H	WASPS (Courage League)	W	36	12
24 Feb	A	BRISTOL (Pilkington Cup quarter-final)	W	19	12
15 Mar	A	Pontypridd	L	14	22
19 Mar	H	The Army	L	16	27
23 Mar	H	GLOUCESTER (Pilkington Cup semi-final)	W	19	10
30 Mar	A	BRISTOL (Courage League)	W	43	5
06 Apr	H	HARLEQUINS (Courage League)	W	41	15
10 Apr	A	GLOUCESTER (Courage League)	L	10	16
13 Apr	A	SARACENS (Courage League)	W	21	15
20 Apr	A	ORRELL (Courage League)	W	44	11
27 Apr	H	SALE (Courage League)	D	38	38
04 May	–	LEICESTER (Pilkington Cup Final)	W	16	15
Played 34;	**won 26;**	**drawn 1;**	**lost 7.**	**1005**	**562**

Courage League Division 1: Champions

(excludes Cross Code challenge v Wigan)

LEAGUE TABLES

1987-88	P	W	D	L	F	A	Pts
Leicester	10	9	0	1	225	133	37
Wasps	11	8	1	2	218	136	37
Harlequins*	11	6	1	4	261	128	30
Bath	11	6	1	4	197	156	30
Gloucester	10	6	1	3	206	121	29
Orrell	11	5	1	5	192	153	27
Moseley	11	5	0	6	167	170	26
Nottingham	11	4	1	6	146	170	24
Bristol*	10	4	1	5	171	145	23
Waterloo	10	4	0	6	123	208	22
Coventry	11	3	1	7	139	246	21
Sale	11	0	0	11	95	374	11

Relegated: Sale and Coventry.
Points scoring system: 4 for a win; 2 for a draw; 1 for fulfilling fixture.
*John Player Cup final counted towards league points.

1989-90	P	W	D	L	F	A	Pts
Wasps	11	9	0	2	250	106	18
Gloucester	11	8	1	2	214	139	17
Bath	11	8	0	3	258	104	16
Saracens	11	7	1	3	168	167	15
Leicester	11	6	0	5	248	184	12
Nottingham	11	6	0	5	187	148	12
Harlequins	11	6	0	5	218	180	12
Orrell	11	5	0	6	221	132	10
Bristol	11	4	0	7	136	144	8
Rosslyn Park	11	4	0	7	164	243	8
Moseley	11	2	0	9	138	258	4
Bedford	11	0	0	11	70	467	0

Relegated: Bedford.

1988-89	P	W	D	L	F	A	Pts
Bath	11	10	0	1	263	98	20
Gloucester	11	7	1	3	215	112	15
Wasps	11	7	1	3	206	138	15
Nottingham	11	6	1	4	142	122	13
Orrell	11	6	1	4	148	157	13
Leicester	11	6	1	4	189	199	13
Bristol	11	6	0	5	188	117	12
Harlequins	11	5	0	6	194	184	10
Rosslyn Park	11	5	0	6	172	208	10
Moseley	11	3	0	8	113	242	6
Waterloo	11	1	1	9	120	235	3
Liverpool St Helens	11	1	0	10	116	254	2

Relegated: Liverpool St Helens and Waterloo
Points scoring system: 2 for a win; 1 for a draw.

1990-91	P	W	D	L	F	A	Pts
Bath	12	11	0	1	280	104	22
Wasps	12	9	1	2	252	151	19
Harlequins	12	8	0	4	267	182	16
Leicester	12	8	0	4	244	131	16
Orrell	12	7	0	5	247	115	14
Gloucester	12	6	0	6	207	163	12
Rosslyn Park	12	6	0	6	216	174	12
Nottingham	12	6	0	6	128	194	12
Northampton	12	5	1	6	197	206	11
Saracens	12	5	0	7	151	228	10
Bristol	12	4	1	7	135	219	9
Moseley	12	1	1	10	113	244	3
Liverpool St Helens	12	0	0	12	88	349	0

Relegated: Liverpool St Helens.

League Tables

1991-92	P	W	D	L	F	A	Pts
Bath*	12	10	1	1	277	126	20
Orrell	12	10	0	2	204	95	20
Northampton	12	9	1	2	209	136	19
Gloucester	12	7	1	4	193	168	15
Saracens	12	7	1	4	176	165	15
Leicester	12	6	1	5	262	216	13
Wasps	12	6	0	6	177	180	12
Harlequins	12	5	1	6	213	207	11
London Irish	12	3	3	6	147	237	9
Bristol	12	4	0	8	192	174	8
Rugby	12	2	3	7	124	252	7
Nottingham	12	2	1	9	133	204	5
Rosslyn Park.	12	0	1	11	111	258	1

Relegated: Rosslyn Park and Nottingham.
*Bath deducted 1pt for fielding unregistered player.

1992-93	P	W	D	L	F	A	Pts
Bath	12	11	0	1	355	97	22
Wasps	12	11	0	1	186	118	22
Leicester	12	9	0	3	220	116	18
Northampton	12	8	0	4	215	150	16
Gloucester	12	6	0	6	173	151	12
Bristol	12	6	0	6	148	169	12
London Irish	12	6	0	6	175	223	12
Harlequins	12	5	1	6	197	187	11
Orrell	12	5	1	7	175	183	10
London Scottish	12	3	1	8	192	248	7
Saracens	12	3	0	9	137	180	6
West Hartlepool	12	3	0	9	149	236	6
Rugby	12	1	0	11	104	368	2

Relegated: London Scottish, Saracens, West Hartlepool, Rugby.

1993-94	P	W	D	L	F	A	Pts
Bath	18	17	0	1	431	181	34
Leicester	18	14	0	4	425	210	28
Wasps	18	10	1	7	362	340	21
Bristol	18	10	0	8	331	276	20
Northampton	18	9	0	9	305	342	18
Harlequins	18	8	0	10	333	287	16
Orrell	18	8	0	10	327	302	16
Gloucester	18	6	2	10	247	356	14
London Irish	18	4	0	14	217	391	8
Newcastle-Gosf.	18	2	1	15	190	483	5

Relegated: London Irish, Newcastle-Gosforth.

1994-95	P	W	D	L	F	A	Pts
Leicester	18	15	1	2	400	239	31
Bath	18	12	3	3	373	245	27
Wasps	18	13	0	5	470	313	26
Sale	18	7	2	9	327	343	16
Orrell	18	6	3	9	256	326	15
Bristol	18	7	0	11	301	353	14
Gloucester	18	6	1	11	269	336	13
Harlequins	18	6	1	11	275	348	13
West Hartlepool	18	6	1	11	312	412	13
Northampton	18	6	0	12	267	335	12

Relegated: Northampton.

1995-96	P	W	D	L	F	A	Pts
Bath	18	15	1	2	575	276	31
Leicester	18	15	0	3	476	242	30
Harlequins	18	13	0	5	524	314	26
Wasps	18	11	0	7	439	322	22
Sale	18	9	1	8	365	371	19
Bristol	18	8	0	10	329	421	16
Orrell	18	7	0	11	323	477	14
Gloucester	18	6	0	12	275	370	12
Saracens	18	5	0	13	284	451	10
West Hartlepool	18	0	0	18	288	634	0

No relegation.